TOWARDS A REGIME OF RESPONSIBILITY OF ARMED GROUPS IN INTERNATIONAL LAW

Human Rights Research Series, Volume 90.

The titles published in this series are listed at the end of this volume.

TOWARDS A REGIME OF RESPONSIBILITY OF ARMED GROUPS IN INTERNATIONAL LAW

Laura Íñigo Álvarez

INTERSENTIA

Cambridge – Antwerp – Chicago

Intersentia Ltd
8 Wellington Street
Cambridge | CB1 1HW | United Kingdom
Tel.: +44 1223 736 170 | Fax: +44 1223 736 169
Email: mail@intersentia.co.uk
www.intersentia.com | www.intersentia.co.uk

Distribution for the UK and Ireland:
NBN International
Airport Business Centre, 10 Thornbury Road
Plymouth, PL6 7 PP
United Kingdom
Tel.: +44 1752 202 301 | Fax: +44 1752 202 331
Email: orders@nbninternational.com

Distribution for Europe and all other countries:
Intersentia Publishing nv
Groenstraat 31
2640 Mortsel
Belgium
Tel.: +32 3 680 15 50 | Fax: +32 3 658 71 21
Email: mail@intersentia.be

Distribution for the USA and Canada:
Independent Publishers Group
Order Department
814 North Franklin Street
Chicago, IL60610
USA
Tel.: +1 800 888 4741 (toll free) | Fax: +1312 337 5985
Email: orders@ipgbook.com

Towards a Regime of Responsibility of Armed Groups in International Law

ISBN 978-1-83970-004-0 (paperback)
ISBN 978-1-83970-005-7 (PDF)
D/2020/7849/102
NUR 828

British Library Cataloguing in Publication Data. A catalogue record for this book is available from the British Library.

ACKNOWLEDGEMENTS

Throughout the writing of this book I have received a great deal of support and assistance from a number of people and institutions. Firstly, I would like to thank my supervisors, Prof. Dr. Cedric Ryngaert, Prof. Dr. Carmen Márquez Carrasco and Dr. Katharine Fortin. I am indebted to Prof. Dr. Carmen Márquez Carrasco for her constant support, motivation and guidance, and for giving me the opportunity to engage in this PhD journey that began at the University of Seville. I am also grateful to Prof. Dr. Cedric Ryngaert and Dr. Katharine Fortin for their willingness to co-supervise my thesis. Their expertise was invaluable in formulating the research topic and methodology. Besides my supervisors, I would like to thank the members of my reading committee, Prof. Dr. Joaquín Alcaide Fernández, Prof. Dr. Terry Gill, Prof. Dr. Seline Trevisanut, Prof. Dr. Gerd Oberleitner and Dr. Brianne McGonigle Leyh for their insightful comments and suggestions for improving my manuscript. To my paranymphs, Yulia Levashova and Solène Guggisberg, I owe a huge debt of gratitude. Thank you for your friendship and for standing by my side at every moment I needed. My appreciation also goes to Anna Ledvinka for editing and proofreading this book.

This work would not have been possible without the financial support provided by the University of Seville Research Plan and the EU Project FRAME during the first years of research; and the Postgraduate Fellowship from La Caixa Banking Foundation during the last two years I spent in Utrecht. Likewise, I am grateful for the funds provided by the Stimulation Fund for Dissertations from Utrecht University that assisted in organising the PhD ceremony. My sincere thanks also go to the Ius Commune Research School and the Netherlands Network for Human Rights Research for the training and feedback provided from several prestigious professors in the Netherlands. I also appreciate the feedback offered by the IHCL Platform at the Asser Institute, especially by Dr. Christophe Paulussen. In addition, I received generous support from the PhD Programme at the University of Seville Law School and its coordinator Prof. Dr. Fernando H. Llano Alonso.

I would also like to acknowledge my colleagues at the IER Department of Utrecht University and the Utrecht Centre for Accountability and Liability Law (UCALL) who supported me and were always willing to help. Special thanks go to Wen Duan, Julie Fraser, Maddalena Visser, Friederycke Haijer, Kai Liu, Congrui Qiao, Machiko Kanetake, Diana Odier-Contreras, Tao Tang, Andrea Minto, Mita Mulia, Marloes van Rijsbergen, Elmar Schmidt, Vivian Aiyedogbon, Laurens van Kreij and Hye-Min Kim. Likewise, I want to thank my colleagues from the Ius Commune training programme,

Elif Durmus, Charlotte Mol, Tim Bleeker, Tom Vos, Tom Verdonk, Andrew Sweeney, Friso Bostoen, Erin Jackson, Luisa Cortat, Pieter Gillaerts, and Niels Graaf for their warm encouragement and all the good moments we spent during those lunches and dinners. My appreciation also goes to my colleagues at the Department of Public International Law of the University of Seville and the Research Group SEJ055, Laura García, Luis Rodríguez-Piñero, Rocío Alamillos, Elisa Medici, Nora Loozen, Francisco A. Domínguez, Libia Arenal, Pablo Gavira, Cristina Zamora, Marta Bordignon, Simona Fanni, Daniel Iglesias and Paula Schmid.

My friends and colleagues from the summer course at the Hague Academy of International Law have been another important source of inspiration and encouragement throughout this journey, including Jorge Crespo, Tetevi Davi, Jamilla Abdulle, Landry Femtchou, Luisa Scarpelli, Paola Reyes, Ezéchiel Amani, Wiliander F. Salomão, Walter Arévalo, Carolina Soler, Xuexia Liao and Kimberley Graham, as well as the coordinators of the programme, Monique Legerman and Anna Vasilyeva. Moreover, I also want to offer my thanks to my friends in Seville, Olga González, Ana Espinós, Cristina Valverde, Jose Ignacio López, and Jose Emilio Fernández; and my friends in the Netherlands, Barbra Bodnar, Olga Sorkin, Manuel Álvarez, Hrvoje Greguric, Attila Gulyas, Raquel León, Chelsea Woit, Patricio Rogat, Eva Hureau, Carlos Ronda, Arno Koehler, Pedro J. Montaño, Kristian Lenger, and Amal Nassar. Friends are the family one chooses, and I am truly grateful to have had them by my side all these years.

Finally, and most importantly, I owe my deepest gratitude to my parents Guillermina and José Ramón. Thank you for teaching me the value of hard work and always supporting me in pursuing my goals. My life would not have been the same without your knowledge and your love towards arts and culture. This look back to my origins makes me recall a verse by the Sevillian poet Antonio Machado that was found in his pocket when he passed away: "Estos días azules y este sol de la infancia".

Seville – Utrecht

CONTENTS

Chapter V.
The Obligation to Provide Reparations by Armed Groups 157

ABBREVIATIONS

ACHPR	African Charter on Human and Peoples Rights
ACHR	American Convention on Human Rights
AFRC	Armed Forces Revolutionary Council (Sierra Leone)
ANSAs	Armed Non-State Actors
AOGs	Armed Opposition Groups
ARIO	Articles on the Responsibility of International Organizations
ASR	Articles on State Responsibility
ATCA	Alien Tort Claim Act
CDF	Civil Defense Forces (Sierra Leone)
CMAs	Civil/Military Administrators
DDR	Disarmament, Demobilization and Reintegration
ECHR	European Convention on Human Rights
ELN	Ejército de Liberación Nacional (Colombia)
EMC	Estado Mayor Central
FARC-EP	Fuerzas Armadas Revolucionarias de Colombia – Ejército del Pueblo
FIS	Front Islamique du Salut (Algeria)
FMLN	Frente Farabundo Martí para la Liberación Nacional (El Salvador)
FSA	Free Syrian Army
GAM	Free Aceh Movement (Indonesia)
GMC	General Military Council
ICC	International Criminal Court
ICCPR	International Covenant on Civil and Political Rights
ICJ	International Court of Justice
ICL	International Criminal Law
ICRC	International Committee of the Red Cross
ICTR	International Criminal Tribunal for Rwanda
ICTY	International Criminal Court for the Former Yugoslavia
IHL	International Humanitarian Law
IHRL	International Human Rights Law
ILA	International Law Association
ILC	International Law Commission
IRA	Irish Republican Army
JCE	Joint Criminal Enterprise
KLA	Kosovan Liberation Army
LRA	Lord's Resistance Army

LTTE	Liberation Tigers of Tamil Eelam (Sri Lanka)
MILF	Moro Islamic Liberation Front (Philippines)
MLC	Mouvement de Libération du Congo
NDFP	National Democratic Front of the Philippines
NIAC	Non-International Armed Conflict
NPA	New People's Army (Philippines)
OCHA	UN Office for the Coordination of Humanitarian Affairs
OHCHR	United Nations Office of the High Commissioner of Human Rights
PCIJ	Permanent Court of International Justice
RUF	Revolutionary United Front (Sierra Leone)
SCSL	Special Court for Sierra Leone
SLA	Sudan Liberation Army
SPLM/A	Sudan People's Liberation Movement/Army
TRC	Truth and Reconciliation Commission
UNBPG	UN Basic Principles and Guidelines on the Right to a Remedy and Reparations
UPC	Union de Patriotes Congolais
UDHR	Universal Declaration of Human Rights
VCLT	Vienna Convention on the Law of Treaties

CHAPTER I
INTRODUCTION

1. INTRODUCTION

The role of armed groups has emerged as an essential topic of discussion in the areas of international humanitarian law (IHL) and international human rights law (IHRL). This increase in attention has been motivated by the increase in the number of non-international armed conflicts (NIACs) during the past decades and the necessity to address the multiple legal challenges that armed groups pose. According to *The War Report,* in 2017 there was a total of 55 armed conflicts, out of which 38 were considered NIACs; in 2018, 51 of the 69 armed conflicts were considered to be NIACs.[1] Consequently, the majority of armed conflicts are now non-international, involving the participation of a series of armed groups. In this regard, the UN Secretary-General has emphasised the effects of this proliferation and the multiple violations committed by armed groups by indicating that:

> The consequences for civilians have been devastating, as armed groups have often sought to overcome their military inferiority by employing strategies that flagrantly violate international law. These range from deliberate attacks against civilians, including sexual violence, to attacks on civilian objects such as schools, to abduction, forced recruitment and using civilians to shield military objectives.[2]

Likewise, the International Council on Human Rights Policy identified the most common violations committed by armed groups, including arbitrary deprivation of the right to life; disregard for the protection owed to civilians caught up in conflict; torture and ill-treatment; abuses against children; abuses against women; and arbitrary deprivation of liberty and due process.[3] Most violations have been committed by armed groups in Afghanistan, Central African Republic, Colombia, Democratic

---

1 A. Bellal (ed), 'The War Report: Armed Conflicts in 2017' (The Geneva Academy of International Humanitarian Law and Human Rights, March 2018); A. Bellal (ed) 'The War Report: Armed Conflicts in 2018' (The Geneva Academy of International Humanitarian Law and Human Rights, April 2019).

2 Report of the Secretary-General on the Protection of Civilians in Armed Conflict (10 November 2010) S/2010/579, para. 8.

3 International Council on Human Rights, 'Ends and Means: Human Rights Approaches to Armed Groups' (International Council on Human Rights, Geneva 2000) 10 available at <www.ichrp.org/files/reports/6/105_report_en.pdf> accessed 12 May 2019.

Republic of Congo, Mali, Nigeria, Sudan and Syria, among others.[4] The harm which armed groups can cause requires that the international legal regulation becomes more effective in addressing their actions and also attaches reparative consequences thereto. In particular, the UN Secretary-General has reiterated 'the need to ensure accountability for violations, for both parties to conflict and individual perpetrators' as well as provide justice to victims.[5] He has furthermore pointed to the development of 'further measures to promote the responsibility of armed groups and non-State actors' as one of the priorities in the protection of civilians in conflict.[6] Similarly, in a recent report on armed non-state actors (ANSAs) and the protection of the right to life, the Special Rapporteur on extrajudicial, summary or arbitrary executions explained that 'the current legal framework to address ANSAs presents unacceptable limitations' and 'it is unjust to the victims of ANSAs violations and ineffective at addressing protection gaps'.[7]

The proliferation of armed groups and the repeated violations of international humanitarian law and human rights law have created several challenges for contemporary international law, in particular in the determination of international legal obligations and the international responsibility of these entities. This book will analyse, firstly, if a regime of responsibility in international law is necessary to address violations committed by armed groups and, secondly, how the responsibility of armed groups can be established in international law in terms of attribution and the legal consequences thereof.

1.1. THE QUEST FOR RESPONSIBILITY OF ARMED GROUPS IN INTERNATIONAL LAW

Scholarly debates regarding armed groups in international law initially covered the question of recognition of insurgency and the legal status of rebels.[8] Traditionally, insurgents were considered holders of international rights and obligations by those states that recognised them as having such status. Today, many authors claim that the rules of recognition of belligerency have been, at least to a certain extent, abandoned

4 Report of the Secretary-General on the Protection of Civilians in Armed Conflict (18 June 2015) S/2015/453, 3–10.

5 Report of the Secretary-General on the Protection of Civilians in Armed Conflict (10 May 2017) S/2017/414, para. 33.

6 Report of the Secretary-General to the Security Council on the Protection of Civilians in Armed Conflict (28 May 2004) S/2004/431, para. 16.

7 Report of the Special Rapporteur on Extrajudicial, Summary or Arbitrary Executions on Armed Non-State Actors: the Protection of the Right to Life (5 June 2018) UN Doc. A/HRC/38/44, para. 7.

8 See H. Lauterpacht, 'Recognition of Insurgents as a *De Facto* Government' (1939) 3 *Modern Law Review* 1, 2; L. Oppenheim, *International Law: A Treatise, Vol. I* (7th edn, Longmans, Green & Co 1948) 248–253; A. Cassese, 'The Status of Rebels Under the 1977 Geneva Protocol on Non-International Armed Conflicts' (1981) 30 *International and Comparative Law Quarterly* 2, 416–439; L. Moir, *The Law of Internal Armed Conflict* (Oxford University Press 2002).

and consequently, 'these recognition regimes have been replaced by compulsory rules of international humanitarian law which apply when the fighting reaches certain thresholds'.[9] To this end, the question that emerged next related to the applicability of IHL obligations to armed groups. Although there are still a number of theories explaining this link, consensus has been established with regards to the fact that armed groups fighting in a NIAC bear international obligations under Common Article 3 of the Geneva Conventions, Additional Protocol II and Customary International Humanitarian Law.[10] More recently, the focus has turned to their possible human rights obligations.[11] The UN Human Rights Council has recognised that armed groups that exercise control over territory and have certain state-like functions are subject to a gradated scale of human rights obligations.[12] International obligations, both in terms of IHL and IHRL, are also part of ceasefire and peace agreements between Governments and armed groups.[13]

If armed groups as such have international obligations, it is only logical to ask if they also hold responsibility under international law. However, the question of whether the violation of primary obligations of international law (in particular IHL) entails any legal consequences for armed groups as collective entities and what these consequences might be, still remains controversial.[14] The International Committee of the Red Cross (ICRC) study on customary IHL has stated that armed groups 'incur responsibility for acts committed by persons forming part of such groups', admitting however that 'the consequences of such responsibility are not clear'.[15] More recently,

---

9 A. Clapham, 'Human Rights Obligations of Non-State Actors in Conflict Situations' (2006) 88 *International Review of the Red Cross* 863, 491–523, at 492. See also I. Detter, *The Law of War* (2nd edn, Cambridge University Press 2000) 43.

10 S. Sivakumaran, 'Binding Armed Opposition Groups' (2006) 55 *International & Comparative Law Quarterly* 2, 369–394; J. K. Kleffner, 'The Applicability of International Humanitarian Law to Organized Armed Groups' (2011) 93 *International Review of the Red Cross* 882, 443–461; C. Ryngaert, 'Non-State Actors in International Humanitarian Law' in J. D'Aspremont (ed), *Participants in the International Legal System: Multiple perspectives on Non-State Actors in International Law* (Routledge 2011) 284–294.

11 A. Clapham, *Human Rights Obligations of Non-State Actors* (Oxford University Press 2006) 271–316. More recently, D. Murray, *Human Rights Obligations of Non-State Armed Groups* (Hart Publishing 2016) and K. Fortin, Accountability of Armed Groups under Human Rights Law (Oxford University Press 2017).

12 UN Human Rights Council, Report of the International Commission of Inquiry to Investigate All Alleged Violations of International Human Rights Law in the Libyan Arab Jamahiriya (1 June 2011) A/HRC/17/44, para. 72.

13 See C. Bell, *Peace Agreements and Human Rights* (Oxford University Press 2000); S. Sivakumaran, *The Law of Non-International Armed Conflict* (Oxford University Press 2012) 125–133.

14 V. Bílková, 'Establishing Direct Responsibility of Armed Opposition Groups for Violations of International Humanitarian Law?' in N. Gal-Or, C. Ryngaert & M. Noortmann (eds), *Responsibilities of the Non-State Actors in Armed Conflict and the Market Place: Theoretical Considerations and Empirical Findings* (Brill Nijhoff 2015) 263 (hereafter V. Bílková, 'Direct Responsibility of Armed Opposition Groups').

15 J. M. Henckaerts & L. Doswald-Beck, *Customary International Humanitarian Law, Volume I: Rules* (Cambridge University Press 2005), Rule 149 (hereafter, J. M. Henckaerts & L. Doswald-Beck, *Customary International Humanitarian Law*).

in the 2016 Commentary to Common Article 3 the ICRC affirmed that 'international law is unclear as to the responsibility of a non–State armed group, as an entity in itself, for acts committed by members of the group'.[16] Additionally, the Articles on the State Responsibility (ASR) left the door open to armed groups incurring responsibility, explaining in their commentary that '[a] further possibility is that the insurrectional movement *may itself be held responsible* for its own conduct under international law, for example for a breach of international humanitarian law committed by its forces'.[17] However, this statement has not been further developed which consequently reinforces the lack of clarity on the issue. This dissonance between the obligations and responsibility of armed groups points to a gap within the international legal system.

Since the publication of the well-known study on the accountability of armed opposition groups in international law by Zegveld in 2002[18], little effort has been paid to the analysis of the international responsibility of armed groups in a book-length study. As indicated by Kleffner:

> In contrast to [...] other non-state actors, no efforts are currently being undertaken to codify the legal dimensions of accountability of organized armed groups in (quasi-)legal instruments and these dimensions have received considerably less attention in academic literature.[19]

In particular, the question of attribution of acts to armed groups has been barely examined by the practice or the scholarship. Reports of the United Nations (UN) Security Council and UN Human Rights Council focus on primary rules and when they refer to secondary rules they do not mention clear rules of attribution.[20] In this context, several authors have called for a clarification of the rules and principles relating to the direct responsibility of armed groups for violations of IHL.[21] Similarly, the

---

16 International Committee of the Red Cross, 'Commentary on Common Article 3 of the Geneva Convention for the Amelioration of the Condition of the Wounded and Sick in Armed Forces in the Field' (2016), para. 892.

17 Art. 10 of the Draft Articles on Responsibility of States for Internationally Wrongful Acts, UN Doc. No. A/56/83 (9 August 2001) commentary para. 16.

18 L. Zegveld, *Accountability of Armed Opposition Groups in International Law* (Cambridge University Press 2002) (hereafter L. Zegveld, *Accountability of Armed Opposition Groups).*

19 J. K. Kleffner, 'The Collective Accountability of Organised Armed Groups for System Crimes', in A. Nollkaemper & H. Van der Wilt (eds), *System Criminality in International Law* (Cambridge University Press 2015) 240 (hereafter J.K Kleffner, 'The collective accountability of organised armed groups').

20 An example of a reference to 'responsibility' of armed groups made by the UN Special Procedures can be found in UN Doc. A/50/569 (16 October 1996) para. 73 where the Special Rapporteur on human rights in Sudan found that the Sudanese People's Liberation Army 'bore responsibility for the violations and atrocities committed in 1995 by local commanders from its own ranks'.

21 M. Sassòli, 'Taking Armed Groups Seriously: Ways to Improve Their Compliance with International Humanitarian Law' (2010) 1 *Journal of International Humanitarian Legal Studies,* 5–51, at 45 (hereafter M. Sassòli, 'Taking Armed Groups Seriously'); C. Ryngaert & A. Van De Meulebroucke 'Enhancing and Enforcing Compliance with International Humanitarian Law by Non-State Armed Groups: an Inquiry into Some Mechanisms' (2012) 16 *Journal of Conflict & Security Law,* 443–472; J. K Kleffner, 'The Collective Accountability of Organised Armed Groups', 20.

Committee on Non-State Actors of the International Law Association has stated that 'the mechanism of direct responsibility of armed opposition groups therefore seems to be, at the very best, a doctrine in *statu nascendi*', adding that 'it remains controversial [...] whose conduct would be attributable to an armed opposition group, or what the content of the responsibility would be'.[22]

In sum, the question of the international responsibility of armed groups requires a comprehensive study. Several gaps in the study of this topic can be identified. Firstly, it is noted that certain questions related to the responsibility of armed groups have been addressed by the scholarship, such as the sanctions imposed on armed groups or the possible obligation to provide reparation.[23] However, this analysis has been done in a rather disconnected manner from the notion of international responsibility. The question of the international responsibility of armed groups requires a unitary approach in its analysis, in order to avoid fragmentation leading to contradictory and conflicting outcomes. Specifically, the question of attribution and its legal consequences needs to be considered in a unitary study, rather than in watertight compartments. Secondly, no study has been done that connects the responsibility of armed groups with an analysis of their organisational structure. Previous efforts have focused exclusively on indirect mechanisms for holding armed groups accountable such as state responsibility or individual criminal responsibility.[24] If we want to further elaborate on the international responsibility of armed groups, we need to understand how these groups work in practice to determine how rules can be better adapted to the new realities these groups bring about.[25] More importantly, the special characteristics that make them different from other entities have to be considered. Although some solutions have been proposed, the operationalisation of the international responsibility of armed groups has not been developed in a systematic manner.

In this respect, there could be several potential advantages to the establishment of a responsibility regime for armed groups. A responsibility regime that frames armed groups as collective entities increases the possibility of victims obtaining full reparations, thereby giving the rights of victims full acknowledgement.[26] Indeed, enabling victims to obtain reparations by providing accountability and suggesting remedies was one of the key recommendations by the UN Secretary-General when

---

22 International Law Association Committee on Non-State Actors, 'Third report on the Obligations and Responsibility of Non-State Actors in International Law' (Washington Conference 2014)11.

23 See A. La Rosa & C. Wuerzner, 'Armed Groups, Sanctions and the Implementation of International Humanitarian Law' (2008) 90 *International Review of the Red Cross* 870, 327–341; R. Dudai, 'Closing the Gap: Symbolic Reparations and Armed Groups' (2011) 93 *International Review of the Red Cross* 883, 783–808.

24 V. Bílková, 'Direct Responsibility of Armed Opposition Groups', 265–266.

25 Verhoeven has emphasised the need for more study on the organisational structure and decision-making by insurrectional movements. See S. I. Verhoeven, 'International Responsibility of Armed Opposition Groups: Lessons from State Responsibility for Actions of Non-State Armed Groups' in N. Gal-Or, C. Ryngaert, & M. Noortmann (eds) *Responsibilities of the Non-State Actor in Armed Conflict and the Market Place: Theoretical Considerations and Empirical Findings* (Brill Nijhoff 2015) 303.

26 K. Mastorodimos, *Armed Non-State Actors in International Humanitarian and Human Rights Law: Foundation and Framework of Obligations, and Rules on Accountability* (Routledge 2015) 3.

addressing the issue of the protection of civilians in conflicts.[27] Furthermore, group responsibility has the potential to create a culture of deterrence and compliance. Although deterrence can be obtained through individual criminal prosecutions, holding an armed group responsible as a collective entity enables the targeting of its financial and organisational structure.[28] As such, enhancing compliance by non-state armed groups is currently one of the five core challenges listed by the UN Secretary-General in the protection of civilians.[29]

1.2. BEYOND THE STATE-CENTRIC SYSTEM OF INTERNATIONAL LAW

The debate on the obligations and responsibilities of armed groups is embedded in the broader discussion of the role of non-state actors in international law. International law has been traditionally created and applied by and for states. However, the phenomenon of globalisation, privatisation and the changing nature of armed conflicts have brought new actors to the international scene which has challenged this traditional Westphalian legal order.[30] Those actors range from non-governmental organisations, transnational corporations, armed opposition groups, terrorist groups and religious associations, amongst others. The responses given to address the issue of non-state actors and their configuration in international legal terms depend on one's approach to international law.

According to Clapham, one of the leading scholars in the study of non-state actors, there are three main approaches to tackling this question.[31] The first one conceives states as the main subjects in the international legal system and the only bearers of obligations under international law. This represents the traditional positivist view of international law.[32] The second approach focuses on the fact that states have lost their monopoly and power over international relations and consequently, attention has shifted towards international institutions and non-state actors. This has been translated into a necessity to establish new ways to understand justice and law in order

---

27 Report of the Secretary-General on the Protection of Civilians in Armed Conflict (22 May 2012) S/2012/376, para. 64.

28 See D. Amoroso, 'Armed Opposition Groups' (and Foreign Fighter) Abidance by International Human Rights Law: The Issue of Compliance in Syria and Iraq' in A. de Guttry, F. Capone and C. Paulussen (eds) *Foreign fighters under International Law and Beyond* (TMC Asser Press 2016).

29 Report of the Secretary-General on the Protection of Civilians in Armed Conflict (29 May 2009) S/2009/277, para. 38–47.

30 See F. Mégret, 'Globalization and International Law' *Max Planck Encyclopedia of International Law* (Oxford University Press 2009) at <https://papers.ssrn.com/sol3/papers.cfm?abstract_id=1200782> accessed 12 May 2019. See also P. Alston, 'The "Not-a-Cat" Syndrome: Can the International Human Rights Regime Accommodate Non-State Actors? in P. Alston (ed), *Non-State Actors and Human Rights* (Oxford University Press 2005) 17–18.

31 A. Clapham, *supra note* 11, 25–29.

32 D. Anzilotti, *Cours de Droit International* (Recueil Sirey 1929); J. Crawford, *Brownlie's Principles of Public International Law* (8th edn, Oxford University Press 2012).

to respond to the problems created by the globalisation.[33] Finally, Clapham suggests an intermediate third approach towards non-state actors, by explaining that:

> My approach retains as a starting point the principles and rules of public international law with its origins in the law-making power of the nation-state. But I want to go beyond the traditional narrow, state-focused approach and argue that some of the obligations found in public international law, and traditionally only applied to states, also apply to non-state actors. I recognise the importance of non-state actors and their influence without suggesting that they have achieved the role of law-maker. We should indeed examine their activity and their interaction with states and others to determine the duties and rights that states have fixed them with.[34]

This book takes this third approach to international law as a point of departure, recognising the central role of states in the international legal system but incorporating an acknowledgement of the interactions between states, international organisations and non-state armed groups. The international legal order has shifted from law-making processes that are based exclusively on the adoption of treaties by states and the development of customary international law to a more pluralistic legal order where different entities co-exist and interact with states. As explained by Pronto, 'although states remain the primary makers of international law, they are joined by other participants such as international organizations and judges as well as entities which are influential in the making of international law, including non-governmental organizations (NGOs) and even individuals'.[35] In fact, non-state actors are not seen exclusively as objects of international law but are progressively being considered as 'participants' of the international legal system.[36] This pluralisation *ratione personae* in international law 'has disrupted the original unity and homogeneity of the State centric system'.[37]

As Higgins points out, international law is not just a neutral application of rules, but a process based on authoritative decision-making.[38] In acknowledging the aforementioned new realities, international law has a potential role to play. In particular, when dealing with the progressive development of law, international law has to be adapted 'as far as possible to the contemporary conditions of international life' and 'has to fill in gaps in, and amend, the law in the light of new developments'.[39] With this in mind, this book looks at the new reality created by non-state armed groups and the necessity that international law adapts to cover these entities and fill the responsibility gap.

---

33 See G. Teubner, *Global Law Without a State* (Aldershot 1997).

34 A. Clapham *supra note* 11, 28.

35 A. N. Pronto, 'Some Thoughts on the Making of International Law' (2008) 19 *The European Journal of International Law* 3, 601–616, at 602.

36 For a comprehensive study on non-state actors as participants in law-making and law-enforcement processes see J. D'Aspremont (ed), *Participants in the International Legal System – Multiple Perspectives on Non-State Actors in International Law* (Routledge 2011).

37 International Law Association Committee on Non-State Actors, 'Final report on Non-state actors' (Johannesburg Conference 2016) 3, para. 9.

38 R. Higgins, *Problems and Process: International Law and How We Use it* (Clarendon Press 1994).

39 United Nations, 'The Work of the International Law Commission, Vol. 1' (New York 2012) 143, 162.

2. AIM AND OBJECTIVES

The above sections have pointed to the existence of considerable uncertainty regarding the framework of responsibility for armed groups in international law. While much has been written regarding their international (primary) obligations, the possibility of a responsibility framework under international law is underexplored. Consequently, the overall aim of this research is to examine how the principles of international responsibility can be developed and adapted to account for armed groups as collective entities. In particular, this general aim is divided into three specific objectives.

First, it seeks to describe and analyse the concept of responsibility in international law and assess the legal and practical reasons in favour of developing such a regime for armed groups. In this context, the notion of responsibility will be critically analysed from a theoretical perspective, drawing on research not only from international law but also from philosophical and political science studies. In particular, the focus will be on the relationship between individual and organisational/group responsibility; the legal and ethical reasons of the necessity of a responsibility regime; and the practical implications and challenges of this possible regime.

Second, the book examines the viability of establishing a responsibility regime for armed groups based on rules of attribution. Attribution is one of the key elements for holding collective entities accountable. The requirement of imputation or attribution was first emphasised by Triepel and Anzilotti and has been a key element in the regime of state responsibility and that of international organisations.[40] Similarly, for international criminal law it is also an essential component to determine the degree of liability of persons involved in the commission of international crimes.[41] With regard to armed groups, we still lack certain legal criteria against which we can determine whether the conduct of an individual or a group can be traced to an armed group, and therefore, if rules of attribution can be designed for them. To this end, it is necessary to determine whether similar rules of attribution to those of states could be applied for armed groups, whether these rules need adaptations to the characteristics of armed groups or whether new rules need to be designed.

Third, the research explores the possible legal consequences of responsibility applicable to armed groups. The principal aim of holding an entity responsible is the possibility to claim reparations, which is the natural legal consequence of responsibility.[42] Traditionally, reparations have been only owed by states. However, the reality of contemporary armed conflicts has shifted the discussion to the position of armed groups in providing compensation to victims. Although there have been cases of armed groups, such as the Revolutionary Armed Forces of Colombia or the

40 D. Anzilotti, *Corso di Diritto Internazionale, vol. 1* (CEDAM 1955) 285–286; H. Triepel, *Völkerrecht und Landesrecht* (C. L. Hirschfeld 1899) 324–371.

41 M. Jackson, 'The Attribution of Responsibility and Modes of Liability in International Criminal Law' (2016) 29 *Leiden Journal of International Law* 3, 879–895.

42 C. Ferstman, 'Reparations' *Oxford Bibliographies* available at <www.oxfordbibliographies.com/view/document/obo-9780199796953/obo-9780199796953-0003.xml> accessed 12 May 2019.

Lord's Resistance Army in Uganda that committed to pay reparations, it still not clear under which legal basis an obligation to provide reparations by armed groups can be established in international law and which forms it should take.[43]

3. TERMINOLOGY AND SCOPE OF THE STUDY

The scope of this study largely depends on the definition of certain key notions such as 'armed groups', 'violations', and 'responsibility'. Since there is a lack of uniformity in the use of these notions, and certain branches of public international law offer differing definitions, it is essential to determine the understanding of these concepts this book will take from the outset.

3.1. THE NOTION OF ARMED GROUPS

It should be noted that while there is a definition of armed forces of States provided by Article 43 of Additional Protocol I to the Geneva Conventions dealing with international armed conflicts, there is no general definition of armed groups.[44] Common Article 3 of the Geneva Conventions refers to the 'parties' to the conflict while Additional Protocol II applies to 'dissident armed forces or other organised armed groups which, under responsible command, exercise... control over part of its territory [...]'.[45] Other policy documents use different terminology such as rebels, insurgents, guerrillas, armed opposition groups and armed non-state actors.[46] The UN Office for the Coordination of Humanitarian Affairs (OCHA) in its manual on '[h]umanitarian negotiation with armed groups' has outlined the main characteristics of non-state armed groups indicating that:

> [T]hey have the potential to employ arms in the use of force to achieve political, ideological or economic objectives; are not within the formal military structures of States, State-

---

43 See L. Moffett 'Beyond Attribution: Responsibility of Armed Non-State Actors for Reparations in Northern Ireland, Colombia and Uganda in Gal-or, N. Ryngaert, C. & Noortmann, M. *Responsibilities of the Non-State Actor in Armed Conflict and the Market Place: Theoretical Considerations and Empirical Findings* (Brill Nijhoff 2015).

44 According to Art. 43 Additional Protocol I of the Geneva Conventions, 'armed forces of a Party to a conflict consists of all organized armed forces, groups and units which are under a command responsible to that Party for the conduct of its subordinates, even if that Party is represented by a government or an authority not recognized by an adverse Party. Such armed forces shall be subject to an internal disciplinary system which, "inter alia", shall enforce compliance with the rules of international law applicable in armed conflict'. Moreover, Art. 4 A (1), (2), and (3) of the Third Geneva Convention Relative to the Treatment of Prisoners of War refers to the main characteristics of State armed forces.

45 See Art. 1(1) Additional Protocol II to the Geneva Conventions 1949.

46 On the different terminology see DCAF & Geneva Call, 'Armed Non-State Actors: Current Trends and Future Challenges' DCAF Horizon 2015 Working paper No. 5 (2011) 7–8.

alliances or intergovernmental organizations; and are not under the control of the State(s) in which they operate.[47]

For the purpose of this study, the term 'armed groups' and 'non-state armed groups' will be used interchangeably and will refer to collective entities which fight in opposition to a Government or other armed groups operating within the context of a non-international armed conflict (NIAC).[48] Consequently, the study refers to armed groups with a sufficient degree of organisation whether or not they exercise control of a territory. In this regard, the International Criminal Tribunal for the former Yugoslavia (ICTY) has identified several key elements or factors that characterise an armed group as 'organised', including, the presence of a command structure; the ability to define a unified military strategy and use military tactics; or the ability to speak with one voice and negotiate and conclude agreements such as cease-fire or peace accords.[49] On the contrary, the study does not cover paramilitary organisations that fight alongside or with the support of a government, nor does include armed groups which operate in situations of internal disturbances and tensions, such as riots and isolated or sporadic acts of violence.[50]

3.2. VIOLATIONS OF INTERNATIONAL LAW

As far as violations of international law are concerned, the study focuses mainly on violations of IHL because there is a major consensus on its applicability to armed groups based on treaty law, case-law, the practice of the UN and the opinions of relevant authors.[51] In particular, the UN Security Council, the UN Secretary-General and the UN Human Rights Council have systematically referred to the necessity of non-state armed groups to respect the rules of IHL. Although recent practice of the UN Human Rights Council has encouraged armed groups with territorial control to respect fundamental human rights of the persons living in those areas, and while a great number of scholars argue that there is a legal basis for the applicability of human rights duties to armed groups, there is less certainty regarding their scope of application.[52] Moreover, it is still unclear whether breaches of human rights law by

47 UN Office for the Coordination of Humanitarian Affairs (OCHA), 'Humanitarian Negotiations with Armed Groups. A Manual for Practitioners' (January 2006), at 6, available at <https://www.unocha.org/sites/dms/Documents/HumanitarianNegotiationswArmedGroupsManual.pdf> accessed 12 May 2019.

48 'An armed conflict exists whenever there is [...] protracted armed violence between governmental authorities and organised armed groups or between such groups within a State'. *Prosecutor v. Tadić* (Decision on the Defence Motion for Interlocutory Appeal on Jurisdiction) ICTY Case No. IT-94-I-T, (2 October 1995) (*Tadić* Jurisdiction Decision) para 70.

49 See *Prosecutor v. Boskovski and Tarculovski* (Trial Judgment) ICTY Case No. IT-04–82-T (10 July 2008) para 194–15.

50 Art. 1(2) Additional Protocol II to the Geneva Conventions 1949.

51 See S. Sivakumaran, *The Law of Non-International Armed Conflicts* (Oxford University Press 2012).

52 See Geneva Academy of International Humanitarian Law and Human Rights, 'Human Rights Obligations of Armed Non-State Actors: An Exploration of the Practice of the UN Human Rights

armed groups should be conceived as 'abuses' or as 'violations'.[53] It has been argued that 'the word "violation" is broadly understood to refer to the breach of a hard legal obligation whereas the word "abuse" refers to the breach of a soft, non-binding norm'.[54] Consequently, this study considers violations of IHL as the first step into the analysis of violations of international law committed by armed groups and its legal framework in terms of responsibility. This does not, however, preclude the idea that further research could be conducted into the issue of responsibility of armed groups for human rights breaches. In fact, some of the reports analysed in this study refer simultaneously to breaches of both IHL and IHRL.

3.3. NOTIONS OF RESPONSIBILITY

With regard to the notion of responsibility, this book takes into consideration three conceptions of responsibility, namely state responsibility; individual criminal responsibility; and collective/organisational responsibility. In this respect, state responsibility affirms 'the general conditions under international law for the State to be considered responsible for wrongful actions or omissions, and the legal consequences which flow therefrom'.[55] Under classic international law, states were the only subjects that could be held responsible for violations of international law. Regarding individual criminal responsibility, this concept deals with natural persons who commit an international crime and who are held individually responsible and liable for punishment.[56] This is a more recent notion in international law which derives from the famous statement of the Nuremberg Tribunal affirming that '[c]rimes against international law are committed by men, not by abstract entities, and only by punishing individuals who commit such crimes can the provisions of international law be enforced.'[57]

Finally, collective/organisational responsibility is a broader notion that refers to 'the responsibility of a group, consisting of two or more persons for a particular act

Council' (Geneva, December 2016); Harvard Law School Program on International Law and Armed Conflict, 'Armed Non-State Actors and International Human Rights Law: An Analysis of the Practice of the UN Security Council and the UN General Assembly' (June 2017).

53 A. Constantinides, 'Human Rights Obligations and Accountability of Armed Opposition Groups: The Practice of the UN Security Council' (2010) 4 *Human Rights and International Legal Discourse*, 89–110, at 98.

54 K. Fortin, *Accountability of Armed Groups under Human Rights Law* (Oxford University Press 2017) 16 (hereafter K. Fortin, *Accountability of Armed Groups under Human Rights Law*).

55 Draft articles on Responsibility of States for Internationally Wrongful Acts, with commentaries 2001, *Yearbook of the International Law Commission* (2001), Vol. II; UN Doc. No. A/56/83, Part Two, at 31, para. 1.

56 Art. 25 (1)(2) Rome Statute of the International Criminal Court.

57 Judgment of the International Military Tribunal, in *The Trial of German Major War Criminals: Proceedings of the International Military Tribunal sitting at Nuremberg, Germany*, Part 22, London (1950), 447.

or acts committed by individual members of the group or by the group as a whole'.[58] This concept does not originally derive from public international law but rather from philosophical and political science studies.[59] However, it has been used by some organisations and authors to emphasise the duties of the group under international law or the involvement of the structures of the group in the commission of violations of international law.[60] In this respect, references to the responsibility of armed groups have been made in terms of 'direct responsibility' in contrast to the indirect responsibility applied by the mechanisms of state responsibility and individual criminal responsibility[61]; 'collective responsibility' in contrast to the responsibility of individual members of the group[62]; or simply 'group responsibility'.[63] This study will further elaborate on this conception of organisational responsibility of the armed group for violations of IHL.

4. RESEARCH QUESTIONS AND METHODOLOGY

The main purpose of the book is to inquire how international law could be better adapted to the reality of armed groups and their responsibility as collective entities. To this end, the main research question is:

> *How can and should international law develop a responsibility framework for armed groups for violations of international humanitarian law (IHL)?*

In order to answer this question, the following sub-questions are proposed:

> 1. *To what extent is a regime of responsibility for armed groups necessary under international law?*

---

58 S. Darcy, *Collective responsibility and Accountability under International Law* (Transnational Publishers 2007) xvi.

59 See G. F. Mellena, *Collective Responsibility* (Brill Rodopi 1997); see also Stanford Encyclopedia of Philosophy, 'Collective Responsibility' (August 2005, revised in March 2017).

60 For instance, The Panel of Experts on Accountability in Sri Lanka referred to the organisational responsibility of the LTTE as 'a concept that recognizes that international humanitarian law also places duties on non-state armed groups'; see Report of the Secretary General's Panel of Experts on Accountability in Sri Lanka (31 March 2011), para. 191.

61 International Law Association Committee on Non-State Actors, 'Third report on the Obligations and Responsibility of Non-State Actors in International Law' (Washington Conference 2014); see also A. Bellal, 'Establishing the Direct Responsibility of Non-State Armed Groups for Violations of International Norms: Issues of Attribution' in N. Gal-Or, C. Ryngaert & M. Noortmann. *Responsibilities of the Non-State Actor in Armed Conflict and the Market Place: Theoretical Considerations and Empirical Findings* (Brill Nijhoff 2015).

62 J. K. Kleffner *supra note* 19.

63 K. Schmalenbach, 'International Responsibility for Humanitarian Law Violations by Armed Groups' in H. Krieger (ed) *Inducing Compliance with International Humanitarian Law. Lessons from the African Great Lake Region* (Cambridge University Press 2015).

2. *Which methodology can and should be used to develop a responsibility framework for armed groups under international law?*

3. *In terms of attribution, under which conditions can and should acts of formal or de facto members of an armed group be attributed to the group itself?*

4. *In terms of legal consequences, can the armed group be under an obligation to provide* reparations to victims?

This book conducts doctrinal legal research which clarifies the current legal framework applicable to armed groups by analysing authoritative texts based on primary and secondary sources.[64] The doctrinal research will serve to find the gaps and inconsistencies in the current regulation. Accordingly, legal and policy documents on international humanitarian law (IHL), international human rights law (IHRL) and international criminal law (ICL) applicable to NIACs are analysed in conjunction with secondary sources, such as case law, literature and doctrine. Both, IHL and IHRL are considered applicable during armed conflicts.[65] While IHL is the branch of international law that specifically deals with the regulation of armed conflicts, IHRL applies at all times, both in peace time and in situations of armed conflicts.

The proposals to fill these normative gaps are based on two main methodological tools, namely, analogical reasoning and interpretative techniques. Analogy is an effective way to fill normative gaps and consists of identifying similarities and deciding if these similarities are relevant.[66] In particular, analogy has been applied between the draft articles on the international responsibility of states and international organizations, on the one hand, and the possible responsibility of armed groups, on the other. Interpretation deals with 'the process of assigning meaning to texts and other statements for the purposes of establishing rights, obligations, and other consequences relevant in a legal context'.[67] However, interpretation does not only involve assigning meaning. It is also a creative process and constitutes an important factor in shaping and making international law. In this respect, according to Provost, 'the interpretation of international law can thus be seen to involve a diverse range of legal actors, both states

---

64 M. McConville & W. H. Chui, *Research Methods for Law* (Edinburgh University Press 2007) 4.

65 See *Legal Consequences of the Construction of a Wall in the Occupied Palestinian Territory* (Advisory Opinion) [2004] ICJ Rep 136, 9 July 2004, para. 106. See also C. Droege, 'The Interplay between International Humanitarian Law and International Human Rights Law in Situations of Armed Conflict' (2007) 40 *Israel Law Review* 2, 310–355.

66 S. Vöneky, 'Analogy in International Law' in Max Planck Encyclopedia of Public International Law (February 2008) para. 5, available at <http://opil.ouplaw.com/view/10.1093/law:epil/9780199231690/law-9780199231690-e1375> accessed 12 May 2019 (hereafter S. Vöneky, 'Analogy in International Law').

67 M. Herdegen, 'Interpretation in International Law' in Max Planck Encyclopedia of Public International Law (March 2013) para. 1, available at <http://opil.ouplaw.com/view/10.1093/law:epil/9780199231690/law-9780199231690-e723> accessed 12 May 2019.

and non-state, operating on the basis of a range of interpretative practices, both formal and informal'.[68]

The aforementioned methodologies are applied to each of the above research questions as follows. In relation to the first research question, the book critically examines the notion of responsibility from a theoretical perspective, drawing on research from international law and its historical evolution and also from philosophical and political science studies, with a particular focus on the issue of collective responsibility. The study also conducts a systematic review of the main responses given by international law to tackle violations committed by armed groups as collective entities. This part is predominantly descriptive and serves to enquire how these mechanisms reflect the question of the responsibility of armed groups. Particularly, the purpose of this part is to determine whether the current legal framework is suitable to address the behaviour of armed groups as such and to examine the gaps and inconsistencies in its regulation. Once the current legal framework has been described, the book evaluates whether the rules work in practice or whether they are in accordance with desirable legal and ethical principles.[69] In this context, the applicable regulation will be measured against a series of evaluative yardsticks or principles: the rule of law principle, the prevention of impunity and the victims' rights to reparation. The rule of law is a governing principle in international law which predicates that all persons, institutions and entities are accountable to just, fair and equitable laws. Preventing impunity refers to the necessity of bringing perpetrators to account and is directly linked to the obligation to provide reparation to victims of armed conflict and their right to receive it.

The second question is exploratory, looking for new fruitful paths in legal research that better include issues of responsibility of armed groups in international law.[70] The departing point is the examination of the methodology employed by the International Law Commission (ILC) to develop the responsibility of states (via the Articles on State Responsibility – ASR) and the responsibility of international organisations (via the Articles on the Responsibility of International Organizations – ARIO) and to question whether the same methodology could be applied to armed groups. The research examines the extent to which possible analogies could be applied between the ASR and the ARIO on the one hand, and the responsibility of armed groups, on the other. In this regard, the ILC has considered traditional sources of international law, namely international treaties, customary international law, general principles of international law and secondary sources, such as judicial and arbitral decisions, and the opinions of relevant jurists. Due to the insufficiency of traditional sources of international law dealing with the conduct of armed groups, this book will explore additional materials. In particular, this section will take into account the relevant

---

68 R. Provost, 'Interpretation in International Law as a Transcultural Project' in A. Bianchi, D. Peat & M. Windsor (eds), *Interpretation in International Law* (Oxford University Press 2015) 303.

69 M. Van Hoecke (ed) *Methodologies of Legal Research* (Hart Publishing 2011) v.

70 *Ibid.*

practice of UN monitoring bodies such as the reports of the UN Human Rights Council and its Special Rapporteurs, and the reports of UN Commissions of Inquiry and Fact-Finding Missions which assess the situation of IHL and human rights violations committed during non-international armed conflicts with a particular focus on the conduct of non-state armed groups. Even if considered as non-binding or *soft*-law, the reports provided by these state-empowered entities are of particular relevance for two reasons. First, they are produced by bodies created and empowered by states to carry out particular functions. In this sense, their work-product can be traced back to states, including 'law-making and law-shaping activities'.[71] Second, they offer an authoritative interpretation because their competence to apply international law derives from their mandates and they follow legal argumentation based on conformity with principles of international law.[72] Additionally, the practice of armed groups (also known as 'other practice' by the ICRC) consisting of unilateral declarations, special agreements and codes of conduct will be analysed.[73] The book will pay particular attention to the study of the legal value of this practice, whether it should be included in the formation of customary international law or whether it should be considered as a tool to contribute to the interpretation and adaptation of the rules of responsibility. These materials could inform not only the discussions on primary obligations applicable to armed groups but also the possible international responsibility of the group as such.

In relation to the third research question relating to attribution, the purpose of this part is to determine which minimum rules of attribution from the ASR and the ARIO could be applied to armed groups and whether they need further adaptation. Adaptations need to take into account the specific features of armed groups and the existence of relevant practice on the matter. In this sense, one of the main features of armed groups is their structural disparity, which could be divided into centralised and decentralised armed groups.[74] The organisational structure of armed groups is a key element to be considered in terms of attribution which has not yet been incorporated

---

71 See S. Sivakumaran, 'Beyond States and Non-State Actors: The Role of State-Empowered Entities in the Making and Shaping of International Law' (2017) 55 *Columbia Journal of Transnational Law* 2, 343–394.

72 See C. Hardwood, 'Contributions of International Commissions of Inquiry to Transitional Justice' (2016) Grotius Centre Working Paper 2016/054-ICL, 15–19. See also, I. Venkze, 'Semantic Authority' (2016) Amsterdam Law School Research Paper No. 2016–06.

73 The ICRC has expressively declared that '[t]he practice of armed opposition groups, such as codes of conduct, commitments made to observe certain rules of international humanitarian law and other statements, does not constitute State practice as such. While such practice may contain evidence of the acceptance of certain rules in non-international armed conflicts, its legal significance is unclear and it has therefore been listed under "Other Practice"'. See J. M. Henckaerts & L. Doswald-Beck, *Customary International Humanitarian Law*, at xlii.

74 On this division see T. Rodenhäuser, *Organizing Rebellion: Non-State Armed Groups under International Humanitarian Law, Human Rights Law, and International Criminal Law* (Oxford University Press 2018), 74–78. Sivakumaran also refers to pyramidal and decentralised groups based on their organisational structure. See S. Sivakumaran, *The Law of Non-International Armed Conflict* (Oxford University Press 2012). See also International Committee of the Red Cross, 'The Roots of Restraint in War' (Geneva, 2018).

in the scholarly debates on the matter.[75] Taking into account the structural disparity of armed groups will help in adapting international law to the current reality of armed conflicts. Bearing in mind the practice of UN monitoring bodies and the special features and practice of armed groups, the study will conclude with the identification of possible rules or principles of attribution for armed groups.

As regards the fourth research question on the legal consequences of responsibility, and in particular the issue of reparations, new patterns in recent practice and the literature of armed groups being held responsible will be explored. This practice consists of bilateral agreements between states and armed groups such as peace and cessation of hostilities agreements; unilateral declarations by armed groups; *soft law* instruments; and reports of UN Commissions of Inquiry and Fact-Finding Missions. The legal value of this practice will be examined in terms of their normative value and their possible role in the formation of customary international law. Finally, the potential obligation to provide reparation by armed groups and its legal basis will be examined as a question for the progressive development of international law.

5. STRUCTURE OF THE STUDY

This book is structured into five chapters, in addition to this introduction which provides the background and motivation of the current research and sets out the key concepts and the research questions of the study, as well as the overarching methodology. Chapter 2 answers the first research question on the necessity of a responsibility regime for armed groups in international law. This chapter deals with the concept of responsibility and the current legal framework applicable to armed groups. It concludes with an assessment of the legal and practical reasons for developing a responsibility regime for armed groups. Chapter 3 examines the methodology used by the ILC to develop the Articles on State Responsibility and the Articles on the Responsibility of International Organisations and considers whether a similar method could be applied by analogy to armed groups. Chapter 4 explores the question of the attribution of conduct to armed groups and suggests minimum rules of attribution for armed groups taking into account the special features of armed groups and the relevant practice on the matter. Chapter 5 examines the legal consequences of responsibility for armed groups. In particular, this chapter analyses the current legal framework of reparations in international law and considers examples of armed groups that have been held responsible to pay reparations or situations where there has, at least, been an attempt to do so. This chapter provides discussion on the legal basis for the obligation to afford reparations to victims on behalf of armed groups and the possible forms that these reparations can take. Finally, chapter 6 contains the main conclusions of the research and offers possible legal paths to adapt international law and international responsibility to the reality of armed groups that commit violations of IHL.

75 S. I. Verhoeven *supra note* 25, 303.

CHAPTER II

THE NECESSITY OF A RESPONSIBILITY REGIME FOR ARMED GROUPS IN INTERNATIONAL LAW

1. INTRODUCTION

This study starts from the premise that there is a lack of development of the rules regulating the responsibility of armed groups as such in international law. While armed groups are gaining power and control over territories globally, many of their actions remain unaddressed by international law in a systematic manner. Indeed, although there are certain rules regulating the conduct of armed groups during armed conflict, the existing legal framework seems to be fragmented. There are primary obligations deriving from IHL for NIAC; there are provisions for successful insurrectional movements that become a new state or government in a territory; and there are rules on the criminal responsibility of members of armed groups. Nevertheless, there is no comprehensive set of rules that regulates the consequences of violations of international law committed by armed groups. At the same time, there has been extensive scholarly attention to the issue of primary obligations of armed groups, but the question of their international responsibility remains largely underexplored.

For the purpose of this chapter, it is key to understand the existing framework of responsibility in international law, its evolution and the actors that this regime covers. The chapter will first describe the concept of responsibility and its evolution in international law from a historical point of view. This is essential to understand why this topic was considered relevant for codification under international law and why it was necessary to develop this concept separately in international law. This historical overview will be complemented with an analysis of this notion from a philosophical and political science point of view. Philosophical and political science studies provide a rich understanding of the issue of responsibility both from an individual and collective perspective. In particular, the notion of 'collective responsibility' has been analysed by these fields that have developed several theories to justify its application. They could, therefore, bring additional insights into the current research and offer a more conceptually grounded legal analysis of the notion of responsibility in international law.[1]

---

1 R. Pierik, 'Shared Responsibility in International Law: A Normative-Philosophical Analysis' in A. Nollkaemper, *A Distribution of Responsibility in International Law* (Cambridge University Press 2015) 38.

Secondly, the chapter will provide a systematic review of the current legal framework applicable to armed groups as well as the mechanisms that directly or indirectly address violations of international law committed by such groups. Those mechanisms consist of the application of international criminal law; monitoring and reporting mechanisms, such as truth-seeking mechanisms and naming and shaming techniques; and the imposition of sanctions. The purpose of this section is to analyse how international law responds to violations committed by armed groups and to discuss the extent to which the current legal framework suitably addresses the behaviour of armed groups as collective entities. Consequently, this section identifies gaps and inconsistencies in their regulation.

Thirdly, following this systematic review, the chapter will focus on answering the first research question of the study, namely, 'to what extent is a regime of responsibility for armed groups necessary under international law?' In other words, what are the legal and practical reasons in favour of developing such a regime? This assessment considers the rule of law as a governing principle of international law together with the obligation to provide reparation and preventing impunity. Moreover, the factors that render ICL an inadequate tool to address the whole range of violations committed by armed groups will be also examined. Finally, this chapter tackles the issue of complementarity between individual criminal responsibility and the international responsibility of the group as such, and the legal and practical challenges that a regime of responsibility for armed groups poses for the international legal order. In this respect, the findings from philosophical and political science studies will inform the discussion on the complementarity between the different layers of responsibility. The first and second part of this chapter are descriptive in nature as the main purpose is to identify the foundations of international responsibility and to map how international law responds to violations committed by armed groups. The third section is evaluative, and considers the added value that a responsibility regime for armed groups could bring to international law from both a legal and practical point of view.

2. THE CONCEPT OF RESPONSIBILITY

Responsibility is a central notion in international law and has been connected with the existence of primary duties and obligations. It is a well-known principle of international law that duties are followed by responsibilities or, in other words, that the violation of an obligation entails the emergence of responsibility. In a report on the *Spanish zone of Morocco Claims*, Judge Huber said '[...] if the obligation in question is not met, responsibility entails the duty to make reparations'.[2] The Permanent Court of International Justice (PCIJ) also established in the *Chorzów Factory* case that '[i]t is a principle of international law that the breach of an engagement involves an obligation to

2 *Great Britain v. Spain, 2 R.I.A.A* (1924) (Spanish Zone of Morocco Claims) 615, 641.

make reparation in an adequate form'.[3] It can therefore be inferred that the consequence of a violation of an international obligation is the necessity to provide reparations.

From this perspective, classic literature on the matter has based responsibility in international law on the premise of the existence of international obligations. For instance, Anzilotti claimed that 'the existence of an international order postulates that the subjects on which duties are imposed should equally be responsible in the case of a failure to perform those duties'.[4] Moreover, responsibility has been called by Pellet as a 'necessary corollary of law' based on the maxim *ubi responsabilitas, ibi jus*.[5] Similarly, Nollkaemper states that 'responsibility is inherent to the notion of obligation'.[6]

The issue of responsibility was one of the first in the list of topics for codification by the League of Nations and later by the International Law Commission as it will be shown in the following sections. As traditional international law was incumbent only over the relations between states, the concept of international responsibility referred first to the responsibility of states considered as collective entities. However, responsibility in international law has subsequently been developed not only in relation to states, but also in relation to international organisations and individuals. Both the Articles on State Responsibility (ASR) and the Articles on the Responsibility of International Organizations (ARIO) have followed the model of primary and secondary rules, establishing responsibility where the state or international organisation has committed an internationally wrongful act, i.e. has violated an international obligation.[7] In particular, the ARIO (2011) emphasises that:

> The draft articles thus rely on the basic distinction between primary rules of international law, which establish obligations for international organizations, and secondary rules, which consider the existence of a breach of an international obligation and its consequences for the responsible international organization. Like the articles on State responsibility, the present draft articles express secondary rules.[8]

In addition, in the twentieth century, responsibility in international law started taking into account not only collective entities but also individuals. In particular, the Nuremberg trials referred to the criminal responsibility of individuals, declaring that

---

3 *Case Concerning the Factory at Chorzów* (Germany v Poland) (Merits) PCIJ Rep Series A No 17, 13 September 1928, at 33.

4 D. Anzilotti, *Cours de Droit International* (Panthéon-Assas/LGDJ 1999) 467.

5 A. Pellet, 'The Definition of Responsibility in International Law' in J. Crawford, A. Pellet & S. Olleson (eds), *The Law of International Responsibility* (Oxford University Press 2010) 4.

6 A. Nollkaemper, 'Responsibility' (2017) Amsterdam Law School Legal Studies Research Paper No. 2017-04.

7 Art. 2 ASR and art. 4 ARIO establish that the elements of an internationally wrongful act such as an act or omission: a) attributable to a State or an International Organization; b) which constitutes a violation of an international obligation.

8 Draft Articles on the Responsibility of International Organizations, with Commentaries, *Yearbook of the International Law Commission* (2011), Vol. II, UN Doc A/66/10, Part Two, General commentary, para. 3.

'crimes against international law are committed by men, not by abstract entities'.[9] In this sense, international criminal law (ICL) is also based on the existence of a violation of international law, particularly where there is a violation of IHL and IHRL which translates into the commission of an international crime. Therefore, ICL is specifically applied to violations committed by individuals. According to Pellet, 'the international responsibility of individuals shares a common characteristic with that of States (and international organizations): its source is the violation of an obligation (of abstention) arising under international law'.[10] It follows that the initial concept of responsibility focused on the idea of collective responsibility, that is, the responsibility of states as collective entities, which later developed into the possibility of holding individuals responsible under international law. The notion also evolved to consider the responsibility of international organisations by analogy with the state. The question remains as to whether other collective entities, such as non-state actors, can also be held responsible under international law.

2.1. THE EVOLUTION OF INTERNATIONAL RESPONSIBILITY

While the concept of responsibility has become central in international law, for a long time this notion was given scarce attention. Early international authors treated responsibility as a mere incident of substantive law that would only appear indirectly in mechanisms by which states would claim their rights through the use of reprisals or war.[11] It was not until the 19th and early 20th century that international responsibility was considered a separate subject for study, mainly due to the work of Triepel and Anzilotti.[12] Early international law writers had touched upon the issue of responsibility but only indirectly. However, some of their findings are nevertheless worth mentioning.

Grotius did not identify international responsibility as a separate legal category. He did, nevertheless, acknowledge responsibility for war in the context of individual leaders and their punishment, and he promulgated general principles on civil liability. These civil law principles were not, however, included in his work on the law of nations. In his Chapter XVII of Book II he developed the issue of the damage done by an injury and the obligation to make reparation, but made no distinction between individual and state responsibility.[13] Moreover, when he referred to the obligations of sovereigns to

9 Nuremberg International Military Tribunal: Judgment and Sentences (1947) 41 *Americal Journal of International Law*, 172, 221.

10 A. Pellet, 'The definition of responsibility in international law' in J. Crawford, A. Pellet & S. Olleson (eds), *The Law of International Responsibility* (Oxford University Press 2010) 8.

11 J. Crawford, *State Responsibility* (Cambridge University Press 2013) 3.

12 *Ibid*, 24. See H. Triepel, *Völkerrecht und Landesrecht* (C. L. Hirschfeld 1899); D. Anzilotti, 'La Responsabilité Internationale des États à Raison des Dommages Soufferts par les Étrangers' (1906) Revue Générale de Droit Internationale Public, 5–29.

13 H. Grotius, *De Iure Belli ac Pacis* (1625) (Oceana Publications Wildy & Son 1964) Ch. XVII, 884.

make reparation for the damage done by their soldiers, such reparation was considered only under civil law.[14]

The lack of interest on the issue of responsibility in international law at the time of Grotius is explained by Crawford as follows:

> One reason why none of the early writers identified responsibility as a legal category, or dealt with it other than incidentally, was the virtual absence of procedures and institutions at the international level that might have required clear distinctions to be drawn between the state and its nationals, or that might have focused on excuses for nonperformance or on the content of the obligation of reparation.[15]

In the period after Grotius, a number of authors focused on the notion of international obligations arising from the breach of treaties and other wrongs. For instance, in 1764 Wolff touched on some aspects of responsibility in his *Ius Gentium*. He established that in case of a violation, the 'right belongs to a party to a treaty against the violator of a treaty'.[16] Consequently, the violator acquires a secondary obligation, that is, to make reparation to the party violated. Additionally, he referred to the attribution of the conduct of private citizens to the state when the private citizen 'acts by order of the ruler of that state, whom he obeys as a superior'.[17] Similarly, Vattel considered that acts against a citizen should be seen as injuries to their state and therefore, the corresponding state should 'punish the aggressor, and, if possible, oblige him to make full reparation'.[18] In this regard, Vattel described different means of enforcing the right to reparation prior to the commencement of war, such as retaliation, retorsion and reprisals.[19]

One of the first attempts to formulate a system of international responsibility is found in *Le Droit Internationale Public de L'Europe* written by Heffter in 1857.[20] Although he did not create a comprehensive system of international responsibility, the merit of his work derives from his attempt to transfer the structure of the civil law of extra-contractual liability into the sphere of international law. In this vein, he distinguishes between obligations that derive from treaties, and obligations that originate from other acts.[21] In the section entitled 'Faits Illicites' he establishes that violations of fundamental rights, especially the rights to freedom, honor and property, are considered illicit acts that gives rise to the obligation to make reparation.[22]

---

14 *Ibid*, 895.

15 J. Crawford, *supra note* 11, 10.

16 C. Wolff, *Ius Gentium methodo scientifica pertractatum: in quo jus gentium naturale ab eo quod voluntarii, pactitii et consuetudinarii est accurate distinguitur* (Aere Societatis Venetae, 1764), Ch. III, 195.

17 *Ibid*, Ch. III, 161.

18 E. Vattel, *Le Droit des Gens ou Principes de la loi naturelle, appliqués à la conduite et aux affaires des Nations et des Souverains*, Vol. 1 (London, 1758), Book II, Ch. VI, 298.

19 *Ibid*, Book II, Ch. XVIII, 458 – 67.

20 A. W. Heffter, *Le Droit International Public de l'Europe, tr. par Jules Bergson* (E.H. Schrœder 1857).

21 *Ibid*, Ch. III, section I and II.

22 *Ibid*, 203–204.

Interestingly, he also discusses obligations owed to the international community as a whole.[23]

As already stated, it was not until the late 19th and early 20th centuries that the modern doctrine of international responsibility started to take shape in the writings of Triepel and Anzilotti. The importance of their work was in establishing rules of attribution (or imputation) as an integral element of international responsibility.[24] In *Völkerrecht und Landesrecht,* Triepel reflects on international responsibility, considering it in the context of the federal state[25], and elaborates on questions about the imputation of acts of individuals and state organs.[26] Anzilotti's primary concern was the responsibility for injuries to foreigners.[27] He stressed the importance of determining rules of attribution, claiming that the idea of attribution was not a mere system of causation, but a process of law which needed its own rules.[28] Moreover, he also referred to the consequence of responsibility as the obligation to make reparation. Later on, in 1912 Oppenheim considered that the consequence of the commission of an international wrong, or in his words 'an international delinquency' for failing to comply with an international duty was the possibility of the violated State to compel the delinquent State to comply with its international duties through reprisals or even war.[29]

During the beginning of the 20th century, scholarly research became more inclined to discussing the issue of responsibility. In particular, the work of Eagleton (1928) entitled *The Responsibility of States in International Law* stresses the importance of the topic:

> States, like individuals, have ever been concerned with their rights rather than their duties. It is nevertheless surprising that so little attention has been given to the subject of the responsibility of states in international law. Only in this century have efforts been made to give it a detached treatment.[30]

According to Eagleton, international responsibility should be considered a distinct topic in international law. He argued that the source of international responsibility was the exclusive territorial jurisdiction of the state, which was also a complement of its independence. He specifically claimed that:

> The exclusive territorial control enjoyed by a state under international law is attended by a corresponding responsibility, which is distinctive of states only. No ordinary person, liable at

23 *Ibid*, 104.

24 J. Crawford *supra note* 11, 23.

25 H. Triepel, *Völkerrecht und Landesrecht* (C.L. Hirschfeld 1899).

26 *Ibid*, 324–371.

27 D. Anzilotti, 'La responsabilité internationale des États à raison des dommages soufferts par les étrangers', (1906) RGDIP, 5–29.

28 D. Anzilotti, *Corso di Diritto Internazionale: Vol. I: Introduzione e Teorie Generali* (3rd edn, Athenaeum 1928) 228.

29 L. Oppenheim, *International Law: A Treatise, Vol. I* (Longmans, Green & Co 1912) 243–244.

30 C. Eagleton, *The Responsibility of States in International Law* (The New York University Press 1928) vii.

> civil law for damages done by other persons, could wield over them the power which the state has over those within its territories.[31]

In practice, the responsibility of the state was to be 'ascertained from the duties of control within its territorial limits and over its agents'.[32] Consequently, it appears that the development of the international responsibility was linked to notions of sovereignty and territorial control. As explained later by Brownlie, it was 'the inconvenience of private reprisals, the development of rules restricting forcible self-help, and the work of the International Court' which called for a notion of responsibility from the point of view of the rule of law.[33] On the other hand, Crawford argues that the emergence of the topic was 'a response to the ruinous world of the Great War, and a recall of the practice of responsibility as applied in the last decades of the nineteenth century, from the Alabama arbitration to the Venezuelan claims and the two Hague peace conferences'.[34]

An overview of the scholarship reveals that international responsibility has been the product of two sources. On the one hand, it comes from the law of extra-contractual liability deriving from the civil codes of European countries which require the obligation to compensate or pay reparation.[35] On the other hand, it is connected with the international law of reprisals which acknowledges that the violation of an international duty gives rise to a reaction by the affected state.[36] Furthermore, the reasons for developing such a regime were demonstrably both theoretical and practical. The theoretical basis related to three issues: the obligation to make reparation in case of injury derived from civil law and transferred to the state as a collective entity; the consequences of the lack of compliance with international obligations derived from the international law of reprisals; and the state's duties of control by virtue of its sovereignty over its territory. As elaborated by Anzilotti and Triepel, the practical or operational reason was mainly the necessity to establish rules of imputation or attribution of the state's actions, the state being a collective entity which acts through its agents.

2.2. THE CODIFICATION PROCESS OF INTERNATIONAL RESPONSIBILITY

Following the aforementioned doctrinal approaches, the codification efforts of the state responsibility were initiated by the League of Nations during the period between

31 *Ibid*, 6–7.

32 *Ibid*, 8.

33 I. Brownlie, *Principles of Public International Law* (Clarendon Press 1998) 236–237.

34 J. Crawford *supra note* 11, 26.

35 B. Sabahi, *Compensation and Restitution in Investor-State Arbitration: Principles and Practice* (Oxford University Press 2011) 13–41.

36 The notion of reprisals has considerably changed in recent times and has, to a large extent, been replaced by the concept of countermeasures.

1924 and 1930.[37] A committee of experts was appointed to identify those areas of international law that were considered suitable for codification. In September 1927, the Assembly of the League voted to submit the topic of state responsibility together with the issue of nationality and territorial waters to the first codification conference which took place in The Hague in 1930. The existence of the general rule that responsibility attaches to any internationally wrongful act by a State was clearly expressed in Point II of the request for information addressed to Governments by the Preparatory Committee for the 1930 Hague Conference for the Codification of International Law. At the end of the discussion, the Third Committee of the Conference unanimously approved ten articles. Article 1 laid down that:

> International responsibility is incurred by a State if there is any failure on the part of its organs to carry out the international obligations of the State which causes damage to the person or property of a foreigner on the territory of the State.[38]

However, the Conference was unable to adopt any conventions on the topic of state responsibility because the time assigned for its work was not sufficient. It was not until 1949 when the ILC included this topic in its first period of sessions as an appropriate subject for codification whose process started in 1955 and lasted until 2001. The first codification attempts by the first Special Rapporteur García-Amador focused on state responsibility for injury to aliens and their property, and were based on the provisions of investor protection. Nevertheless, in 1962 Ago recommended a broader focus on the definition of general rules governing the international responsibility of the state, rather than on the narrow topic of the injuries to aliens.[39] In his first report, he emphasised that:

> At some stage, however, it unquestionably became essential to isolate the subject of responsibility *stricto sensu*, together with the relevant principles, and to divorce it from any other body of substantive rules of international law. The continued confusion of State responsibility with other topics was undoubtedly one of the reasons which prevented it from becoming ripe for codification.[40]

The ILC produced the first Draft Articles on State Responsibility (ASR) in 1996 consisting of 60 articles.[41] Nonetheless, there were a number of controversial questions which hampered the adoption of the draft articles and required a second reading. In

---

37 Report on International Responsibility by Mr. F. V. Garcia-Amador, Special Rapporteur (20 January 1956) UN Doc. A/CN.4/96, 177 – 178.

38 *Ibid*, 177 – 178, Annex 3.

39 International Law Commission Yearbook (1963), Vol. II, UN. Doc. A/CN.4/SER.A/1963/ADD.1, 228.

40 First report on State Responsibility by Roberto Ago, Special Rapporteur – Review of Previous Work on Codification of the Topic of the International Responsibility of States (7 May 1969 and 20 January 1970) UN. Doc. A/CN.4/217 and Corr. 1 and Add. 1, at 127, para. 6.

41 International Law Commission Yearbook (1996), Vol. II (2), UN. Doc. A/CN.4/SER.A/1996/Add.l (Part 2) 58–83.

particular, there were two critical issues which are relevant for the purpose of research carried out in this study: one was the establishment of international crimes of states in former Article 19; and the second was the establishment of international responsibility of insurgent groups in former Article 14.

In relation to the first question, wrongful acts were divided into two categories: international delicts and international crimes, depending on the seriousness of the violation. Any violation of an international obligation was considered an internationally wrongful act while a serious breach of specific essential obligations constituted an international crime. There was a list of obligations (or prohibitions) whose violation was considered so grave to entail the commission of a state crime. They related, more specifically, to four topics: the maintenance of international peace and security, such as the prohibition of aggression; the right of self-determination of peoples; slavery, genocide and apartheid; and the preservation of the human environment, such as massive pollution of the atmosphere and the seas. Due to the impossibility of finding a consensus on the substantive consequences that such a distinction would entail, the second version of the ASR (2001) aimed to avoid such divisions and deleted the notion of state crimes. Consequently, all violations of international law committed by the state as a collective entity are to be regarded as wrongful acts while the notion of international crimes is reserved for the area of ICL and individuals.

With regard to the issue of responsibility of insurrectional movements, it was considered that 'the existence of an insurrectional movement *per se* creates certain specific problems which cannot be ignored in a draft codification of the rules of international law governing State responsibility'.[42] These rules were based on the premise that the state was not responsible, in principle, for the acts of individuals or groups engaged in a struggle against it. The reason behind this standpoint was 'the impossibility of attributing to the State the unlawful conduct of an entity which is by definition structurally and functionally independent from it'.[43] The first reading therefore established a safeguard clause in Article 14(3) indicating that the conduct of an organ of an insurrectional movement could be attributed to the movement itself 'in any case in which such attribution may be made under international law'.[44] The commentary to this article made clear that to the extent that insurrectional movements were able to gain an existence separate from the state, they would be able to commit wrongful acts of their own.[45] Although the ILC recognised that this imputation of responsibility was more difficult to establish than those of states, they offered examples of claims presented by third states to some insurrectional movements for injuries caused to them or their nationals during the end of the 19th century and beginning of the 20th century. Three examples in particular were mentioned: a claim by Great Britain against the Confederate insurgents in 1861 during the American Civil War; a request for reparation by the United

---

42 Articles on State Responsibility, First Reading (1996) Art. 14, Commentary para. 5.

43 G. Cahin, 'Attribution of Conduct to the State: Insurrectional Movements' in J. Crawford, A. Pellet & S. Olleson (eds), *The Law of International Responsibility* (Oxford University Press 2010) 252–253.

44 Articles on State Responsibility, First reading (1996) Art. 14(3).

45 *Ibid*, Commentary Art. 14, p. 71, para. 4.

States against an insurrectional movement controlled by General Huerta in Mexico in 1914; and finally, several requests for reparation from the British Government against the Nationalist authorities in 1937 and 1938 during the Spanish Civil War.[46]

In the first case, the British Secretary of State for Foreign Affairs, Earl Russell, exchanged a note with the United States Ambassador Adams in relation to a series of complaints made by the United States. More precisely, these complaints concerned the relations that Great Britain maintained with the Confederate insurgents acting against the Federal Government. In this note of 26 November 1861, Ear Russell indicated that:

> Her Majesty's Government hold it to be an undoubted principle of international law, that when the persons or the property of the subjects or citizens of a state are injured by a *de facto* government, the state so aggrieved has a right to claim from the *de facto* government redress and reparation; and also that in cases of apprehended losses or injury to their subjects states may lawfully enter into communication with *de facto* governments to provide for the temporary security of the persons and property of their subjects.[47]

The second example relates to the arrest of the crew members of a United States' vessel in Tampico, Mexico, on 9 April 1914 by an armed band belonging to the forces of General Huerta, who had temporarily seized power. In response to this event, the United States admiral in command requested various forms of reparation from the authorities of that Government.[48] The third example concerns the requests made by the British government to the Nationalist authorities for reparations as a result of the destruction of a British steamer and a cargo ship during the Spanish civil war.[49] According to Fortin, '[t]he fact that the British pursued the Franco authorities for these claims constitutes evidence that as a matter of policy, the British considered the Franco insurgents responsible for the incidents as a matter of law despite there being no specific agreement to that effect'.[50] There were also other requests for reparation to the Nationalistic authorities from Norway and Portugal based on similar grounds.[51]

However, the final version of the ASR deleted former Article 14 arguing, firstly, that this article only established a negative rule of attribution and, secondly, that the subject matter of the articles was the State rather than other entities.[52] The only provision that was finally included related to the conduct of insurrectional movements who become the new government or create a new state (Article 10 of the ASR). In

---

46 *Ibid*, p. 77–78, para. 28.

47 J. B. Moore, *A Digest of International Law*, Vol. I (US Government Printing Office, Washington D.C. 1906) 209.

48 G. H. Hackworth, *Digest of International Law*, Vol. II (U.S. Government Printing Office, Washington, D.C. 1941) 420–421.

49 C. Rousseau, 'La Non-Intervention en Espagne' (1938) 3 *Revue de Droit International et de Législation Comparée* 217, 278 fn 105–107.

50 K. Fortin, *Accountability of Armed Groups under Human Rights Law* (Oxford University Press 2017) 106.

51 C. Rousseau, *supra note* 49, 279–280.

52 First report on State responsibility by James Crawford, Special Rapporteur (7, 24 April, 1, 5, 11 and 26 May, 22 and 24 July, 12 August 1998) UN. Doc. A/CN.4/490 and Add. 1–, at 51–53, para. 272–273.

such a case, the new state would be held responsible for the wrongful acts committed by the insurrectional movement against third states during the armed struggle for independence. This rule is based on the principle of continuity of the government.[53] However, the application of this article is impeded by two obstacles. First, this provision is only applicable to armed groups who succeed in the formation of a new government or state but not to armed groups who are defeated even though they could have been active for decades.[54] Second, it is not applicable 'in the case of governments of national reconciliation, formed following an agreement between the existing authorities and the leaders of an insurrectional movement'.[55] The article has been also criticised on a number of issues, such as the scarce practice that is based on, and the lack of clarity on its scope of application given that the notion of 'insurrectional movements' remains vague.[56] Therefore, the application of this provision is quite limited and does not match the reality of contemporary non-international armed conflicts.

Finally, the ASR were approved on the second reading in 2001, comprising of fifty-nine provisions and an associated commentary. On 12 December 2001, the United Nations General Assembly took note of the Articles, annexed the text to General Assembly Resolution 56/83 and recommended it to all governments without prejudice to their future adoption.[57] Even if the ASR were not formally adopted as an international convention, they are considered to be part of the customary international law through state practice, decisions of courts and tribunals, and writings.[58]

The responsibility of international organisations was, on the other hand, left untouched under the draft articles 'without prejudice to any question of the responsibility under international law of an international organization, or of any State for the conduct of an international organization'.[59] In 2000, the ILC decided to include the topic of the responsibility of international organisations in its long-term programme of work. The first Special Rapporteur, Mr. Giorgio Gaja, started his study with the same elements of international responsibility by analogy with the ASR. In particular, he declared that:

> It would be unreasonable for the Commission to take a different approach on issues relating to international organizations that are parallel to those concerning States, unless there are specific reasons for doing so. This is not meant to state a presumption that the issues are to be regarded

53 See P. Dumberry, 'New State Responsibility for Internationally Wrongful Acts by an Insurrectional Movement' (2006) 17 *The European Journal of International Law* 3, 605–621, at 609.

54 G. Cahin, *supra note* 43, 252–253.

55 Articles on State Responsibility, Second reading (2001), Art. 10, Commentary 7, 51.

56 I. Verhoeven, 'International Responsibility of Armed Opposition Groups: Lessons from State Responsibility for Actions of Non-State Armed Groups' in N. Gal-Or, C. Ryngaert, & M. Noortmann (eds) *Responsibilities of the Non-State Actor in Armed Conflict and the Market Place: Theoretical Considerations and Empirical Findings* (Brill Nijhoff 2015) 287–288.

57 UN General Assembly Resolution 56/83, 12 December 2001.

58 See *Application of the Convention on the Prevention and Punishment of the Crime of Genocide (Bosnia and Herzegovina v. Yugoslavia)* (Merits) [2007] Judgment, ICJ Rep, 26 February 2007, para. 379. See also S. Olleson 'The Impact of the ILC's Articles on Responsibility of States for Internationally Wrongful Acts – Preliminary Draft' (British Institute of International and Comparative Law 2007).

59 Articles on State Responsibility, First reading (1996), Art. 57.

> as similar and would lead to analogous solutions. The intention only is to suggest that, should the study concerning particular issues relating to international organizations produce results that do not differ from those reached by the Commission in its analysis of State responsibility, the model of the draft articles on responsibility of States for internationally wrongful acts should be followed both in the general outline and in the wording of the new text.[60]

There has been certain criticism against the Draft Articles on the Responsibility of International Organizations (ARIO) that were finally adopted in 2011. Most of these criticisms refer to the lack of sufficient practice on the topic[61], the existence of different types of international organisations, and the lack of third-party dispute settlement mechanisms.[62] However, the ARIO are still considered a starting point for addressing violations of international law committed by international organisations and they have the potential of enhancing their compliance and preventing future violations.[63] Although not cited as much as the ASR, the ARIO have been referred to by the European Court of Human Rights, the House of Lords and the Supreme Court of The Netherlands.[64] Additionally, the International Law Association also worked on the issue of accountability of international organisations, taking a wider stance but nevertheless also referring to the 'responsibility arising out of acts or omissions which do constitute a breach of a rule of international law'.[65] In this regard, although primarily focused on the state, international law has evolved to acknowledge the responsibility of other collective entities such as international organisations.

2.3. PHILOSOPHICAL AND POLITICAL SCIENCE APPROACHES TO COLLECTIVE RESPONSIBILITY

The previous section examined the concept of responsibility from an international law perspective focusing mainly on the notion of state responsibility. To complement this

60 First Report on Responsibility of International Organizations by Giorgio Gaja, Special Rapporteur (26 March 2013) UN Doc. A/CN.4/532, at 5, para. 11.

61 J. Alvarez, 'Book Review of Dan Sarooshi: International Organizations and Their Exercise of Sovereign Powers', (2007) 101 *American Journal of International Law*, 676–677.

62 J. Klabbers, *An Introduction to International Institutional Law* (2nd edn, Cambridge University Press 2009), 292. See also Chatham House, 'Legal Responsibility of International Organizations in International Law', Summary of the International Law Discussion Group meeting held at Chatham House on Thursday, 10 February 2011.

63 See K. Daugirdas, 'Reputation and the International Responsibility of International Organizations' (2015) 25 *European Journal of International Law* 4, 991–1018.

64 See *Behrami and Behrami v. France* and *Saramati v. France, Germany and Norway* (Decision on Admissibility) European Court of Human Rights, Application No 71412/01 and 78166/01 (2 May 2007); *R. (on the application of Al-Jedda) v. Secretary of State for Defence* [2007] UKHL 58; *Mothers of Srebrenica et al. v. State of The Netherlands and the United Nations*, Supreme Court of The Netherlands, Judgment, Case no. 10/04437 (13 April 2012); *The State of the Netherlands v. Hasan Nuhanovic*, Supreme Court of The Netherlands, Judgment, Case no. 12/03324 (6 September 2013).

65 International Law Association, 'Final Report on Accountability of International Organizations' (Berlin Conference 2004) 5.

approach, the perspective of related fields, such as philosophical and political science, could bring useful insights into the enquiry that looks at how responsibility operates and how we can ascribe responsibility to different entities. These fields are considered specifically relevant since law is based on moral and philosophical concepts of justice and accountability.[66] Moreover, the notion of 'collective responsibility' has been extensively studied by these fields that offer different theories for its application. Since the purpose of this study is to conceive the international responsibility of armed groups as collectivities, it could be helpful to incorporate a normative-philosophical basis for its development.

There are several notions of responsibility in philosophical legal studies. For instance, in his monograph on *Punishment and Responsibility*, Hart distinguishes four different conceptions of responsibility, including a) role-responsibility; b) causal-responsibility; c) liability-responsibility; and d) capacity-responsibility.[67] According to Hart, the perspective used by the law is the 'liability-responsibility'. He asserts that:

> when legal rules require men to act or abstain from action, one who breaks the law is usually liable, according to other legal rules, to punishment for his misdeeds, or to make compensation to persons injured thereby, and very often he is liable to both punishment and enforced compensation.[68]

According to philosophical approaches, responsibility can be understood both in terms of individual and collective responsibility. Individual responsibility has traditionally been closely linked to criminal responsibility. Collective responsibility has, however, generated debate amongst moral and legal philosophers for centuries.[69] The crux of this debate is how to connect the two levels of responsibility, i.e. the individual and the collective. The connection has been justified in several ways. In this sense, the reductionist or methodological individualist approaches consider the individual a means for establishing collective responsibility. In other words, ascribing responsibility to collectivities will, in the end, be reduced to identifying the responsibility of individuals.[70] This means that every member's actions contribute to the actions of the group and it is the aggregation of the actions of individuals that leads to the commission of a harm.

---

66 See A. Boldizar and O. Korhonen, 'Ethics, Morals and International Law' (1999) 10 *European Journal of International Law* 2, 279–311; J. Rawls, *A Theory of Justice* (Harvard University Press 1971) 206–213.

67 H. L. A. Hart, *Punishment and Responsibility. Essays in the Philosophy of Law* (Oxford University Press 2008) 212.

68 *Ibid*, 215.

69 See L. May & S. Hoffman (eds), *Collective Responsibility: Five Decades of Debate in Theoretical and Applied Ethics* (Rowman & Littlefield Publisher 1991). See also M. Smiley, 'Collective Responsibility', *The Stanford Encyclopedia of Philosophy* (Summer 2017 Edition), Edward N. Zalta (ed), available at <https://plato.stanford.edu/archives/sum2017/entries/collective-responsibility> accessed 20 May 2018.

70 See R. Albin, 'Collective Responsibility: Organizations as Organic Entities' (2016) 6 *Open Journal of Philosophy*, 392–405, at 393–397; D. E. Cooper, 'Collective Responsibility (A Defence)' in L. May & S. Hoffman (eds), *Collective Responsibility: Five Decades of Debate in Theoretical and Applied Ethics* (Rowman & Littlefield Publishers 1991) 37–38.

Other approaches have focused on collective responsibility based on factors that explain how the group acts in a unified manner. These 'organic' approaches claim that collective responsibility is possible so far as the group of persons act as an autonomous unit following the so-called agent theory. For instance, Pierik states that a 'collective can be held responsible when its members, through their cooperation, can mimic the performance of a single unified agent'.[71] In a similar vein, Albin develops a notion of collective responsibility based on organisations as organic entities in the sense of considering these organisations not as mere aggregations of individuals, but as 'organic modes of human existence'.[72] The rationale for such a strategy is that some groups resemble persons in such a way that they can properly be treated as individuals. The organisation is then taken as a whole which transcends the sum of its component parts. In this sense, the intentions of the group are different from those of its individual members. In most of these cases, those groups have created decision-making processes within their structures which allow them to act in a uniform manner.[73] This theory has traditionally been applied to corporations but could be applied to other type of entities, whose organisational structure and actions allow for it to be considered a uniform entity.

Another approach applied by scholarship is that group action is based on the common interests or needs of group members. This means that there may be sufficient solidarity to allow the group to engage in collective actions.[74] For instance, to justify collective responsibility, Feinberg focuses on the common interests of a group rather than on the decision-making processes. In his view, the existence of solidarity within a group entails a community of interest among all the members in the sense that 'each party's integrated set of interests contains as one of its components the integrated interest-set of the other'.[75] The problem of this theory, however, is that it can only be applied to small organisations where a strong degree of solidarity already exists.

All these approaches share one common element, namely the importance of establishing membership which in turn justifies collective responsibility. In short, the key matter is the explanation of how a group acts uniformly through its members via its decision-making processes or the ability to establish the existence of common interests or needs. Moreover, individual and collective responsibility can coexist. In this context, Pettit argues that 'even when all the relevant enactors in a group have been identified and held responsible, still it may be important to hold the group agent responsible as

71 R. Pierik, 'Shared Responsibility in International Law: A Normative-Philosophical Analysis' in A. Nollkaemper, *A Distribution of Responsibility in International Law* (Cambridge University Press 2015) 38.

72 R. Albin, *supra note* 70, 392–405.

73 L. May & S. Hoffman, 'Introduction' in L. May & S. Hoffman (eds), *Collective Responsibility: Five Decades of Debate inTtheoretical and Applied Ethics* (Rowman & Littlefield Publisher 1991) 2–3.

74 *Ibid*, 3.

75 J. Feinberg, 'Collective Responsibility (Another Defense)' in L. May & S. Hoffman, *Collective Responsibility: Five Decades of Debate inTtheoretical and Applied Ethics* (Rowman & Littlefield Publisher 1991) 62.

well'.[76] This is deemed necessary as without the arrangements and organisation enabled by the group as a whole, the harm caused would have not happened. In other words, the group organised itself in such a way that such harm was likely or inevitable.[77]

Certain arguments from philosophical studies go further and consider that entities such as corporations and even looser organisations such as religious groups have responsibilities to the extent that they are acting as a unified single agent. The benefits of conceiving the level of collective responsibility are several. First, it is useful to claim collective responsibility of an entity when the victims cannot identify the persons involved or when the perpetrator, belonging to that organisation, is deceased. Often, the victims bear the burden of identifying the perpetrator of violations which are, in essence, a collection of actions and where it is difficult to identify the role of each member involved.[78] Second, punishing individual members for individual acts cannot cover the whole action since the organisation has taken specific decisions and tactics in such a way that a violation was likely to occur.[79] Indeed, the reason for establishing two levels of responsibility is that collectives follow different goals than the individuals themselves.

In a certain way, the notion of collective responsibility has also been introduced in international law through the application of state responsibility and the responsibility of international organisations on the basis that they function as organic entities. In this line, other entities acting in the international legal order with a certain level of organisation and coordination, such as armed groups, could follow the same reasoning for collective responsibility. To the extent that armed groups act in a unified manner with a minimum level of organisation and coordination of its members, the same notion of collective responsibility could be applied to them. The main issue remains establishing of who is and is not a member and determining which actions can be imputed to the responsibility of the group.

Alongside philosophical science, the issue of responsibility has also arisen in the field of political science, which also provides a number of views on how to deal with the responsibility of complex organisations. In particular, political science approaches are concerned with the analysis of political and governmental institutions and processes. On the one hand, with regard to the so-called 'problem of many hands', which considers the difficulties in identifying who is responsible for political outcomes when different officials contribute to decisions and policies of a government, the mainstream reply has focused on allocating responsibility to specific individuals.[80] According to Thompson, even if it is desirable to hold organisations and other collectivities responsible in certain ways, especially for financial sanctions, this could have negative consequences on individuals because it could risk including individuals who are not responsible,

---

76 P. Petit, 'Responsibility Incorporated' (2007) 38 *Netherlands Journal of Legal Philosophy* 2, 90–117, at 111.
77 *Ibid*, 113.
78 R. Albin, *supra note* 70, 401.
79 P. Petit, *supra note* 76, 112.
80 See D. F. Thompson, 'Responsibility for Failures of Government: The Problem of Many Hands' (2014) 44 *American Review of Public Administration* 3, 259–273.

or exonerating those who may be partly responsible.[81] He therefore argues for strengthening the role of individual responsibility.

On the other hand, some scholars have recently considered the organisational bases of collective actions from the point of view of the principal-agent theory. The principal-agent theory emerged in the field of economics but was soon translated to other fields such as political science and international relations.[82] This theory is based on the delegation of authority where the agent acts on behalf of, or as a representative of, the principal, whereby the principal delegates tasks and responsibilities to its agents. There have been a number studies on the application of this theory to civil-military relations to explain the dynamics of armed forces and government security forces.[83] More precisely, Butler, Gluch and Mitchell studied the application of the principal-agent theory to the issue of sexual violence committed by security forces and how the degree of control over the agents can determine whether more or fewer incidents of sexual violence will take place.[84]

The principal-agent theory has also been applied to armed groups. Armed groups have in many cases political goals and can be considered an embryonic form of government.[85] Many of the issues that emerge in relation to states are, therefore, applicable to similar types of organisations by analogy. As an illustration, the work of Haer elaborates on the application of this theory to armed groups.[86] Although she does not specifically consider the topic of responsibility, Haer's work is relevant as it tries to explain 'to what extent organizational characteristics of armed groups relate to the level of perpetrated civilian killings'.[87] In this sense, it is interesting to look at the organisational structures of armed groups to understand how violations are committed and, therefore, how responsibility can be attributed to them. Armed groups can, and are, perceived as organised units. To this end, Vinci claims that an armed group can be considered a 'structured, cohesively organised, singular actor' since it can command and direct an organisation in an autonomous manner.[88] In a similar vein, Weinstein considers that one key difference between group-level violence and individual-level violence is the intention, planning, and systematicity applied, and that individual motivations for killing are different from group-level causes.[89]

---

81 *Ibid*, 2.

82 G. Miller, 'The Political Evolution of Principal-Agent Models' (2005) 8 *Annual Review of Political Science* 1, 203–225.

83 See S. Gates, 'Recruitment and Allegiance: The Microfoundations of Rebellion' (2002) 46 *Journal of Conflict Resolution* 1, 111–130.

84 C. K. Butler, T. Gluch & N. J. Mitchell, 'Security Forces and Sexual Violence: A Cross-National Analysis of a Principal-Agent Argument' (2007) 44 *Journal of Peace Research* 6, 669–687.

85 See Z. C. Mampilly, *Rebel Rulers. Insurgent Governance and Civilian Life during War* (Cornell University Press 2011) 50–58.

86 R. Haer, *Armed Group Structure and Violence in Civil Wars: The Organizational Dynamics of Civilian Killing* (1st ed, Routledge 2015).

87 *Ibid*, 173.

88 A. Vinci, *Armed Groups and the Balance of Power: The International Relations of Terrorists, Warlords and Insurgents* (1st ed, Routledge 2008) 20–21.

89 J. M. Weinstein, *Inside Rebellion. The Politics of Insurgent Violence* (Cambridge University Press 2007) 31–42.

Some political science scholars have referred to the possibility to establish collective responsibility as different from criminal responsibility, which is mainly individual. For instance, Ainley argues that a broader conception of responsibility for atrocities is required, one which goes beyond criminal and legal responsibility. She explores the possibilities that politics can bring to the discussion, and proposes new processes where both collective and individual accountability are taken into account.[90] Accordingly, Truth Commissions could be re-labelled as Responsibility and Truth Commissions and have the authority to hold to account not just individuals but also groups.[91]

Analogously to philosophical approaches, political science studies tried to explain the divide between individuals and collectives in terms of their corresponding responsibilities. Both approaches have a tendency to look at the role and responsibilities of complex organisations and how they work through their members. Consequently, for a discussion on the topic of the responsibility of collective entities, including armed groups, to take place, it is necessary to consider who the members of such organisations are, as well as the dynamics within the group. Additionally, although some potential in the arguments presented can be indeed acknowledged, certain notions of collective responsibility should be nevertheless avoided international law. Those notions relate to the moral responsibility of a society (e.g. the so-called German guilt)[92] or those that refer exclusively to collective punishments.[93] Therefore, terms such as 'organizational' or 'group responsibility' are preferred.

2.4. CONCLUDING REMARKS ON THE CONCEPT AND EVOLUTION OF RESPONSIBILITY

Several conclusions can be drawn from the analysis of the historical development of the topic of international responsibility. First, the responsibility of international legal entities has historically emerged after the recognition of rights and obligations. Initially, international responsibility was a rather incidental subject which complemented the exercise of rights and obligations. The reasons for developing responsibility as a separate and unitary topic related to the powers that states could exercise over territories and persons under their control, on the one hand; and the necessity to offer a reaction or a consequence for the violation of international duties, on the other. Second, during the codification process of the ASR, the issue of responsibility of insurrectional movements was presented as a concern in the legal regulation of responsibility, though it was left unsettled. The precedent work of the ILC on insurrectional movements shows that

---

90 K. Ainley, 'Excesses of Responsibility: The Limits of Law and The Possibilities of Politics' (2011) 25 *Ethics & International Affairs*, 407–431.

91 *Ibid*, 28–32.

92 See K. Jaspers, *The Question of German Guilt. Perspective in Continental Philosophy* (2nd edn, Fordham University Press 2001).

93 Collective punishments are prohibited under the Geneva Conventions and the Additional Protocols.

the question of their international responsibility is 'neither recent nor radical'.[94] Although such observations illustrate that there has been indirect recognition of the responsibility of armed groups for violations of IHL, these have never been developed. Third, the issue of international responsibility has evolved from an inter-state system to a system that takes into consideration the appearance of new subjects and actors, such as international organisations and individuals, which deserve regulation by the international legal order. Once an entity has gained limited legal personality in the international legal order and its actions can be assessed as a separate entity from their individual members, responsibility must follow as a logical consequence. In this regard, the same understanding could be applied to entities such as non-state armed groups.

On the other hand, philosophical and political science approaches have contemplated the possibility of establishing collective responsibility of entities, such as corporations and armed groups, in cases where they act in an autonomous and cohesive manner. These approaches have laid down to reasons in particular as to why certain entities, including armed groups, should be held collectively responsible. First, the collective responsibility of an entity is important when victims are not able to identify the persons involved or when the perpetrator, belonging to the organisation, is deceased. Second, punishing individual members for individual acts does not cover the whole set of actions performed by the organisation, that has employed certain means and tactics in such a manner that a violation was likely to occur. Moreover, both philosophical and political science studies consider it necessary to explain the relationship between the group and its individuals and the decision-making processes within the group. Therefore, any study of the question of responsibility of collective entities should take into account the interactions between the group and its members. Finally, these studies show that individual and collective responsibility could be conceived as complementary, which in turn could help to fill the responsibility gap and offer financial support to victims. These ideas will be further considered in section 4 in relation to the assessment of a responsibility regime for armed groups in international law. Nevertheless, collective responsibility of the group should be premised on the violation of international standards, and not on a mere account of moral responsibility. To avoid any assimilation with moral or ethical concepts, the terms 'organisational' or 'group responsibility' are preferred.

3. CURRENT LEGAL FRAMEWORK APPLICABLE TO ARMED GROUPS

Having considered the importance and the reasons for assigning responsibility to collective entities under international law and under philosophical and political

94 E. Heffes, 'The Responsibility of Armed Opposition Groups for Violations of International Humanitarian Law: Challenging the State-Centric System of International Law' (2013) 4 *Journal of International Humanitarian Legal Studies*, 81–107, at 106.

sciences approaches, it is necessary to enquire how international law currently addresses violations committed by armed groups. As explained in the introduction, there are primary norms of IHL applicable to armed groups and direct and indirect mechanisms that address the violations committed by them. To this extent, this section consists of a systematic review of the mechanisms and responses provided by international law to react to violations committed by armed groups which reflect, in a certain way, an underlying notion of responsibility. The purpose of this section is to find the gaps and inconsistencies in the regulation of the actions of armed groups that have prevented international law from developing a coherent response. In addition, it is necessary to give acknowledgement to the scholarly debates that recognise the disconnection between primary and secondary rules relating to armed groups. To this effect, it is essential to briefly summarise the existence of primary rules of international law applicable to armed groups. This constitutes the underlying basis to considering their responsibility or the secondary rules applicable to them. Indeed, in relation to states and international organisations, discussions on rights and obligations always predate deliberations on the issues of responsibility. From that perspective, there are a number of recent debates that have emerged in relation to the possibility of holding armed groups responsible, which merit examination. These too will be discussed in the following sections.

3.1. MECHANISMS ADDRESSING VIOLATIONS COMMITTED BY ARMED GROUPS

The international legal system has offered certain responses to the commission of IHL violations by armed groups. The main response has been the application of ICL to prosecute the leaders and members of the armed group.[95] The literature has, however, identified additional mechanisms that directly or indirectly tackle the commission of violations by armed groups as collective entities.[96] Those mechanisms whose main purpose is to assess the conduct of states and armed groups against international legal rules are considered 'direct' mechanisms. These consist of monitoring compliance mechanisms, including truth seeking mechanisms, and reporting mechanisms with the purpose of naming and shaming. 'Indirect' mechanisms refer to those mechanisms that deal with a variety of topics where the responsibility of armed groups is subjacent.

95 The ILA Report on Non-State Actors considers the determination of international criminal responsibility an indirect instrument because it focuses on the individual but not on the group.

96 Among these authors, A. Clapham, 'Focusing on Armed Non-State Actors' in A. Clapham & P. Gaeta, *The Oxford Handbook of International Law in Armed Conflict* (Oxford University Press 2014) 793–808; J. K Kleffner, 'The Collective Accountability of Organised Armed Groups', 250–257; C. Ryngaert & A. Van De Meulebroucke 'Enhancing and Enforcing Compliance with International Humanitarian Law by Non-State Armed Groups: an Inquiry into some Mechanisms' (2012) 16 *Journal of Conflict & Security Law* 3, 456–461; A. Bellal, 'Non-State Armed Groups in Transitional Justice Processes Adapting to New Realities of Conflict', in R. Duthie and P. Seils (eds), *Justice Mosaics: How Context Shapes Transitional Justice in Fractured Societies* (International Centre for Transitional Justice, 2017).

The imposition of sanctions to armed groups or its members is an example of such a mechanism as it will be explained below. The following sections will undertake a systematic review of those mechanisms that cover the commission of IHL violations by armed groups in both a direct and indirect manner. The purpose of this section is to examine how these instruments have reflected the question of responsibility from the point of view of their collective action and identify the gaps and inconsistencies in the assessment provided by them.

3.1.1. International criminal law

ICL has contributed to the fight against impunity for international crimes committed by armed groups, and in particular, for war crimes and crimes against humanity. In relation to the prosecution of armed groups, six of the eleven situations currently before the International Criminal Court (ICC) refer to acts committed by leaders and members of armed groups. These six cases are those of the Central African Republic (two situations), Mali, Darfur (Sudan), Uganda, and the Democratic Republic of the Congo.[97] In fact, the first trial heard by the ICC was against the leader of an armed group, Thomas Lubanga Dyilo. In January 2009, Lubanga, the former leader of the rebel movement Union des Patriotes Congolais (UPC), was convicted for recruiting children under the age of 15 during the clashes in the Democratic Republic of the Congo between September 2002 and August 2003.[98]

International criminal responsibility covers the actions of natural persons but not those of legal persons and refers to individual responsibility as expressed by Article 25(1) of the ICC Statute. The working group in charge of drafting the Statute contemplated the idea of including certain organisations, such as companies, political parties or racist groups, but this idea was finally ruled out as it was considered that it could result in the criminalisation of mere passive membership in an organisation, which was against the basic principles of criminal law.[99] Although the criminal responsibility of armed groups is only conceived in terms of individual responsibility, the commission of certain international crimes requires the existence of collective action. The appeals judgment in the first case before the ICTY describes this issue as follows:

> Most of the time [international] crimes do not result from the criminal propensity of single individuals but constitute manifestations of collective criminality: the crimes are often carried out by groups of individuals acting in pursuance of a common criminal design. Although only some members of the group may physically perpetrate the criminal act

97 All the situations and cases under investigation before the ICC can be found at <https://www.icc-cpi.int/pages/situations.aspx> accessed 30 April 2019.

98 *Prosecutor v. Thomas Lubanga Dyilo*, (Decision on Sentence Pursuant to Article 76 of the Statute) ICC-01/04-01/06-2901 (10 July 2012).

99 M. C. Bassiouni (ed), *International Criminal Law. Volume 1: Crimes* (Transnational 1999) 24. A. Clapham, 'Extending International Criminal Law beyond the Individual to Corporations and Armed Opposition Groups' (2008) 6 *Journal of International Criminal Justice*, 899–926, at 919.

> [...], the participation and contribution of the other members of the group is often vital in facilitating the commission of the offence in question.[100]

This statement seems to acknowledge the argument provided by philosophical studies which encourage the establishment of the responsibility of the group for having organised things in such a way that a violation was likely to occur.[101] In relation to crimes against humanity, Article 7(2)(a) of the ICC Statute requires the existence of 'a State or an organization policy to commit such an attack' as a key element. In this sense, crimes against humanity have been considered crimes of a collective nature since their perpetration requires a series of institutions, personnel and resources. According to the current wording of the Statute, crimes against humanity may be committed not only under the control and coordination of the State but also under the control of another type of organisation, among which armed groups may be included. Particularly, in the case of *Prosecutor v. Tadić*, the ICTY affirmed that crimes against humanity had evolved to include, as perpetrators, not only legitimate governments but also those entities exercising *de facto* control over a particular territory.[102] This example demonstrates that individual responsibility for committing certain international crimes is linked to the collective actions of a group because without such support the individual would not have the means to commit it. In this vein, Mégret points out that the international criminal responsibility of individuals derives from leading or obeying the state or an organised armed group, but does not arise in isolation.[103] Smeulers also argues that it is crucial to match the collective nature of international crimes with mechanisms of collective responsibility which better reflect the actual features of these crimes.[104] Therefore, it is legitimate to question if such actions respond to the coordinated policy of a group, why then should responsibility be relegated only to several individuals?

Having said that, there are certain answers provided by ICL to tackle the collective nature of international crimes. In this respect, different modes of liability have been applied, that are aimed at addressing the collective nature of a crime, namely superior or command responsibility and joint criminal enterprise (JCE). Superior or command responsibility has been long established in international law and is now included in Article 28 of the ICC Statute. According to this provision, a military commander or superior will be held responsible for the acts committed by any subordinates who were or should have been under his or her effective authority or control. On the other hand, the doctrine of JCE was developed by the *Tadić* Appeals Chamber judgment and considers each member of an organised group individually responsible for crimes

---

100 *Prosecutor v. Tadić* (Appeal Chamber Jurisdiction Decision) ICTY Case No. IT-94-I-T (15 July 1999) (*Tadić* Appeal Judgment), para. 191.

101 See section 2.3 of this chapter.

102 *Prosecutor v. Tadić*, (Trial Judgment) ICTY Case No. IT-94-I-T (7 May 1997) (*Tadić* Trial Judgment), para. 654.

103 F. Mégret, 'The Subjects of International Criminal Law' in P. Kastner (ed), *International Criminal Law in Context* (Taylor and Francis 2017) 9.

104 A. Smeulers, 'Punishing the Enemies of All Mankind' (2008) 21 *Leiden Journal of International Law* 4, 971–993, at 983.

committed following a common plan or purpose, even if the particular individual did not physically participate in the crime or crimes.[105] A similar version of the doctrine of JCE has been included in Article 25(3)(d) of the ICC Statute, according to which:

> A person shall be criminally responsible and liable for punishment for a crime within the jurisdiction of the Court if that person: [...] d) In any other way contributes to the commission or attempted commission of such a crime by a group of persons acting with a common purpose. Such contribution shall be intentional and shall either: (i) Be made with the aim of furthering the criminal activity or criminal purpose of the group, where such activity or purpose involves the commission of a crime within the jurisdiction of the Court; or (ii) be made in the knowledge of the intention of the group to commit the crime.

This article refers to the contribution of an individual to the commission of a crime by a group of persons having a common purpose. The similarity with the JCE can be seen in the common purpose element but this mode does require an individual contribution to the crime so it is understood as a form of assistance to a group crime. In the case of *Prosecutor v. Mbarushimana*, the ICC established that a person who participates in a crime can be both a member of the said organisation or an 'outside contributor'.[106] One of the requirements for considering such participation punishable is the fact that the crime is included within the jurisdiction of the ICC and is committed by *a group of persons*. As a consequence, as Fortin explains, '[a]rticle 25(3)(d)(i) of the Rome Statute seems implicitly to recognize the possibility that a "group" may commit crimes under international law'.[107] Therefore, it could be said that the crime of reference is committed by a collectivity or a group, but only certain contributions are punishable.

In relation to these modes of liability, one clarification needs to be made. These mechanisms seem to focus on holding one person responsible for the action of others, but not on holding the group responsible as such. The logic behind these modes of liability is that 'an individual member of the collective may be made criminally responsible for crimes committed by the group even where the punishable acts may have been outside the scope of the agreed criminal plan'.[108] Moreover, there has been strong criticism against the use of extended forms of JCE mainly because the mental element, or *mens rea*, is not properly assessed, which makes prosecution too easy (this has been known as 'just convict everyone').[109] Due to the fact that international crimes represent the

105 See G. Bigi, 'Joint Criminal Enterprise in the Jurisprudence of the International Criminal Tribunal for the Former Yugoslavia and the Prosecution of Senior Political and Military Leaders: The *Krajišnik* Case' in A. von Bogdandy and R. Wolfrum (eds), *Max Planck Yearbook of United Nations Law*, Vol. 14 (Koninklijke Brill 2010) 51–83.

106 *Prosecutor v. Mbarushimana* (Decision on the Confirmation of Charges) ICC-01/04-01/10-465-Red (16 December 2011), para. 273.

107 K. Fortin, *Accountability of Armed Groups under Human Rights Law*, 299.

108 S. Darcy, *Collective Responsibility and Accountability under International Law* (Transnational Publishers 2007) 198.

109 See M. L. Badar, '"Just Convict Everyone!" – Joint Perpetration: From Tadic to Stakic and Back Again' (2006) 6 *International Criminal Law Review*, 293–302.

most serious violations of international law, the culpability requirements have to be strict. In this regard, several authors pointed to the deficiencies of the JCE mechanism. According to Ohlin, there are three key problems with this doctrine: insufficient treatment of the concept of intentionality, inadequate treatment of foreseeability, and the imposition of equal culpability for all members of a JCE.[110] As for the new configuration in Article 25(3)(d) of the ICC Statute, doubts still remain as to the quality or nature of the contribution that is required to be held criminally responsible.[111] In relation to the mechanism of superior responsibility, the ICC Statute added one form of *mens rea*, that is, those military superiors who might not have known of the crimes committed by the subordinates but 'owing to the circumstances at the time, should have known [...]'.[112] The scope of this new form of *mens rea* has also been subject to criticism. For instance, Ambos claims that 'the peculiar structure of superior responsibility leads to a stunning contradiction between the negligent conduct of the superior and the underlying intent crimes committed by the subordinates'.[113] Even the ICTY has expressed concern with the expansive use of collective modes of liability arguing that the prosecutor should prove subjective awareness or at least recklessness in order to hold an individual criminally responsible as a direct perpetrator.[114] Additionally, Darcy argues that 'using the extended forms of joint criminal enterprise and superior responsibility may compromise prospects for deterrence and even the legitimacy of the institutions of international criminal justice' as they could cast doubts on established principles of criminal liability and fair trial.[115]

To sum up, ICL represents a tool that deals with responsibility issues but focuses only on the most serious violations of international law and in particular on the liability of individual persons. Collective modes of liability under ICL are still subject to controversy, in particular due to the insufficient treatment of the concept of intentionality of the crime. Moreover, these modes of liability rely on holding one person responsible for the action of others, but not on holding the group responsible as such. Therefore, focusing on the international criminal responsibility of the most responsible individuals could leave certain actions unpunished.

3.1.2. *Truth seeking mechanisms*

In addition to the criminal responsibility of individuals, monitoring compliance mechanisms in the field of IHL and IHRL are increasingly focusing on the actions

---

110 J. D. Ohlin, 'Three Conceptual Problems with the Doctrine of Joint Criminal Enterprise' (2007) 5 *Journal of International Criminal Justice*, 69–90.

111 See K. Ambos, 'The ICC and Common Purpose: What Contribution is Required Under Article 25(3)(d)?' in C. Stahn (ed), *The Law and Practice of the ICC: A Critical Account of Challenges and Achievements* (Oxford University Press 2015).

112 Art. 28 (a)(i) Rome Statute.

113 K. Ambos, 'Superior Responsibility' in A. Cassese, P. Gaeta, J. R. W. D. Jones (eds) *The Rome Statute of the International Criminal Court: A Commentary, Vol. 3* (Oxford University Press 2002) at 834.

114 *Prosecutor v. Blaškić* (Judgment) ICTY Case No. IT-95-14-A (29 July 2004), para. 43.

115 S. Darcy, 'Imputed Criminal Liability and the Goals of International Justice' (2007) 20 *Leiden Journal of International Law* 2, 377–404, at 403.

carried out not only by states, but also by armed groups. Among these instruments, truth seeking mechanisms are a key tool to establishing events and facts during armed conflicts, identifying alleged perpetrators, and providing recommendations on to how to address violations of IHL and IHRL.[116] Truth seeking mechanisms include commissions of inquiry, fact-finding missions, and truth and reconciliation commissions. Commissions of inquiry and fact-finding missions serve to identify serious violations of IHL and IHRL, as well as to promote accountability and combat impunity.[117] They tend to include in their mandates the requirement of responsibility and the identification of perpetrators of such violations. Similarly, truth commissions are non-judicial bodies that investigate violations of human rights committed over a period of time in a particular country, including violations 'by the military or other government forces or armed opposition forces'.[118] They are officially authorised or sanctioned by the state. The purpose of these commissions is to prepare a final report and make recommendations. Truth commissions have traditionally documented only the actions of states but some have also considered the actions of armed groups involved in such violations. Generally, the situations considered by truth commissions are periods of dictatorship or armed conflict. As these mechanisms analyse and report violations of IHL committed by both parties to an armed conflict, this section examines how these instruments reflect on the responsibility of armed groups as collectivities. For the purpose of this section, a number of reports have been selected. These will be detailed in the sub-sections below.

Commissions of inquiry, fact-finding missions and other investigating missions

The UN has been active in establishing these investigative mechanisms through the resolutions and reports of the Security Council, the Secretary-General, the General Assembly, the Human Rights Council, and the Office of the High Commissioner for Human Rights (OHCHR).[119] While the missions mandated by the UN Security Council and the UN Secretary General related more specifically to issues of maintenance of peace and security, some of them also touched upon violations of IHL and IHRL taking place during armed conflicts.[120] Since 2006 the UN Human Rights Council has become prolific in establishing these inquiries, having set up a total of twenty-eight

---

116 A. Bellal, 'Non-State Armed Groups in Transitional Justice Processes Adapting to New Realities of Conflict', in R. Duthie and P. Seils (eds), *Justice Mosaics: How Context Shapes Transitional Justice in Fractured Societies* (International Centre for Transitional Justice 2017).

117 See C. Hardwood, 'Contributions of International Commissions of Inquiry to Transitional Justice' (2016) Grotius Centre Working Paper 2016/054-ICL, 15–19.

118 P. B. Hayner, 'Fifteen Truth Commissions – 1974 to 1994: A Comparative Study' (1994) 16 *Human Rights Quarterly* 4, 597–655, at 558.

119 See Office of the High Commissioner for Human Rights, 'Commissions of Inquiry and Fact-Finding Missions on International Human Rights and Humanitarian Law: Guidance and Practice', UN Doc. HR/PUB/14/7(2015) <www.ohchr.org/Documents/Publications/CoI_Guidance_and_Practice.pdf> accessed 29 April 2019.

120 C. Harwood, *supra note* 117, 5.

commissions of inquiry and fact-finding missions.[121] Their mandates have assessed situations of serious violations of IHL and IHRL protracted or resulting from sudden events, and have promoted accountability for such violations.

In this context, this section examines how these mechanisms deal with the responsibility of armed groups as such. For the purpose of this study, 30 inquiries have been selected. Particular focus has been placed on the reports of missions mandated by the UN Human Rights Council since they deal specifically with monitoring violations of IHL and IHRL. These inquiries have been selected based on the existence of a non-international armed conflict and consist of 24 missions resulting in one or several final reports dealing with situations in Burundi (three missions), Central African Republic (CAR), Cote D'Ivoire, Darfur, Democratic Republic of Congo (DRC), Iraq, Libya (two missions), Myanmar, Occupied Palestinian territories and Israel (seven missions), South Sudan (two missions), Sri Lanka, Syria (two missions) and Yemen.[122] Moreover, six additional missions mandated either by the OHCHR (Mali and Nigeria)[123], the UN Security Council (Darfur and CAR)[124] and the Secretary General (Sri-Lanka and DRC)[125] have also been included as their reports refer to violations of IHL and IHRL committed during non-international armed conflicts. This analysis has considered whether the aforementioned reports acknowledge any of the following circumstances: the application of primary obligations for armed groups; the responsibility of the individual members of the armed group; or the responsibility of the armed group itself. From the 30 selected commissions of inquiry and fact-finding missions, it was concluded that 23 of them refer in their reports to violations of international law committed by armed groups either directly or indirectly. In particular, it is possible to extract the following findings.

Firstly, most reports refer to primary obligations of armed groups indicating the necessity to respect IHL and human rights standards. References to IHL and IHRL frameworks are made in terms of 'requirements of human rights and humanitarian law', the 'obligation to ensure respect for international humanitarian law and human

---

121 See the list of 28 HRC-mandated Commissions of Inquiries/Fact-Finding Missions & Other Bodies at <www.ohchr.org/EN/HRBodies/HRC/Pages/ListHRCMandat.aspx> accessed 30 April 2019. The Fact-finding Mission on the human rights situation in the Occupied Palestinian Territory (6 July 2006) was not implemented and so has been excluded from the present analysis.

122 From the referred list of 28 missions, the missions in Lebanon, DPRK and Eritrea do not deal with non-international armed conflict and they have therefore been excluded from this study. Moreover, the second mission in the Kasai region in the DRC (2018) has yet to produce a report and so has also been excluded.

123 OHCHR Fact-finding mission on the situation of human rights in Mali 2012; OHCHR Fact-finding mission to investigate atrocities committed by the terrorist group Boko Haram and its effects on human rights in the affected States [Cameroon, Chad, the Niger, Nigeria] 2015.

124 The 2004 International Commission of Inquiry on Darfur (UNSC Resolution 1564, 2004); The 2013 International Commission of Inquiry on the Central African Republic (UNSC Resolution 2127, 2013).

125 The Mapping exercise of the most serious violations of human rights and international humanitarian law committed within the territory of the Democratic Republic of the Congo between March 1993 and June 2003, established by the UN Secretary General on 8 May 2007; the 2010 Secretary-General's Panel of Experts on Accountability in Sri Lanka established by the UN Secretary-General (22 June 2010) SG/SM/12967.

rights law', 'provisions of Common Article 3 of the Geneva Conventions and Additional Protocol II', 'fundamental human rights', 'human rights obligations constituting peremptory international law', and 'fundamental human rights forming customary international law', among others. Specific obligations under IHL are also examined, such as the principle of distinction, the necessity to take feasible precautions, or the prohibition of indiscriminate attacks. More precisely, these examples relate to the armed groups in the conflict in Darfur (rebel groups such as SLA and JEM)[126], the Gaza conflict (Palestinian armed groups)[127], the armed conflict in Libya (opposing forces such as the Free Libyan Army; armed groups affiliated with Ansar al-Sharia; groups pledging allegiance to ISIL; and tribal armed groups in the South)[128], the armed conflict in Syria (anti-government armed groups like the Free Syrian Army; the IS of Iraq and Al-Sham; and Kurdish armed groups)[129], the armed conflict in CAR (non-state armed groups such as the Séléka forces and the Anti-balaka)[130], the armed conflict in Sri Lanka (the LTTE)[131], or the armed conflict in Myanmar (the ethnic armed organizations such as the KIA, the SSA-S, the SSA-N, the TNLA, the AA, and the MNDAA).[132]

Secondly, most reports refer to patterns in the commission of violations relating to the organisational structure or the territorial control of these groups. Violations of IHL and human rights during armed conflicts are not isolated incidents. On the contrary, they are committed by the application of a series of strategies governed by the hierarchy of the armed group and, in some cases, in the areas controlled by them. Commissions of inquiry have elaborated on the collective actions carried out by armed groups in the course of the commission of these violations. In this sense, they talk about the 'effective overall control over military personnel' by rebel groups in Darfur[133]; attacks that constitute 'a pattern of organized violence' by armed groups under the control of the Gaza authority[134]; armed groups in control of many detention facilities in Libya committing arbitrary detentions and abductions[135]; a clear pattern of targeting

126 References to primary rules are included in the Report of the Commission of Inquiry in Darfur 2004 and the High-Level Mission, 2006.

127 References to primary rules are included in the Report of the UN Fact-Finding Mission to the Gaza conflict in 2009 and the Commission of Inquiry, 2014.

128 References to primary rules are included in the Report of the Commission of Inquiry in Libya 2011 and the OHCHR Investigation in Libya, 2015.

129 References to primary rules are included in the Reports of the Commission of Inquiry in Syria from 2011 to present.

130 References to primary rules are included in the Reports of the Commission of Inquiry in CAR 2013 and the OHCHR Fact-Finding Mission in CAR 2014.

131 References to primary rules are included in the Report of the Panel of experts on Accountability in Sri Lanka in 2011.

132 References to primary rules are included in the Report of the Independent International Fact-Finding Mission on Myanmar in 2018.

133 Report of the International Commission of Inquiry on Darfur to the United Nations Secretary-General, Pursuant to Security Council Resolution 1564 of 18 September 2004, Geneva (25 January 2005) para. 564.

134 Report of the United Nations Fact-Finding Mission on the Gaza Conflict (25 September 2009) A/HRC/12/48, para. 80.

135 Report of the OHCHR Investigation on Libya (15 February 2016) A/HRC/31/47, para. 12.

schoolyards by anti-government armed groups or the creation of training camps to recruit children by the ISIS in Syria[136]; or the development of a 'well-structured international strategy' by the LTTE in Sri Lanka through the use of conventional tactics and extensive intelligence apparatuses.[137]

Thirdly, almost all reports refer to individual criminal responsibility of the leaders and members as the exclusive accountability mechanism for armed groups. After mapping the violations committed by both state and non-state armed groups, commissions of inquiry usually reserve a final section on legal responsibility. In some cases, issues of responsibility are dealt with in the final section dealing with conclusions and recommendations. Where violations are committed by the state, this section normally refers to state responsibility for the conduct of its organs and individual criminal responsibility. However, with regard to armed groups, this section only considers the individual criminal responsibility of its leaders and members. This is the case of the reports on Gaza, Libya, Iraq, Central African Republic, South Sudan, Cote D'Ivoire, Democratic Republic of Congo, Mali, Myanmar, Nigeria, and Yemen.

Fourthly, only two inquiries, namely the Commission of Inquiry in Darfur and the Panel of Experts on Accountability in Sri Lanka, point to the direct international responsibility of the armed groups as such. The Commission of Inquiry in Darfur dealt with the violations committed by the Sudan Liberation Movement/Army (SLM/A) and the Justice and Equality Movement (JEM). In its section on the categories of international crimes, the Commission explained the possibility of dual responsibility and the obligation to provide reparations by both parties in the following terms:

> Serious violations of human rights law and humanitarian law may amount to international crimes, subject to the conditions set out by the ICTY in Tadić (Interlocutory Appeal) and largely codified in the ICC Statute. In other words, these violations may entail the individual criminal liability of their author or authors. These violations may *also involve the international responsibility of the State or of the international non-state entity* to which those authors belong as officials (or for which they acted as de facto organs), with the consequence that *the State or the non-state-entity may have to pay compensation* to the victims of those violations.[138]

The Panel of Experts on Accountability in Sri Lanka also recognised the international responsibility of the Liberation Tigers of Tamil Eelam (LTTE) as such for violations of IHL. Specifically, the panel distinguished three types of legal responsibility:

> The Panel considers three forms of responsibility. State responsibility concerns whether the State of Sri Lanka would be responsible for violations were the alleged facts found to be true.

136 Report of the Independent International Commission of Inquiry on the Syrian Arab Republic (13 August 2014) A/HRC/27/60, para. 94–95.

137 Report of the Secretary General's Panel of Experts on Accountability in Sri Lanka (31 March 2011) para. 33.

138 Report of the International Commission of Inquiry on Darfur to the United Nations Secretary-General, Pursuant to Security Council Resolution 1564 of 18 September 2004, Geneva (25 January 2005), para. 175, emphasis added.

> Under international law, state responsibility applies only to the acts of the State of Sri Lanka. Actions by non-state actors such as paramilitary groups or private citizens who act under the instructions of, or are directed or controlled by, the State are imputable to the State. *Organizational responsibility is a concept that recognizes that international humanitarian law also places duties on non-state armed groups, including in this case the LTTE.* Individual responsibility generally concerns whether particular individuals regardless of their affiliation in an armed conflict would be criminally responsible for violations. Criminal responsibility attaches to certain acts, regardless of whether the individual was acting on behalf of the Government or the LTTE (or neither).[139]

More subtly, the Commission of Inquiry in Syria indirectly recognised the responsibility of anti-government armed groups and not only of individual members. This is observable in two reports. In section IV on responsibility, the report of August 2012 distinguished between state responsibility, responsibility of anti-government armed groups and individual criminal responsibility.[140] However, the sub-section on anti-government armed groups only reflected the primary rules of IHL and the criminal responsibility of their members. In the report of February 2013, the Commission recommended that armed groups 'ensure the accountability of those who violate international human rights and humanitarian law, and provide effective redress for victims based on international standards'.[141] This last part indirectly bears in mind the responsibility of the group for the actions of individuals who violate the law and the obligation to provide reparations.

With regards to the missions launched in Gaza, their reports have usually referred to the responsibility of the Gaza authorities for the actions of the armed groups operating in its territory in a similar way to the due diligence obligations of states. In particular, the UN Fact-Finding Mission on the Gaza conflict in 2009 claimed that:

> The Mission notes, more importantly, that, [...] the Gaza authorities are obliged under international law to control the activities of armed groups operating on the territory under their control. If they failed to take the necessary measures to prevent the Palestinian armed groups from endangering the civilian population by conducting hostilities in a manner incompatible with international humanitarian law, *they would bear responsibility* for the damage done to the civilians living in Gaza.[142]

Fifthly, some reports refer to state responsibility for the actions of non-state actors, in particular where the armed groups in question support or are in coalition with the state;

---

139 Report of the Secretary General's Panel of Experts on Accountability in Sri Lanka (31 March 201) para. 191, emphasis added.

140 3rd Report of the International Commission of Inquiry on the Syrian Arab Republic (15 August 2012) A/HRC/21/50, 21–22, para. 131–142.

141 4rd Report of the International Commission of Inquiry on the Syrian Arab Republic (5 February 2013) A/HRC/22/59, para. 177 (d).

142 Report of the United Nations Fact-Finding Mission on the Gaza Conflict, A/HRC/12/48 (25 September 2009), para. 498, emphasis added.

or where the insurrectional group becomes the new government. In this regard, reports attribute the actions of non-state armed groups to the state according to the rules of effective control under Article 8 ASR or to the actions of the successful insurrectional movement under Article 10 ASR. This is the case of the exercise of 'effective control' by the Burundian State over the non-state actor Imbonerakure, the youth wing of Burundi's ruling party, which was aligned with the Government's policy[143]; and the Séléka, which after it seized power, engaged the state responsibility of the Central African Republic for all violations committed by its members in the country during the armed conflict.[144] In other cases, the dependence of these non-state actors on the state could not be proved, as was the case in Iraq, as additional information was needed to establish the link between the militia forces and the Government.[145]

To summarise, when determining violations of international law committed by armed groups, commissions of inquiry and fact-finding missions pay special attention to detailing the collective actions carried out by armed groups in a specific section for the violations committed by them, separate from the section dedicated to state violations. Moreover, these mechanisms emphasise the primary obligations of armed groups according to humanitarian and human rights law standards. However, in the section of conclusions and recommendations most of these reports only refer to the criminal responsibility of individuals. Only two of the twenty-three cases dealing with violations committed by armed groups have referred to the possible international responsibility of the group as such. This idea was already emphasised by Zegveld when she stated that international bodies had given priority to individual criminal responsibility over group responsibility.[146] It therefore appears that disconnect remains between the responsibility of individual members and the armed group itself, which is not clearly addressed by these mechanisms. If violations of IHL are committed following certain patterns or policies that are facilitated by the structures of the group, then the recommendation section should also address this aspect in a similar manner to those dedicated to state violations.

Finally, there are some important limitations in the work performed by commissions of inquiry and fact-finding missions. These mechanisms assess violations committed during a specific time-frame of the armed conflict prescribed by the specific mandate of the mission. As such, their scope is limited to specific facts and events. Another problem, raised by Bellal, is that in a number of armed conflicts there are a huge number of non-state armed groups, such as in DRC, Libya and Syria, and consequently, 'it can prove difficult for these mechanisms to address all the violations committed by all the actors at a given time, leaving many violations unaccounted for'.[147]

---

143 Report of the Commission of Inquiry on Burundi (11 August 2017) A/HRC/36/54, para. 23–27.

144 Report of the United Nations High Commissioner for Human Rights (12 September 2013), A/HRC/24/59, para. 25.

145 Report of the Office of the United Nations High Commissioner for Human Rights on the human rights situation in Iraq in light of the abuses committed by the so-called Islamic State in Iraq and the Levant and associated groups (13 March 2015) A/HRC/28/18, para. 51.

146 L. Zegveld, *Accountability of Armed Opposition Groups*, 223.

147 A. Bellal, *supra note* 116, 5.

Truth and reconciliation commissions

This section analyses the work of truth and reconciliation commissions in terms of their considerations of the responsibility of armed groups as collective entities. The information for this section has been gathered from the United States Institute of Peace's Truth Commissions Digital Collection which contains each commission's final reports as well as links to other official legislative texts.[148] In addition, other secondary sources have been used to complement the information provided by the reports, namely, the section on Truth Commissions from the two-year project headed by Professor Bassiouni on 'Conflicts, Victimization and Post-Conflict Justice'[149]; and the thematic issue on Truth and Reconciliation Commissions of the International Review of the Red Cross in 2006.[150] The reports considered in this section have been selected on the basis of the existence of a non-international armed conflict and there being a submitted final report. Most of the truth commissions deal with situations of dictatorship, authoritarian regimes or the existence of a military regime where violations by the state have been attributed based on the rules of state responsibility.[151] Other truth commissions either did not conclude with a final report or the report was not publicly available.[152] Consequently, the selection of truth commissions that address violations committed during a NIAC are considerably fewer than the ones analysed in the previous section. The reports selected for this section are the Report of the Commission on the Truth for El Salvador; the Report of the Commission for Historical Clarification in Guatemala; the Final Report Truth and Reconciliation Commission of the Republic of Liberia; the Report of the Truth and Reconciliation Commission in Peru; and the Final Report of Sierra Leone's the Truth and Reconciliation Commission. Their analysis reveals the following findings.

In the case of El Salvador, the 1993 report details the violations of IHL and IHRL carried out by the Frente Farabundo Martí para la Liberación Nacional (FMLN). It covers the use of violence against non-combatants and the execution of alleged criminals without due process. Interestingly, the report tries to explain patterns in the manner in which these violations were carried out, including how they were adopted by

148 See the United States Institute of Peace's Truth Commissions Digital Collection at <https://www.usip.org/publications/2011/03/truth-commission-digital-collection> accessed 30 April 2019.

149 E. Wiebelhaus-Brahm, 'Truth Commissons and other Investigative Bodies' in M. Cherif Bassiouni (ed) *The Pursuit of International Criminal Justice: A World Study on Conflicts, Victimization, and Post-Conflict Justice* (Intersentia 2010) 477–574.

150 See the Special Issue on Truth and Reconciliation Commission, *International Review of the Red Cross* (2006) Vol. 88, No. 862 at <https://www.icrc.org/en/international-review/truth-and-reconciliation-commissions> accessed 30 April 2019.

151 This is the case of the truth commissions in Argentina, Chad, Chile, Ecuador, Ghana, Haiti, Honduras, Morocco, Nigeria, Panama, Paraguay, South Korea, Timor Leste and Uruguay. The truth commission in South Africa deals with non-state paramilitary formations such as such as the ANC's self-defence units and the IFP's self-protection units (SPUs). However, the Commission found that '[t]he preponderance of responsibility rests with the state and its allies'. See the Truth and Reconciliation Commission of South Africa Report, Vol. 5, Chapter 6, p. 210.

152 This is the case of the truth commissions in Kenya, Rwanda and Uganda.

the hierarchy and executed by local commanders. For instance, in the case of summary executions of mayors, the Commission found that:

> 1. There is full evidence that the FMLN General Command approved and adopted a policy of murdering mayors whom it considered to be working against it.
> 2. There is full evidence that members of the ERP [Ejército Revolucionario del Pueblo] leadership, among others, carried out the policy and ordered their local commanders to murder mayors whom they considered to be working against FMLN.
> [...]
> 5. There is full evidence that local ERP commanders, either under orders from the leadership or with its approval and backing, murdered the mayors listed in this summary.
> 6. There is full evidence that the murders of mayors [...] were part of an established pattern, based on a deliberate FMLN policy, and were carried out by local ERP commanders on orders from and with the express approval of members of the ERP leadership.
> 7. There is full evidence that the mayor of Guatajigua, José Alberto López, was murdered in October 1988, while in the power of commander "Amadeo".
> 8. The execution of mayors by FMLN was a violation of the rules of international humanitarian law and international human rights law.[153]

This particular example demonstrates the existence of a group policy that was executed by its local commanders and which was attributed to a specific commander as an official member of the armed group. In the recommendation section, the FMLN was mandated to stop the use of armed violence and to provide compensation to victims in those cases where it was found to have been responsible in a similar way to a state. Specifically, the Commission found that the 'FMLN must provide such compensation where it is found to have been responsible, while this obligation devolves on the State in cases where the actions or omissions of the public authorities or their agencies were among the causes of the acts of violence described [...]'.[154] Accordingly, responsibility was distributed between the state and the armed group.

The Commission for Historical Clarification in Guatemala (1999), although mostly focused on violations committed by the state, also refers to human rights violations committed by insurgent armed groups. In terms of primary rules, the Commission emphasised that armed groups have the obligation to respect the minimum standards of IHL that apply to armed conflicts, as well as general principles common to IHRL.[155] The Commission also found out that arbitrary executions were decided upon at different levels in the organic structure of the guerrilla organisations with the participation of both high military commanders and local delegates.[156] However, in terms of responsibility, the report only focuses on the leaders of the armed groups claiming

153 UN Security Council, 'From Madness to Hope: The 12-year war in El Salvador: Report of the Commission on the Truth for El Salvador' (1 April 1993) Annex, UN Doc. S/25500, 144–45.

154 *Ibid*, 177.

155 *Guatemala Memoria del Silencio, Resumen ejecutivo, conclusiones y recomendaciones*, vol. II, 27 April 1999, UN Doc. A/53/928 Anexo, 312–313, para. 127.

156 *Ibid*, para. 130.

that 'the superior levels of the organic structure of the guerrillas hold undeniable responsibility'.[157]

The report of the Truth and Reconciliation Commission in Peru (2003) points out that the Shining Path group was the principal perpetrator of crimes and human rights violations, responsible for 54% of deaths, while the Túpac Amaru Revolutionary Movement was only responsible for 1.5% of deaths.[158] The Commission emphasised that attacks were committed in a calculated, generalised and systematic manner by the Shining Path.[159] Its strategy was not based on the control of territory but the control of the population. Here, the recommendation section focuses on the individual criminal responsibility of the leaders and members of the Shining Path and the Túpac Amaru Revolutionary Movement.[160] The report did not address the responsibility of the group as such in the recommendation section.

In the case of Liberia, the Commission's report (2009) considered the application of both Common Article 3 and Additional Protocol II to the Geneva Conventions. It found that a list of armed groups, rebel groups or warring factions as well as their financers, leaders, commanders, combatants and advisors were responsible for committing 'gross' violations of human rights and 'serious' humanitarian law violations in Liberia between January 1979 and October 2003.[161] In the section on 'Determinations', the Commission refers to four types of perpetrators, namely individual perpetrators, group perpetrators dealing with armed groups, corporate perpetrators dealing with corporations, and government perpetrators dealing with the Government of Liberia from 1979 to 2003.[162] The recommendation section states that while prosecutions and public sanctions were applicable to all individuals, reparations were only imposed on the state of Liberia.[163] One can again perceive a disconnect between the individual responsibility of group members and the group responsibility.

In the Final Report of the Truth and Reconciliation Commission of Sierra Leone (2009) the Commission determined that all armed groups involved in the conflict were responsible for human rights violations, especially the Revolutionary United Front (RUF) that was considered responsible for 60.5% of violations.[164] In particular, the Commission found that:

> [T]he leadership of the RUF, the [Armed Forces Revolutionary Council] AFRC, the [Sierra Leone Army] SLA and the [Civil Defence Forces] CDF to be responsible for: a) either authorising or instigating human rights violations against civilians; b) alternatively, for

[157] *Ibid*, para. 143.
[158] Report of the Truth and Reconciliation Commission in Peru (2003) vol. 2, 1, 430.
[159] *Ibid*, Vol. 6, p. 16.
[160] *Ibid*, Vol. 9, p. 107.
[161] Truth and Reconciliation Commission of Liberia, 'Final Report: Volume II: Consolidated Final Report' (2009) vol. II, 10.
[162] *Ibid*, 265–266.
[163] *Ibid*, 276.
[164] Final Report of Sierra Leone's the Truth and Reconciliation Commission (2004), vol. II, chapter II, 38.

> failing to stop such practices or to speak out against them; c) and for failing to acknowledge the atrocities committed by their followers or members.[165]

In the section on methodology, the Commission's priority was to establish the responsibility of individual perpetrators. It explains that:

> In presenting the normative of the conflict, the Commission made several findings concerning the responsibility of the respective factions and certain individuals. These findings were based on empirical evidence linking the perpetrator to the violations. Where the evidence was inconclusive, the Commission declined to make a finding. Most of the Commission's findings were made against the armed factions that participated in the conflict rather than against individual perpetrator. However, where the information at the disposal of the Commission pointed conclusively to the role of an individual in the conflict, the person in question was named.[166]

In this report, the Commission tried to link the commission of violations with the armed factions of the conflict. However, it did not explain the specific process of attribution of such violations to the group itself. The main findings were made against the leadership of the armed groups and against some individual perpetrators. Similarly to the work of commissions of inquiry and fact-finding missions, the priority of truth commissions is to determine the criminal responsibility of the leaders and members of armed groups for violations of IHL and IHRL committed during non-international armed conflicts. Only the Truth Commission for El Salvador truly recognised the responsibility of the armed group by firstly, attempting to explain the attribution of violations to specific members and local commanders, and therefore to the group itself; and secondly, by inferring the obligation to provide reparations by the group which was directly linked to its group responsibility for the violations committed. Nevertheless, these mechanisms also pay attention to the patterns and organisational strategies performed by armed groups.

One limitation of truth commissions is the lack of uniformity among these mechanisms. Indeed, the work of truth commissions highly depends on the specific context in which they are created and the configuration through which they have been established. The scope of their results vary depending on their design and the differences in their funding.[167] In addition, their main focus is not only determining who the perpetrators are but also establishing past events as well as understanding the patterns and origins of the violations.[168] Consequently, in some cases establishing the truth could be prioritised over determining the exact legal responsibility of all the entities involved.

---

165 *Ibid*, 28.

166 *Ibid*, Vol. 1, Chapter 5, para. 66.

167 A. Bellal, *supra note* 116, 5.

168 *Ibid*.

3.1.3. *Naming and shaming*

Another means by which violations committed by armed groups can be addressed is the naming and shaming of perpetrators of specific violations. This method has been applied by the UN Secretary-General in the process of reporting violations committed against children rights and sexual violence during armed conflicts. In this connection, the Secretary General has appointed a Special Representative on the issue of children in armed conflict who submits an annual report to the General Assembly and the Human Rights Council containing relevant information.[169] One of the sections within these reports lists a number of 'persistent perpetrators'. 'Persistent perpetrators' are those who have been listed for at least five years for the commission of violations against children.[170] They include both state security forces and non-state armed groups. As of 2018, 69 actors in 14 country situations have been listed as parties that recruit, use, kill or maim children, commit rape and other forms of sexual violence against children, engage in attacks on schools and/or hospitals, or abduct children in situations of armed conflict.[171] Out of these 69 actors, 59 are non-state armed groups in Afghanistan, Central African Republic, Democratic Republic of Congo, Iraq, Mali, Myanmar, Somalia, South Sudan, Sudan, Syria, Yemen, Colombia, Nigeria and the Philippines.[172]

This exercise ultimately aims to hold perpetrators accountable and encourages them to comply with child protection standards. According to Nyamutata '[t]he philosophical objective of the strategy was to inflict stigmatization through public exposure. Because of the attendant reputational costs, the offenders would desist from violation of children's rights during warfare'.[173] In order to be de-listed, parties must prepare and implement an action plan with concrete and time-bound activities to halt the violations.[174] Additional measures consist of the imposition of sanctions by the Security Council on military and political leaders of these groups in order to end impunity and to prevent the commission of these violations.[175]

---

169 The current Special Representative of the Secretary-General for Children and Armed Conflict is Virginia Gamba, named by Secretary-General Antonio Guterres in April 2017. She is the fourth person to hold this position. See Office of the Special Representative of the Secretary-General on Children and Armed Conflict available at <https://childrenandarmedconflict.un.org/about-us/special-representative/virginia-gamba/> accessed 20 April 2019.

170 Report of the Secretary-General on Children in Armed Conflict (26 April 2012) A /66/782–S /2012/26, para. 221.

171 Report of the Secretary-General on Children in Armed Conflict (16 May 2018) A/72/865–S/2018/465, Annex I and II, 38–42.

172 *Ibid.*

173 C. Nyamutata, 'Engaging or Shaming? An Analysis of UN's Naming and Shaming of Child Abusers in Armed Conflict' (2013) 4 *Journal of International Humanitarian Legal Studies* 1, 151–173, at 155.

174 Office of the Special Representative of the Secretary-General on Children and Armed Conflict, available at <https://childrenandarmedconflict.un.org/our-work/action-plans/> accessed 20 April 2019.

175 See C. Márquez Carrasco, L. Íñigo Álvarez, N. Loozen & E. Salmón, *Survey Study on Human Rights Violations in Conflict Settings*, EU FP7 Research Project, Deliverable No. 10.1 (30 September 2014)

The method of naming and shaming has also been implemented more generally in the area of sexual violence in armed conflicts. Since 2012, the UN Secretary-General has been reporting on conflict-related sexual violence with the support of the Special Representative and the Team of Experts on the Rule of Law and Sexual Violence in Conflict.[176] Similarly to the field of children in armed conflict, these reports contain a list of parties who are 'credibly suspected of committing or being responsible for patterns of rape and other forms of sexual violence in situations of armed conflict'.[177] The last report of March 2018 listed 51 actors, of which 39 represent non-state armed groups in countries such as the Central African Republic, Cote d'Ivoire, Democratic Republic of Congo, Iraq, Mali, Somalia, Sudan, South Sudan, Syria and Nigeria.[178] The Secretary-General recommended the inclusion of commissions of sexual violence a criterion for the imposition of sanctions and 'that any person or entity who transfers funds to Islamic State in Iraq and the Levant (ISIL) directly or indirectly in connection with sexual violence or exploitation would be eligible for listing'.[179]

As for some limitations, these mechanisms have been only employed in certain areas such as children rights and sexual violence during armed conflicts, as these areas are considered some of the most serious violations of IHL. Consequently, not all violations of IHL are included as a basis for naming and shaming. Furthermore, these mechanisms are conceived as policy instruments rather than legal tools that would determine the legal responsibility of armed groups. The object is the reputational cost of these actions for states and non-state entities and the prevention of future violations. Consequently, although they represent useful tools to encourage the compliance with IHL, they are not conceived as legal instruments through which one is able to assess the international responsibility of armed groups.

3.1.4. Sanctions

In the context of the sanctions imposed by the UN Security Council under Chapter VII of the UN Charter, sanctions have been directed not only against states but also against certain non-state armed groups. Sanctions consist of 'reactive measures taken in an institutionalized context to a breach of an international obligation having serious consequences for the international community as a whole'.[180] These sanctions may include complete or partial interruption of economic relations and other means of

152–154 available at <www.fp7-frame.eu/wp-content/uploads/2016/08/08-Deliverable-10.1.pdf> accessed 20 April 2019.

176 Report of the Secretary-General on Conflict-related Sexual Violence (13 January 2012) A /66/657–S /2012/33, 1.

177 *Ibid*, 1.

178 Report of the Secretary-General on Conflict-related Sexual Violence (23 March 2018) S/2018/250, Annex, 33–35.

179 Report of the Secretary-General on Conflict-related Sexual Violence (15 April 2017) S/2017/249, 28.

180 V. Goelland-Debbas, 'Responsibility and the United Nations Charter' in J. Crawford, A. Pellet & S. Olleson (eds), *The Law of International Responsibility* (Oxford University Press 2010) 133.

communication, such as the freezing of assets, weapons embargoes, travel restrictions and the severance of diplomatic relations.[181]

With regards to non-state entities, the Security Council has imposed sanctions on a number of groups including the Bosnian Serb forces in the former Yugoslavia, the non-state parties in the conflict in Sierra Leone in 1992, the Taliban in Afghanistan and the Congolese and foreign armed groups and other militias operating in the Democratic Republic of Congo.[182] The aim of measures such as the freezing of assets and weapons embargoes is primarily the weakening of the financial basis of armed groups.[183] Furthermore, other international organisations such as the European Union and a number of individual states have also adopted sanctions against several armed groups.[184] Consequently, through the imposition of these types of sanctions, international organisations have indirectly tried to bring to account different non-state armed groups.

It should be emphasised that these measures are not designed to deal with issues of international responsibility but to preserve peace and security.[185] However, many of these aforementioned situations have resulted in the commission of grave violations of international law by both states and non-state armed groups. These sanctions indirectly highlight the responsibility of the group as such. More precisely, the very fact that the international community chooses to react by imposing sanctions against certain non-state armed groups demonstrates that there is an implicit recognition that the collective actions of groups deserve responses that go beyond the individual criminal responsibility of their members.

3.2. ACADEMIC DISCUSSION ON THE DISCONNECTION BETWEEN PRIMARY AND SECONDARY RULES

There has been extensive literature regarding the question of the obligations of armed groups under international law and the primary rules applicable to them.[186] Specifically,

---

181 Art. 41 UN Charter.

182 In relation to the former Yugoslavia, Security Council Resolution 942 (1994); in relation to Sierra Leone, Security Council Resolution 1132 (1997) and 1171 (1998); in relation to Afghanistan, Security Council Resolution 1267 (1999); in relation to the DR Congo, Security Council Resolution 1493 (2003) and 1807 (2008); See also J. K. Kleffner, 'The collective accountability of organised armed groups', 253.

183 D. Amoroso, 'Armed Opposition Groups' (and Foreign Fighters) Abidance by International Human Rights Law: The Issue of Compliance in Syria and Iraq' in A. de Guttry, F. Capone & C. Paulussen (eds) *Foreign Fighters under International Law and Beyond* (TMC Asser Press 2016), 219.

184 Council Decision 2005/930/EC of 21 December 2005 implementing Art. 2(3) of Regulation (EC) No. 2580/2001 on specific restrictive measures directed against certain persons and entities with a view to combating terrorism and repealing Decision 2005/848/EC. The list of groups and entities include: Hamas, New Peoples Army (NPA), the Kurdistan Workers' Party (PKK), the Colombian National Liberation Army (Ejercito de Liberacion Nacional), Revolutionary Armed Forces of Colombia (FARC), or the Shining Path (SP).

185 J. K Kleffner, 'The collective accountability of organised armed groups', 253.

186 See A. Clapham, 'Human Rights Obligations of Non-state Actors in Conflict Situations' (2006) 88 *International Review of the Red Cross* 863, 491–523; C. Ryngaert, 'Non-state Actors in International Humanitarian Law' in J. D'Aspremont (ed), *Participants in the International Legal System – Multiple*

IHL obligations are applied to both parties in non-international armed conflicts i.e. governments as well as organised armed groups, through Common Article 3, Additional Protocol II, and Customary IHL.[187] International practice has consistently recognised the necessity of armed groups to respect rules of IHL. For instance, in the *Nicaragua case*, the International Court of Justice (ICJ) affirmed that the acts of the *contras* towards the Nicaraguan government were governed by the law applicable to conflicts not of an international character.[188] In 2004, the Special Court for Sierra Leone (SCSL) also emphasised that all parties to an armed conflict, i.e. both state and non-state actors, are bound law by IHL.[189] In a similar vein, since the late 1990s, the UN Security Council and other organs of the United Nations have repeatedly called upon armed groups to abide by IHL provisions.[190]

Moreover, certain armed groups have expressly accepted these rules through unilateral declarations and special agreements.[191] Ceasefire and peace agreements between the parties to a NIAC have also established obligations in terms of IHL and IHRL.[192] Additionally, in cases where the armed group exercises control over territory, the practice of the UN Human Rights Council has indicated that armed groups should also respect human rights law during armed conflicts. This was considered in particular during the armed conflict in Libya in which the International Commission of Inquiry stated that 'it is increasingly accepted that where non-state groups exercise *de facto* control over territory, they must respect fundamental human rights of persons in that territory'.[193] Consequently, there is a consensus in relation to the fact that armed groups fighting in a NIAC bear international obligations.

Perspectives on Non-State Actors in International Law (Routledge 2011) 284–294; J. K. Kleffner, 'The Applicability of International Humanitarian Law to Organized Armed Groups' (2011) 93 *International Review of the Red Cross* 882, 443–461.

187 See J. M. Henckaerts & L. Doswald-Beck, *Customary International Humanitarian Law.*

188 *Military and Paramilitary Activities in and against Nicaragua* (Merits) [1984] Judgment ICJ Rep 392, 26 November 1984, para 219.

189 *Prosecutor v. Sam Hinga Norman* (Decision on Preliminary Motion Based on Lack of Jurisdiction) (Child Recruitment) Case No. SCSL-2004-14-AR72(E) (31 May 2004), para. 22.

190 For instance, UN Security Council Resolution 1214 (1998) on the conflict in Afghanistan reiterated that 'all parties to the conflict are bound to comply with their obligations under international humanitarian law and in particular under the Geneva Conventions of 12 August 1949'. UN Security Council Resolution 1216 (1998) called on all parties of the conflict in Guinea-Bissau, including the Government and the Self-Proclaimed Military Junta, to respect strictly the relevant provisions of international humanitarian law.

191 For instance, the commitments made by the FMLN in El Salvador in 1988 and the NDFP in the Philippines in August 1991 to comply with Common Article 3 and Additional Protocol II. In addition, the NGO Geneva Call has stimulated the signing of so-called 'Deeds of Commitment' by armed groups to express their adherence to specific humanitarian norms. The list of armed groups who have signed the Deeds of Commitment is available at <https://genevacall.org/how-we-work/armed-non-state-actors> accessed 13 June 2017.

192 See C. Bell, *Peace Agreements and Human Rights* (Oxford University Press 2000).

193 UN Human Rights Council, Report of the International Commission of Inquiry to investigate all alleged violations of international human rights law in the Libyan Arab Jamahiriya (1 June 2011), A/HRC/17/44, para. 72. See also UN Secretary-General, Report of the Secretary-General's Panel of Experts on Accountability in Sri Lanka (31 March 2011) para. 188.

The existing consensus on the IHL primary rules applicable to armed groups contrasts with the lack of agreement that exists in relation to the application of secondary rules. This is also referred to as the 'responsibility gap'.[194] As explained before, the actions of armed groups fighting in a NIAC will not be covered by the ASR unless the armed group is successful and becomes the new government or a new state.[195] Additionally, the ASR will cover armed groups acting as instruments of the state, either empowered by the law of the state to exercise elements of governmental authority or acting under its effective control.[196] However, the ASR do not deal with armed groups fighting *against* the state.[197] In this context, states can only respond for their own failure to act, or also called due diligence, which is difficult to enforce in the context of armed conflicts.[198] For these reasons, the Committee on Non-State Actors of the International Law Association concluded that the mechanism of state responsibility to hold armed groups responsible is 'of limited use' since armed groups most commonly fight against states.[199] Consequently, the provisions of the ASR appear to be more suitable for paramilitary organisations or for those armed groups supporting the actions of the state.

The recognition of the international responsibility of armed groups as such has been considered by the scholarship and the practice only briefly. The ICRC study on customary international humanitarian law acknowledges that armed groups hold responsibility for violations of IHL and that violations committed by persons forming part of those groups should be attributed to the armed group as such.[200] In this sense, there is an underlying recognition of the possibility that armed groups bear international responsibility as a group. However, this assertion is not further developed or operationalised. Similarly, the commentary to the ASR left the door open for the possible responsibility of insurrectional movements.[201] One of the first authors to address this issue was Zegveld in her book on the accountability of armed opposition groups in international law in 2002.[202] She believes that '[i] n its current form, international law is unable to make armed opposition groups

194 K. Schmalenbach, 'International Responsibility for Humanitarian Law Violations by Armed Groups' in H. Krieger (ed), *Inducing Compliance with International Humanitarian Law: Lessons from the African Great Lake Region* (Cambridge University Press 2015) 495–496. This is also referred to as an 'accountability gap' in L. Zegveld, *Accountability of Armed Opposition Groups*.

195 See Art. 10 of the Articles on State Responsibility (ASR). See also G. Cahin, *supra note* 43.

196 These provisions are established in Art. 5 (Conduct of persons or entities exercising elements of governmental authority), Article 8 (Conduct directed or controlled by a State), and Article 9 (Conduct carried out in the absence or default of the official authorities).

197 Expressing a different view on this, see K. Fortin, *Accountability of Armed Groups*, 268–284. She argues that certain acts of certain armed groups could be considered under Art. 9 ASR.

198 V. Bílkova, 'Direct Responsbility of Armed Opposition Groups', 271. See also C. M. J. Ryngaert & A. Van De Meulebroucke, *supra note* 96, 463.

199 International Law Association Committee on Non-State Actors, 'Third report on the Obligations and Responsibility of Non-State Actors in International Law' (Washington Conference 2014) 8.

200 J. M. Henckaerts & L. Doswald-Beck, *Customary International Humanitarian Law*, Rule 149, p. 536.

201 Art. 10 of the Articles on State Responsibility (ASR), Commentary para. 16.

202 See L. Zegveld, *Accountability of Armed Opposition Groups*.

themselves fully accountable for their abuses against the civilian population'.[203] She considers the notion of accountability as a broader concept that encompasses 'both the substantive obligations of the relevant actors and their responsibility for breaches of these obligations'.[204] However, in terms of international responsibility *stricto sensu* she mainly focuses on the responsibility of the State and individual leaders of armed groups, dedicating only a short section to the responsibility of the armed group as such.[205] Regarding the responsibility of the group itself, she points to the existence of one main difficulty, that is, the determination of the conduct that is capable of being attributed to armed groups; and a procedural hurdle, that is, finding a suitable forum with jurisdiction to bring claims against them.[206]

Since Zegveld's contribution, there has been a preliminary examination of the issue in a number of journal articles and book chapters.[207] Sassòli emphasises the disconnection between primary and secondary norms indicating that '[w]hile it is today uncontroversial that armed groups are internationally responsible for violations of IHL, the exact rules on attribution, content and implementation of such responsibility are not yet clarified'.[208] Similarly, Heffes considers that even if armed opposition groups have international obligations and can breach them, 'the current international legal framework does not directly approach this issue'.[209] In this line, Kleffner warns that the lack of a legal framework of responsibility of armed groups is unsatisfactory for a legal system that should be governed by the rule of law.[210] Likewise, Bellal points to the lack of clear rules that 'will contribute to the difficulty of establishing and efficient and legitimate system of accountability for non-state actors'.[211] Moreover, it is still uncertain which type of responsibility framework should be applied for armed groups as collective entities. Although some preliminary solutions have been offered by the scholarship, more clarification can be gained through a thorough examination of the operationalisation of such a regime of international responsibility for non-state armed groups.

203 *Ibid*, 164.
204 *Ibid*., 5.
205 *Ibid*., 152–163.
206 *Ibid*., 152–154; 157–163.
207 Namely V. Bílková, 'Direct Responsibility of Armed Opposition Groups'; J. K Kleffner, 'The collective accountability of organised armed groups'; E. Heffes, *supra note* 92; S. I. Verhoeven, *supra note* 56; K. Schmalenbach *supra note* 194; A. Bellal, 'Establishing the Direct Responsibility of Non-State Armed Groups for Violations of International Norms: Issues of Attribution' in N. Gal-or, C. Ryngaert, C. & M. Noortmann, *Responsibilities of the Non-State Actor in Armed Conflict and the Market Place: Theoretical Considerations and Empirical Findings* (Brill Nijhoff 2015); K. Mastorodimos, *Armed Non-State Actors in International Humanitarian and Human Rights Law. Foundation and Framework of Obligations, and Rules on Accountability* (Routledge 2015) 112–137.
208 M. Sassòli, 'Taking Armed Groups Seriously', 44.
209 E. Heffes, *supra note* 92, 107.
210 J. K Kleffner, 'The collective accountability of organised armed groups', 258–260.
211 A. Bellal, *supra note* 207, 309.

3.3. CONCLUDING REMARKS ON MECHANISMS ADDRESSING ARMED GROUPS' VIOLATIONS

This section has analysed the current international legal framework applicable to armed groups and more specifically, the responses given by international law to address these violations. In that respect, four main mechanisms have been examined namely, ICL, truth seeking mechanisms, naming and shaming procedures, and sanctions. While all these instruments directly or indirectly acknowledge the responsibility of armed groups for violations of IHL, they do not cover the full range of their actions. ICL only addresses the actions of individual members of armed groups. Particularly, when dealing with collective modes of liability, ICL only covers the responsibility of specific persons for the actions of others, but not the conduct of the group as such. This contrasts with the requirement of an organisational policy for the commission of crimes against humanity or the commission of a crime by a group of persons. If such actions respond to the coordinated policy of a group or a common plan, why is responsibility only relegated to several individuals? The exclusive focus on the international criminal responsibility of individual members could leave certain actions unpunished.

In relation to truth seeking mechanisms such as commissions of inquiry and truth and reconciliation commissions, the above sections have demonstrated that they are useful tools in determining the facts and violations which have been committed during an armed conflict by both states and non-state armed groups. They are able to describe in considerable detail patterns in the commission of violations and the strategies of armed groups. However, when referring to accountability, they tend to focus predominantly on the establishment of individual criminal responsibility. Only a few examples, including the Commission of Inquiry in Darfur, the Accountability Panel in Sri Lanka, and the Truth Commission in El Salvador actually acknowledge the organisational responsibility of the armed group together with the responsibility of its individual members. They have nevertheless some limitations in their scope of action, such as the specific time-frame during which they operate, or the lack of uniformity among them.

Another response given by international law has been the naming and shaming of armed groups that have committed violations against children's rights and sexual violence offences during armed conflict. The listing of groups has sometimes been followed by sanctions to force armed groups to comply with humanitarian and human rights standards. However, they only cover specific types of IHL violations, namely those related to children rights and sexual violence in conflict as these violations are considered the most serious ones. Moreover, they are conceived as policy tools rather than legal instruments to assess the responsibility of the armed group. Finally, sanctions have been imposed on different non-state entities in the framework of Chapter VII of the UN Charter. These are aimed at weakening the financial basis of these groups. As a limiting factor, sanctions are not specifically aimed at establishing the international legal responsibility of those entities but rather focus on preserving peace and security.

All the aforementioned mechanisms offer certain responses to bring armed groups to account either by targeting their leaders and individual members through criminal prosecutions, stigmatising them through naming and shaming, or weakening their financial basis with the imposition of sanctions. Implicitly, these mechanisms acknowledge the existence of collective and organised action carried out by armed groups. Some of them even affirm the organisational responsibility of the armed group. Nonetheless, these accountability instruments are not accompanied by a legal framework against which it would be possible to assess the responsibility of the armed group as a collective entity. Consequently, it can be argued that the existing legal framework is fragmented and presents inconsistencies when addressing the violations of international law committed by non-state armed groups.

Finally, this section addresses the disconnection between primary and secondary rules applicable to armed groups. While there is a consensus among the practice and the scholarship regarding the existence of primary obligations of IHL for armed groups, such agreement does not seem to exist in relation to secondary norms or norms of international responsibility. Nevertheless, a number of authors have called for a clarification of such norms as a necessity to implement a legal framework that is coherent and effective in addressing violations of international law.

4. A RESPONSIBILITY REGIME FOR ARMED GROUPS UNDER INTERNATIONAL LAW: AN ASSESSMENT

After ascertaining the gaps and inconsistencies in the international legal framework regarding armed groups and their responsibility, this section will evaluate how the lack of clear and coherent rules affects key governing principles of international law. The evaluation considers the rule of law as a governing principle in international law together with the prevention of impunity and the obligation to provide reparation to victims of armed conflict. As it will be explained, the rule of law predicates that all persons, institutions and entities are accountable to just, fair and equitable laws. The obligation to provide reparation is both a consequence of responsibility and a fundamental right of victims of armed conflict. Moreover, this section assesses whether the requirements of ICL are sufficient to address the full range of violations of international law committed by armed groups. Finally, the prospects of a responsibility regime for armed groups will take into account the possible complementarity between individual and collective responsibility mechanisms as well as the legal and practical challenges to developing such a regime. In particular, this assessment will take into consideration the findings of the previous sections about the added value of collective/organisational responsibility and will serve to answer the first sub-question of this study, namely, why is a responsibility regime for armed groups necessary under international law?

4.1. THE RESPONSIBILITY GAP AND THE RULE OF LAW

The previous section demonstrated that there is a partial regulation of different aspects of the responsibility of armed groups, such as the criminal responsibility of individual members or the sanctions imposed on them but there is no coherent set of rules which addresses armed groups in a collective manner. This entails the so-called problem of the 'responsibility gap' which was already outlined by a number of authors.[212] At the same time, there is strong pressure by the United Nations to make armed groups comply with international standards during armed conflict and to promote the responsibility of armed groups and other non-state actors.[213] This has been one of the key challenges in the protection of civilians in the last decades.

The lack of clear rules addressing the responsibility of armed groups directly clashes with the idea of an international legal order governed by the rule of law.[214] The principle of the rule of law is embedded in the Universal Declaration of Human Rights (UDHR) and the Charter of the United Nations. In its preamble, the UDHR states that 'human rights should be protected by the rule of law'.[215] The UN Charter also states that one of the aims of the UN is 'to establish conditions under which justice and respect for the obligations arising from treaties and other sources of international law can be maintained'.[216] This is a principle supported both at the national and international level.[217] In 2004, the UN Secretary-General called for the strengthening of the rule of law in conflict and post-conflict situations and defined the rule of law as:

> [A] principle of governance in which all persons, institutions and entities, public and private, including the State itself, are accountable to laws that are publicly promulgated, equally enforced and independently adjudicated, and which are consistent with international human rights norms and standards.[218]

More specifically, it was considered that the rule of law requires:

> [M]easures to ensure adherence to the principles of supremacy of law, equality before the law, accountability to the law, fairness in the application of the law, separation of powers, participation in decision-making, legal certainty, avoidance of arbitrariness and procedural and legal transparency.[219]

---

212 See section 3.2 on the disconnection between primary and secondary rules.

213 See Report of the Secretary-General to the Security Council on the protection of civilians in armed conflict (28 May 2004) S/2004/431, para. 16; Report of the Secretary-General on the protection of civilians in armed conflict (10 May 2017) S/2017/414, para. 33.

214 J. K. Kleffner, 'The collective accountability of organised armed groups', 259.

215 Universal Declaration of Human Rights (1948), Preamble, para. 3.

216 UN Charter, Preamble, para. 1.

217 S. Chesterman, 'An International Rule of Law' (2008) 56 *American Journal of Comparative Law*, 331–362.

218 Report of the UN Secretary-General, The rule of law and transitional justice in conflict and post-conflict societies (23 August 2004) UN Doc. S/2004/616, para. 6.

219 *Ibid.*

In this context, the lack of a legal framework of responsibility for armed groups causes damage to the legal certainty, transparency and legitimacy of the international legal order since the absence of 'certain, predictable and stable rules' also endangers the remaining requirements of fairness and accountability to the law. In addition, a recent resolution of the UN General Assembly has emphasised the commitment to the rule of law in relation to two topics, namely international peace and security and human rights.[220] In relation to armed conflicts, the focus of the resolution has been on three areas: reaffirming the obligation of all states and all parties to armed conflict to respect and ensure respect for international humanitarian law in all circumstances; incorporating a full range of judicial and non-judicial measures to ensure accountability, serve justice, and provide remedies to victims; and fighting against impunity for violations of international humanitarian law and gross violations of human rights law.[221] These areas have to be considered in the context of contemporary armed conflict, where not only states but also non-state armed groups participate and often commit violations that need to be addressed. However, without proper rules against which these violations can be assessed, the requirements of the rule of law cannot be met. Joint efforts need to be employed that will aid in fighting against impunity in a manner that fully respects the international rule of law.

Consequently, clarifying the legal framework in this field would contribute to strengthening legal certainty and accountability to the law. It can also aid to facilitating the transparency of monitoring compliance and other accountability mechanisms that deal with reporting violations of IHL and IHRL, particularly given the current disconnect between reporting and monitoring processes and their encompassing conclusions and recommendations. If the responsibility of armed groups as such is recognised, then it is necessary to establish rules of attribution and legal consequences that can be applied by these mechanisms. Finally, group responsibility could create a culture of deterrence and compliance since only the group as a whole may take preventive steps.[222] In the end, the existence of measures that tackle the whole group could help to improve compliance with international norms.

4.2. PREVENTION OF IMPUNITY AND THE RIGHT TO REPARATION OF VICTIMS OF ARMED CONFLICT

The prevention of impunity goes hand in hand with the provision of effective remedies to victims. In this context, impunity is often linked to the denial of effective remedies for victims. The possibility of establishing collective responsibility of an armed group would directly benefit the victims of armed conflict. In the last decades, the

220 UN General Assembly, Resolution 67/1 Declaration of the High-level Meeting of the General Assembly on the Rule of Law at the National and International Levels (30 November 2012).
221 *Ibid*, 3–4.
222 See K. Mastorodimos, *supra note* 201, 3.

right to reparation for violations committed during armed conflict has emerged as a fundamental right of victims.[223] Particularly, reparations now constitute an essential element in transitional justice processes where serious violations of IHL and IHRL have been committed. In this regard, Evans indicates that 'the need to translate consequences of serious violations, such as reparations, in favour of individual victims has become an important aspect of affirming the legitimacy and credibility of the international legal order and human rights standards'.[224]

As explained above, the commission of an internationally wrongful act gives rise to a secondary obligation to provide reparation in order to remedy the damage caused. As a result, reparation is the natural consequence of responsibility and it has been considered a general principle of national and international law. The commission of international crimes also entails the provision of reparations by convicted individuals. Moreover, recent soft law standards are introducing the right of victims to reparations without having to take into account whether the responsible party is a state or a non-state entity. For instance, the UN Basic Principles and Guidelines on the right to a remedy and reparation for victims of gross violations of International Human Rights Law and serious violations of International Humanitarian Law (UNBPG) have recognised the right of victims irrespectively of whether the offender is a person, a legal person or other entity.[225]

Since armed conflicts are now fought by both states and non-state entities and there have been many instances of armed groups committing violations of IHL and IHRL, it seems necessary to find ways to coalesce several aims: the legal consequences of responsibility, the fight against impunity and victims' rights to reparation. In the end, reparations for victims of armed conflict are better addressed if the respondent is a collective entity, whether that be a state or an armed group.[226] From the point of view of the victim, it is irrelevant if the offender is a state agent or a member of an armed group. Moreover, the difficulties in identifying individual perpetrators or the leaders should not be an obstacle for providing full reparations to victims. This has been acknowledged by philosophical and political science approaches as studied in the previous section. According to these fields, establishing the collective responsibility of the group would be beneficial when victims cannot identify the individual perpetrators or when the perpetrator has not been found. In this sense, Carrillo-Santarelli has proposed the application of common norms, principles of responsibility and reparations, regardless of who the violators are.[227] The issue of reparation and victims' rights will

223 See C. Evans, *The Right of Reparation in International Law for Victims of Armed Conflict* (Cambridge University Press 2012).

224 *Ibid*, 2.

225 Resolution 60/147 on Basic Principles and Guidelines on the Right to a Remedy and Reparation for Victims of Gross Violations of International Human Rights Law and Serious Violations of International Humanitarian Law adopted and proclaimed by the UN General Assembly on 16 December 2005.

226 K. Mastorodimos, *supra note* 207, 3.

227 N. Carrillo-Santarelli, *Direct international human rights obligations of non-state actors: A legal and ethical necessity* (Wolf Legal Publishers 2017) 341–343 (hereafter N. Carrillo-Santarelli, *Direct international human rights obligations of non-state actors)*.

be fully developed in Chapter 5. At this stage, it suffices to point out that developing a responsibility regime for armed groups as collective entities is in accordance with the general obligation to provide reparations at the national and international level, which in turn would aid in contributing to remedy the damage caused. Moreover, it would also serve to strengthen the rights of victims of serious violations of IHL in accordance with the developments of soft law standards and in the prevention of impunity.

4.3. THE INSUFFICIENCY OF INDIVIDUAL CRIMINAL RESPONSIBILITY

As mentioned earlier, international criminal responsibility has been considered the mainstream answer when dealing with violations of international law committed by armed groups. However, there are important reasons to question whether international criminal law could be conceived as the ideal mechanism to address violations committed by these groups. In particular, there are a number of reasons to question its adequacy to hold to account armed groups as collective entities. These reasons are analysed by reference to four aspects of ICL: personal scope of application, material scope of application, purposes of criminal prosecution, and procedural difficulties.

In relation to the personal scope of application, the previous section outlined that ICL only covers the action of individuals as natural persons, but not groups.[228] Moreover, the different modes of liability established to cope with crimes of a collective nature, such as superior responsibility and JCE, have been subject to criticism. In this connection, the main criticism has related to the risk of diminishing the *mens rea* standard for the purpose of prosecuting more persons involved in the crime, and consequently imposing equal culpability of all members.[229] The possibility of prosecuting a collective entity under ICL would cope with the same issues relating to the culpability requirements and the difficulties in proving the mental element of such entities. This concern is shared by a number of scholars who warn against using ICL as the best alternative to fill the gap of corporate human rights responsibility.[230]

---

228 See Article 25(1) ICC Statute; Article 6 ICTY Statute; Article 5 ICTR Statute; Article Statute of the Special Court for Sierra Leone; Article 3 Statute Special Tribunal for Lebanon; Article 29 Extraordinary Chambers in the Courts of Cambodia; Article 14(1) Special Panels of the Dili District Court East Timor. Interestingly, according to Article 46C of the *Protocol on Amendments to the Protocol on the Statute of the African Court of Justice and Human Rights* is entitled 'Corporate Criminal Liability' and establishes that 'the Court shall have jurisdiction over legal persons, with the exception of States.' However, the Protocol is still not in force.

229 J. D. Ohlin, 'Three Conceptual Problems with the Doctrine of Joint Criminal Enterprise' (2007) *Cornell Law Faculty Publications*, Paper 30, 69–90.

230 See L. van den Herik and J.L. Černič, 'Regulating Corporations under International Law: From Human Rights to International Criminal Law and Back Again' (2010) 8 *Journal of International Criminal Justice*, 725–743; E. Brabandere, 'Non-state Actors and Human Rights: Corporate Responsibility and the Attempts to Formalize the Role of Corporations as Participants in the International legal System' in J. D'Aspremont, M. W. Reisman & M. Noortmann, *Participants in the International Legal System: Multiple Perspectives on Non-State Actors in International Law* (Routledge 2011) 268–283.

With regard to the crimes that are subject to the prosecution of international courts and in particular that of the ICC, not all violations of IHL are considered international crimes and are therefore, punishable.[231] The provisions of the ICC Statute only cover the most serious violations of the Geneva Conventions and the Additional Protocols including genocide, war crimes and crimes against humanity. Consequently, some violations do not reach the level of international crimes. For instance, as explained by Heffes, several provisions included in Additional Protocol II are not taken into account for the determination of international criminal responsibility, including those related to the persons whose liberty has been restricted.[232] This has also been acknowledged by the UN Special Rapporteur on Extrajudicial, Summary or Arbitrary Executions who has pointed to the limitations of ICL to address violations committed by ANSAs explaining that '[a] final and obvious limitation with ICL is that not all crimes committed by ANSAs meet the required ICL threshold'.[233]

Another limitation is that international criminal proceedings appear to focus mainly on retribution and deterrence. According to the preamble of the Rome Statute, the goal of the ICC is 'to put an end to impunity for the perpetrators of these crimes and thus to contribute to the prevention of such crimes'.[234] However, it is not clear to what extent international criminal prosecutions are satisfactorily dealing with these objectives. With regard to retribution, there are several obstacles to the realisation of this objective, such as the selectivity of prosecutions, the variability in sentencing and the possibility of plea bargaining.[235] Even when an international criminal court has been established, the selection of cases can be based on discretionary decisions favouring those cases that are more likely to secure a conviction or those related to inherently grave crimes.[236] In relation to deterrence, there has not been sufficient empirical evidence that proves that criminal prosecutions had actually reduced the likelihood that another person in the same or different place would commit another offence in the future.[237]

On the contrary, transitional justice approaches call for a multidisciplinary approach to mass atrocity not only through international criminal proceedings, but also through restitution and reparations. According to Dudai, ICL and individual prosecutions do not address the full range of victims' needs.[238] In this vein, Drumbl proposes to include a tort for violations of state responsibility and, potentially, for organisational or group liability outside the structures of the state. He argues that this 'might provide an additional layer of justice insofar as the criminal law does not directly

---

231 V. Bílková, 'Direct Responsibility of Armed Opposition Groups', 273.

232 See E. Heffes, *supra note* 92, 84–85. He refers, for instance, to Art. 5(1)(e) AP II.

233 Report of the Special Rapporteur on extrajudicial, summary or arbitrary executions on armed non-State actors: the protection of the right to life (5 June 2018) A/HRC/38/44, para. 32.

234 Preamble of the Rome Statute of the International Criminal Court, para. 5.

235 M. A. Drumbl, *Atrocity, Punishment and International Law* (Cambridge University Press 2007)150–169.

236 *Ibid*, 151.

237 *Ibid*, 169.

238 R. Dudai, 'Closing the Gap: Symbolic Reparations and Armed Groups' (2011) 93 *International Review of the Red Cross* 883, *785*.

reach the state or organization as an actor'.[239] Therefore, while prosecuting individuals for the commission of international crimes is an important aim in itself, there are other purposes in serving justice, such as truth-seeking, restitution and providing remedies to victims which could be met through additional judicial and non-judicial mechanisms.

In addition, as criminal proceedings are long and require a strict system of evidence, sometimes victims are unable to obtain reparations. Bellal considers that the length of international trials and the limited breath of action of ICL are 'insufficient to rely on individual criminal responsibility to address violations of international law committed by armed non-state actors'.[240] More particularly, the person who committed the violation, with the support of the group, may be deceased, which prevents them from obtaining reparations. Indeed, according to Bassouni, less than 1 percent of perpetrators of international crimes have been brought to justice.[241]

To summarise, these features point to the inadequacy of international criminal proceedings to address all the aspects of violations committed by armed groups, in terms of the persons that are subject to prosecution, the type of violation considered and the purpose of the prosecution. Additionally, the high standards of evidence make proceedings long and often victims are unable to obtain full and adequate reparation. Therefore, the insufficiency of ICL to address the full range of violations committed by armed groups opens the door for exploring new mechanisms that consider their collective actions as well as the needs of the victims.

4.4. COMPLEMENTARITY BETWEEN INDIVIDUAL CRIMINAL RESPONSIBILITY AND STATE/COLLECTIVE RESPONSIBILITY

If individual criminal responsibility is not able to fully tackle violations committed by collective entities, and in particular by armed groups, then it is necessary to examine whether both levels of responsibility could be complementary. In principle, state responsibility has been declared compatible with the individual responsibility of its agents. Although both arise from the same act, they serve different purposes. Individual criminal responsibility aims to combat impunity and punish the perpetrators of such violations while state responsibility responds to the need to restore international order to its *status quo* and repair the damage caused. According to Nollkaemper, the fact that the individual agent is prosecuted separately does not affect the reparative functions of the state.[242] In addition, state responsibility plays a systemic function as 'it may be more

---

239 M. A. Drumbl, 'Collective Responsibility and Post-Conflict Justice' in T. Isaacs & R. Vernon (eds) *Accountability for Collective Wrongdoing* (Cambridge University Press 2011) 39.

240 A. Bellal, *supra note* 207, 305.

241 M. C. Bassiouni (ed) *The Pursuit of International Criminal Justice: A World Study on Conflicts, Victimization, and Post-Conflict Justice* (Intersentia 2010) 3–39.

242 A. Nollkaemper, 'Concurrence between Individual Responsibility and State Responsibility in International Law' (2003) 52 *International and Comparative Law Quarterly*, 615–640, at 622.

important for the enforcement of "the provisions of international law" to address states, rather than to confine legal responses to single individuals who carry out a state policy'.[243]

This complementarity is derived from Article 58 ASR, Article 66 ARIO and Article 25 (4) of the ICC Statute. According to Article 58 ASR, '[t]hese articles are without prejudice to any question of the individual responsibility under international law of any person acting on behalf of a State'. The commentary to this article specifically notes that in the case of crimes against international law committed by State officials, there is a large probability that the state itself would be responsible for the acts in question or for failure to prevent or punish them. In the same vein, Article 66 ARIO establishes that '[t]hese draft articles are without prejudice to any question of the individual responsibility under international law of any person acting on behalf of an international organization or a State'. While Article 25 (4) of the ICC Statute affirms that '[n]o provision in this Statute relating to individual criminal responsibility shall affect the responsibility of States under international law'.

In practice, this complementarity can be seen in the *Application of the Genocide Convention* case where the conviction of individual agents of the former Yugoslavia before the ICTY and other national courts for the acts committed during the armed conflict between 1991 and 1995 did not prevent the International Court of Justice (ICJ) from examining the responsibility of Serbia in the genocide.[244] The Court commented on the interaction between individual criminal responsibility and state responsibility for genocide, explaining that the duality of responsibility is a 'constant feature of international law'.[245] In a separate opinion, Judge Bennouna found a close relationship between the two and noted that establishing criminal responsibility of those who lead the state could subsequently lead to state responsibility.[246] In particular, he expressed an optimistic understanding of the importance of civil sanction and justice. In addition, the Commission of Inquiry in Darfur also declared the complementarity between state and individual responsibility, indicating that '[t]he importance of determining individual criminal responsibility for international crimes whether committed under the authority of the State or outside such authority stands in addition to State responsibility'.[247] Similarly, in the Lockerbie case, al-Megrahi, a Libyan agent, was convicted for the aerial incident in question while compensation claims were also requested from Libya by the United Kingdom and the United States. Libya finally accepted its civil liability by offering $2.7 billion to compensate the victims of the attack.[248]

243 *Ibid*, 625.

244 *Application of the Convention on the Prevention and Punishment of the Crime of Genocide (Bosnia and Herzegovina v. Yugoslavia)* (Merits) [2007] Judgment, ICJ Rep, 26 February 2007. See also A. Nollkaemper, 'A Concurrence between Individual Responsibility and State Responsibility in International Law' (2003) 52 *International and Comparative Law Quarterly*, 615–640.

245 *Ibid*, para. 173–174.

246 *Ibid*, Déclaration de M. le Juge Bennouna, 3.

247 Report of the International Commission of Inquiry on Darfur to the United Nations Secretary-General, Geneva, 25 January 2005, para. 407.

248 *Her Majesty's Advocate v Al Megrahi*, Scottish High Court of Justiciary at Camp Zeist (The Netherlands) 40 ILM 582 (31 January 2001). See also 'Libya admits Lockerbie blame', *BBC News*

This understanding could also be applied *mutatis mutandis* to armed groups that commit violations of international law. Moreover, if the criminal responsibility of some of their members has been established, it would be easier to hold the armed group responsible for the purposes of tort liability or reparations in an analogous manner to state responsibility. In this connection, according to Drumbl, 'there is no reason criminal trials cannot be held for the most responsible members while the group as a whole is also sanctioned'.[249] Other authors have also called for the complementarity between individual criminal responsibility and the responsibility of the collective actor. In this respect, Carrillo-Santarelli notes that:

> [T]he possibility of a collective entity having international legal responsibility does not detract from the possibility of individualizing responsibility, which is important because on the one hand individualization permits identifying all the persons that planned and participated in abuses, thus helping to avoid generalized accusations and to make the consequences of responsibility more effective and accurate.[250]

In fact, the Commission of Inquiry in Darfur and the Panel of Experts on Accountability in Sri Lanka have already recognised the possibility of holding armed groups responsible alongside the state with the corresponding obligation to provide compensation to victims.[251] In addition, holding the group responsible for the purposes of reparation would avoid the concerns outlined above in relation to corporate criminal responsibility and the element of intentionality. As indicated by authors from philosophical studies, even if the individuals belonging to the group have been held responsible, there are important reasons to hold the group responsible as well, in particular, due to the development and implementation of such organisational policy.[252]

4.5. CHALLENGES OF A RESPONSIBILITY REGIME FOR ARMED GROUPS

In the process of assessing whether a responsibility regime for armed groups should be established, it is essential to look both at the challenges that such a regime could present for the international legal order as well as at other practical considerations. Similarly to the issues raised during the codification process of the responsibility of international organisations, a number of legal obstacles has been pointed out with regard to the possibility of establishing a responsibility regime for armed groups. These concerns

(16 August 2003) available at <http://news.bbc.co.uk/2/hi/uk_news/scotland/3155523.stm> accessed 23 April 2017.

249 M. A. Drumbl, 'Collective Responsibility and Post-Conflict Justice' in T. Isaacs & R. Vernon (eds) *Accountability for Collective Wrongdoing* (Cambridge University Press 2011) 54.

250 N. Carrillo-Santarelli, *Direct international human rights obligations of non-state actors*, 353.

251 See section 3.1.2 of this chapter.

252 See P. Petit, 'Responsibility Incorporated' (2007) 38 *Netherlands Journal of Legal Philosophy* 2, 90–117, at 11. See also section 2.2.3. of this chapter.

relate to substantive issues, namely the question of the international legal personality of armed groups, their structural disparity and their temporal existence; as well as procedural obstacles such as the lack of international judicial forum to address their actions. These concerns are examined in the next paragraphs.

First of all, when considering the obligations and responsibilities of armed groups we face the question of determining their legal personality.[253] In classic international law, responsibility has been connected to international legal personality, meaning that a person or entity is capable of possessing international rights and obligations and has the capacity to carry out certain actions at the international level.[254] However, the concept of international legal personality is a circular one. As explained by Nollkaemper, '[t]he ability of actors to bear obligations, to have rights, and to enter into legal relationships and indeed to be subject of international responsibility can both be seen as manifestations of personality as they can be seen as conditions of personality'.[255] In a globalised world, it is necessary to consider the reality of the actors operating in the international legal order and their corresponding obligations beyond the strict categories of subjecthood. In this context, there have been proposals that suggest to overcome the formality of the notion of subjects due to its lack of functional purpose.[256] D'Aspremont has further elaborated on the proposals of the policy-oriented school of New Haven to look at a more dynamic concept like the one of 'participants' in the international legal system, rather than the restricted concept of subjects.[257] The notion of participants derives from the idea of law conceived as a 'process of decision-making rather than a defined set of rules and obligations'.[258]

In any case, armed groups involved in a NIAC do enjoy limited legal personality or at least some aspects of legal personality.[259] According to Fortin, armed groups could enjoy different levels of legal personality depending on their capacities, their relations with third parties, and the circumstances in which they operate.[260] In this sense, the ICJ has already stated in the *Reparations* case that recognising that different entities are subjects of international law does not mean that they hold the same rights, duties, and capacities as states.[261] Consequently, it is possible to look at the different degrees of obligations that each entity has, which in turn helps determine their corresponding

253 See, for example, K. Fortin, *The Accountability of Armed Groups*, 152–173.

254 For a comprehensive analysis of the question, see J. E. Nijman, *The Concept of International Legal Personality: An Inquiry Into the History and Theory of International Law* (T. M. C. Asser Press 2004).

255 A. Nollkaemper, 'Responsibility' (2017) *Amsterdam Law School Legal Studies Research Paper* No. 2017-04, 9.

256 R. Higgins, *Problems and Process: International Law and How We Use It* (Clarendon Press 1994) 49; A. Clapham, *Human Rights Obligations of Non-State Actors* (Oxford University Press 2006) 59–63.

257 J. D'Aspremont (ed), *Participants in the International Legal System – Multiple Perspectives on Non-State Actors in International Law* (Routledge 2011) 2.

258 *Ibid*, 2.

259 A. Cassese, *International Law in a Divided World* (Clarendon Press 1986) 84. See also L. Zegveld, *Accountability of Armed Opposition Groups*, 57.

260 K. Fortin, *The Accountability of Armed Groups*, 154.

261 *Reparation for Injuries Suffered in the Service of the United Nations* (Advisory Opinion) [1949] ICJ Rep 174, 11 April 1949, at 178.

level of responsibility. At a minimum, armed groups are bound by the obligations derived from Common Article 3 of the Geneva Conventions. Those obligations become more comprehensive for armed groups that have control over territory, and who are subsequently subject to Additional Protocol II to the Geneva Conventions. Additional Protocol II extends the protection afforded to civilians, detainees and medical personnel, and includes key provisions related to the care of children and their education, judicial guarantees for those prosecuted in connection with an armed conflict, protection of civilian objects indispensable to the survival of the civilian population, protection of cultural objects, and the prohibition of forced movement of civilians.[262]

Another consideration is the difficulty in establishing a uniform regime of responsibility for armed groups as a result of their structural disparity.[263] There is a wide range of armed groups that vary in terms of their structure. While some armed groups adopt a state-like structure, others follow a looser organisation. In particular, traditional centralised armed groups share similar characteristics in terms of hierarchy and strict control of their members. Emerging armed groups appear to follow a non-centralised structure based on autonomous cells. According to Sinno, armed groups adopt different structures including centralised, descentralised, networked, patron-client, multiple, and fragmented structures.[264] Indeed, this is one of the key challenges that any potential responsibility framework needs to address in order to provide an answer to the new reality of contemporary armed conflicts. Although it is acknowledged that it is almost impossible to analyse every type of organisational structure of armed groups, there are two main categories that have been described for IHL purposes by the ICRC and the literature, that is, centralised and decentralised armed groups, also referred to as 'pyramidal' and 'horizontal' armed groups respectively.[265] Any potential system of responsibility will need to take into account these structural differences in order for such a framework to be realistic. These elements will be particularly considered in Chapter 4 dealing with the attribution of conduct to armed groups.

In addition, one of the main concerns during the drafting of the articles on insurrectional movements in the ASR was the question of the temporal existence of armed groups.[266] The first reading of the ASR established a divide between those groups that succeed in becoming the government or new state and those that do not

262 Articles 4, 5, 6, 13, 14, 15, 16, 17 of Additional Protocol II tot he Geneva Conventions.

263 A. Bellal, *supra note* 207, 306–307.

264 See A. H. Sinno, 'Armed Groups' Organizational Structure and their Strategic Options' (2011) 93 *International Review of the Red Cross* 882, 311–332.

265 See ICRC, *The Roots of Restraint in War* (Geneva 2018). See also T. Rodenhäuser, *Organizing Rebellion: Non-State Armed Groups under International Humanitarian Law, Human Rights Law, and International Criminal Law* (Oxford University Press 2018) 61–112; S. Sivakumaran, *The Law of Non-International Armed Conflicts* (Oxford University Press 2012) 172– 174; A. S. Hashim, *Insurgency and Counter-Insurgency in Iraq* (Hurst 2006) 152.

266 Fourth report on State responsibility by Mr. Roberto Ago, Special Rapporteur, International Law Commission Yearbook (30 June 1972 and 9 April 1973) UN Doc. A/CN.4/264 and Add.1., para. 154.

succeed in their objectives.[267] Only those groups that succeed in creating a new state or government were finally included in the second reading of the ASR under current Article 10. However, the reality of contemporary armed conflicts is quite different. Indeed, certain armed groups operate in their respective territories for decades, as is the case with the LTTE in Sri Lanka or the FARC-EP in Colombia.[268] This issue was also examined by Verhoeven who pointed out that:

> [...] the temporary existence of insurrectional movements does not preclude that they may exist for a significant amount of time. Armed opposition groups typically emerged in weak or failing States which do not have the necessary resources to suppress them. At the same time armed opposition groups may not have sufficient resources and support to achieve their objectives. The result is a stalemate and sporadic, fighting for years or decades. In such instances the temporary nature of the insurrectional movement is no bar the invocations of international responsibility.[269]

Thus, it can be argued that this temporary existence cannot be considered an obstacle in itself for attributing responsibility to the armed group as such. Nevertheless, in order to develop a workable system of responsibility for armed groups, their temporary nature needs to be addressed. More particularly, it is necessary to consider whether responsibility can be invoked if the entity as such ceases to exist or if the armed group transitions into a new type of organisation, for instance, a political party.

Finally, some scholars refer to the absence of an international forum that would address violations committed by non-state armed groups.[270] In relation to violations of IHL, there is no institutionalised international mechanism through which victims can claim their rights, not even for violations committed by states.[271] Therefore, the problem is not the impossibility of finding a forum for the actions of armed groups but the inexistence of an international forum for victims of armed conflict in general, regardless of whether the perpetrator is a state or a non-state armed group. The only mechanism available for this purpose is the International Humanitarian Fact-Finding Commission established by Article 90 of Additional Protocol I of the Geneva Conventions, which only investigated its first case in May 2017 in Ukraine.[272] Nevertheless, the procedures

---

267 Articles on State Responsibility, Art. 14 and 15, First Reading (1996). See also G. Cahin, *supra note* 43, 252–253.

268 The Liberation Tigers of Tamil Eelam (LTTE) have been active since 1976. See 'Tamil Tigers' in Encyclopedia Britannica <https://www.britannica.com/topic/Tamil-Tigers> accessed 20 April 2019. The peace agreement between the Government of Colombia and the FARC put an end to more than 40 years of civil conflict. See 'Who are the FARC?' *BBC News* (24 November 2016) available at <www.bbc.com/news/world-latin-america-36605769> accessed 20 April 2019.

269 S. I. Verhoeven, *supra note* 56, 296.

270 L. Zegveld, *Accountability of Armed Opposition Groups*, 157–163; V. Bílková, 'Direct Responsibility of Armed Opposition Groups', 282.

271 L. Zegveld, 'Remedies for Victims of Violations of International Humanitarian Law' (2003) 85 *International Review of the Red Cross* 851, 497–526, at 514.

272 C. Azzarello & M. Niederhauser, 'The Independent Humanitarian Fact-Finding Commission: Has the "Sleeping Beauty" Awoken?' in *ICRC Humanitarian Law & Policy* (January 2018).

do not allow individual victims of IHL violations to bring cases before the Commission. The inexistence of an institutionalised international mechanism should not be an obstacle to address the responsibility of armed groups since alternative non-judicial procedures can be found. In particular, UN Commissions of Inquiry, Fact-Finding Missions and Truth Commissions could be useful tools in determining the attribution of acts by armed groups. Indeed, some scholars have already proposed the use of Commissions of Inquiry and Truth Commissions as preliminary steps in establishing the responsibility of non-state armed groups.[273] Besides, some domestic courts are able to prosecute organisations and other private entities as collective entities or deal with torts committed by different organisations, not just individuals.[274]

4.6. CONCLUDING REMARKS ON THE ASSESSMENT OF A RESPONSIBILITY REGIME FOR ARMED GROUPS

This section has highlighted that the lack of clear rules regarding the responsibility of armed groups as collective entities could cause damage to key governing principles of international law. Particularly, the insufficiency of legal certainty is incompatible with an international legal order based on the rule of law. Without clear rules of attribution and legal consequences for armed groups, the prospects of a legitimate, fair and transparent legal order cannot be met. Moreover, preventing impunity and ensuring victim's rights to remedy and reparation provide an additional legal foundation for the establishment of a regime of responsibility for armed groups. The commission of a violation of international law gives rise to a secondary obligation to provide reparation to victims as a general principle of international law. Due to the increase in the number of NIACs, those violations can now stem from the actions of not only states, but also non-state armed groups. In this context, the identity of the perpetrator of such violations should not be an obstacle in obtaining reparations. Therefore, the rights of victims of armed conflict could be strengthened if the responsibility of the armed group is also included as an additional layer of accountability.

Furthermore, it has been argued that international criminal responsibility is not sufficient to deal with violations committed by armed groups. There are a number of key limitations including those relating to the personal and material scope of application of ICL, the purposes of prosecutions and further procedural barriers. These restrictions allow for the consideration of the compatibility of the collective/organisational responsibility of armed groups with the individual criminal responsibility of their members. The possibility of dual responsibility has already been established for

273 See A. Bellal, 'Non-State Armed Groups in Transitional Justice Processes Adapting to New Realities in Conflict' in R. Duthie & P. Seils (eds) *Justice Mosaics: How Context Shapes Transitional Justice in Fractured Societies* (International Centre for Transitional Justice 2017) 4. See also K. Ainley, 'Excesses of Responsibility: The Limits of Law and The Possibilities of Politics' (2011) 25 *Ethics & International Affairs* 407.

274 These options are analysed in Chapter 5 on reparations and possible enforcement mechanisms.

states and international organisations. Importantly, the ICJ has defined this duality as a feature of international law. In principle, other entities with obligations under international law could follow a similar approach.

To summarise, a regime of international responsibility for armed groups is necessary for the following reasons: the need for the clarification of rules of responsibility for armed groups according to the requirements of the rule of law; the obligation to provide reparations to victims of non-international armed conflicts and prevent impunity; and the insufficiency of ICL to deal with the full range of violations committed by armed groups. The other side of the coin is the identification of a number of legal obstacles and practical challenges to the establishment of a responsibility regime for armed groups. These obstacles refer to issues of legal personality, structural disparity, temporal existence and lack of international forum applicable to armed groups. To respond to these challenges, this study has opted to avoid the strict notion of 'subject' and focus on the existence of obligations under IHL applicable to armed groups as the underlying legal basis. As for the issue of structural disparity, this study will pay particular attention to two main categories of armed groups in terms of their organisational structure, namely centralised and decentralised groups. In relation to the question of their temporal existence, this concern is not considered an obstacle in itself for attributing responsibility to the group as such, but it will be reflected in Chapters 4 and 5 of this book. Armed groups that have been operating in a territory for a considerable amount of time will be particularly examined. And, finally, with regard to a possible forum for armed groups, existing monitoring mechanisms can be used as a preliminary step, together with the responses given by domestic systems. This will be further analysed in Chapter 5.

5. CONCLUSIONS

This chapter has provided a response to the first research question, namely 'to what extent a regime of responsibility for armed groups is necessary under international law?' In answering this question, this chapter has reflected on the broader notion of international responsibility and its evolution over time. International responsibility developed as a necessary complement to the rights and obligations of states taking the extra-contractual civil liability model from domestic law as a source of inspiration. International responsibility is premised on the commission of an internationally wrongful act, that is, a violation of an obligation of international law. This notion evolved to include other subjects of international law such as international organisations. In principle, other entities that exercise powers over territory or control over people could follow a similar understanding of international responsibility. For Nollkaemper, there is a strong relationship between power and responsibility. He particularly notes that 'the proposition that power breeds (or should breed) responsibility seems to underlie much of international law'.[275] To complement this approach, political science and philosophical studies have proposed that collective entities other than states should also bear responsibility.

As regards armed groups, the main response given by international law to tackle the violations committed by them seems to focus on the criminal responsibility of their individual members, leaving untouched the possible responsibility of the group. At the same time, monitoring mechanisms have started to deal with the actions of armed groups, by reporting on the strategies and organisational policies of these groups. However, there is no legal framework in place against which the conduct of armed groups qua collective entities could be assessed by these mechanisms. This lack of clarity and transparency endangers an international legal order based on the rule of law. Ascribing international responsibility to armed groups as collective entities could serve to bridge the so-called 'responsibility gap' by strengthening the rule of law and benefiting the right to reparation of victims of non-international armed conflict. In fact, establishing several layers of responsibility between the individual and the collective entity could be more effective in addressing the whole range of actions carried out by non-state armed groups. Finally, connecting the factual power of armed groups with a coherent response by the international legal order would also serve to fight against impunity.

275 A. Nollkaemper, 'Power and Responsibility' (2014) Amsterdam Law School Legal Studies Research Paper No. 2014–35, 6.

CHAPTER III

DEVELOPING A RESPONSIBILITY REGIME FOR ARMED GROUPS IN INTERNATIONAL LAW

1. INTRODUCTION

The previous chapter concluded that in order to fill the responsibility gap and to answer to the rights of victims of non-international armed conflicts a framework that addresses the responsibility of armed groups under international law is required. Following from these discussions, it is now necessary to inquire how principles of responsibility, and in particular of attribution, could be developed in relation to armed groups. In this sense, the sub-question addressed in this chapter is 'which methodology can and should be used to develop a responsibility framework for armed groups under international law?'. In principle, there appear to be two possible alternatives: extending international criminal responsibility to collective entities, including armed groups; or using the previous framework of the Articles on State Responsibility (ASR) created by the International Law Commission (ILC) as a starting point. In this context, the International Law Association (ILA) has posed the question of whether 'the direct responsibility of AOGs [Armed Opposition Groups] would be construed in analogy with the responsibility of states or rather with individual criminal responsibility'.[1] Similarly, Bílková notes that one of the main issues of uncertainty is choosing a model between state responsibility and individual criminal responsibility or building a new type of responsibility.[2]

Following this reasoning, some authors have suggested extending ICL to organised entities. In particular, Clapham proposes to extend ICL to armed opposition groups based on the fact that armed groups are able to violate not only IHL obligations but also those expressed in terms of international criminal law associated with crimes against humanity and genocide.[3] This suggestion relates to the fact that criminal responsibility of collective entities is recognised in some domestic legal systems.

---

1 International Law Association Committee on Non-State Actors, 'Third report on the Obligations and Responsibility of Non-State Actors in International Law' (Washington Conference 2014) 11.

2 V. Bílková, 'Direct Responsibility of Armed Opposition Groups', 278–279.

3 A. Clapham, 'Extending International Criminal Law beyond the Individual to Corporations and Armed Opposition Groups' (2008) 6 *Journal of International Criminal Justice*, 899–926, at 925.

However, as noted in the previous chapter, there are several difficulties in extending ICL in such a way, particularly in relation to the wide range of violations committed by armed groups. In fact, a combination of international criminal responsibility of individual members and international responsibility of the collectivity was preferred for the reasons already explained. On the contrary, other authors, such as Kleffner, Verhoeven and Heffes, have suggested applying the ASR to non-state armed groups by analogy due to the similarities between states and armed groups.[4] Nevertheless, these doctrinal attempts encounter some limitations. As a first constraint, these proposals tend to focus exclusively on the ASR as inspiration or departing point but do not consider the rules adopted for international organisations, nor do they examine how the process has been translated to international organisations. Moreover, these propositions do not explain the extent or circumstances under which the application of analogical reasoning is suitable for the conduct of armed groups and the possible limitations of these analogies.

In this respect, if the purpose of this book is to propose a methodology to be followed in relation to armed groups and their international responsibility, this study needs to consider, first, whether the model developed by the ILC regarding states and international organizations is adequate for armed groups as well. To this extent, this chapter provides an analysis of the methodology that the ILC employed to develop the rules on responsibility in the ASR and the ARIO. This part will highlight the lessons learned in relation to the development of such rules as well as the main critiques these rules have attracted. The aim of this chapter is to address the potential of applying analogical legal reasoning between the common principles of responsibility of states and international organizations, and the conduct of armed groups. This issue is examined in three steps. First, the question of analogies in international law will be explored in order to determine its conditions, advantages and limitations. The application of analogical legal reasoning needs to consider the similarities and differences between the proposed cases and decide whether a similar approach could be taken in relation to armed groups. This first step is justified because previous studies did not offer a systematic argumentation about the advantages and limitations of analogies. If such path is followed, these principles would need to be adapted to the characteristics of armed groups and the relevant practice on the matter. Second, in the process of finding this relevant practice, the potential role of non-traditional sources of international law will be examined, namely reports from non-judicial monitoring mechanisms and the practice of armed groups. Within this context, it is also necessary to assess the legal value of these additional sources of international law. Do these instruments contribute

---

4 See J. K Kleffner, 'The collective accountability of organised armed groups'; I. Verhoeven, 'International Responsibility of Armed Opposition Groups: Lessons from State Responsibility for Actions of Non-State Armed Groups' in N. Gal-Or, C. Ryngaert, & M. Noortmann (eds) *Responsibilities of the Non-State Actor in Armed Conflict and the Market Place: Theoretical Considerations and Empirical Findings* (Brill Nijhoff 2015); E. Heffes, 'The Responsibility of Armed Opposition Groups for Violations of International Humanitarian Law: Challenging the State-Centric System of International Law' (2013) 4 *Journal of International Humanitarian Legal Studies*, 81–107.

to customary international law or are they regarded as interpretative tools? Third, the last section of this chapter will offer a proposal in relation to the methodology that can be used to develop a responsibility framework for armed groups under international law. In sum, this method will be based on the application of an analogous approach which considers minimum principles of responsibility and attribution as the main basis where the necessary adjustments are introduced.

2. THE METHODOLOGY OF THE ILC ON SECONDARY NORMS OF INTERNATIONAL RESPONSIBILITY

The following section analyses the methodology that has been applied by the ILC to develop secondary norms on international responsibility in relation to states and international organisations. This analysis will serve to examine how the rules of state responsibility were developed and how they were adapted to the characteristics of international organisations. In this regard, this process of adaptation can be seen as a future prospect for developing the international responsibility of other collective entities such as organised armed groups. It also aids in outlining the possible legal obstacles and the limitations that the ILC has encountered in this process.

As explained in the previous chapter, the ILC followed the work of the League of Nations in the codification process on the issue of state responsibility. One of the main changes was the decision to regulate the principles of state responsibility in general and not only in one specific area. The purpose was to eliminate the reference to the status of aliens that was traditionally linked to the topic of state responsibility and rely on 'responsibility *per se*'.[5] Moreover, the emphasis of the ASR was not placed on defining the rules that establish obligations for states but on whether an obligation has been violated and what the consequence of such a violation should be.[6] Accordingly, rules of responsibility have been defined as 'secondary rules' as opposed to 'primary rules' consisting of international obligations.[7]

The main methodological tool employed by the ILC in drafting the ASR was inductive legal reasoning, that is, 'drawing inferences from specific observable

5 First Report on State Responsibility by Mr. Roberto Ago, Special Rapporteur: Review of Previous Work on Codification of the Topic of the International Responsibility of States (7 May 1969 and 20 January 1970) UN Doc. A/CN.4/217, Corr. 1 and Add.1, para. 65.

6 Second Report on State Responsibility by Mr. Roberto Ago, Special Rapporteur: The Origin of International Responsibility (20 April 1970) UN Doc. A/CN.4/233, 12, para. 7.

7 Articles on State Responsibility, General Comment, para. 1: 'These articles seek to formulate, by way of codification and progressive development, the basic rules of international law concerning the responsibility of States for their internationally wrongful acts. The emphasis is on the secondary rules of State responsibility: that is to say, the general conditions under international law for the State to be considered responsible for wrongful actions or omissions, and the legal consequences which flow therefrom'.

phenomena to general rules'.[8] Induction is the process of generalising rules based on the observance of specific cases. It consists of reviewing previously decided cases with the purpose of determining applicable rules.[9] The use of the inductive method requires the existence of a substantive amount of case material so that reasonable generalisations can be reached.[10] This technique has been used in the formation of treaties, customary international law and general principles of law.[11] However, this method was not always explicitly addressed in the reports of the different rapporteurs. Only a small number of references in the reports of the Special Rapporteur Roberto Ago can be found. For instance, in the third report, he expressed the preference 'for an essentially inductive method, rather than for the deduction of theoretical premises'.[12] In addition, in the fifth report he emphasised that:

> In preparing the material to be included in chapter III, it is logical to rely mainly on the inductive method, which has already proved so useful and which consists, in connexion with the various points, in first analysing international judicial decisions and State practice and then making use of the specific results of this analysis when formulating rules. This method has proved so useful in the previous stages of our work that it would be absurd to reject it without good reason.[13]

Similarly, the first reading of the ASR refers to the inductive method as the method followed by the Special Rapporteur in his reports which was aimed at formulating rules from an analysis of state practice and international judicial decisions.[14] Nevertheless, the current text of the ASR does not explicitly refer to the methodology employed by the ILC in drafting these articles. The determination of the ASR rules was based on the analysis of judicial decisions (particularly from the PCIJ and the ICJ), arbitral decisions (from mixed claim commissions and arbitral tribunals), state practice and the relevant literature on the matter.[15] Thus, it was clear that its law-making methods were

---

8 W. T. Worster, 'The Inductive and Deductive Methods in Customary International Law Analysis: Traditional and Modern Approaches' (2014) 45 *Georgetown Journal of International Law*, 456.

9 K. Sinclair, 'Legal Reasoning: In Search of an Adequate Theory of Argument' (1971) 59 *California Law Review* 3, 827.

10 G. Schwarzenberger, 'The Inductive Approach to International Law' (1947) 60 *Harvard Law Review* 4, 541.

11 *Ibid*, 562–566.

12 Third Report on State responsibility by Mr. Roberto Ago, Special Rapporteur: The Internationally Wrongful Act of the State – Source of International Responsibility (5 March, 7 April, 28 April and 18 May 1971) UN Doc. A/CN.4/246 and Add. 1–3, at 202, para. 13.

13 Fifth Report on State Responsibility by Mr. Roberto Ago, Special Rapporteur: The Internationally Wrongful Act of the State – Source of International Responsibility (continued) (14 April and 4 May 1976) UN Doc. A/CN.4/291 and Add. 1 & 2 and Corr. 1, 22 March, at 5, para. 11.

14 Draft Articles on State Responsibility with Commentaries adopted by the International Law Commission in its First Reading, January 1997, at 87, para. 13.

15 The commentary of the ASR makes systematic references to arbitral and judicial decisions, state practice and the opinion of jurists as the basis for the establishment of these rules at p. 32 para. 2, p. 36, paras. 12–13, p. 37, para. 4, p. 39, para. 6, p. 45, para. 3, p. 46, para. 4, in p. 50, para. 3, p. 51, para. 12, p. 52, paras. 2–3, p. 58, para. 4, p. 66, para. 7, p. 70, para. 7, p. 75, para. 2, p. 83, para. 14, p. 93, para.

based on the traditional sources of international law as established by Article 38 of the ICJ Statute, including state practice contributing to customary international law, and secondary sources such as judicial decisions and the writings of publicists.

With regards to the drafting process of the ARIO, the ILC took as a reference its previous work elaborated in relation to states. However, the ILC considered the ARIO an autonomous project from the ASR, claiming that:

> While the present draft articles are in many respects similar to the articles on State responsibility, they represent an autonomous text. Each issue has been considered from the specific perspective of the responsibility of international organizations. Some provisions address questions that are peculiar to international organizations. When in the study of the responsibility of international organizations the conclusion is reached that an identical or similar solution to the one expressed in the articles on State responsibility should apply with respect to international organizations, this is based on appropriate reasons and not on a general presumption that the same principles apply.[16]

Despite the alleged autonomy of the ARIO rules, the main methodological tool employed by the ILC was analogical legal reasoning. This can be inferred from the reports of Special Rapporteur Giorgio Gaja. In particular, in his first report he notes that the ARIO would follow the same approach as the ASR both in its general outline and the wording of the text.[17] In other reports, the Special Rapporteur called for the application of analogy with the ASR in cases not specifically covered by the ARIO, for instance, eventual cases of attribution of conduct to an international organisation.[18] The reason for following this unitary approach was to bring coherence and predictability to the issue of international responsibility.[19] In this respect, the ILC explicitly recognised that the 'concept of responsibility', which refers to the consequences under international law for carrying out an internationally wrongful act, was also the same for international organisations.[20]

Consequently, the premise of the ILC to draft the ARIO was the application of analogies as far as possible and the adaptation of norms where required. The ILC specifically justified the necessity of adjustments in the following way:

> The need for coherency in the Commission's work requires that a change, in respect of international organizations, in the approach and even the wording of what has been said

12, p. 94, para. 3, p. 99, paras. 2–3, p. 108, para. 7, p. 110, para. 4, p. 112, para. 2, p. 114, para. 6, p. 128, para. 3, p. 134, para. 2.

16 Articles on the Reponsibility of International Organisations, General Commentary, para. 4.

17 First Report on Responsibility of International Organizations by Mr. Giorgio Gaja, Special Rapporteur (26 March 2013) UN Doc. A/CN.4/532, at 5, para. 11.

18 Second Report on Responsibility of International Organizations by Mr. Giorgio Gaja, Special Rapporteur (2 April 2004) UN Doc. A/CN.4/541, at 28, para. 64.

19 C. Ahlborn, 'The Use of Analogies in Drafting the Articles on the Responsibility of International Organizations: An Appraisal of the "Copy-Paste Approach"' (2012) *SHARES Research Paper* 13, Amsterdam Centre for International Law, 2012–14.

20 Report of the Commission to the General Assembly on the Work of its Fifty-Fourth Session, Vol. II, Part II, *Yearbook of the International Law Commission* (2002) at 93, para. 465.

> with regard to States, needs to be justified *by differences in the relevant practice or in objective distinctions in nature.*[21]

Therefore, those adjustments were based on the peculiarities relating to the nature of international organisations or the existence of differing practice on the matter. The practice that was included in these articles was that of states and international organisations as well as judicial decisions (mainly from the ICJ). In this regard, the ILC used the same sources of international law as previously done with the ASR but also included the practice of international organisations, especially that of the United Nations. For instance, the statement of the United Nations Legal Counsel sums up the United Nations practice in relation to the 'control of the deployment of national contingents in a peacekeeping force' and the conduct of organs or agents.[22] Moreover, a memorandum by the Office of Legal Affairs of the United Nations that concerned claims involving off-duty acts of the members of peacekeeping forces was considered for the attribution of *ultra vires* acts.[23] Another example is provided by an internal document issued on the 12th October 2009 by the United Nations Legal Counsel as providing evidence of the practice of aid or assistance by an international organisation.[24] In summary, although the ARIO is based on the same traditional sources of international law, it did consider additional sources such as the practice of international organisations as the main subjects of the rules. Where the practice of states and international organisations was coincident, the rule was kept in the same form. Where the practice was divergent, or certain special features of international organisations required further consideration, the rule was adapted or eliminated. In any case, it can be said that the ARIO rules have a high degree of coincidence with the rules of state responsibility and only in certain limited aspects they were adjusted to their specific circumstances. This is the case in particular in relation to rules of attribution, as will be explained in the following chapter.

2.1. LESSONS LEARNED FROM THE WORK OF THE ILC ON INTERNATIONAL RESPONSIBILITY

As it has been seen above, the work of the ILC on the question of international responsibility was initiated with the state as the main subject of study and was then expanded to international organisations. In relation to states, the ILC relied on a substantive amount of practice from states, arbitral tribunals and international courts. It therefore mainly codified the existing practice with regards to secondary norms

21 Second Report on Responsibility of International Organizations by Mr. Giorgio Gaja, Special Rapporteur (2 April 2004) UN Doc. A/CN.4/541, para. 5 (emphasis added).

22 Articles on the Reponsibility of International Organisations, General Commentary, para. 6.

23 Articles on the Reponsibility of International Organisations, General Commentary, Article 8, para. 9.

24 Articles on the Reponsibility of International Organisations, General Commentary, Article 14, para. 6.

on international responsibility. Particularly, the aim of the ILC was to 'undertake the codification of the "principles of international law governing State responsibility"'.[25] However, the ILC also clarified that 'it is necessary to do something more than "to codify"; it is necessary to change and adapt traditional law so that it will reflect the profound transformation which has occurred in international law'.[26] Therefore, even though its main effort pertained to the codification of existing law, some degree of law creation was also necessary, and indeed, accepted.

As regards international organisations, it has been seen that the aim of the ILC was to set out general principles concerning their international responsibility.[27] However, several authors claim that the ARIO were not based on a sufficient level of practice in comparison to the work of the ASR.[28] In fact, this was already recognised by the ILC, which justified this position by emphasising that their role was not to exclusively codify international law but to work on the progressive development of international law.[29] Consequently, the ILC noted that the authority of the rules 'will depend upon their reception by those to whom they are addressed'.[30] In this context, it has been argued that international law has to be adapted 'as far as possible to the contemporary conditions of international life' and 'has to fill in gaps in, and amend, the law in the light of new developments'.[31] On this aspect, it is important to highlight that the ILC did consider the practice of international organisations together with the practice of states as the main sources of the final product of the ARIO.

The final text of the ARIO was subject to further criticism. These criticisms relate, in particular, to the lack of clearly established primary rules, the diversity of international organisations and the lack of third-party dispute settlement mechanisms.[32] It has been argued that many primary rules are still controversial for international organisations, and consequently, drafting secondary rules is premature.[33] However,

---

25 Report on International Responsibility by Mr. F. V. Garcia-Amador, Special Rapporteur (20 January 1956) UN Doc. A/CN.4/96, para. 1.

26 *Ibid.*, para. 10.

27 First Report on Responsibility of International Organizations by Mr. Giorgo Gaja, Special Rapporteur, (26 March 2013) UN Doc. A/CN.4/532, para. 2.

28 J. E. Alvarez, 'Book Review of Dan Sarooshi: International Organizations and Their Exercise of Sovereign Powers' (2007) 101 *American Journal of International Law*, 676–677.

29 In the General Commentary of the ARIO, the ILC recognised that '[t]he fact that several of the present draft articles are based on limited practice moves the border between codification and progressive development in the direction of the latter'. See Articles on the Reponsibility of International Organisations, General Commentary, p. 2, para. 5.

30 *Ibid.*, para. 5.

31 United Nations, 'The Work of the International Law Commission, Vol. 1' (New York 2012) 143, 162.

32 See M. Möldner, 'Responsibility of International Organizations: Introducing the ILC's DARIO' (2012) 16 *Max Planck Yearbook of United Nations Law*, 322–326; K. Daugirdas, 'Reputation and the International Responsibility of International Organizations' (2015) 25 *European Journal of International Law* 4, 991–1018.

33 See J. E. Alvarez, 'Book Review of Dan Sarooshi: International Organizations and Their Exercise of Sovereign Powers' (2007) 101 *American Journal of International Law*, 676–677.

the fact that some international obligations are still emerging for international organisations does not preclude the creation of secondary rules as there are many other obligations that have already been established, including those developed by virtue of the ratification of treaties by international organisations, that result in the imposition of obligations on them.[34] Moreover, it has been stated that the ARIO do not take into account the diversity of international organisations, for instance, with regards to economic integration organisations such as the European Union.[35] The approach of the ILC was to cover a broad spectrum of international organisations but at the same time to recognise that 'the specific, factual or legal circumstances pertaining to the international organization concerned should be taken into account, where appropriate'.[36] Accordingly, special features of international organisations are to be taken into consideration. Other authors claim that the ILC should have justified closer analogies between both sets of articles and should have focused more on the similarities rather than on the differences between states and international organisations, with the possibility of establishing a unitary set of rules.[37] Finally, as per some procedural aspects, Klabbers refers to the practical difficulties regarding the enforceability of the responsibility of international organisations before international tribunals.[38]

Remarkably, the arguments that were put forward against the codification of secondary rules for international organisations and the work-product of the ILC are the same as those that are now being raised against a possible framework of responsibility for armed groups based on the lack of clarity of primary rules, the structural diversity of armed groups and the lack of a judicial forum, as was explained in Chapter 2.[39] One has to acknowledge that both sets of articles were meant to develop 'general principles', not strict rules, since the possibility of special rules was opened for both states and international organisations.[40] Moreover, the legal significance of such rules could only be determined at a later stage according to the degree of use and application made by the legal operators. In any case, both sets of rules have served as a basic framework for attributing wrongful acts.

---

34 M. Möldner, 'Responsibility of International Organizations: Introducing the ILC's DARIO' (2012) 16 *Max Planck Yearbook of United Nations Law*, 325.

35 E. Paasivirta & P. Kuijper, 'Does One Size Fit All? The European Community and the Responsibility of International Organizations' (2005) 36 *Netherlands Yearbook of International Law* 1, 169–226, at 206.

36 Articles on the Reponsibility of International Organisations, General Commentary, Article 2, para. 15.

37 C. Ahlborn, 'The Use of Analogies in Drafting the Articles on the Responsibility of International Organizations: An Appraisal of the "Copy-Paste Approach"' (2012) *SHARES Research Paper* 13, Amsterdam Centre of International Law, 2012–14, 11–12.

38 J. Klabbers, *An Introduction to International Institutional Law* (2nd ed, Cambridge University Press 2009) 292.

39 See Section 4.5 of Chapter 2.

40 Article 55 of the Articles on State Responsibility and Article 64 of the Articles on the Responsibility of International Organisations on *lex specialis*.

3. ANALOGICAL LEGAL REASONING IN RELATION TO SECONDARY NORMS ON INTERNATIONAL RESPONSIBILITY AND ARMED GROUPS

Having analysed the methods followed by the ILC, one can conclude that the ILC wanted to keep the issue of international responsibility in a coherent and unitary system while adjusting certain principles to the characteristics of international organisations. In this regard, the process of adaptation of the state's rules of responsibility to international organisations could be seen as a possible method to follow in relation to the conduct of armed groups. As concerns international organisations, some rules were directly transposed by analogy, others required some adaptation and others were not transposed at all. Those adjustments were justified due to the existence of differences in the relevant practice or objective distinctions in nature. As suggested, the process of development of rules of responsibility for international organisations based on analogies could be seen as a departing point. However, to proceed with a similar approach, it is first necessary to explore the conditions, advantages and limitations to apply analogies in international law, before determining the extent to which this analogous approach can be applied to the conduct of armed groups. Moreover, it will also require addressing the possible obstacles and critiques that were mentioned previously. The following sections will elaborate on these questions.

3.1. ANALOGIES IN INTERNATIONAL LAW: CONDITIONS, ADVANTAGES AND LIMITATIONS

Reasoning by analogy is a well-known technique in domestic law, especially in common law systems.[41] It consists of the application of an existing rule to a new situation that shares similar characteristics but does not fall within the wording of that rule.[42] In international law, the use of analogical legal reasoning has been reflected in the decisions of international courts and arbitral tribunals, in soft law instruments, and in the writings of scholars. For example, in the well-known *Continental Shelf* case, the ICJ identified the 200-nautical-mile distance criterion as a new rule by way of analogical deduction from the existing 200-nautical-mile distance criterion already applicable to the exclusive economic zone.[43] Similarly, in the *Nicaragua* case, the Court established that the right of immediate termination of declarations should be treated

41 See A. Rigoni, 'Common-Law Judicial Reasoning and Analogy' (2014) 20 *Legal Theory*, 133–156. More recently, K. Stevens, 'Reasoning by Precedent: Between Rules and Analogies' (2018) 24 *Legal Theory* 3, 216–254.

42 K. Sinclair, 'Legal Reasoning: In Search of an Adequate Theory of Argument' (1971) 59 *California Law Review* 3, 828.

43 *Continental Shelf (Libyan Arab Jamahiriya/Malta)* [1985] Judgment ICJ Rep 13, 3 June 1985, at 29, para. 27.

'by analogy, according to the law of treaties'.[44] Analogous reasoning is also common in international investment law where arbitral tribunals have established analogies from public international law and domestic systems in a wide range of issues.[45] Analogies have also been proposed in certain soft law instruments. For instance, in the Guiding Principles on Internal Displacement, refugee law was offered as a useful source to be applied for the protection of internally displaced people.[46] In the field of IHL, the development of customary rules on non-international armed conflicts has been mainly based on the parallel IHL rules applicable to international armed conflict.[47] Therefore, analogies have been used not only by courts and tribunals but also as tools to influence the development of international law.

According to Sivakumaran, the use of analogies represents a useful technique for filling gaps. As he explains, '[i]f a gap is identified in the law, it will likely be seen as more appropriate to rely on an equivalent rule or a related understanding in a different body of law rather than to draw up a rule from scratch'.[48] Therefore, the first pre-condition for the application of an analogy is the existence of a *lacuna*, that is, a particular situation that is not covered by law. The second condition for the application of an analogy is the existence of similarities between the cases which are the object of analysis. In this respect, Vöneky suggests applying analogous reasoning in a three-step process:

> [...] by, first, comparing the regulated and the unregulated cases; by, secondly, identifying the similarities between the cases, and by, thirdly, rationally deciding that the similarities of the cases compared have to be seen as being relevant for their legal evaluation and their differences as being irrelevant.[49]

The key step in the process of comparison is to determine whether those similarities are sufficient and relevant enough to justify the same legal treatment. As also explained by Sunstein, 'for analogical reasoning to operate properly, we have to know that A and B are "relevantly" similar and that there are not "relevant" differences between them'.[50] For the evaluation of the relevance of those similarities and irrelevance of their differences, it is necessary to develop some kind of criterion or theory. On this matter, Vöneky proposes the examination of 'the specific object and purpose of the rule in

44 *Military and Paramilitary Activities in and against Nicaragua* (Merits) [1984] Judgment ICJ Rep 392, 26 November 1984, at 420, para. 63.

45 See V. Vadi, *Analogies in International Investment Law and Arbitration* (Cambridge University Press 2015).

46 Guiding Principles on Internal Displacement (Guiding Principles), annexed to UNGA Resolution 46/182 (1991).

47 S. Sivakumaran, 'Techniques in International Law-Making: Extrapolation, Analogy, Form and the Emergence of an International Law of Disaster Relief' (2017) 28 *European Journal of International Law* 4, 1097–1132, at 1118.

48 *Ibid*, 1120.

49 S. Vöneky, 'Analogy in International Law', para. 5.

50 C. R. Sunstein, 'On Analogical Reasoning' (1993) 106 *Harvard Law Review* 3, 741–791, at 745.

question'.[51] This goes in consonance with the general rule of interpretation of treaties established in Article 31(1) of the Vienna Convention on the Law of Treaties (VCLT). According to this rule, '[a] treaty shall be interpreted in good faith in accordance with the ordinary meaning to be given to the terms of the treaty in their context and in the light of *its object and purpose*'. The analysis of the object and purpose of the rules could be seen as a useful tool to establish criteria against which their similarities and differences could be evaluated, and to afterwards decide if the comparison is reasonable in legal terms. These elements can be found in the *travaux préparatoires* of the treaty in question or in the preamble and commentaries of the norm.

The main advantage of reasoning by analogy is that it fosters coherence within the international legal system which also serves the purpose of predictability.[52] When similar cases are treated in the same way, the consistency of the legal order is consolidated, thereby ensuring cases do not escape the rule of law. In this regard, filling gaps in such a way contributes to strengthening legal certainty. Moreover, it can be useful in providing creative solutions to emerging facts and situations. It has been similarly argued that 'analogical reasoning may be especially desirable in contexts in which we seek moral evolution over time'.[53] To this end, analogy could be helpful because it serves to give reply to new concerns in contemporary international law.

Nevertheless, analogous reasoning has a number of limitations. In particular, analogous reasoning relies excessively on existing convictions and frameworks which may also contain weaknesses.[54] This constitutes an important limitation to be born in mind. Applying the same legal framework could perpetuate a legal solution that may not be adequate in view of new developments in the particular area. In addition, it has been noted that legal analogies serve to compare cases but they do not provide the final criterion to decide whether or not to proceed with the extrapolation of solutions.[55] To provide an answer to these concerns, it is important to remember that analogical reasoning is not an automatic process. Rather, it requires a certain level of abstraction. However, this can also be said for other forms of legal reasoning such as induction, which also relies on deciding whether a rule can be derived from particular cases. Therefore, although reasoning by analogy may not be the perfect tool, it can still help in offering creative solutions to new cases not covered by the law.

3.2. APPLYING ANALOGICAL LEGAL REASONING TO THE CONDUCT OF ARMED GROUPS

As explained above, analogical legal reasoning has advantages and limitations like any other method of legal reasoning. This section will attempt to apply this analogous

51 S. Vöneky, 'Analogy in International Law', para. 17.
52 C. Ahlborn, *supra note* 37, 4.
53 C. R. Sunstein, *supra note* 50, 782.
54 *Ibid*, 769.
55 *Ibid*, 773.

approach between the rules on international responsibility for states and international organisations on the one hand, and the conduct of armed groups on the other. This analysis will be conducted in a two-step process: first, through exploring the similarities and differences between the proposed cases; and second, by assessing whether the similarities are relevant enough. As an explanatory note, the rules of responsibility of states and international organisations will be specifically considered as a unitary system to this effect.

3.2.1. Similarities and differences between the proposed cases

The first condition for the application of analogous reasoning is the existence of a *lacuna*. In this context, a *lacuna* was identified in the previous chapter regarding the responsibility of armed groups under international law, and in particular, the lack of attribution rules applicable to these groups. The second condition is based on the existence of similarities between two cases, one which is actually regulated and the other which is not. Therefore, for the theoretical application of analogical reasoning to the question of responsibility of armed groups, it will be necessary to examine what the similarities and differences between the proposed cases are. For this purpose, the study will look at states and international organisations, on the one hand, and armed groups, on the other.

With regard to the similarities between states, international organisations, and armed groups, the main common element is that they are all collective entities with at least a minimum organisational structure. As abstract legal entities, they can only act through human beings.[56] In this regard, to become an armed group for the purposes of Common Article 3 of the Geneva Conventions, some kind of hierarchical and organised structure needs to be in place. In particular, the ICTY has defined several indicators to determine the degree of organisation that armed group must comply with to reach the threshold of a non-international armed conflict. These indicators are: the existence of a command structure; the ability to exercise military operational capacities; a minimum level of logistical capacities; the existence of disciplinary rules and the ability to implement the basic obligations of Common Article 3; and the ability to speak with one voice.[57] These factors indicate that a group of people act as a unit and therefore as an organisation. Moreover, certain armed groups control portions of territory and perform governmental functions in a similar manner to states. This has been referred to as 'insurgent or rebel governance'.[58] These similarities are more evident in relation to armed groups constituting *de facto* regimes. *De facto* regimes are those organised

56 L. Zegveld, *Accountability of Armed Opposition Groups*, 152.

57 *Prosecutor v. Boškoski & Tarčulovski* (Trial Judgment) Case No. ICTY-04-82-T (10 July 2008) (hereafter *Boškoski Trial Judgment*), paras. 194–203. See also K. Fortin, *Accountability of Armed Groups under Human Rights Law*, 127–137.

58 See Z. C. Mampilly, *Rebel Rulers: Insurgent Governance and Civilian Life during War* (Cornell University Press 2011); K. Fortin, 'The Application of Human Rights Law to Everyday Civilian Life Under Rebel Control' (2016) 63 *Netherlands International Law Review* 2, 161–181.

entities that have control over specific territories and claim to be the official government in such territories.[59] According to the UK House of Lords in the *Arantzazu Mendi* case, having *de facto* control means 'exercising all the functions of a sovereign government, in maintaining law and order, instituting and maintaining courts of justice, adopting or imposing laws regulating the relations of the inhabitants of the territory to one another and to the government'.[60]

Secondly, armed groups share similar obligations to states under international humanitarian law. In a non-international armed conflict, both parties are required, as a minimum, to treat persons not taking active part in hostilities humanely, with a series of specific prohibitions against the life and dignity of such persons, and to collect and take care of the wounded and sick.[61] Consequently, in the context of non-international armed conflicts 'international humanitarian law makes no distinction between the obligations of states and those of the armed groups concerned'.[62] Additional Protocol II to the Geneva Conventions does, however, acknowledge the differences in capabilities regarding those responsible for the internment or detention of the persons.[63] In addition, in the field of children and armed conflict, the UN Special Representative of the Secretary-General has established parallel obligations for states and non-state armed groups in the action plans addressing the six-grave violations against children's rights. These obligations range from issuing military command orders prohibiting the recruitment and use of children and criminalising these actions, to investigating and prosecuting those who recruit and use children.[64]

Thirdly, some armed groups are more organised than others and, consequently, perform more tasks than others. Indeed, this too can be said of international organisations. Not all international organisations share the same internal organisation, neither do they perform the same functions. They are characterised by the principle of speciality. This diversity was already acknowledged by the ILC, which indicating the following:

> International organizations are quite different from States, and in addition present great diversity among themselves. In contrast with States, they do not possess a general competence and have been established in order to exercise specific functions ('principle of speciality'). There are very significant differences among international organizations with regard to their powers and functions, size of membership, relations between the organization

59 See J. A. Frowein, '*De facto* regime' in *Max Planck Encyclopedia of Public International Law* (March 2013), available at <http://opil.ouplaw.com/view/10.1093/law:epil/9780199231690/law-9780199231690-e1395?rskey=f19NuL&result=1&prd=EPIL> accessed 20 May 2019. Also, J. Van Essen, '*De Facto* Regimes in International Law' (2012) 28 *Utrecht Journal of International and European Law* 74, 31–49.

60 *The Arantzazu Mendi* [1939] A.C. 256 reproduced in 1942 ILR 60, at 65 et seq.

61 These obligations derive from Common Article 3 of the Geneva Conventions.

62 A. La Rosa & C. Wuerzner, 'Armed Groups, Sanctions and the Implementation of International Humanitarian Law' (2008) 90 *International Review of the Red Cross* 870, 327–341, at 328.

63 Article 5(2) Additional Protocol II of the Geneva Conventions.

64 See Office of the Special Representative of the Secretary-General for Children and Armed Conflict, 'Actions Plans' at <https://childrenandarmedconflict.un.org/tools-for-action/action-plans/> accessed 30 May 2019.

> and its members, procedures for deliberation, structure and facilities, as well as the primary rules including treaty obligations by which they are bound.[65]

In relation to armed groups, the main requirement – according to Common Article 3 of the Geneva Conventions – is that they have a minimum level of organisation, namely a military structure that is able to conduct hostilities, with the possibility of a judicial branch. For the application of Additional Protocol II, armed groups controlling territory are likely to have a civil or administrative unit which adopts rulings for the population under their control.[66] Some examples of armed groups with this type of civil and administrative units are the Revolutionary United Front (RUF) in Sierra Leone, the Liberation Tigers of Tamil Eelam (LTTE) in Sri Lanka, the Revolutionary Armed Forces of Colombia – People's Army (FARC-EP), and the Sudan People's Liberation Movement/Army (SPLM/A), among others.[67] Although the diversity of the internal organisation was identified as a sensitive issue for the development of secondary rules of international organisations, the ILC opted for emphasising common and minimum principles of responsibility and acknowledging that other special rules could be applied depending on the circumstances.

As for the differences between these entities, there are two main considerations to bear in mind. As a first concern, armed groups are, in most cases, considered illegal entities. They are often labelled as 'criminal' or 'terrorist' groups by states and international organisations, creating problems of engagement.[68] As Sassòli notes '[...] armed groups involved in ongoing conflicts are by definition illegal under the law of the State where they fight and often also under the law of third States. This is even more so the case due to the recent practice of States and international organizations of labelling many groups as "terrorist" [...]'.[69] Likewise, Kleffner specifically refers to this issue and explains that:

> Organized armed groups do not have a right to exist under international law and, as a consequence, the objectives pursued by establishing a legal framework governing their legal responsibility may be more far-reaching than those pursued by holding states responsible.[70]

In contrast to states and international organisations that are legally recognised in the international arena, armed groups are usually regarded as illegitimate entities. This entails problems in the regulation of their actions from a normative perspective. However, legitimacy concerns can vary depending on the case. For instance, according

---

65 Articles on the Reponsibility of International Organisations, General Commentary, para. 7.

66 For instance, Art. 6 AP II implies the existence of rebel laws and courts.

67 S. Sivakumaran, 'Re-envisaging the International Law of Internal Armed Conflict' (2011) 22 *European Journal of International Law* 1, 219–264.

68 A. Bellal, 'Non-State Armed Groups in Transitional Justice Processes Adapting to New Realities of Conflict' in R. Duthie and P. Seils (eds), *Justice Mosaics: How Context Shapes Transitional Justice in Fractured Societies* (New York 2017) 1.

69 M. Sassòli, 'Taking Armed Groups Seriously', 20.

70 J. K Kleffner, 'The collective accountability of organised armed groups', 260.

to political and sociological studies, the legitimacy of armed groups can be assessed through the study of 'dynamic relational processes', that is, their relationship with the civilian population it seeks to represent, the government of the state where it operates or the international community.[71] As these studies suggest, the relationship between armed groups and states can be categorised into three types: collusive, conciliatory and conflictual.[72] In conciliatory relations, the state recognises the existence and control exerted by the armed group. As Podder explains:

> In conciliatory relationships, the state accepts the autonomy of non-state armed actors because of shortcomings. It either lacks the military capacity to recapture territory under the control of armed groups or considers such territory to be non-strategic in nature.[73]

The relationship between the armed group and the international community can also vary based on factors such as the political objectives that the armed group seeks or its ability to control territory and population. In this sense, 'a relational approach offers flexibility in analysing the important relationships and how these shape legitimacy over time'.[74] Consequently, legitimacy or illegitimacy considerations about armed groups are not always self-evident and can change over the course of the conflict.

Another main difference between states and international organisations on the one hand, and armed groups, on the other, rests on the stability of their structures. The organic structure of armed groups is not always clear and is subject to constant evolution. As Mastorodimos points out, unlike states that enjoy a stable organisation, armed groups are 'operating in a rather informal and secretive context'.[75] In this regard, while states and international organisations enjoy a stable organisation with a more or less clear set of functions, armed groups' structures could vary over the course of time, having a more rudimentary organisation at the beginning of the armed struggle and becoming more sophisticated in later years or vice versa, by simplifying their structures over time. However, this does not mean that the group does not enjoy a minimum level of organisation. If the armed group does not have a minimum organised structure, it will not comply with the requirements for it to be considered a party to the conflict. In fact, it has been argued that 'when the criteria of "intensity" and "organization" no longer exist, the armed conflict comes to an end'.[76] In some cases armed groups have been active for several decades causing considerable impact in the areas under their influence. Therefore, even if the structure of armed groups cannot

71 S. Podder 'Understanding the Legitimacy of Armed Groups: A Relational Perspective' (2017) 28 *Small Wars & Insurgencies* 4–5, 686–708, at 687.

72 *Ibid*, 694.

73 *Ibid*, 695.

74 *Ibid*, 701.

75 K. Mastorodimos, *Armed Non-State Actors in International Humanitarian and Human Rights Law: Foundation and Framework of Obligations, and Rules on Accountability* (Routledge 2015) 122.

76 *R. Bartels, 'From* Jus In Bello *to* Jus Post Bellum: *When do Non-International Armed Conflicts End?' in C. Stahn, J. S. Easterday, and J. Iverson (eds)* Jus Post Bellum: Mapping the Normative Foundations *(Oxford University Press 2014) 309.*

completely replicate that of a state or an international organisation, there is a level of organisation in place that allows it to operate. In this line, Verhoeven has noted that 'insurrectional movements will not be as sophisticated and bureaucratically organized as States, but they need a minimal, hierarchical organization, required to fight in a non-international armed conflict'.[77] In particular, this organisation allows the armed group to operate as a unit with common goals. As established by the ICTY, one of the factors which serves to determine whether an armed group is organised enough to be a party to a NIAC is the ability 'to speak with one voice, such as its capacity to act on behalf of its members in political negotiations with representatives of international organisations and foreign countries; and its ability to negotiate and conclude agreements such as cease fire or peace accords'.[78]

The last and most important step in the process of applying analogical legal reasoning is to evaluate whether the similarities between the cases are considered relevant and whether the differences are irrelevant. To this end, the suggested criterion was the analysis of the object and purpose of the rule or rules in question to assess what the underlying rationale behind it is, and what the value or concern that the norm aims to protect is. Accordingly, the next section will examine the object and purpose of the rules of responsibility in international law taking into consideration the *travaux préparatoires* and their accompanying commentaries.

3.2.2. Assessment: the object and purpose of the rules of international responsibility

The object and purpose of a treaty or a norm represent a unitary concept that refers to the goals that the drafters of the treaty aimed to achieve.[79] In fact, most scholars treat the 'object and purpose' of a treaty as a joint notion.[80] In relation to the articles on international responsibility, it has been understood that the underlying aim of the draft articles of both states and international organisations was to bring coherence and predictability to the issue of international responsibility. Indeed, this is what was meant by the Special Rapporteur, Roberto Ago, when he noted the need to study 'responsibility *per se* without reference to any particular sector'.[81] While responsibility was initially related solely to the conduct of aliens, the ILC decided to explore responsibility in general eliminating 'the continued confusion between international responsibility

77 I. Verhoeven, 'International Responsibility of Armed Opposition Groups: Lessons from State Responsibility for Actions of Non-State Armed Groups' in N. Gal-Or, C. Ryngaert, & M. Noortmann (eds) *Responsibilities of the Non-State Actor in Armed Conflict and the Market Place: Theoretical Considerations and Empirical Findings* (Brill Nijhoff 2015) 299.

78 Boškoski Trial Judgment, para. 203.

79 D. S. Jonas and T. N. Saunders, 'The Object and Purpose of a Treaty: Three Interpretive Methods' (2010) 43 *Vanderbilt Journal of Transnational Law* 3, 565–609, at 578.

80 I. Buffard & K. Zemanek, 'The "Object and Purpose" of a Treaty: An Enigma?' (1998) 3 *Austria Revue of International & European Law,* 311, 325.

81 First Report on State Responsibility by Mr. Roberto Ago, Special Rapporteur: Review of Previous Work on Codification of the Topic of the International Responsibility of States' (7 May 1969 and 20 January 1970) UN Doc. A/CN.4/217, Corr. 1 and Add. 1, para 65.

and the status of aliens'.[82] Moreover, the ILC also emphasised 'the overriding need to ensure clarity in the examination of the topic'.[83] When the ILC began its work on the responsibility of international organisations and defined the main elements of responsibility, it declared that there were no reasons to take a different approach than the one used for states.[84] In fact, the ILC stressed 'the need for keeping some coherence in the Commission's output'.[85] In this way, the ILC was trying to keep a unitary approach to the question of international responsibility and consequently, ensure predictability.

In contrast to primary norms, secondary norms on international responsibility do not serve to determine the content of the international obligation which has been violated but who, i.e. which person or entity in particular, has caused it. In this sense, a substantive part of the draft articles is dedicated to the creation of rules of attribution or imputation as one of the essential elements of international responsibility. The aim of the rules of attribution is to establish a line between the actions that should be considered as official actions of the states or international organisation in question, and those of a private character. As explained by the Office of Legal Affairs of United Nations, although in theory the conduct of all human beings could be connected with a state via nationality or residence, this approach is not accepted in relation to the question of responsibility in international law.[86] Rather, rules of attribution are established 'with a view to limiting responsibility to conduct which engages the State as an organization, and also so as to recognize the autonomy of persons acting on their own account and not at the instigation of a public authority'.[87] Consequently, the rules of attribution serve to distinguish between actions of individuals of a private character and actions of international collective entities such as states and international organisations.

The aim to bring predictability and coherence to the issue of international responsibility will not be damaged if additional entities with a limited level of international legal personality are also included. In fact, clarifying who is an official member or which actions could be attributed to an armed group will serve the same objective of determining which entity (who) is to carry the blame. Furthermore, bringing certainty to the issue of international responsibility of armed groups will keep the distinction between primary norms (obligations) and secondary norms (responsibility) and will preserve the coherence of the international legal order.

---

82 *Ibid*, para. 65.

83 Second Report on State Responsibility by Mr. Roberto Ago, Special Rapporteur: Origin International Responsibility' (20 April 1970) UN Doc. A/CN.4/233, at12, para. 5.

84 First Report on Responsibility of International Organizations by Mr. Giorgio Gaja, Special Rapporteur (26 March 2013) UN Doc. A/CN.4/532, paras. 35–36.

85 International Law Commission Report, Fifty-fourth Session (2002), UN Doc. A/57/10, 232, para. 475.

86 United Nations Legislative Series, *Materials on the Responsibility of States for Internationally Wrongful Acts* (United Nations 2012) 27.

87 *Ibid*, 27.

3.3. CONCLUDING REMARKS ON THE APPLICATION OF ANALOGICAL LEGAL REASONING TO THE CONDUCT OF ARMED GROUPS

It can be concluded that, as for the similarities between the proposed cases, states, international organisations and armed groups have to develop a minimum level of organisation to operate in a unified manner. Furthermore, both states and armed groups share parallel obligations under international humanitarian law. However, some key differences exist among these entities. As opposed to states and international organisations, armed groups are not considered legitimate and legal entities. To address this concern, it must be acknowledged that, regardless of their legal status, they enjoy a factual existence and their actions have far-reaching effects among the population under their influence, circumstances that cannot be ignored by international law. Moreover, considerations about the legitimacy or illegitimacy of armed groups can vary depending on a number of factors or over the course of the time. Another difference relates to the instability of the internal structures of armed groups. Their organisation changes over the course of the struggle, often adapting to the circumstances of the armed conflict, sometimes losing members and territories, other times reinforcing their contingencies. This can cause indeterminacy as regards the definition of their members and internal structures in comparison to the formal structures of states and international organisations.

With regard to the assessment of these similarities and differences, the analysis of the object and purpose of the rules of international responsibility can offer some insight. As concerns the purpose of the draft articles on international responsibility, the main idea is to bring predictability and coherence to the international legal system. More specifically, the aim of the rules of attribution or imputation is to help distinguishing between the acts of an organisation and the acts of isolated individuals. In other words, these rules serve to define the acts that are performed on behalf of the organisation. Consequently, including additional collective entities would entail further coherence within the issue of international responsibility and would help determine who should be considered as a part of the organisation of the armed group and who should be excluded.

In principle, there seems to be no policy reasons against the development of similar rules or guidelines in relation to armed groups and their international responsibility as long as these entities have reached a minimum level of organisation and are bound by a limited set of obligations under international law. Nevertheless, one limitation has to be introduced: armed groups differ widely from states and international organisations so a plain transposition of the applicable rules would not be advisable. There are important notions that need to be clarified, such as the organisational structure of the armed group or how its members and/or organs should be defined. In such case, although the common bases of attribution from states and international organisations could be taken as a starting point, major adjustments would need to be introduced to incorporate the peculiarities and specificities of armed groups. In this line, Kleffner explains that certain rules on attribution could potentially be applied to armed groups by analogy 'provided the necessary adjustments are made'.[88]

Another limitation relates to the application of analogical legal reasoning as a suitable method to the development of new rules. As explained in the previous section, the application of analogies has the weakness of perpetuating an existing framework of law that may not be perfect and can also contain inadequacies. An alternative solution does not have to derive from the framework suggested by the ILC and rather, a new paradigm for the international responsibility of armed groups could be created. Nevertheless, the application of analogical legal reasoning is preferred as it appears to strike a fair balance between keeping the unity and coherence of the international legal system and acknowledging the peculiarities and capabilities of organised armed groups.

4. FROM TRADITIONAL TO NON-TRADITIONAL SOURCES OF INTERNATIONAL LAW

The previous section addressed the possibility of applying analogical legal reasoning to the question of international responsibility and the conduct of armed groups by reference to the work done by the ILC. States and international organisations were compared to armed groups in relation to their basic structure as a unified organisation and their international obligations under IHL. It was concluded that, even if these rules can be taken as a starting point, major adjustments need to be introduced. Similarly to the work done in connection to international organisations, those adjustments would need to take into account the special features of armed groups as well as the relevant practice on the matter. In contrast to international organisations where there was at least certain practice on the matter by states and international organisations, the practice concerning armed groups is more limited. Consequently, one might wonder whether the same traditional sources of international law are suitable to introduce those adjustments for armed groups. As explained earlier, the law-making methods used by the ILC for the development of the rules on state responsibility were based on traditional sources of international law as established in Article 38 of the ICJ Statute, such as state practice contributing to customary international law, and secondary sources such as judicial decisions and the writings of publicists. With regards to the ASR, the ILC also analysed decisions from arbitral tribunals that contributed to a substantive part of the final text. In relation to the ARIO, the ILC did consider the practice of international organisations where this practice was coincident with the practice of states.[89] Thus, in order to develop and adjust the general principles on international responsibility, the ILC included additional sources of international law which do not fit clearly in the list contained in Article 38 of the ICJ Statute.

---

88 J. K. Kleffner, 'The collective accountability of organised armed groups', 262.

89 See Section 2 of this chapter.

In fact, the formal system of ascertaining rules in international law has recently been the subject of debate, in part due to the influence of non-state actors within the legal order.[90] The line that divides law from non-law has become blurred. Moreover, there has been a tendency over the development of the so-called *soft law* instruments.[91] These concerns have been described by D'Aspremont as follows:

> The retreat from the question of ascertainment has been dramatically accentuated by the undeniable finding that much of the international normative activity takes place outside the remit of traditional international law, and that only a limited part of the exercise of public authority at the international level nowadays materializes itself in the creation of norms which can be considered international legal rules according to a classical understanding of international law.[92]

With regard to armed groups, the traditional sources of international law rarely deal with the conduct of such groups. However, there are 'other sources' and non-judicial mechanisms that have tackled the conduct of armed groups. These materials have been taken into consideration when discussing the primary obligations of armed groups. The ICRC refers to them as 'other practice' including unilateral declarations, special agreements, codes of conduct and other internal ruling of armed groups.[93] Similarly, Sivakumaran has referred to these instruments as 'less traditional sources of the law of non-international armed conflicts' as they do not correspond to the classic sources of international law.[94] In particular, he notes that:

> The existence of these less traditional "sources", especially those of non-state armed groups, tends to be overlooked. This is not a conscious decision on the part of the international community. Rather, they are forgotten because, oftentimes, they do not have a counterpart in international armed conflict.[95]

In this regard, this material may also contain elements that help clarify secondary rules for armed groups, particularly with respect to the factual organisation of the armed group. Moreover, non-judicial monitoring mechanisms dealing with violations committed by armed groups could include information that offers assistance in linking the actions of individuals with the group. However, the question remains as to the legal value of such materials and the extent to which this practice can be used to define secondary rules. These issues will be addressed in the following sections.

---

90 See M. Noortmann, A. Reinisch & C. Ryngaert, *Non-State Actors in International Law* (Hart Publishing 2015).

91 See D. Shelton (ed) *Commitment and Compliance: The Role of Non-Binding Norms in the International Legal System* (Oxford University Press 2000).

92 J. D'Aspremont, *Formalism and the Sources of International Law: A Theory of the Ascertainment of Legal Rules* (Oxford University Press 2011) 2.

93 J. M. Henckaerts & L. Doswald-Beck, *Customary International Humanitarian Law*, xlii.

94 S. Sivakumaran, *The Law of Non-International Armed Conflicts* (Oxford University Press 2012) 107.

95 *Ibid*, 107.

4.1. THE LEGAL SIGNIFICANCE OF THE PRACTICE OF ARMED GROUPS

As the ILC has considered the practice of international organisations, such as official statements or internal rules, as a source to modulate the rules on international responsibility, the question arises as to whether the own practice of armed groups could be used to similarly adjust these rules. For this purpose, it is essential to clarify what normative value can be ascribed to the practice of armed groups, including unilateral declarations, special agreements, codes of conduct and internal rulings. In principle, there are three main questions that can be taken into consideration: a) whether this practice has a clear normative value; b) whether it could contribute to the formation of customary international law in a direct or indirect manner; or c) whether it could be used as an interpretative tool to clarify certain rules or notions.

4.1.1. Uncertainty about the normative value of the practice of armed groups

Due to the problems of legitimacy and legality of armed groups, the normative value of their practice has always been considered uncertain. This has been explicitly recognised by the ICRC stating that 'its legal significance is unclear'.[96] In terms of primary obligations in international law, some armed groups have committed to comply with certain rules through unilateral declarations or special agreements, have established their own internal rules about their organisation and/or disciplinary systems through codes of conduct.[97] As regards unilateral declarations issued by armed groups, the main question is whether they have a binding nature. With respect to states, the ICJ recognised in the *Nuclear Tests* case that 'declarations made by way of unilateral acts, concerning legal or factual situations, may have the effect of creating legal obligations'.[98] On the contrary, unilateral declarations issued by armed groups have been criticised for their supposedly weak effectiveness and their use for propaganda purposes.[99]

Nevertheless, international organisations have acknowledged the significance of unilateral declarations made by armed groups. For instance, several UN reports have considered unilateral declarations as being binding for armed groups and have determined the need to supervise such commitments.[100] In addition, the Inter-American Commission on Human Rights also reflected on the relevance of declarations

96 J. M. Henckaerts & L. Doswald-Beck, *Customary International Humanitarian Law*, xlii.

97 M. Mack, *Increasing Respect for International Humanitarian Law in Non-International Armed Conflict* (ICRC, Geneva 2008).

98 *Nuclear Tests* (*Australia v. France*) [1974] ICJ Rep 253, 20 December 1974, para. 43–46.

99 M. Mack, *supra note* 97, 20.

100 See Additional Report of the Special Representative of the Secretary-General for Children and Armed Conflict (9 February 2000) UN Doc. E/CN.4/2000/71, para. 20; Report of the Special Rapporteur on Extrajudicial, Summary or Arbitrary Executions (27 March 2006) U.N. Doc. E/CN.4/2006/53/Add.5, para. 30. See also Report of the Secretary-General on the Protection of Civilians in Armed Conflict (29 May 2009) UN Doc. S/2009/277, 29/05/2009, para. 42, where the Secretary-General mentioned

made by armed groups in its third report on the human rights situation in Colombia.[101] In 2001, the European Parliament underlined the significance of declarations made by armed opposition groups relating to total mine-bans, and expressed its support for the Deed of Commitment mechanism created by the NGO Geneva Call.[102] Another example is provided by international courts that have drawn attention to the statements of certain armed groups committing to IHL. In particular, the ICJ mentioned that the unilateral declaration to comply with the Fourth Geneva Convention made by Palestine was considered 'valid' by the depository.[103] Similarly, in the *Akayesu* case the International Criminal Tribunal for Rwanda (ICTR) addressed a statement made by the Rwandan Patriotic Front (RPF) to the ICRC where the RPF declared itself to be bound by IHL rules.[104] There are also some references by the scholarship in relation to the binding effect of unilateral declarations made by non-state actors. For instance, Ryngaert notes that 'there is no reason not to extend the binding nature of unilateral acts to other actors whose international legal personality is functionally necessary for the international community to function adequately'.[105] Likewise, Clapham and Klabbers point that non-state actors can bind themselves at the international level.[106] Apart from committing to comply with IHL rules, unilateral declarations could potentially serve to express the international responsibility of the armed group or contribute to the attribution of conduct to the group as such.

In relation to the normative status of special agreements concluded between states and armed groups, these agreements do not, in principle, fall within the conventional

unilateral undertakings by armed groups as a useful tool for promoting engagement with already existing obligations incumbent on these groups.

101 See Inter-American Commission on Human Rights, Third Report on the Situation of Human Rights in Colombia (1999), OEA/Ser.L/V/II.102, Doc. 9 rev. 1, at 78, para. 20, n. 11.

102 European Parliament Resolution of 6 September 2001, on measures to promote a commitment by non-State actors to a total ban on anti-personnel landmines, B5-0542, 0561, 0568, 0575, 0590 and 0599/2001, para. 5-6.

103 *Legal Consequences of the Construction of a Wall in the Occupied Palestinian Territory* (Advisory Opinion) [2004] ICJ Rep 136, 9 July 2004, para. 91, 'La Palestine s'est par ailleurs engagée unilatéralement, par déclaration du 7 juin 1982, à appliquer la quatrième convention de Genève. La Suisse, en qualité d'Etat dépositaire, a estimé valable cet engagement unilatéral'.

104 *Prosecutor v. Jean-Paul Akayesu* (Judgment) Case No. ICTR-96-4-T (2 September 1998), para. 627.

105 C. Ryngaert, 'Non-State Actors in International Humanitarian Law', in J. D'Aspremont (ed), *Participants in the International Legal System: Multiple Perspectives on Non-State Actors in International Law* (Routledge 2011) 289–290.

106 According to Clapham, 'One can make the case that such a declaration, whether or not it is written and witnessed, could be considered binding under international law and therefore a further source of obligation; this would be the case even in a situation where the relevant treaty made no provision for declarations with the depositary'. See A. Clapham, 'The Rights and Responsibilities of Armed Non-State Actors: The Legal Landscape & Issues Surrounding Engagement', Geneva Academy of International Humanitarian Law and Human Rights (February 2010) 19–20. As for Klabbers, '[o]f course, non-state entities may make unilateral declarations even in the absence of a specific provision to that effect, and following general international law, it may very well be that by making unilateral declarations those entities bind themselves on the international level'. See J. Klabbers, '(I Can't Get No) Recognition: Subjects Doctrine and the Emergence of Non-State Actors', in J. Petman & J. Klabbers (eds) *Nordic Cosmopolitanism: Essays in International Law for Martii Koskenniemi* (Martinus Nijhoff 2003) 351–69, at 351.

regime of the law of treaties. Nonetheless, as indicated by Article 3 of the Vienna Convention on the Law of Treaties (VCLT), this fact shall not affect the legal force of such agreements.[107] In this vein, the ICTY affirmed in the *Tadić* case that it was authorised to apply any agreement which 'was unquestionably binding on the parties' and 'was not in conflict with or derogating from peremptory norms of international law'.[108] According to Clapham, these types of undertakings were considered representative of international agreements by the Darfur Commission of Inquiry, and could give rise to international rights and obligations.[109] Some scholars have conceived special agreements as treaties, while others have emphasised their mixed legal nature, both internal, on the basis of the parties involved, and, international because of the existence of a subject of international law that guarantees their implementation.[110] Agreements between states and armed groups can take the form of ceasefire or peace agreements where the parties could establish the international responsibility for the violations committed by each side as well as the legal consequences of such responsibility.

Finally, in relation to codes of conduct, their normative significance is even more uncertain as they usually only have internal value. However, they could be considered as having two important purposes. First, they can have a direct impact on the dissemination of the rules and on the training of armed group members.[111] Second, they could be regarded as essential instruments in the determination of the organisational structure of the armed group and its chain of command in a similar way to the military manuals or the internal regulation of states. In this respect, they could have a similar role to the 'rules of the organization' for international organisations in the ARIO.[112]

4.1.2. The contribution of the practice of armed groups to customary international law

The second question relates to the possible contribution of the practice of armed groups to the formation of customary international law. In this regard, although the ICRC

---

107 Although the VCLT applies to international agreements between states, it does not preclude recognition of international agreements between other subjects of international law. See Article 3 VCLT: The fact that the present Convention does not apply to international agreements concluded between States and other subjects of international law or between such other subjects of international law, or to international agreements not in written form, shall not affect: […] c) The application of the Convention to the relations of States as between themselves under international agreements to which other subjects of international law are also parties.

108 *Tadić* Jurisdiction Decision, para. 143.

109 A. Clapham, *supra note* 106, at 19.

110 On the category of treaties see L. Vierruci, 'Applicability of the Conventions by Means of Ad Hoc Agreements', in A. Clapham, P. Gaeta & M. Sassòli (eds) *The 1949 Geneva Conventions: A Commentary* (Oxford University Press 2015) 516–517. On the mixed nature see P. Kooijmans, 'The Security Council and Non-State Entities as Parties to Conflicts', in K. Wellens (ed), *International Law: Theory and Practice, Essays in Honour of Eric Suy* (Martinus Nijhoff 1998) 338.

111 M. Mack, *supra note* 97, 22.

112 See Article 2(b) Articles on the Responsibility of International Organisations: "rules of the organization" means, in particular, the constituent instruments, decisions, resolutions and other acts of the international organization adopted in accordance with those instruments, and established practice of the organization.

has admitted that the legal significance of the practice of armed groups is unclear and that it does not constitute state practice, it nevertheless recognised that it 'may contain evidence of the acceptance of certain rules in non-international armed conflicts'.[113] In the case of anti-personnel mines, a great number of armed groups have signed the Geneva Call's Deed of Commitment prohibiting the use of mines through internal regulations.[114] This can be seen as an example of acceptance of international norms and, therefore, as declaratory of customary rules. In particular, the ICTY examined unilateral declarations, bilateral agreements and internal regulations by armed groups and considered the behaviour of insurgents as 'instrumental in bringing about the formation of customary rules'.[115]

Other authors have gone further suggesting that the practice of armed groups should be taken into account for the formation of future customary rules governing non-international armed conflicts. In this context, Sassòli has proposed taking the practice of non-state armed groups into consideration for these purposes since 'non-international armed conflicts are by definition fought at least as much by armed groups as by governmental armed forces'.[116] He further explains that:

> In my view, customary law is based on the behaviour of the subjects of a rule, in the form of acts and omissions, or in the form of statements, mutual accusations and justifications for their own behaviour. Non-State actors would logically be subject to customary law which they contribute to creating.[117]

Likewise, Roberts and Sivakumaran call for armed groups to play a role in the creation of what they label 'quasi-custom', indicating that '[...]one way forward would be to develop a theory of quasi-customary international law that would be based on the practices and views of states plus actors other than states, including, in the present context, armed groups'.[118] This question has been recently examined by the ILC and his Special Rapporteur Michael Wood on the issue of the identification of customary international law.[119] Special Rapporteur Wood analysed the role of actors other than states in the formation of customary international law, concluding that even if certain non-state actors can play an important role in promoting international law, 'their actions are not "practice" for purposes of the formation or evidencing of customary

113 J. M. Henckaerts & L. Doswald-Beck, *Customary International Humanitarian Law*, xlii.
114 To date, 50 non-state armed groups have signed the commitment on the prohibition of anti-personnel mines. See <https://genevacall.org/how-we-work/deed-of-commitment/> accessed 30 May 2019.
115 *Tadić* Jurisdiction Decision, para. 107–108.
116 M. Sassòli, 'Taking Armed Groups Seriously', 12.
117 *Ibid*, 18.
118 A. Roberts & S. Sivakumaran, 'Lawmaking by Nonstate Actors: Engaging Armed Groups in the Creation of International Humanitarian Law' (2012) 37 *Yale Journal of International Law* 1, 107–152 at 150.
119 *See Analytical Guide to the Work of the International Law Commission on the Identification of Customary International Law at <http://legal.un.org/ilc/guide/1_13.shtml> accessed 7 June 2019.*

international law'.[120] In Draft Conclusion 4 on the requirement of practice, paragraph 3 notes that the '[c]onduct of other actors is not practice that contributes to the formation, or expression, of rules of customary international law, but may be relevant when assessing the practice referred to in paragraphs 1 and 2'.[121] In its commentary, the ILC clarified this statement explaining that:

> Paragraph 3 makes explicit what may be implicit in paragraphs 1 and 2, namely that the conduct of entities other than States and international organizations - for example, NGOs, non-State armed groups, transnational corporations and private individuals - is neither creative nor expressive of customary international law. As such, their conduct does not serve as direct (primary) evidence of the existence and content of rules of customary international law. The paragraph recognizes, however, that such conduct may have an important indirect role in the identification of customary international law, by stimulating or recording practice and acceptance as law (*opinio juris*) by States and international organizations. Although the conduct of non-State armed groups is not practice that may be said to be constitutive or expressive of customary international law, the reaction of States to it may well be. Likewise, the acts of private individuals may also sometimes be relevant, but only to the extent that States have endorsed or reacted to them.[122]

Consequently, the ILC has recognised the conduct of non-state actors as having an indirect role not in the formation but in the identification of customary international law. Moreover, it stated that although the conduct of armed groups does not constitute practice for the formation or creation of customary international law, the reaction of states to such conduct may be included. As regards the conduct of non-state armed groups, the Russian Federation indicated that:

> [I]t was not entirely clear why, in addition to non-governmental organizations (NGOs) and private individuals playing an important [...] role in the identification of rules of customary international law, reference was also made [in the commentary to paragraph 3] to non-State armed groups and transnational corporations.[123]

It further suggested a clarification to the effect that 'only the reaction of States to the behaviour of such actors was important'.[124] The answer of the Special Rapporteur on this issue was rather ambiguous arguing that '[a]ny reference to non-State armed groups and transnational corporations would need to be considered as well'.[125] Therefore, the question is yet to be solved.

---

[120] Second Report on Identification of Customary International Law by Mr. Michael Wood, Special Rapporteur (22 May 2014) UN Doc. A/CN.4/672, at 32, para. 45.

[121] International Law Commission Report, Sixty-eighth Session (2016) UN Doc. A/71/10, 88.

[122] *Ibid*, 89–90, para. 9.

[123] Fifth Report on Identification of Customary International Law by Mr. Michael Wood, Special Rapporteur (14 March 2018) UN Doc. A/CN.4/717 18–19, para. 40.

[124] *Ibid*, 18.

[125] *Ibid*, 22, para. 49.

Although desirable, the incorporation of the practice of armed groups into customary rules is a complex endeavour. There are several issues that cause difficulties regarding, on the one hand, the identification of the so-called practice of armed groups and, on the other hand, the conceptualisation and methodology of customary international law. In relation to the first issue, the main issue is how the practice of several armed groups could be identified and generalised so as to represent a single category of actors. This question has been posed by Fortin who affirms that 'it is hard to envisage a situation where it could be comfortably said that the practice or views of several armed groups could be said to be representative of all armed groups'.[126] However, this concern can be also applied to the conduct of states that are also very heterogenous and who can also offer contradictory views on a wide variety of topics. In fact, if a critical perspective is taken on the formation of some customary norms, it is evident that less powerful states, especially non-western states, have played a less significant role in the formation of certain international legal norms. This seems to be the case with regard to the international minimum standard for compensation for expropriation and the conflicted history of customary international law of the territorial sea.[127] As Kelly explains, '[i]f a particular customary rule or standard is formed without the participation of a significant number of states or their interests and concerns are ignored or treated as irrelevant to norm formation, then a rule or standard may be seen not only as lacking general acceptance but also as lacking democratic legitimacy'.[128] Accordingly, if we aim to include the conduct and views of armed groups, we would need to make sure that there is a significant amount of practice, as well as an *opinio juris* element to ensure a fair balance. More particularly, this would mean the inclusion of a variety of armed groups from different geographical regions and with different organisational structures.

Regarding the conceptualisation and methodology of customary international law, some authors have pointed to other legal hurdles. For instance, Clapham fears that incorporating such practice would transform the international legal system 'into a more descriptive normative framework where the law reflects existing cannons of behaviour by all concerned, rather than generating injunctions for non-state actors'.[129] Similarly, Rondeau notes that the current system of norm creation through customary international law do not necessarily need to include the practices of actors other than states. In particular she claims that 'to open the door for input from different stakeholders would lead to the presence of multiple levels of customary norms in international law, as well as differently tailored boundaries of the rules, depending on

126 K. Fortin, 'How to Cope with Diversity While Preserving Unity in Customary International Law? Some Insights from International Humanitarian Law' (2018) 23 *Journal of Conflict & Security Law* 3, 337–358, at 351.

127 See J. P. Kelly, 'Customary International Law in Historical Context: The Exercise of Power without General Acceptance' in B. D. Lepard (ed) *Reexamining Customary International Law* (Cambridge University Press 2017), 47–85.

128 *Ibid*, 49.

129 A. Clapham, *supra note* 106, at 43.

who is involved'.[130] To mitigate those concerns, some proposals and clarifications have been introduced into the discussions.

One idea is to draw inspiration from the so-called regional customary rules which are developed for particular geographical regions.[131] In this regard, Hiemstra and Nohle propose that non-regional special customary law can be developed for non-state armed groups due to the fact that not all subjects of international law are bound by the same customary rules.[132] This would lead to a special customary regime binding only between non-state armed groups. There are also other proposals that intend to strike a fair balance between the practice of states and armed groups. Roberts and Sivakumaran have suggested establishing certain limitations with regards to the weight given to the practice and views of armed groups.[133] One limitation would be that armed groups would not have the power to create a new custom or undermine or change an existing custom without consensus between armed groups and states.[134] Another constraint could be that the practice of armed groups could not be treated as equal to the practice of states and, consequently, the role of states in the formation of customary international law should still be prioritised over other actors.[135]

To sum up, it can be argued that although the practice and *opinio juris* of states should be given a primary role in the formation of customary international law, non-state actors are not totally excluded from complementary or additional roles. Specifically, the ILC in its current study on customary international law has recognised the indirect role of non-state actors in the identification of norms. Moreover, in relation to armed groups, it is necessary to distinguish two categories of practice: their conduct in relation to states; and their conduct in relation to other armed groups. With regards to their relationship with states, custom could be eventually created if there was some kind of consensus or coincident practice among states and armed groups, keeping the leading role of states in the formation of customary international law. As for the relationship with other armed groups, there could be a special regime of customary international law which is binding among these entities themselves. Similarly to states, the practice and *opinio juris* of armed groups could be identified not only by looking at their physical actions in the field but also by analysing their public statements and internal rulings.[136] Moreover, account should be given to a sufficient number of armed groups representing different sizes and geographical regions so the general acceptance of a norm can be properly assessed.

---

130 S. Rondeau, 'Participation of Armed Groups in the Development of the Law Applicable to Armed Conflicts' (2011) 93 *International Review of the Red Cross* 883, 649–672, at 668.

131 Third Report on Identification of Customary International Law by Mr. Michael Wood, Special Rapporteur (27 March 2015) UN Doc. A/CN.4/682, at 54–56.

132 H. Hiemstra and E. Nohle, 'The Role of Non-State Armed Groups in the Development and Interpretation of International Humanitarian Law' (2017) 20 *Yearbook of International Humanitarian Law*, 3–35, at 22.

133 A. Roberts & S. Sivakumaran, *supra note* 118, 149–152.

134 *Ibid*, 151.

135 *Ibid*, 151.

136 A. Bellal and E. Heffes, 'Yes, I do": Binding Armed Non-State Actors to IHL and Human Rights Norms through their Consent' (2018) 12 *Human Rights & International Legal Discourse* 1, 120–136, at 126.

4.1.3. *The role of the practice of armed groups as an interpretative tool*

Another question is whether the practice of armed groups can be used as a way to interpret the norms applicable in non-international armed conflicts. According to Sivakumaran, this practice 'must be acknowledged and used to inform interpretations of the law'.[137] From this standpoint, their perspectives on the interpretation of IHL rules could be considered complementary to the current debates in different fora, as their views reflect their actual experiences as parties to armed conflict.[138] In fact, including armed groups' views could be valuable since they could provide important information regarding their actual capabilities and their reasons for complying or dissenting with a norm. As it has been argued, as far as 'the humanitarian core of the norm is respected, NSAGs should be granted some latitude when interpreting certain IHL rules, permitting consideration of their factual capabilities and particular dilemmas and aspirations'.[139]

Certain primary IHL norms require contextualisation due to the different capacities of armed groups and their lack of 'official legislation' to implement some obligations. This can be seen in the provision of judicial guarantees in Common Article 3 to the Geneva Conventions which require a 'previous judgment pronounced by a regularly constituted court, affording all the judicial guarantees which are recognized as indispensable by civilized peoples'.[140] Article 6(2) of Additional Protocol II also demands the passing of a sentence by 'a court offering the essential guarantees of independence and impartiality'. In interpreting this provision, the FMLN in the armed conflict in El Salvador claimed that the 'type of tribunal and law required by Protocol II have had to have been adapted to the existence and capacity of the contending party'.[141] The need for contextualisation would also be required in relation to secondary norms on international responsibility applicable to armed groups. In this sense, the practice and conduct of armed groups could serve in the process of contextualising these and future norms.

There have been a number of examples where the conduct and views of armed groups have been actually used as a source of interpretation in order to discuss the existing challenges in the international legal framework. For instance, the Geneva Academy of International Humanitarian Law and Human Rights has undertook a project on 'Reactions to Norms: Armed Groups and the Protection of Civilians'.[142] The report considers the reaction of more than 30 armed groups to international norms

137 S. Sivakumaran, *The Law of Non-International Armed Conflict* (Oxford University Press 2012) 110.

138 M. Sassòli, 'Taking Armed Groups Seriously', 20.

139 H. Hiemstra and E. Nohle, *supra note* 132, 27.

140 Art. 3(1)(d) Common to the Geneva Conventions.

141 Letter from Commander Nidia Diaz, Director of the FMLN Secretariat for the Promotion and Protection of Human Rights (19 October 1988) partially reproduced in Americas Watch, *Violation of Fair Trial Guarantees by the FMLN's Ad Hoc Courts* (Americas Watch 1990) 510.

142 See Geneva Academy of International Humanitarian Law and Human Rights, *Reactions to Norms. Armed Groups and the Protection of Civilians* (Geneva 2014) available at <https://www.geneva-academy.ch/joomlatools-files/docman-files/Publications/Policy%20Briefing/Geneva%20Academy%2

taking into account 'different types of conflict, their intensity, a range of geographical contexts, and the various motivations that cause groups to use violence'.[143] Similarly, the NGO Geneva Call has organised a project entitled 'The Garance Talks' which bring together representatives from non-state armed groups and experts in order to discuss the current challenges faced by these groups to comply with humanitarian norms.[144] Moreover, another example of research engaging with different actors including armed groups is the project 'Viewpoints' organised by the Centre for Humanitarian Dialogue which dealt with peace processes. This project was useful in collecting the views and opinions of different stakeholders including, among others, former members of armed groups, academics, policy advisers, NGOs, mediators, and former diplomats.[145] Although in the end these processes did not result in norm-creation, these collections of views offered important insights regarding the capabilities of armed groups which could be eventually considered for future norm interpretation.

Therefore, as a minimum, the practice of armed groups can be regarded as an interpretative tool aiding in the clarification and adjustment of primary and secondary norms applicable in non-international armed conflicts. In fact, the inclusion of the views and practice of armed groups in the process of interpretation could be more easily accepted since this would not challenge the role of states as primary law-makers.[146] Moreover, it would also serve to create a sense of ownership of these norms by armed groups.[147]

4.1.4. *The possible contribution of the practice of armed groups to secondary norms on international responsibility*

As explained earlier, the legal significance of the practice of armed groups has usually been studied in relation to primary IHL obligations. However, this practice may also include elements that are relevant to the development of secondary norms on international responsibility. Some armed groups have developed internal rulings and codes of conduct which could serve to clarify the organisational structure and hierarchy of the group. In particular, internal rulings and statutes of armed groups could offer insights into the question of membership and the possible existence of armed groups'

0Policy%20Briefing%201_Amed%20Groups%20and%20the%20Protection%20of%20Civilians_April%202014.pdf> accessed 9 June 2019.

143 *Ibid*, 6.

144 The first edition of the *Garance Talks* was organised in Geneva on 26 November 2015 on the issue of the positive international law obligations of ANSAs. See <https://www.genevacall.org/wp-content/uploads/dlm_uploads/2016/08/GaranceTalks_Issue01_Report.pdf> accessed 30 May 2019. On 22 November 2017, Geneva Call held its second session on the administration of justice by ANSAs. See <https://genevacall.org/wp-content/uploads/dlm_uploads/2018/09/GaranceTalks_Issue02_Report_2018_web.pdf> accessed 30 May 2019.

145 C. Buchanan (ed), *Viewpoints: Volume 2 – Negotiating Disarmament* (Centre for Humanitarian Dialogue, November 2008) available at <https://www.hdcentre.org/wp-content/uploads/2016/08/75ViewpointsEdition2-November-2008.pdf> accessed 9 June 2019.

146 H. Hiemstra and E. Nohle, *supra note* 132, 27.

147 A. Bellal and E. Heffes, *supra note* 136, 7.

organs. These documents could be analogous to the internal law of states or the rules of the organisation for international organisations that are used for the purpose of attribution.[148] Unilateral declarations have also been issued by armed groups in relation to incidents in which they have participated. Moreover, special agreements and peace agreements between armed groups and states could serve to evidence existing practice by both parties regarding legal consequences of responsibility. In this sense, this material can be instrumental in adapting or interpreting possible rules of responsibility for armed groups.

4.2. THE LEGAL SIGNIFICANCE OF NON-JUDICIAL MONITORING MECHANISMS

The second relevant source relates to non-judicial mechanisms in the field of IHL and human rights that have monitored the violations committed by both states and non-state armed groups during non-international armed conflicts. Among these mechanisms, the work of the UN Commissions of Inquiry and Fact-Finding Missions can be highlighted. Moreover, the special procedures of the UN Human Rights Council have also documented IHL violations committed by non-state armed groups. The Human Rights Council has expressly addressed those actions that violate international humanitarian law.[149] Specifically, the Special Rapporteur on Extrajudicial, Summary and Arbitrary Executions has stated that IHL falls within her mandate and her predecessors' reports.[150] Other mechanisms such as Truth and Reconciliation Commission have also addressed issues of accountability by states and non-state parties. Finally, certain NGOs, such as Geneva Call, have established monitoring processes in relation to the actions of non-state armed groups.

In particular, UN mechanisms have denounced the commission of IHL and human rights violations by armed groups and, in some cases, characterised them as international crimes. As indicated in the previous chapter, these reports do not usually focus on issues of responsibility and attribution of armed group as such. However, they can offer insights into the factual link that exists between individuals and the group itself. As noted by Bellal, 'some elements of analysis can be considered as "lessons learned" in the view of a possible elaboration of formal rules of legal responsibility for

148 Art. 4 ASR considers the internal law of the state to define state's organs. Similarly, Art. 6 ARIO refers to the rules of the organization to clarify the functions of the organs and agents of international organizations.

149 UN Human Rights Council Resolution 9/9 'Protection of human rights of civilians in armed conflict' (18 September 2008) A/HRC/RES/9/9. The former Commission on Human Rights also treated international humanitarian law as lying within its mandate.

150 Report of the Special Rapporteur on Extrajudicial, Summary or Arbitrary Executions 'Armed Non-State actors: the Protection of the Right to Life' (5 June 2018) A/HRC/38/44, para. 26; See also P. Alston, J. Morgan-Foster & W. Abresch, 'The Competence of the UN Human Rights Council and its Special Procedures in Relation to Armed Conflicts: Extrajudicial executions in the "War on Terror"' (2008) 19 *European Journal of International Law* 1, 183–209.

non-state actors should an international judicial forum be established in the future with jurisdiction over collective entities other than States'.[151] Since the ILC relied on judicial and arbitral decisions together with state practice (and the practice of international organisations for the ARIO), reports from monitoring mechanisms could be analogous to the former material and could provide essential information regarding violations committed by armed groups.

Once again, the question that arises relates to the normative value of these non-judicial reports. In principle, they do not fit within the classic understanding of sources of international law established by Article 38 of the ICJ Statute. They are different from judicial decisions as they are not binding and do not often decide on individual claims. Nonetheless, their findings are often considered relevant by courts and also attract the attention of scholars.[152] In particular, the work of Commissions of Inquiry has been essential in urging parties to an armed conflict to comply with international obligations and encouraging accountability mechanisms. Their reports have also been cited by courts and scholars. For instance, the ICC relied on the factual findings of the Commission of Inquiry in Darfur, and the report of the Yugoslavia Commission was cited by the Pre-Trial Chamber of the ICC.[153] Although not considered formal sources, monitoring mechanisms engage in the evaluation of facts and the practice of interpreting international law. In this regard, some authors have emphasised their value as interpreters of the law or even as 'quasi-judicial' bodies.[154] In the case of Commissions of Inquiry, Darcy notes that 'Commissions' reports can be considered subsidiary sources of law or should be analogised as such, as they are a hybrid of doctrine and jurisprudence'.[155] As for special procedures, independent experts and special rapporteurs have engaged in country visits and have also acted on individual cases where they commented on the applicable law. Likewise, some authors have emphasised the role of Special Rapporteurs in the development of international law.[156]

It can be argued that these mechanisms have a certain degree of legitimacy in their task of interpreting the law to the situations under their examination. First, as organs

---

151 A. Bellal, 'Establishing the Direct Responsibility of Non-State Armed Groups for Violations of International Norms: Issues of Attribution' in N. Gal-Or, C. Ryngaert & M. Noortmann. *Responsibilities of the Non-State Actor in Armed Conflict and the Market Place: Theoretical Considerations and Empirical Findings* (Brill Nijhoff 2015) 310.

152 C. Harwood, 'International Commissions of Inquiry as Law-Makers' (2016) *ESIL Research Forum*, Conference Paper No. 1/2016, 9.

153 See *Prosecutor v. Al Bashir* (Second Decision on the Prosecution's Application for a Warrant of Arrest) ICC-02/05-01/09, PTC I (12 July 2010); also *Prosecutor v. Bemba Gombo* (Decision Pursuant to Article 61(7)(a) and (b) of the Rome Statute) ICC-01/05-01/08, PTC II (15 June 2009), para. 431.

154 R. Buchan, 'The Mavi Marmara Incident and the Application of International Humanitarian Law by Quasi-Judicial Bodies', in D. Jinks *et al* (eds), *Applying International Humanitarian Law in Judicial and Quasi- Judicial Bodies: International and Domestic Aspects* (Springer 2014) 481.

155 S. Darcy, 'Laying the Foundations: Commissions of Inquiry and the Development of International Law', in C. Henderson (ed), *Commissions of Inquiry: Problems and Prospects* (Hart Publishing 2017) 3.

156 S. P. Subedi, S. Wheatley, A. Mukherjee & S. Ngane, 'The role of the special rapporteurs of the United Nations Human Rights Council in the Development and Promotion of International Human Rights Norms' (2011) 15 *The International Journal of Human Rights* 2, 155–161.

or bodies of international organisations, their competence to interpret and apply international law derive from their mandates.[157] Sivakumaran considers these types of entities as state-empowered entities, that is, entities that states have empowered to carry out particular functions, including among others, the UN Human Rights Committee, the ILC or the ICRC.[158] In this respect, it is the mandate from states that distinguishes them from non-state actors but also 'from mere *fora* for discussion'.[159] Second, the value of the statements and reports by appointed experts and special rapporteurs rests on the independence and impartiality of their evaluations.[160] Accordingly, an entity that is comprised of impartial experts will likely be considered an authoritative source. Finally, their reports follow legal argumentation based on conformity with principles of international law or the application of jurisprudence.[161] Therefore, if a particular monitoring mechanism produces reports that are well-reasoned and substantiated in law, there is more chance that it will be generally accepted by the international community or at least 'the community of international lawyers will read that particular output with the entity's reputation in mind'.[162] Moreover, the output of some of these monitoring mechanisms could stimulate the reaction of states expressing their support. For some authors, the silence or lack of reaction of states to these reports and materials could eventually represent an implied acquiescence with its content.[163]

This legitimacy to interpret the law is closely connected to the notion of 'semantic authority' developed by Venkze. According to this theory, 'semantic authority' refers to the capacity of certain actors to 'have a significant impact on the making of international law within the everyday practice of its discourse'.[164] In his view 'international lawmaking is not a matter of the recognized sources of international law alone, but that it unfolds in the communicative practice of its everyday operation'.[165] Semantic authority can be derived not only from international courts and tribunals but also from organs of international organisations, NGOs, domestic courts or international lawyers. Similarly, D'Aspremont also acknowledges that 'social practice' shapes law-ascertainment through the work of law-applying authorities.[166] He refers

157 C. Harwood, *supra note* 152, 16.

158 S. Sivakumaran, 'Beyond States and Non-State Actors: The Role of State-Empowered Entities in the Making and Shaping of International Law' (2017) 55 *Columbia Journal of Transnational Law* 2, 343–394, at 346.

159 *Ibid*, 356.

160 V. Koutroulis, 'The Prohibition of the Use of Force in Arbitrations and Fact-Finding Reports' in M. Weller (ed), *The Oxford Handbook of the Use of Force in International Law* (Oxford University Press 2015) 612.

161 C. Harwood, *supra note* 152, 16–17.

162 S. Sivakumaran, *supra note* 158, 370.

163 *Ibid*, 385.

164 I. Venkze, 'Semantic Authority' (2016) Amsterdam Center for International Law No. 2016–03, Amsterdam Law School Research Paper No. 2016–06, 3 available at <https://papers.ssrn.com/sol3/papers.cfm?abstract_id=2723851> accessed 30 May 2019.

165 *Ibid*, 4.

166 J. D'Aspremont, 'Non-State Actors and the Social Practice of International Law', in M. Noortmann, A. Reinisch and C. Ryngaert (eds), *Non-state Actors in International Law* (Bloomsbury 2015) 12–14.

to international courts, arbitral tribunals and domestic courts as law-applying authorities, but he also considers other entities such as the ICRC and international legal scholars as having an impact, and as contributing actors to the social practice of law-ascertainment.[167] Similarly, Sivakumaran claims that these entities do not only interpret the law but also serve to make and shape international law. He explains that:

> The precise lawmaking and law-shaping role of state-empowered entities varies and includes, *inter alia*, creating, developing, interpreting, applying, and proposing changes to the law. State-empowered entities shape hard law, through actions like the development and interpretation of treaties or the identification of custom, and also shape soft law, through actions like the creation of principles or guidelines.[168]

Therefore, although not having a place in the formal system of sources of international law, the reports of monitoring mechanisms in the field of IHL and human rights can be regarded as a legitimate source of interpretation of both the facts and the applicable law in question. In particular, since there is no specific judicial forum against which we can evaluate the conduct of non-state armed groups, the role of Commissions of Inquiry and other monitoring mechanisms such as the special procedures at the UN Human Rights Council becomes the only instrument available to find some elements of analysis for the purposes of ascribing international responsibility to armed groups. These materials contain information regarding the patterns of violations committed by armed groups or the factual links between the members and the group. In view of this, these materials could inform not only discussions on primary obligations applicable to armed groups but also the possible international responsibility of the group as such.

4.3. THE ROLE OF INTERPRETATION IN SHAPING AND DEVELOPING INTERNATIONAL LAW

According to the previous section, both the practice of armed groups and the work of non-judicial monitoring mechanisms can be considered instrumental in the process of interpreting and adapting international law to armed groups. In this regard, the role of interpretation could be essential in the development of contemporary international law without challenging the primacy of the traditional sources of international law. As Harwood explains, '[w]hile the theory of formal sources remains generally useful to demarcate law from non-law, it does not capture how interpretation incrementally develops the law, nor does it reflect the plethora of actors which participate in this process'.[169] In fact, there is a thin line between interpretation and development of the law. In this context, several authors have argued that international legal interpretation goes beyond having a mere expository function, and rather gives rise to some creative

167 *Ibid*, 20–31.
168 S. Sivakumaran, *supra note* 158, 358.
169 C. Harwood, *supra note* 152, 3.

elements. For instance, Kolb identifies interpretation and development as a 'joint venture' and considers that the application of law involves a creative process.[170] Similarly, Hollis claims that 'the function of interpretation must extend beyond its classic formulation as a process for "finding the law" to one that may involve its very creation'.[171]

Other authors also acknowledge the existence of various interpretative communities in international law.[172] An important part of IHL has been developed through the interpretative role of international criminal courts and the work of the ICRC. Moreover, other actors are emerging in the task of interpreting IHL, such as independent experts and special rapporteurs. In fact, 'the teachings of the most highly qualified publicists of the various nations' are regarded by Article 38 of the ICJ Statute 'as subsidiary means for the determination of rules of law'. In this respect, the work of independent experts and special rapporteurs could be assimilated to that of highly recognised jurists. Their role is even more authoritative as it counts on the endorsement of the international organisation, namely the United Nations. Consequently, other subsidiary means for the determination and interpretation of international law could potentially be incorporated.

In relation to the possible interpretation provided by armed groups, it is indeed more challenging to confer them an official role in this process. However, taking the practices of armed groups into account could serve to contextualise the norms to the characteristics of armed groups and also make these norms more realistic due to the limited capacities of these entities.[173] Consequently, for the purpose of this study, the 'other practice' of armed groups as well as the work of UN monitoring mechanisms will be considered as interpretative tools which will serve to adjust the general principles of international responsibility to the conduct and characteristics of armed groups.

4.4. CONCLUDING REMARKS ON THE LEGAL SIGNIFICANCE OF NON-TRADITIONAL SOURCES OF INTERNATIONAL LAW

Following the approach of the ILC in the development of rules for international organisations, the special features of armed groups and their relevant practice would need to be taken into consideration in order to introduce the required adjustments and adaptations to the principles on international responsibility. Due to the limitations of traditional sources of international law to provide relevant information regarding the standards of conduct of armed groups and the necessity to incorporate new realities

170 R. Kolb, *Interprétation et création du droit international. Esquisse d'une herméneutique juridique moderne pour le droit international public* (Bruylant 2006) 931.

171 D. B. Hollis, 'Interpretation' in J. D'Aspremont & S. Singh (eds) *Concepts for International Law: Contributions to Disciplinary Thought* (Edward Elgar Publishing 2019) 562.

172 M. Waibel, 'Interpretative Communities in International Law' in A. Bianchi, D. Peat & M. Windsor (eds), *Interpretation in International Law* (Oxford University Press 2015) 147–165.

173 M. Sassòli, 'Taking Armed Groups Seriously', 17.

in contemporary international law, additional sources of international law have been considered for this purpose. These additional materials rest on the so-called 'other practice' of armed groups and the reports from UN monitoring mechanisms. The inclusion of other sources of international law for the development of general principles on international responsibility is not foreign to the methodology followed by the ILC. In particular, the ILC has considered the decisions of arbitral tribunals and the practice of international organisations as sources of information that do not fit within the classic list provided by Article 38 of the ICJ Statute. In this respect, the practice of armed groups can be analogous to the practice and internal rules of international organisations. The reports from UN monitoring mechanisms could be assimilated to the opinion of highly reputed jurists. More importantly, these reports also have the endorsement of the United Nations.

As for the legal significance of the practice of armed groups, three issues have been highlighted as deserving attention. The first one relates to the uncertainty regarding its normative value. The practice of armed groups can be divided into unilateral declarations, special agreements, and codes of conduct and internal rulings. International organisations and scholars have acknowledged the significance of unilateral declarations made by armed groups and have, in some cases, recognised their binding nature. As regards special and peace agreements, they are said to have a mixed legal nature: internal, on the basis of the parties involved; and, international, because of the existence of a subject of international law that guarantees their implementation. Codes of conduct have a mere internal value. However, they could serve to disseminate IHL rules and they could also become essential instruments in the determination of the organisational structure of the armed group and its chain of command.

The second issue refers to the possible contribution of the practice of armed groups to customary international law either directly or indirectly. Although non-state actors do not enjoy a direct role in the formation of customary international law, they are not totally excluded from complementary or additional roles. Particularly, an indirect role of non-state actors in the identification of norms has been recognised by the ILC. Moreover, some proposals can be made in relation to the possible contribution to customary international law by the practice and *opinio juris* of armed groups. In its relationship with states, custom could eventually be created if there is some kind of consensus or coincident practice among states and armed groups. In its relationship with other armed groups, there could be a special regime of customary international law that is binding among these entities themselves. The third issue deals with the role of the practice of armed groups as an interpretative tool. In this context, the inclusion of the views and practice of armed groups in the process of interpretation can be more easily accepted as this would not challenge the role of states as primary law-makers and this could also create a sense of ownership.

Regarding the legal value of reports from non-judicial monitoring mechanisms, it has been argued that these materials enjoy 'semantic authority' in the interpretation of international law. They are considered valuable sources due to the following aspects. First, as organs or bodies of international organisations, their competence to interpret and apply international law derives from their mandates. Second, the value of the statements and reports by appointed experts and special rapporteurs rest on the independence and impartiality of their evaluations. And finally, their reports follow a legal argumentation based on the conformity with principles of international law or the application of jurisprudence. As a minimum, both the practice of armed groups and the reports from non-judicial monitoring mechanisms are regarded as supplementary means for the determination and interpretation of the rules on international responsibility applicable to armed groups.

5. FINDING A SUITABLE METHODOLOGY REGARDING THE INTERNATIONAL RESPONSIBILITY OF ARMED GROUPS: A PROPOSAL

After taking into consideration the findings of the previous sections, this part establishes the methodology that has been suggested for the development of the international responsibility of armed groups. In this regard, the present study proposes the development of an analogous approach to the issue of international responsibility to the one employed by the ILC in the adaptation of norms to international organisations. This analogous approach will be based on common principles of responsibility and attribution shared by states and international organisations. These common principles will act as basic guidance but will be adapted to the specific characteristics of armed groups and the interpretation provided by the so-called 'other practice' and non-judicial mechanisms that have monitored the conduct of armed groups. Although reasoning by analogy has the limitation of perpetuating an existing framework of law which may contain weaknesses, this method has one important advantage, that is, to keep the unity and coherence of the international legal system. In fact, this solution seems to strike a balance between bringing coherence to the system of responsibility in international law and acknowledging the actual differences between diverse entities, such as states, international organisations, and armed groups. This proposal is also in line with the statement of the ICJ in the *Reparations* case according to which not all entities need to enjoy the same rights, obligations and responsibilities.[174]

By incorporating additional sources in the interpretation of norms, this method attempts to avoid the critiques relating to the lack of sufficient practice to develop rules on international responsibility for armed groups.[175] Moreover, to respond to the critiques on the wide disparity of armed groups and the impossibility to identify

174 *Reparation for Injuries Suffered in the Service of the United Nations* (Advisory Opinion) [1949] ICJ Rep 174, 11 April 1949, at 178.

175 This criticism has been raised regarding the rules of responsibility of international organisations but also regarding a possible framework of responsibility for armed groups. See section 2.1 of this Chapter and section 4.5 of Chapter 2.

general rules, this approach would need to consider a number of issues. Among others, it will be essential to determine how to tackle the structural disparity of armed groups, which adjustments need to be introduced and which specific developments have to be considered. In relation to the structural disparity of armed groups, the research will need to analyse the different structures of armed groups, in particular centralised and decentralised armed groups, as well as the issue of membership. Once the different structures have been analysed, the research will focus on the adjustments that are required to match those special features of armed groups. In addition, these adjustments will also take into account the 'other practice' of armed groups and the reports of non-judicial monitoring mechanisms on the matter. The practice of armed groups would need to be based on the conduct of armed groups from different geographical regions. Where the practice of armed groups is coincident with the practice of states and international organisations this could eventually lead to the formation of a norm with customary law status.

In summary, this book attempts to develop a set of basic and minimum guidelines that can be applied to organised armed groups in the process of ascribing international responsibility for IHL violations. To this end, the study will mainly elaborate on the issue of attribution of conduct to armed groups, which is an essential component of the international responsibility of collective entities. The development of these guidelines will be detailed in Chapter 4, which will focus on attribution. As a second component of international responsibility, the book will deal with the question of the legal consequences of responsibility and the obligation to provide reparation in Chapter 5.

6. CONCLUSIONS

This chapter aimed to answer the second sub-question of this study, namely, 'which methodology can and should be used to develop a responsibility framework for armed groups under international law?'. For this purpose, the chapter has inquired into the possible methods that could be applied to develop principles of responsibility for violations of IHL committed by armed groups. The first part of the chapter analysed the methodology used by the ILC when drafting the principles on international responsibility applicable to states and international organisations. The second part of the chapter has questioned if a similar reasoning could be applied to the actions of armed groups as collective entities. To proceed with such an undertaking, the research has inquired to what extent it was possible to apply analogies to the issue of international responsibility between states and international organisations, on the one hand, and armed groups, on the other. In addition, it has analysed the advantages and limitations of this line of reasoning.

It was argued that a similar understanding could be applied to organised armed groups since they are also collective entities that can only act through human beings, they have a minimum level of organisation and similar IHL obligations than states, although a total transposition of these principles was not feasible owing to the key differences that exist among these cases. Therefore, this chapter has proposed to apply an analogous approach that would take the common rules of responsibility and attribution between states and international organisations as a starting point but would adapt them to the specific characteristics of armed groups and the interpretation provided by the secondary materials identified above. In developing these principles and guidelines for armed groups, two basic components will be analysed, that is, the attribution of conduct and the legal consequences of responsibility. The conceptual and operational questions regarding the development of rules of attribution for armed groups will be elaborated in the following chapter. The issue of legal consequences and the obligation to provide reparation will be analysed in Chapter 5.

CHAPTER IV
ATTRIBUTION OF CONDUCT TO ARMED GROUPS

1. INTRODUCTION

The previous chapter established that in order to formulate a responsibility framework for armed groups, the common principles of responsibility between states and international organisations should be considered and adjusted to the characteristics of organised armed groups, while also taking into consideration their own practice and the reports of non-judicial monitoring mechanisms. Accordingly, this chapter will analyse how these principles could be adapted and which special developments need to be contemplated. In this regard, one of the key elements that needs to be explored is the question of attribution that connects the perpetrator of violations of international law with the entity to whom they belong or whom they represent. As such, this chapter will focus on the third sub-question of the study, namely, 'under which conditions can and should acts of formal or *de facto* members of an armed group be attributed to the group itself?'. To answer this question, this part follows an interpretative approach and proposes minimum standards of attribution that could be potentially applied to armed groups.

The chapter starts by exploring the concept of attribution as an essential element in ascribing international responsibility to collective entities and gives account of the academic debate on the question of attribution of conduct to armed groups. Second, it examines the substantive rules of attribution developed for states and international organisations. It provides a comparison between the two and analyses which basic rules of attribution are shared by both states and international organisations. The aim of this analysis is to determine the core principles of attribution that could be potentially applied to collective entities such as organised armed groups.

The following section will consider the application of these core principles to the conduct of armed groups and the adjustments that would need to be introduced. As explained in Chapter 3, the main special feature of armed groups is the issue of their structural disparity. This has been considered as one of the main obstacles to developing general and abstract rules for armed groups. Thus, the chapter will reflect on the different aspects of the structural organisation of armed groups, such as the concurrence of a military and a political wing, the differences between centralised and decentralised groups, and the temporal changes of structures. These aspects are reflected in legal and policy documents on international humanitarian law from the ICRC, political science studies and also in the internal rulings of armed groups themselves. The chapter will then consider the three main principles of attribution identified above, that is, conduct of organs and/or agents; conduct directed and controlled by the armed group; and the acknowledgment of the conduct by the armed group. Following the methodology identified in the previous chapter, the required adjustments will be based on those special features of armed groups, the interpretation provided by the practice of armed groups (in particular, unilateral declarations and codes of conduct), and the reports provided by UN monitoring mechanisms.

With regard to the first principle, the research will explore whether, and if so, how the notion of organs and/or agents could be applied to armed groups; and whether the notion of membership of armed groups is relevant for attributing IHL violations to them. In relation to the second principle, the study will consider which standard of direction and control is applicable to armed groups depending on their different structures. As for the third principle, the analysis will consider whether there are relevant examples of acknowledgment of conduct in the practice of armed groups and the conditions they need to comply with. Finally, some key implications and considerations for future research will be addressed.

2. ATTRIBUTION AS A KEY ELEMENT OF INTERNATIONAL RESPONSIBILITY

One of the central elements of international responsibility is the question of attribution. As examined in Chapter 2, the requirement of imputation or attribution was first emphasised by Triepel and Anzilotti. According to Anzilotti, attribution is not based on factual causation: an act was legally attributed to a subject not because it has been committed by that subject but because the rule attributes it to the state.[1] Similarly, Triepel elaborated on the issue of attribution by establishing the emergence of the responsibility of the state for the acts of individuals, its organs, public law corporations and the responsibility of the federal state for the acts of its member states.[2] In particular, the issue of attribution stands out as being a key element for the responsibility of collective entities. It is not just about declaring the existence of a violation of international law but about imputing it to an entity who is expected to act according to certain international standards. According to De Frouville, attribution serves a double purpose:

> In international law, attribution fulfils a double function in the theory of responsibility. The first consists of designating a responsible person (legal or natural) who will bear the consequences of this responsibility, even though the person in question may not necessarily

1 D. Anzilotti, *Corso di Diritto Internazionale. Vol. 1* (CEDAM 1955) 285–286.
2 H. Triepel, *Droit International et Droit Interne* (Pédone 1920) 321.

be the direct author of the act. The second function lies in the triggering of the application of a particular regime of responsibility: international responsibility of a State or an international organization, where the conduct at issue is attributable to one of these legal persons, or criminal responsibility of the individual where the conduct is attributable to a natural person.[3]

The first aim of attribution is the determination of the responsible person. In this respect, under international law, this connection is not based on a mere exercise of causality but on the development of specific rules that establish the relationship between the individual or group that performs the act (or the omission) and the entity that carries the burden. Consequently, the question of attribution is considered a normative operation.[4] Moreover, this mechanism turns out to be essential in relation to the activities of collective entities. In other words, this element is used to determine the circumstances under which the responsibility of a collective entity could be triggered by the actions or omissions of the individuals or groups to whom they belong or whom represent. As explained by Condorelli and Kress, '[...] none of the subjects of international law belonging to the *genus* of collective entities (States, international organizations, etc) is able to carry out its activities, whatever they may be, other than through individuals'.[5] Therefore, if we want to further elaborate on the international responsibility of armed groups as collective entities, the process of attribution of conduct should be considered one of the key elements of such an analysis.

In relation to the attribution of actions to armed groups as such, only a few authors have tackled this issue. One of the main ideas which has been acknowledged by the doctrine is that this question requires further exploration. In this sense, Zegveld notes that 'the question which acts and omissions can be attributed to armed opposition groups has, however, not been answered in a coherent way by international bodies'.[6] She adds that 'to hold a group accountable for the act of an individual, that act must be attributable to the group on some objective ground'.[7] In its study of the direct responsibility of armed opposition groups (AOGs) and transnational corporations, the International Law Association also concluded that one of the conditions that required further clarification was the issue of 'whose conduct would be attributable to an AOG'.[8] Other authors have also noted that, although it is generally understood that armed groups could be responsible for IHL violations, there is uncertainty regarding the exact rules of attribution.[9]

---

3 O. De Frouville, 'Attribution of Conduct to the State: Private Individuals' in J. Crawford, A. Pellet & S. Olleson (eds) *The Law of International Responsibility* (Oxford University Press 2010) 257.

4 L. Condorelli & C. Kress, 'The Rules of Attribution: General Considerations' in J. Crawford, A. Pellet & S. Olleson (eds) *The Law of International Responsibility* (Oxford University Press 2010) 225–228.

5 *Ibid*, 221.

6 L. Zegveld, *Accountability of armed opposition groups*, 153.

7 *Ibid*, 152.

8 International Law Association Committee on Non-State Actors, 'Third report on the Obligations and Responsibility of Non-State Actors in International Law' (Washington Conference 2014) 11.

9 M. Sassòli, 'Taking Armed Groups Seriously', 44.

Against this background, academics share different views on the possibility of applying the ASR by analogy to armed groups. Kleffner explains that certain rules on attribution from the ASR could potentially be applied to armed groups 'provided the necessary adjustments are made'.[10] Likewise, Heffes claims that 'the internal organization of armed opposition groups can by analogy be considered to be like that of a State'.[11] On the contrary, other authors have been careful about applying the ASR in such a way. In this regard, Sassòli claims that '[w]hile it is tempting to reason by analogy with the well-established rules on State responsibility, there are serious limits to such analogy because of the fundamentally different legal character [...] of an armed group'.[12] Similarly, Bílková warns about the possibility of drawing rules that would be applicable to all armed groups since there is a wide range of different armed groups.[13] In addition, she points to the fact that the concept of organs and members of armed groups remains unclear.

Although these debates represent a timid attempt to respond to the issue of attribution of conduct to armed groups, the question has not been explored in a substantive manner yet. As indicated previously, these doctrinal attempts focus exclusively on the rules of attribution of states as mere inspiration or starting point but do not consider the rules adopted for international organisations. More importantly, these attempts do not address the so-called problem of 'structural disparity' of armed groups and appear to focus on those armed groups that have a state-like structure, while ignoring those groups that have a decentralised structure.[14] For these reasons, an in-depth examination of the potential rules of attribution applicable to armed groups is required. Thereby, this study analyses the substantive rules of attribution for states and international organisations and extracts the core principles of attribution that could be applied to other collective entities. These norms are examined in the following sections.

2.1. RULES OF ATTRIBUTION FOR STATES

Before the adoption of the ASR, international arbitral awards at the beginning of the 20th century had already established the obligation to pay compensation in case of harm caused by the state through its agents, organs, leaders and officials.[15] For instance, in

10 J. K. Kleffner, 'The collective accountability of organised armed groups', 262.

11 E. Heffes, 'The Responsibility of Armed Opposition Groups for Violations of International Humanitarian Law: Challenging the State-Centric System of International Law' (2013) 4 *Journal of International Humanitarian Legal Studies*, 96.

12 M. Sassòli, 'Taking Armed Groups Seriously', 44–45.

13 V. Bílková, 'Direct Responsibility of Armed Opposition Groups', 279.

14 Sassòli refers to those groups with more or less 'State-like' organisations. See, *supra note 9*, at 45.

15 For example, in the award made by the arbitral tribunal in the following cases: *Claim of the Salvador Commercial Company ("El Triunfo Company")*, Reports of International Arbitral Awards, Volume XV (8 May 1902) at 477; *Sambiaggio case*, Mixed Claims Commission (Italy-Venezuela), Reports of International Arbitral Awards, Volume X (13 February and 7 May 1903) at 512; *N. Henriquez case*, Mixed Claims Commission (Netherlands-Venezuela), Reports of International Arbitral Awards,

the arbitral decision presented against the Government of Peru in 1901 it was established that it was a principle of international law universally recognised that the state was responsible for violations of the *ius gentium* committed by its agents.[16] In contrast, in the *Sambiaggio* case, the Commission emphasised that the *Revolutionists* were not agents of the Government since their actions aimed at destroying the Government itself and, therefore, such injuries could not be imputed to the state.[17] With regard to IHL, the Hague Convention of 1907 concerning the Laws and Customs of War on Land stipulates in its Article 3 that '[a] belligerent party which violates the provisions of the said Regulations shall, if the case demands, be liable to pay compensation. It shall be responsible for all acts committed by *persons forming part of its armed forces*'.[18] This article has been transposed to current Article 91 Additional Protocol I of the Geneva Conventions.

Following these precedents, the ASR established the necessity to attribute the act to the subject in question as a fundamental element of the commission of a wrongful act. According to Brownlie, 'responsibility only arises when the act or omission complained of is *imputable* to a state'.[19] Attribution consists of the legal fiction of imputing acts, which are necessarily committed by physical persons, to a legal person. Condorelli and Kress refer to attribution as 'the body of criteria of connection and the conditions which have to be fulfilled, according to the relevant principles of international law, in order to conclude that it is a State (or other subject of international law) which has acted in the particular case'.[20] They also emphasise that attribution represents an indispensable step in the process of establishing responsibility. In this regard, the Permanente Court of International Justice (PCIJ) recognised in 1923 that 'States can act only by and through their *agents and representatives*'.[21]

The ASR were finally adopted in 2001 and established eight rules of attribution for states (from Articles 4 to 11 ASR) that were meant to codify the existing practice. The first and most basic rule is the attribution of acts based on the conduct of state organs (Article 4 ASR), that is, individual or collective entities that make up the organisation of the state and act on its behalf. In the majority of the cases, states will act through their different organs established under domestic law. For the purposes of the ASR, a state organ is 'any person or entity which has that status in accordance with the internal

Volume X (28 February 1903) at 714–715; and *Claim of Finnish shipowners against Great Britain in respect of the use of certain Finnish vessels during the war (Finland, Great Britain)*, Reports of International Arbitral Awards, Volume III (9 May 1934) at 1501.

16 *Sentence arbitrale sur la réclamation numéro 2, présentée par Don Luis Chiessa*, Reports of International Arbitral Awards, Volume XV (30 September 1901) at 399.

17 *Sambiaggio case*, Mixed Claims Commission (Italy-Venezuela), Reports of International Arbitral Awards, Volume X (13 February and 7 May 1903) at 499.

18 The Hague Convention of 1907, Convention (IV) respecting the Laws and Customs of War on Land and its annex: Regulations concerning the Laws and Customs of War on Land (The Hague, 18 October 1907).

19 I. Brownlie, *Principles of Public International Law* (Oxford University Press 2008) 438.

20 L. Condorelli & C. Kress, *supra note* 4, 221.

21 *Questions relating to Settlers of German Origin in Poland* (Advisory Opinion) PCIJ Series B no 6, 10 September 1923, at 22.

law of the State' which 'exercises legislative, executive, judicial or any other functions, whatever position it holds in the organization of the State'.[22] The ICJ also contemplated the possible existence of *de facto* organs of the state by reference to those groups or entities that did not have a formal status of a state organ but that were in 'complete dependence' on the state.[23] However, the court only considered attribution based on this criterion as exceptional.

Another relevant rule is contained within Article 8 ASR, which deals with conduct directed or controlled by the state and which was highly discussed in the *Military and Paramilitary Activities in and against Nicaragua* case and the *Application of the Genocide Convention* case before the ICJ.[24] Article 8 ASR requires the existence of a 'specific factual relationship' between the person or group and the state.[25] Additionally, the conduct in question has to be an integral part of the operations of the state.[26] This has been translated into the so-called *effective control test* according to which specific instructions should be given by the state in each concrete operation in order to attribute the acts of those persons to the state.[27] This conduct could relate to the actions carried by individual persons as well as groups of persons.

The remaining rules can be divided into those related to the exercise of governmental activities by other entities not considered state organs (Articles 5, 6 and 9 ASR); *ultra vires* acts or acts carried out in excess of authority (Article 7 ASR); conduct of successful insurrectional or other movements (Article 10 ASR); and conduct acknowledged and adopted by a state as its own (Article 11 ASR). The actions of other entities can be attributed to the state as far as those persons or groups are authorised to exercise elements of governmental authority (Article 5 ASR), even if it is an organ placed at the disposal of a state by another state (Article 6 ASR) or even if it is carrying out those activities in the absence or in default of the official authorities (Article 9 ASR). For those organs placed at the disposal of another state, their conduct should be 'under its exclusive direction and control, rather than on instructions from the sending State'.[28]

Moreover, the acts of state organs and those entities empowered to exercise governmental functions will also be attributed to the state if they exceed or contravene the orders and instructions given (Article 7 ASR). In relation to insurrectional movements becoming the new state or government, those acts will be attributed to the new entity created following the principle of continuity (Article 10 ASR).[29] Lastly, another possibility is the acknowledgement of the conduct by the state (Article 11

22 Art. 4 ASR.

23 *Application of the Convention on the Prevention and Punishment of the Crime of Genocide (Bosnia and Herzegovina v. Yugoslavia)* (Merits) [2007] Judgment, ICJ Rep, 26 February 2007, para. 392.

24 See A. Cassese, 'The Nicaragua and Tadić Tests Revisited in Light of the ICJ Judgment on Genocide in Bosnia' (2007) 18 *European Journal of International Law* 4, 649–668.

25 Art. 8 ASR, Commentary para. 1.

26 *Ibid*, para. 3.

27 *Application of the Convention on the Prevention and Punishment of the Crime of Genocide (Bosnia and Herzegovina v. Yugoslavia)* (Merits) [2007] Judgment, ICJ Rep, 26 February 2007, para. 400.

28 Art. 6 ASR, Commentary para. 2.

29 This provision was already discussed in Chapter 2.

ASR). The inclusion of this provision as a closing rule is made for the purpose of filling all possible gaps in terms of attribution. This rule refers mainly to actions of private persons or entities which, as a general principle, would not be considered as acts of the state but nevertheless, by way of recognition, are regarded as its own. The ASR establish a number of conditions for the application of this rule. First, the acknowledgement has to be more than a mere support or endorsement.[30] It has to identify the specific conduct as its own, and as such goes beyond general recognition of facts. Second, the act of acknowledgement has to be 'clear and unequivocal'.[31] It could be express, based on words, or inferred from the conduct of the state.

These are the general rules in public international law applicable to states. However, the ASR also refers to the existence of special rules that could replace the application of the general rules in specific fields.[32] In particular, in the field of international humanitarian law a special criterion for attribution appears to be recognized, whereby 'violations of the applicable rules perpetrated in the context of an armed conflict by members of the armed forces of a State are in all circumstances attributable to, and engage the international responsibility of, that State'.[33] This has been derived from the above mentioned Article 91 Additional Protocol I, which establishes the attribution of violations to the state in 'all circumstances'. Therefore, *ultra vires* acts of the members of armed forces will be attributed to the State in any case.[34]

2.2. RULES OF ATTRIBUTION FOR INTERNATIONAL ORGANISATIONS

As regards international organisations, the ARIO did not change the key principles of attribution that continue to be at the core of the notion. Similarly to the state, an international organization is as an abstract entity, and consequently, the general rule of attribution is based on the performance of the organisation through its *organs* or *agents*. This is established by Article 6 ARIO. Even before the ARIO were drafted, the ICJ already referred to the role of the agents of international organisations, in this case the United Nations, taking a comprehensive approach and defining 'the word "agent" in the most liberal sense, that is to say, any person who, whether a paid official or not, and whether permanently employed or not, has been charged by an organ of the organization with carrying out, or helping to carry out, one of its functions – in short, any person through whom it acts'.[35] As the Special Rapporteur Giorgio Gaja explained,

30 Art. 11 ASR, Commentary para. 6.
31 *Ibid*, para. 8.
32 Art. 55 ASR.
33 L. Condorelli & C. Kress, *supra note* 4, 227.
34 M. Sassòli, 'State Responsibility for Violations of International Humanitarian Law' (2002) 84 *International Review of the Red Cross* 846, 401–434, at 405.
35 *Reparation for Injuries Suffered in the Service of the United Nations* (Advisory Opinion) [1949] ICJ Rep 174, 11 April 1949, at 177.

the ICJ gave priority to the fact that a person had been conferred functions by an organ of an international organisation rather than to the fact that a person had or did not have an official status.[36] Therefore, there should be a functional link, which means that a connection must be established between the conduct of the agent and the functioning of the organisation.[37] On the contrary, actions performed by the agent without any reference to their official function would not be attributed to the organisation. The essential feature is that the conduct will be only attributed when the agent is performing tasks on behalf of the organisation but not when the agent is acting in a private capacity.[38]

To this end, the ARIO did not distinguish between organs under normative control (organic structure) or under *de facto* control of the organisation, as was the case in articles 4 and 8 of the ASR.[39] Instead, they refer to both acts of organs or agents. An organ of an international organisation is defined as 'any person or entity which has that status in accordance with the rules of the organization'[40], while an 'agent' means any other person or entity that is not formally included in the rules of the organisation but is 'carrying out, or helping to carry out, one of its functions, and thus through whom the organization acts'.[41] This notion was introduced by reference to the above mentioned advisory opinion of the ICJ in the *Reparations case* that took a wide and flexible understanding of the word 'agent'.[42] Moreover, those actions performed under the instruction, direction or control of an international organisation were assimilated to the conduct of 'agents' of the international organisation and consequently incorporated into the ARIO in Article 6.[43]

This general rule was complemented by three additional rules, incorporated through analogy with the rules on state responsibility, namely the conduct of organs and agents placed at the disposal of an international organisation (Article 7 ARIO); *ultra vires* conduct of organs or agents of an international organisation (Article 8 ARIO); and conduct acknowledged and adopted by an international organisation as its own (Article 9 ARIO). In the case of the conduct of organs and agents at the disposal of an international organisation, this rule required some adjustment. The complete transposition of this rule was not possible due to the fact that the wording 'acting in the exercise of elements of governmental authority' was not appropriate for international

36 Second report on Responsibility of International Organizations by Mr. Giorgio Gaja, Special Rapporteur (2 April 2004) UN Doc. A/CN.4/541, at 7, para. 15.

37 P. Klein, 'The Attribution of Acts to International Organizations' in J. Crawford, A. Pellet & S. Olleson (eds), *The Law of International Responsibility* (Oxford University Press 2010) 304.

38 Art. 6 ARIO, Commentary para. 7.

39 See C. Ahlborn, 'The Use of Analogies in Drafting the Articles on the Responsibility of International Organizations – An Appraisal of the "Copy-Paste Approach"' (2012) *SHARES Research Paper* 13, Amsterdam Centre for International Law, 2012–14, 6–7.

40 Art. 2(c) ARIO.

41 Art. 2(d) ARIO.

42 *Reparation for Injuries Suffered in the Service of the United Nations* (Advisory Opinion) [1949] ICJ Rep 174, 11 April 1949, at 177.

43 Art. 6 ARIO, Commentary para. 11.

organisations.[44] Therefore, as explained in the commentary, the conduct will only be attributed if the organisation exercises effective control over that conduct.[45] This appears to replicate the rationale behind Article 8 ASR, understanding that an individual or entity that does not belong to the organisation can nevertheless trigger the responsibility of that organisation if the individual or entity is acting under its direction or control. The provision was meant to address the cases of states that send military contingents to act on behalf of the United Nations in peacekeeping operations.[46] This is a specific situation relating to the activities of international organisations that need the support of their member states to operate.

With regard to the rule on *ultra vires* acts, this provision only required a minor modification by introducing a reference to the specific functions that international organisations perform, in contrast to the general competence of states (this is also known as the principle of speciality). Consequently, *ultra vires* acts will only be attributed to international organisations if the organ or agent is acting 'within the overall functions of that organization'. The last rule on the acknowledgement of conduct was directly transposed to international organisations without further adaptations. The Commission established that this provision 'mirrors the content of article 11 on the responsibility of States for internationally wrongful acts, which is identically worded [...]'.[47] In particular, the Commission acknowledged that, in principle, there were no policy reasons opposing the application of this rule to international organisations.[48] Moreover, the practice of international organisations was, in this regard coincident with the practice of states.

In conclusion, the rules of attribution were adjusted to the characteristics of international organisations. Moreover, certain rules were not included as they were not easily transposable to international organisations. For instance, the notion of 'governmental authority' in Article 5 ASR did not fit properly with international organisations.[49] In addition, 'conduct carried out in the absence or default of the official authorities' (Article 9 ASR) or 'conduct of an insurrectional or other movement' (Article 10 ASR) presupposed the existence of control over the territory, which was 'a rare event for an international organization'.[50] On the contrary, other questions specifically arose in relation to the actions of international organisations, such as the possibility of joint or shared responsibility between the organisation and its member states.[51]

---

44 Art. 7 ARIO, Commentary para. 4.

45 *Ibid.*, paras. 8–12.

46 Art. 7 ARIO, Commentary para. 1.

47 Art. 9 ARIO, Commentary para. 2.

48 Art. 9 ARIO, Commentary para. 5.

49 Second report on Responsibility of International Organizations by Mr. Giorgio Gaja, Special Rapporteur (2 April 2004) UN Doc. A/CN.4/541, at 7, para. 65.

50 *Ibid*, para. 67.

51 The joint responsibility of an international organization with one or more States is contemplated in Articles 14 to 18 of the ARIO. On this topic, see A. Nollkaemper and I. Plakokefalos, *Principles of Shared Responsibility in International Law* (Cambridge University Press 2014) and A. Nollkaemper

2.3. TOWARDS THE IDENTIFICATION OF CORE PRINCIPLES OF ATTRIBUTION FOR COLLECTIVE ENTITIES

In terms of substantive rules, the responsibility of international organisations includes, on the one hand, general rules applicable to both to states and international organisations and, on the other hand, special rules derived from their specific features.[52] The ARIO are based on the same premise of establishing secondary rules.[53] In this regard, the principles of responsibility applicable to international organisations are essentially the same as those applicable to states. Responsibility is based on the commission of an internationally wrongful act composed of an objective element, the violation of an international obligation, and a subjective element, the attribution of the conduct to the entity in question (Article 2 ASR and Article 4 ARIO).

The specificities of the ARIO are reflected by the introduction of an article with the use of terms, the concept of rules of the organisation and the question of attribution. The ARIO required the clarification of certain notions such as those of 'international organization', 'organ of an international organization' or 'agent of an international organization'.[54] The notion of 'rules of the organization' is of particular interest since they are mentioned in several articles.[55] The definition of rules of the organization goes a bit further than the one contained in the 1986 Vienna Convention on the Law of Treaties between States and International Organizations and between International Organizations because, in addition to decisions and resolutions, it includes 'other acts', thereby reflecting a broader category of acts of contemporary international organisations. In addition, the rules of the organisation do not only have an internal purpose but can also be the source of international obligations according to Article 10 (2) ARIO. Therefore, the notion of the 'internal law of the state' was adapted to the characteristics of international organisations and was given a broader understanding by including other possible acts.

In relation to the question of attribution, in comparison to the eight rules of state responsibility, only four rules were established for international organisations. Several of these rules were adapted, others were directly transposed, and others were eliminated. The rule relating to the conduct of organs was adapted and moulded to the characteristics of international organisations. Particularly, the concept of agent was introduced following a broad functional approach rather than giving a strict consideration of its incorporation in the internal rules of the organization. The rest of the rules were adapted for one of two reasons: either due to the fact that international organisation

---

and I. Plakokefalos, *The Practice of Shared Responsibility in International Law* (Cambridge University Press 2017).

52 See R. Zacklin, 'Responsabilité des organisations internationales' in *Société Française pour le Droit International: La responsabilité dans le système international* (Pedone 1991) 91.

53 Draft Articles on the Responsibility of International Organizations, with Commentaries, *Yearbook of the International Law Commission* (2011), vol. II, Part Two, General commentary, para. 3.

54 Art. 2 ARIO.

55 In Art. 2, 6, 10, 22, 32, 40, 52, 58, 59, and 64 ARIO.

performs specific functions and so the attribution of conduct has to be directly related to the specific area in which that organisation functions; or because the exercise of governmental authority was not suitable for them.[56] The provision on the adoption and acknowledgement of conduct by an international organisation was directly transposed from the state responsibility articles and supported by similar practice on the matter.

Therefore, it can be concluded that the essential principles of responsibility, based on the violation of an obligation and the necessity to attribute this act or omission, are the same for both states and international organisations and these principles have not been disputed by the practice or the scholarship. Moreover, it can be argued that states and international organisations share a minimum set of principles of attribution:

a) Attribution based on the conduct of organs and agents belonging to the organisation, including *ultra vires* acts. This rule can be deducted from Article 4 and 7 ASR in relation to the actions performed by state's organs belonging to its internal structure even if this conduct goes beyond the instructions given by the state. As for international organisations, this rule derives from Article 6 and 8 ARIO that consider the conduct of organs and agents of these organisations, that act within or in excess of the authority given to them.
b) Attribution based on the conduct of other individuals or entities under the direction and control of the organisation. As concerns states, this rule can be derived from Article 8 ASR, which is based on the direction and control that is exercised over individuals and entities other than the state's organs, but also from Article 6 ASR where external organs placed at the disposal of the state have to be under its 'exclusive direction and control'. As regards international organisations, this rule has its basis in the commentary to Article 6 and 7 ARIO, according to which conduct of external organs will be attributed where the international organization's organs and agents are acting under 'the effective control' of that international organisation.[57]
c) Attribution based on the acknowledgement of the conduct of the organisation as its own. This rule is derived from Article 11 ASR and Article 9 ARIO, which share the exact same content.

These three principles can be considered the core principles of attribution for collective entities in international law. The main differences are those that relate to the special features of international organisations, such as the functions they perform (principle of speciality), the types of acts they produce, or the relationship with their members. Consequently, these common principles of responsibility could be potentially applied to other collective entities in international law, including organised armed groups. As far as armed groups have limited personality in IHL and can violate international obligations, similar principles could be applied to them provided that the necessary adjustments are introduced.

---

56 Second report on Responsibility of International Organizations by Mr. Giorgio Gaja, Special Rapporteur (2 April 2004) UN Doc. A/CN.4/541, at 7, para. 65.

57 See Art. 6 ARIO, Commentary para. 11 and Art. 7 ARIO, Commentary paras. 8–12.

3. ADJUSTING THE CORE PRINCIPLES OF ATTRIBUTION TO THE CONDUCT OF ARMED GROUPS

As indicated in the previous chapter, a direct and full transposition of the rules of responsibility of states and international organisations would not be possible because armed groups constitute a different type of entity. In particular, there is considerable uncertainty regarding their internal structures; the definition of their members, representatives or organs; their temporal existence; and the scope of the actions that are likely to be attributed to the group as such. Before proceeding to apply the aforementioned core principles, the next section will examine the main aspects that need to be taken into account to carry out such operation. These features have been identified by legal and policy documents in international humanitarian law from the ICRC, political science studies and the internal rulings of armed groups.

3.1. THE ISSUE OF STRUCTURAL DISPARITY OF ARMED GROUPS

Armed groups are collective entities with a minimum degree of organisation, carrying out different roles within their structures, which could eventually exercise governmental functions and control portions of territory. More rudimentary groups may only be comprised of a military wing but those with a higher degree of organisation also have a political wing. For example, according to the Fifteen-Point Programme of the Sudan People's Liberation Movement (SPLM), the Sudan People's Liberation Army (SPLA) was the military wing of the SPLM, while the SPLM was the political movement 'charged with providing the vision, guidance and leadership for the achievement and consolidation of the New Sudan'.[58] Similarly, according to its internal rules of organisation, the Fuerzas Armadas Revolucionarias de Colombia – Ejército del Pueblo (FARC-EP) was a political-military movement.[59] In this sense, they could resemble the structures of states. Other armed groups follow a decentralised type of organisation and act through semi-autonomous cells such as the anti-balaka militias in Central African Republic or the armed opposition forces that emerged in Libya.[60] These different structures are considered special features of armed groups that need to be analysed in

58 Fifteen-Point Programme of the SPLM, Vision and Programme of the Sudan People's Liberation Movement (SPLM), SPLM Political Secretariat, Yei and New Cush, New Sudan, March 1998, p. 2, available at <http://theirwords.org/media/transfer/doc/sd_splm_a_1998_51-3be918204bb5d36f06c1eb2e8796ae18.pdf> accessed 30 May 2019.

59 Art. 1, FARC-EP Statutes available at <https://www.farc-ep.co/pdf/Estatutos.pdf> accessed 30 May 2019.

60 On the anti-balaka groups see N. Dukhan, *The Central African Republic Crisis* (GSDRC, University of Birmingham 2016). On the armed opposition forces in Libya see B. McQuinn, 'DDR and the Internal Organization of Non-State Armed Groups' (2016) *Stability: International Journal of Security and Development* X(X): X, 1–24.

order to determine how the general principles of attribution could be adapted to the conduct of armed groups. In particular, studying these characteristics will serve to clarify the elements of the organisation of an armed group.

As explained by the report of the ICRC *The roots of restraint in war*, 'an armed group's organizational structure is an important determinant of its behaviour'.[61] Moreover, their organisational structure 'shape and constrain their member's conduct'.[62] In this context, Sinno affirms that 'the organizational structures of armed groups, whether they develop by accident or by design, affect their strategic choices and performance during the conflict [...]'.[63] Therefore, understanding how armed groups behave and organise their contingencies could aid in developing rules that are closer to the reality of contemporary non-international armed conflicts. These organisational elements are analysed in the following sections taking into account the notion of armed groups and their military and political wings; centralised and decentralised types of armed groups; and the changes in structure over time.

3.1.1. *Military and political wing*

One consideration that requires a preliminary examination is the concept of armed group and its components. In particular, armed groups can be comprised of a military wing or both a military and political wing. The question is to what extent the political wing is also considered as part of the armed group for the purposes of attributing IHL violations. From a legal perspective, the ICRC clarifies that:

> The term organized armed group refers exclusively to the armed or military wing of a non-state party to a non-international armed conflict. It does not include those segments of the civilian population that are supportive of the non-state party such as its political wing.[64]

Indeed, the scholarship agrees that NIACs 'are fought between armed forces of states ('states') and the *military wings* of non-state armed groups'.[65] However, from an empirical perspective, there is a blurred line between civilian and military functions performed by members of armed groups. Moreover, some members have both military and political functions. For instance, in the case of the FARC-EP, every military unit was also considered a political cell and every commander had both political and military

---

61 International Committee of the Red Cross, *The Roots of Restraint in War* (Geneva, 2018) 21 (hereafter 'ICRC, *The roots of restraint in war*').

62 See S. E. Parkinson and S. Zaks, 'Militant and Rebel Organization(s)' (2018) 50 *Comparative Politics* 2, 271–293.

63 A. H. Sinno, 'Armed Groups' Organizational Structure and their Strategic Options' (2011) 93 *International Review of the Red Cross* 882, 311–332, at 312.

64 M. Sassòli, A. A. Bouvier & A. Quintin, *How Does Law Protect in War? Cases, Documents and Teaching Materials on Contemporary Practice in International Humanitarian Law* Vol. II (International Committee of the Red Cross 2011) 14.

65 S. Sivakumaran, *The Law of Non-International Armed Conflict* (Oxford University Press 2012) 3, emphasis added.

responsibilities.[66] Similarly, in the case of the SPLM/A, the Commander-in-Chief was in charge of the determination of the political and military objectives of the SPLA.[67] In addition, 'officers from within the SPLA were transferred to specific civil administrative duties as Civil/Military Administrators (CMAs)' and the zonal commanders 'had the overall responsibility for the civil administration of their zones'.[68] On the contrary, the Liberation Tigers of Tamil Eelam (LTTE) distinguished between regional military commanders and district political commissars, whereby both were working at the same organisational level.[69] Consequently, in certain cases there may be some confusion and overlap of the functions performed by these two components.

In principle, the political wing is not considered an integral part of the armed group for the purposes of a NIAC. However, in practice some members perform simultaneous functions within the group. In the process of attributing IHL violations there should be a correlation between the role and responsibilities of the individual and the actions carried out by the group. Consequently, the civilian or military role of the individual could be a factor to be considered when identifying the different standards of attribution for IHL violations. These circumstances need to be taken into account when applying these rules and will be examined in section 4 of this Chapter.

3.1.2. Centralised and decentralised groups

Although armed groups can take different forms and shapes, the main distinction with regard to their organisational structure for the purposes of IHL is based on their centralised or decentralised system.[70] Some armed groups try to resemble national armies and follow a hierarchical and centralised structure. However, due to the different nature of armed conflicts, armed groups do not always have a central hierarchical structure. Instead, other armed groups operate in a more autonomous manner, acting in a horizontal rather than in a vertical way. It is important to remember that the organisational requirement of armed groups fighting in a NIAC is considered flexible enough to adapt to different types of armed groups. In this regard, 'there is no one-size-fits-all definition of such groups'.[71] Moreover, according to the ICTY, organised armed

66 M. M. Ortega, *Acciones y reacciones estratégicas adaptaciones de las FARC a las innovaciones operacionales de las Fuerzas Armadas de Colombia durante la política de defensa y seguridad democrática* (Universidad de los Andes 2011) 51.

67 Section 14, Laws of Southern Sudan, The Sudan People's Liberation Army Act 2009, 10.

68 D. H. Johnson, 'The Sudan People's Liberation Army and the Problem of Factionalism', in C. S. Clapham (ed) *African Guerrillas. Eritrea, Tigrai, Sudan, Somalia, Uganda, Rwanda, Congo-Zaire, Liberia, Sierra Leone* (Indiana University Press 1998) 67.

69 J. Richards, 'An Institutional History of the Liberation Tigers of Tamil Eelam (LTTE)' (2014) Centre on Conflict, Development and Peacebuilding Working Paper (2014), 41.

70 T. Rodenhäuser, *Organizing Rebellion: Non-State Armed Groups under International Humanitarian Law, Human Rights Law, and International Criminal Law* (Oxford University Press 2018), 74–78 (hereafter T. Rodenhäuser, *Organizing Rebellion)*. Sivakumaran also refers to pyramidal and decentralized groups based on their organizational structure. See S. Sivakumaran, *The Law of Non-International Armed Conflict* (Oxford University Press 2012) 172–174.

71 G. Gaggioli, 'Targeting Individuals Belonging to an Armed Group' (2018) 51 *Vanderbilt Journal of Transnational Law* 3, 901–917, at 907.

groups 'do not necessarily need to be as organized as the armed forces of a State'.[72] Nevertheless, the organisation cannot be too loose either. In particular, the group will not comply with the minimum level of organisation if its units or individual members 'act entirely on their own initiative, in total disregard of a countervailing policy espoused by the armed group'.[73] This section will analyse both of the aforementioned categories of armed groups and their characteristics through the study of specific examples. These examples relate to armed groups operating in a NIAC taking place in one country. Accordingly, transnational armed groups are excluded from the analysis. Finally, the differences between both types of structures will be assessed to determine the consequences this may have for the development of rules of attribution.

Centralised armed groups

Centralised armed groups are those characterised by a vertical structure that follow a strict chain of command. According to the recent study of the ICRC, 'centralized non-state armed groups share many of the structural characteristics found in integrated State militias, including a prominent hierarchy, elaborate doctrine and strict discipline'.[74] Centralised armed groups are characterised by an established hierarchy, top-down decision-making processes, and clear signs of military discipline such as uniforms and symbols, saluting, daily schedules, etc.[75] In this context, Haer explains the dynamics of centralised armed groups in the following way:

> The command and control chain in hierarchical organizations follows a formal vertical communication network; downward (directing subordinates) and upward (reporting to management). Vertical communication makes it therefore relatively easy for the leadership to gather information from and to command and control the performance of all agents.[76]

Some examples of centralised armed groups are the FARC-EP in Colombia, the LTTE in Sri Lanka, the National Resistance Army (NRA) in Uganda, the Moro Islamic Liberation Front (MILF) in the Philippines, the Union de Patriotes Congolais (UPC) in Congo, the Lebanese Hezbollah, and the Islamic State Group in Syria and Iraq.[77] In particular, the FARC and the LTTE represent paradigmatic examples of highly centralised and hierarchical groups. In Colombia, the FARC-EP divided the nation into seven blocs, each of them operating in a different region: the Eastern Bloc, the North-

---

72 *Prosecutor v. Orić*, (Judgment) ICTY Case No. IT- 03–68- T (30 June 2006), para 254; *Boškoski Trial Judgment*, para 197.

73 Y. Dinstein, *Non- International Armed Conflicts in International Law* (Cambridge University Press 2014) 140.

74 ICRC, *The roots of restraint in war*, 38.

75 *Ibid*, 24.

76 R. Haer, *Armed Group Structure and Violence in Civil Wars: The Organizational Dynamics of Civilian Killing* (Routledge 2015) 48.

77 See these examples in ICRC, *The roots of restraint in war*, 38–43; T. Rodenhäuser, *Organizing Rebellion*, 74–75; and R. Haer, *supra note* 76, 46–48.

western Bloc, the Middle-Magdalena Bloc, the Southern Bloc, the Caribbean Bloc, the Central Joint Command, and the Western Joint Command.[78] The function of the blocs was to coordinate and unify the activities in a specific geographical area.[79] The military units were further divided into fronts, columns, companies, platoons, and squads and were assisted by commissions and militias.[80] In Sri Lanka, the LTTE 'transformed from a guerrilla organisation to a type of regular army with a conventional fighting force'.[81] Its military wing was based on ground forces and several specialised forces, such as the naval arm (the Sea Tigers), a suicide force (the Black Tigers) and an air force (the Air Tigers).[82] The military structure was completed with an intelligence unit and several auxiliary units. Both share a very similar organisational chart which resembles the structure of a state army as it is shown in the charts below.

Chart 1. The military structure of the FARC-EP in 1993

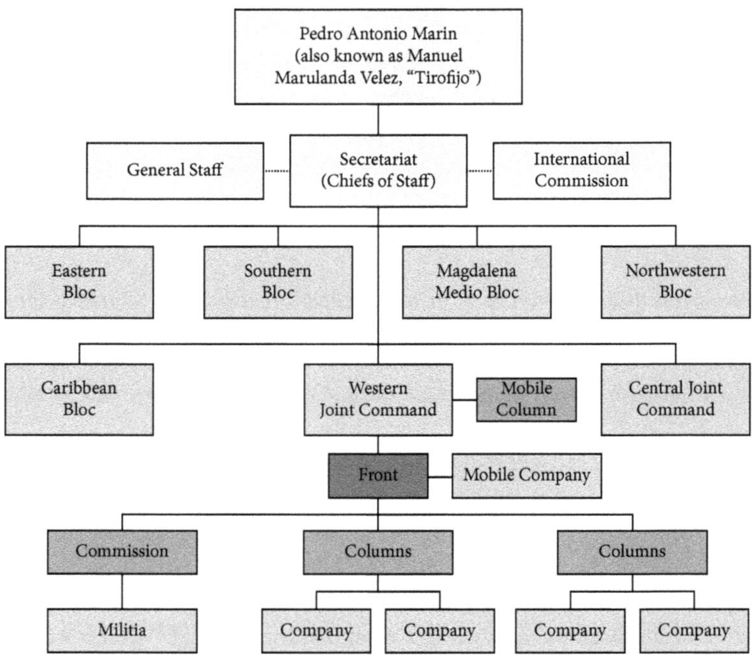

Source: K. R. Burnett, Case Studies in Insurgency and Revolutionary Warfare – Colombia (1964 – 2009) (United States Army Special Operations Command, John Hopkins University. National Security Analysis Department, 2014) 122.

78 J. G. Ferro Medina & G. Uribe Ramón, *El orden de la Guerra: las FARC-EP entre la organización y la política* (Centro Editorial Javariano 2002) 52–53.

79 Art. 3(g) FARC-EP Statutes.

80 Art. 3 FARC-EP Statutes.

81 N. Terpstra and G. Frerks, 'Rebel Governance and Legitimacy: Understanding the Impact of Rebel Legitimation on Civilian Compliance with the LTTE Rule' (2017) 19 *Civil Wars* 3, 279–307, at 286.

82 C. C. Fair, *Urban Battle Fields of South Asia. Lessons Learned from Sri Lanka, India and Pakistan* (Rand Corporation 2004) 24.

Chart 2. The military structure of the LTTE in 2002

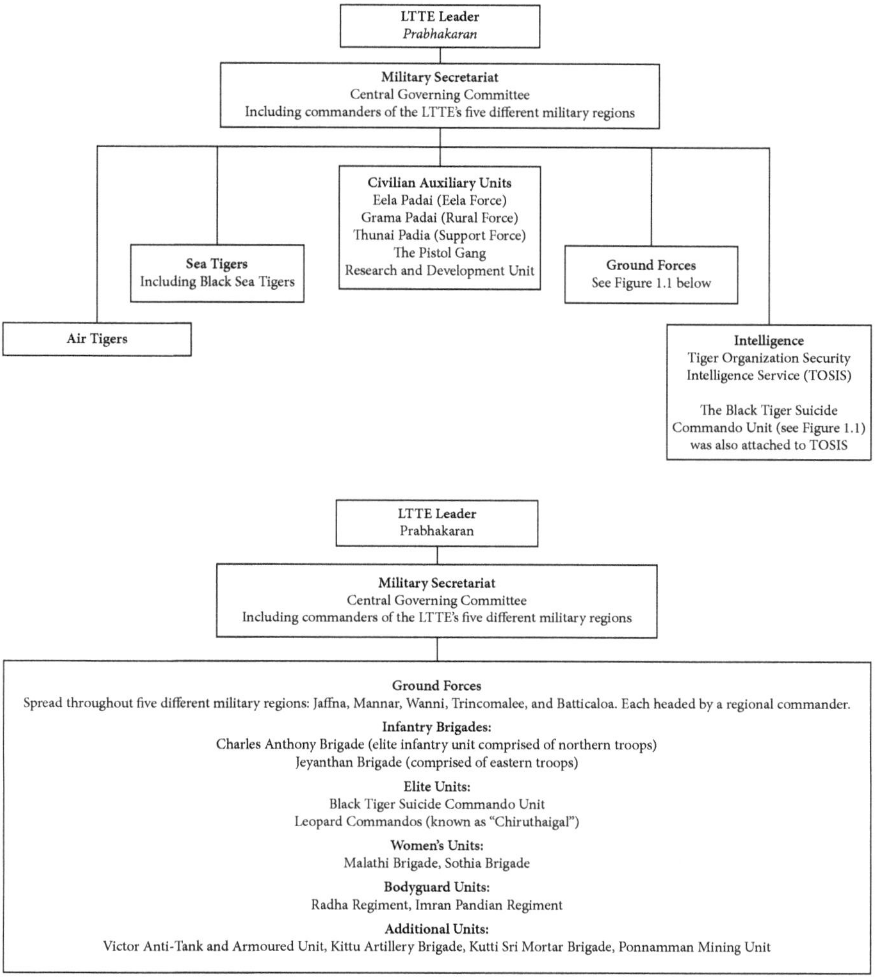

Source: J. Richards, 'An Institutional History of the Liberation Tigers of Tamil Eelam (LTTE)' (2014) *The Centre on Conflict, Development and Peacebuilding*, CCDP Working Paper, 17.

Both groups developed a strict chain of command. As explained by Rodenhäuser in relation to centralised armed groups, 'each unit has a commander who exercises power over subordinates and is subject to the commands of a superior'.[83] In the case of FARC-EP, combatants 'have to obey the formulations, strategies and tactical conceptions at the political level as well as the strategic, operational and tactic conceptions at the military order'.[84] In light of this, bloc and front commanders respond directly, both militarily and financially, to the Secretariat, while the subordinate units respond to

83 T. Rodenhäuser, *Organizing Rebellion*, 74.

84 Internal Ruling on the Disciplinary Regime of the FARC-EP, Preamble, para. 4.

the superior in the command chain.[85] Similarly, in the case of the LTTE, the military units below the regional commanders had to follow the chain of command and report directly to the superior.[86] According to Terpstra and Frerks, the system of discipline in the LTTE 'was extremely rigid'.[87] Consequently, 'the performance of cadres during battle was closely monitored and any unsatisfactory results and breaches of the codes of conduct would be punished'.[88]

Decentralised armed groups

The ICRC defines decentralised armed groups as 'an alliance of small armed groups, whose individual commanders retain considerable decision-making power and responsibility over group members'.[89] They consist of 'semi- autonomous or splinter factions operating under an ill-defined leadership structure'.[90] This typology of groups is characterised by a limited hierarchy, loose coordination and autonomy of unit commanders, and few observable signs of military discipline.[91] However, the fact that armed groups develop a decentralised organisation 'do[es] not preclude the ability to engage in significant military action, to implement strict internal codes, or to control territory'.[92] According to Sinno, the more control the second-level units have over the determination of local decisions, the more decentralised the group will be.[93] Likewise, Weinstein affirmed that '[b]y decentralizing power and resources, rebel leaders place real authority in the hands of their agents to mount operations, organize their troops, and work on behalf of the group's objectives'.[94]

Examples of decentralised armed groups are the Shining Path in Peru, the Frente Farabundo Martí para la Liberación Nacional (FMLN) in El Salvador, anti-balaka groups in Central African Republic (CAR), armed opposition groups in Libya, and Ansar Dine in Mali.[95] The anti-balaka groups in CAR and the armed opposition groups in Libya are particularly good examples of this type of decentralised structure. Anti-balaka is an umbrella term referring to various groups that engage in armed resistance against Séléka rebels, in the north of the CAR, where local leaders act autonomously. It

85 F. Gutiérrez Sanín & A. Giustozzi, 'Networks and Armies: Structuring Rebellion in Colombia and Afghanistan' (2010) 33 *Studies in Conflict & Terrorism* 9, 836–853, at 843.

86 Colombo Embassy Cable 1987, 'Inside the LTTE: A Look at the Tiger's Command Structure', para. 4, available at <http://bharatkalyan97.blogspot.com/2013/04/inside-ltte-look-at-tigers-command_9775.html> accessed 14 June 2019.

87 N. Terpstra and G. Frerks, *supra note* 81, 287.

88 *Ibid*, p. 287.

89 ICRC, *The roots of restraint in war*, 46.

90 T. Rodenhäuser, *Organizing Rebellion*, 75.

91 ICRC, *The roots of restraint in war*, 46.

92 T. Rodenhäuser, *Organizing Rebellion*, 76.

93 A. H. Sinno, *supra note* 63, 316.

94 J. M. Weinstein, *Inside Rebellion. The Politics of Insurgent Violence* (Cambridge University Press 2007) 138.

95 See these examples in ICRC, *The roots of restraint in war*, 46–51; T. Rodenhäuser, *Organizing Rebellion*, 74–75; and R. Haer, *supra note* 76, 46–48.

was not until the 5th December 2013 when they attacked Bangui demonstrating their capacity to conduct a military attack which was 'clearly organized by individuals with military expertise and background' as indicated by the International Commission of Inquiry on CAR.[96] In relation to the level of organisation of the anti-balaka groups the Office of the Prosecutor of the ICC has stated that:

> [...] the Office notes, for example, the coordinated attacks carried out by anti-balaka against Séléka troops in various locations in the Ouham prefecture in September 2013 as well as its armed clashes with Séléka in July and August 2014 when anti-balaka sought to reinforce its positions in the areas in the western and central parts of the country. Such incidents illustrate the group's ability to plan and implement military operations. Additionally, the attack carried out in Bangui on 5 December 2013, in particular, exhibited a significant level of planning, resources, and coordination on the part of anti-balaka forces. The anti-balaka Chief of Staff, with the rank of Lieutenant, directly claimed responsibility for having coordinated the 5 December and 25 December 2013 attacks.[97]

Therefore, even if these groups followed a decentralised organisation, it was demonstrated that they were able to conduct a coordinated military attack. In the case of Libya, there was an alliance of armed groups where 'fighters have received little training and do not operate with the appropriate discipline, command and control systems'.[98] Nonetheless, their ability to sustain hostilities over a period of time, their access to weaponry, and their control over territory at different times made them fulfil the requisite degree of organisation by July 2014.[99] Although one of the first reports of the Commission of Inquiry on Libya seemed to suggest that these armed opposition forces were united under the umbrella of the Libyan National Army, the Commission later indicated that the 'Libyan National Army neither coordinated nor led the military struggle against Qadhafi forces'.[100] Moreover, it also indicated that the anti-Qadhafi forces 'were formed autonomously at the outset of the conflict and in some cases managed over time to fashion their ranks into reasonably well-organized command structures'.[101] According to McQuinn, 'the Thubactis Battalion was the largest group, which had almost two thousand members organized into ten autonomous subgroups'.[102]

---

96 UN Secretary-General, 'Final report of the International Commission of Inquiry on the Central African Republic' (22 December 2014) S/2014/928, 71.

97 Office of the Prosecutor, International Criminal Court, 'Situation of the Central African Republic II, Article 53(1) Report' (24 September 2014) 34–35.

98 Report of the United Nations High Commissioner for Human Rights on the situation of human rights in Libya and on related technical support and capacity-building needs (12 January 2015) A/HRC/28/51, 5.

99 Geneva Academy of International Humanitarian Law and Human Rights, 'Non-international armed conflicts in Libya' in *RULAC: Rule of Law in Armed Conflicts* (2018) <www.rulac.org/browse/conflicts/non-international-armed-conflicts-in-libya#collapse3accord> accessed 12 June 2019.

100 UN Human Rights Council, 'Report of the International Commission of Inquiry on Libya' (2 March 2012) A/HRC/19/68 Annex I, para. 64–66.

101 *Ibid*, para. 61.

102 B. McQuinn, 'DDR and the Internal Organization of Non-State Armed Groups' (2016) *Stability: International Journal of Security and Development* X(X): X, 1–24, at 11.

He further notes that '[t]he leader of the Thubactis Battalion, Salem Jawha, explained in interviews that each of the ten sub-commanders was responsible for organizing his own non-military supplies and that there was little communication'.[103] The military structure of decentralised armed groups has been represented by the ICRC as follows.

Chart 3. Military structure of decentralised armed groups

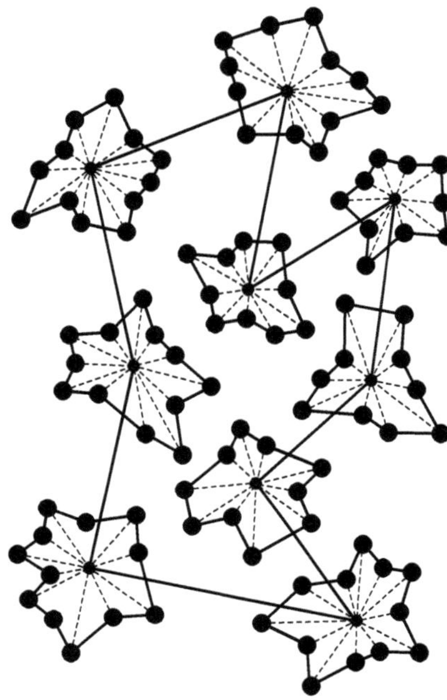

DECENTRALIZED
NON-STATE ARMED GROUPS

Source: ICRC, *The roots of restraint in war* (Geneva, 2018) 46

In conclusion, the differing organisational structures of armed groups will affect their chain of command and their decision-making processes. In centralised armed groups, senior leaders are the central decision-makers and primary contacts for addressing operational and humanitarian concerns, while sub-commanders follow their orders.[104] In contrast, in decentralised groups, each sub-commander retains significant authority over the unit's operations and conduct. In fact, local commanders are key contacts who are in charge of organising the conduct of their units' members.[105] These circumstances could have considerable consequences on the rules of attribution applicable in each case. In particular, the standard of direction and control may differ between both types

103 *Ibid*, 11–12.
104 ICRC, *The roots of restraint in war*, 23.
105 *Ibid*, 23.

of structure since centralised armed groups require strict control over all its military structures and decentralised armed groups retain general coordination over their units but specific decisions are taken by the local commanders. These factors will be further analysed in section 4.2 of this chapter regarding the standard of direction and control.

3.1.3. Changes of structure over the course of time

Another main difference between recognised collective entities such as states and international organisations on the one hand, and armed groups on the other, are the changes of structure over the course of the fight. This makes it difficult to determine the attribution of conduct in a general and stable manner. As a minimum, the armed group has to fulfil the requirements of Common Article 3 to the Geneva Conventions. For instance, in the case of Syria, the Commission of Inquiry considered that by August 2012 the increased organisational capabilities of the anti-government armed groups reached the legal threshold for a non-international armed conflict and, consequently, armed groups became bound by IHL obligations.[106] In those non-international armed conflicts that have been active for decades, such as the those taking place in Colombia, Sudan or Sri Lanka, the structure of the armed groups have fluctuated considerably. In the cases of the FARC-EP and the LTTE, these groups evolved from a rudimentary guerrilla organisation to a sophisticated well-trained organisation with a political and military wing and a civil administration.[107]

On the contrary, other armed groups could see their structures diminish and eventually disappear altogether. In fact, if the armed group ceases to maintain a minimum level of organisation, this could lead to the termination of the NIAC. In that way, while the focus appears to be on the intensity of the armed conflict, Bartels suggests that the criterion of organisation should be considered more relevant in assessing the moment at which an armed conflict is regarded as terminated.[108] Moreover, with the end of the armed conflict, the armed group could be defeated or could transition into another entity such a political party. Arguably, it could be more difficult to attribute violations and ascribe international responsibility when the armed group disappears. This could represent an obstacle in claiming reparations against the armed group, but not in terms of determining the international responsibility of the armed group during the course of the armed conflict and *a posteriori*. Even if the armed group disappears, its responsibility could be later recognised by UN monitoring mechanisms, the peace agreement concluded between the parties or even indirectly through recognition of the

---

106 Report of the Independent International Commission of Inquiry on the Syrian Arab Republic (16 August 2012) A/HRC/21/50, at 6, para. 12.

107 Regarding the FARC-EP see J. G. Ferro Medina & G. Uribe Ramón, *El orden de la Guerra: las FARC-EP entre la organización y la política* (Centro Editorial Javariano, 2002). Regarding the LTTE, see N. Terpstra and G. Frerks, *supra note* 81.

108 R. Bartels, 'From *Jus In Bello* to *Jus Post Bellum*: When do Non-International Armed Conflicts End?' in C. Stahn, J. S. Easterday, and J. Iverson (eds) *Jus Post Bellum: Mapping the Normative Foundations* (Oxford University Press 2014) 310.

international criminal responsibility of some of its members. When the armed group transforms into a political party or other type of association, this new entity could be eventually considered the successor of the armed group. This has been the case of the FARC-EP, the SPLM/A or the FMLN, among others.[109] In any case, the temporal existence of the armed group cannot be an obstacle in itself to attributing violations to them, although it could indeed have consequences on the possible enforcement of reparations. Therefore, attribution of conduct will be context-dependent, that is, it will depend on the specific moment when the conduct takes place and the level of organisation of the group at that point in time.

3.2. CONCLUDING REMARKS ON THE ADJUSTMENT OF PRINCIPLES OF ATTRIBUTION TO ARMED GROUPS

This section has concluded that the main special feature of armed groups, that is, their structural disparity, constitutes a decisive factor to be taken into account when delimiting and adjusting possible rules of attribution. In this regard, attribution of conduct to the armed group as such will depend on several factors. First, armed groups can be comprised of a military wing exclusively or both a political and military wing. Legally, the political wing is not an integral part of the armed group for the purposes of a NIAC. However, from an empirical perspective, there is a blurred line between civilian and military functions performed by members of armed groups. In this respect, the civilian or military character of the individual could determine a different standard of attribution of conduct to the group. Consequently, it is crucial that the role and responsibility of the individual or group is linked to the actions carried out by the group.

Second, armed groups can follow centralised or decentralised organisation structures. Centralised armed groups are those with a hierarchical and vertical structure which follow a strict chain of command. Some examples of this type of armed group are the FARC-EP in Colombia, the LTTE in Sri Lanka, the NRA in Uganda, the MILF in the Philippines, the UPC in Congo, the Lebanese Hezbollah, and the Islamic State Group in Syria and Iraq. Decentralised armed groups consist of semi-autonomous or splinter factions where each sub-commander retains significant authority over the unit's operations and conduct. Some examples are the Shining Path in Peru, the FMLN in El Salvador, anti-balaka groups in Central African Republic (CAR), the armed opposition groups in Libya, and Ansar Dine in Mali. The organisational structure of the armed group will influence the standard of direction and control that could be applied

109 For instance, the FARC-EP transitioned into a political party under the name of 'Fuerza Alternativa Revolucionaria del Común' and participated in the last Colombian legislative elections of 2018. The SPLM became the ruling party of the new republic of South Sudan on 9 July 2011. The FMLN became the opposition's leading political force and went on to win the presidency in March 2009.

to the different members or units, depending on the centralised or decentralised type of organisation.

Finally, attribution of conduct to armed groups is context-dependent. Armed groups evolve during the course of the conflict, fluctuating from rudimentary organisations to more sophisticated organisation resembling state structures. With the end of the armed conflict, the armed group could be defeated or could transition into a different entity such a political party. Nevertheless, the temporal existence of the armed group cannot be considered an obstacle in itself to attribute violations to it, since this can be done during the armed struggle or *a posteriori*. Therefore, the attribution of conduct will depend on the specific moment when the conduct takes place and the level of organisation of the group at that point.

4. APPLICATION OF RULES OF ATTRIBUTION TO ARMED GROUPS

According to the methodology proposed in the Chapter 3, the core principles of attribution could be applied to armed groups after introducing the required adjustments to their special features and the information provided by the own practice of armed groups and the reports of non-judicial monitoring mechanisms. These special features have been examined in the previous section and will be taken into consideration in the formulation of these rules. Moreover, internal rulings, codes of conduct and unilateral declarations of armed groups will serve to interpret the rules of attribution. Other indicators and tools of interpretation can be found in the reports of UN monitoring bodies which have assessed the conduct of non-state armed groups and the IHL violations committed by them. This section analyses whether and how attribution can be based on the three principles of attribution identified earlier, namely: 1) on the conduct of organs and/or agents of the armed group; 2) on the conduct directed and controlled by the armed group; and 3) on the acknowledgement of the conduct by the armed group.

4.1. CONDUCT OF ORGANS AND/OR AGENTS OF THE ARMED GROUP

The first principle of attribution, identified previously as being common for states and international organisations, was based on the actions of its organs and/or agents. In other words, the actions of the members of its internal organisation will be attributed to the entity as such. The application of this rule for armed groups will require the examination of two key questions: first, whether the notion of organs and/or agents could be applied to armed groups and how; and second, whether the notion of membership of armed groups is relevant for attributing IHL violations.

4.1.1. *Do armed groups have organs and/or agents?*

The first question is related to the possibility of applying the notion of organs and agents to armed groups. For the definition of 'organs', both the ASR and ARIO rely on the internal law or rules of the organisation. In principle, these rules are difficult to find in relation to armed groups as they often operate in the shadows, trying to keep their activities hidden. However, certain armed groups have produced their own internal regulations, which could be helpful in clarifying the organisational chart of that group.

The Taliban codes of conduct, also known as the *Taliban layhas,* have a section concerning organisational structures that distinguishes between a military commission, provincial officials and district governors.[110] In particular, the military commission is composed of commanders and is mainly in charge of 'planning, taking into account mujahedin strength, geographic locations, using successful techniques and experience and getting plans to the mujahedin'.[111] The Constitution of the National Democratic Front of the Philippines (NDFP) contains a section on organisational principles, establishing as members all the constituent organisations represented in the founding national conference, as well as other allied organisations, and defining the New People's Liberation Army as the main armed force of the organisation.[112] Moreover, the internal rules of the SPLM distinguished the SPLA as the military wing and the Civil Authority for the New Sudan as the highest political and administrative authority.[113] In this regard, the head of the SPLA is the Commander-in-Chief who is assisted by the General Military Council (GMC). The GMC is composed of 'GHQ senior staff and unit and formation commanders from Battalion level and above' and 'shall be the technical advisory organ to the Commander-in-Chief on technical military affairs and the general conduct of the war including strategy, tactics and administration'.[114]

Other examples of armed groups that define their organs are the FARC-EP in Colombia and the Mouvement de Libération du Congo (MLC). The FARC-EP developed substantive internal rules such as Statutes, internal rules on the disciplinary regime, and internal rules on command.[115] The FARC-EP Statutes defined the 'Estado Mayor Central' (EMC) as the committee that exercised the political and military direction of the organisation.[116] The EMC was composed of 25 members

110 K. Clark, 'The Layha: Calling the Taleban to Account – Appendix 1: The Taleban Codes of Conduct in English'. AAN Thematic Report 6/2011, Afghanistan Analysts Network (June 2011), Section 6, at 8 available at <http://aan-afghanistan.com/uploads/Appendix_1_Code_in_English.pdf> accessed 12 June 2019.

111 *Ibid*, at 9, para. 42.

112 Constitution of the National Democratic Front of the Philippines (July 1994), Article V and VI available at <http://members.casema.nl/ndf/about/ndf_consti.pdf> accessed 12 June 2019.

113 Fifteen-Point Programme of the SPLM, Vision and Programme of the Sudan People's Liberation Movement (SPLM), SPLM Political Secretariat, Yei and New Cush, New Sudan, March 1998, Section 2 and Section 3.

114 *Ibid,* Section 2, 2.

115 These documents are available in Spanish at <https://www.farc-ep.co/octava-conferencia/estatuto-farc-ep.html> accessed 12 June 2019.

116 Art. 2 FARC-EP Statutes.

and a permanent organ of direction called the Secretariat, comprising of 7 members of the EMC – five permanent members and two supplemental members.[117] The MLC also established its own statutes including four organs: the President, the Political-Military Liberation Council, the General Secretariat and a military wing called the 'Liberation Army of Congo'.[118] Articles 12 to 16 of their statutes define the functions of every organ and, amongst others, the general policies of the group at the political and military level, the administration at the regional level, recruitment and communications.

These examples demonstrate the existence of organs in the practice of armed groups. In this sense, Heffes and Frenkel note that the possible existence of non-state organs could serve as a rule to 'attribute their member's acts to the armed groups'.[119] Similarly, Bílkova has stated that 'as a minimum, it is accepted that AOGs [Armed Opposition Groups] must bear responsibility for wrongful acts committed by their organs/members'.[120] Consequently, in those cases where armed groups develop internal regulations with an organisational chart, it would be easier to attribute the conduct of such organs to the group as such, including *ultra vires* acts.

Beyond the existence or not of internal rules of the organisation, organs could also be determined *de facto*, if the person or entity is exercising specific functions or tasks for the group. Some authors have argued that individuals holding a position in the organisation or exercising a 'continuous functional link to the command structure' should constitute sufficient proof for the attribution of conduct to the group.[121] In this vein, Sassòli affirms that '[armed groups] have members and other persons exercising elements of their authority, who act in that capacity'.[122] Similarly, Gaggioli considers members as those individuals with a function in the armed wing of the non-state party to the conflict.[123] This is in line with the concept of 'agent' provided by the ARIO that refers to those persons carrying out activities and acting on behalf of the organisation with independence of their inclusion in the internal structures of the organisation. In cases where an official organic chart that outlines the different roles of the organs and agents concerned is lacking, the question would be on how a functional link with the group could be established. Therefore, the question remains as to how to assess

117 K. R. Burnett, *Case Studies in Insurgency and Revolutionary Warfare – Colombia (1964 – 2009)* (United States Army Special Operations Command, John Hopkins University, National Security Analysis Department, 2014) 121.

118 Mouvement de Libération du Congo, 'Statuts du Mouvement de Libération du Congo' (1999) Art. 11 available in French at <http://theirwords.org/media/transfer/doc/cd_mlc_1999_09-28d0edd1d32a444ad3205b5f82476140.pdf> accessed 12 June 2019.

119 E. Heffes & B. E. Frenkel, 'The International Responsibility of Non-state Armed Groups: In Search of the Applicable Rules' (2017) 8 *Goettingen Journal of International Law* 1, 39–72, at 65.

120 V. Bílková, 'Direct Responsibility of Armed Opposition Groups', 279.

121 K. Mastorodimos, *Armed Non-State Actors in International Humanitarian and Human Rights Law: Foundation and Framework of Obligations, and Rules on Accountability* (Routledge 2015) 124; J. K. Kleffner, 'The collective accountability of organised armed groups', 262–263.

122 M. Sassòli, 'Taking Armed Groups Seriously', 45.

123 G. Gaggioli 'Targeting Individuals Belonging to an Armed Group' (2018) 51 *Vanderbilt Journal of Transnational Law* 901, 901-917, at 912 (hereafter G. Gaggioli, 'Targeting Individuals').

whether a member is acting and/or performing tasks or other activities on behalf of the group.

To this end, it would be useful to find indicators that could help identify and link the actions of individuals with the group. In this sense, the practice of UN monitoring mechanisms can be relevant in clarifying this relationship. In particular, the UN mechanisms seem to understand that, as a minimum, the actions of military units under the command structure of the armed group should be attributed to the group as such. For instance, in the armed conflict in Colombia, the reports of the UN High Commissioner for Human Rights have described several attacks committed by different military units belonging to the FARC-EP, such as fronts and columns, which have been later connected to the group itself. To give some examples, the massacre committed against 8 people in August 2000 was attributed to the 14th Front of the FARC in Caquetá.[124] The death of a 15-year-old girl and her 5-month-old baby caused by an anti-personnel mine in the rural area of Tierradentro (Córdoba) in 2005 was attributed to the 58th front of the FARC.[125] Two civilians were reported injured while working in a water inlet in Samaná (Caldas), when a mine went off in the inlet in May 2005. This incident was attributed to the 47th Front of the FARC.[126] The use of indiscriminate explosive devices by Gabriel Galvis, FARC's Mobile Column, on the 30th July 2014 resulted in the death of a two-year-old girl in her home in Calandaima (Cauca).[127] Moreover, the death of two children and the injuries caused to eight policemen was attributed to Daniel Aldana, FARC's Mobile Column, who threw hand grenades at the football pitch in Chilvi (Nariño) on the 14th May 2014.[128] Implicitly, these reports acknowledged the fact that these military units were acting on behalf of the group since they concluded by establishing the commission of grave breaches of IHL, such as indiscriminate attacks and attacks against civilians, by the group as such. Accordingly, some sort of agency of the armed group and its capacity to act through its military units was recognised.

The Special Rapporteur on the situation of human rights in Sudan has been more explicit, and has referred to the report of the 14th August 1995 by Operation Lifeline Sudan which established that:

> The attack on Ganyiel was a systematic, organized and planned intervention in which a large number of armed and equipped soldiers took part and committed atrocities against the local population. There can be little doubt that the soldiers involved belong to SPLA. While there is no evidence to suggest that the attack was formally sanctioned or approved by military commanders either at the most senior level or locally, it is hard to believe that so many men

124 Report of the United Nations High Commissioner for Human Rights on the Human Rights Situation in Colombia (8 February 2001) E/CN.4/2001/15, at 21, para. 89.

125 Report of the United Nations High Commissioner for Human Rights on the Situation of Human Rights in Colombia (16 May 2006) E/CN.4/2006/9, Annex III, at 56, para. 80.

126 *Ibid*, Annex III, at 58, para. 92.

127 Report of the United Nations High Commissioner for Human Rights on the Situation of Human Rights in Colombia (23 January 2015) A/HRC/28/3/Add. 3, at 11, para. 46.

128 *Ibid*, para. 46.

> could have become involved without the knowledge of the local commander. Nonetheless, responsibility for the attack clearly lies with SPLA/M and, as such, is a clear violation of the new ground rules.[129]

The Special Rapporteur concluded that 'the SPLA bears responsibility for the violations and atrocities committed in 1995 by local commanders from its own ranks, although it has not been proved that they committed these actions on orders from the senior leadership, nor is it known whether they have been or will be pardoned by superiors'.[130] After the peace agreement in Southern Sudan in 2005, the Secretary-General also referred to the direct responsibility of the SPLA indicating that 'the Government and SPLA also bear a direct responsibility when individuals within their command structures recruit children'.[131] In this context, Schmalenbach agrees that '[i]f a military commander can be identified and organizationally linked to the armed group, the conduct of all individual combatants acting under the commander's military command and control are attributable to the group'.[132] In this line, the Commission of Inquiry in Syria recommended anti-government armed groups to discipline individuals under their command who were responsible for IHL violations, such as kidnapping and hostage-taking.[133] Consequently, the action of those individuals under the command of the armed group were directly linked to the group. In Libya, the UN High Commissioner for Human Rights recommended all armed groups 'to remove from active duty those suspected of such actions [IHL and human rights violations]'.[134] Here, the High Commissioner was implicitly considering the responsibility of armed groups for those persons fulfilling duties on behalf of the group.

There could other indicators that help in connecting the actions of individual members with the group, such as the uniforms of the members involved, the means received from the group to carry out certain tasks (equipment, weapons and/or other financial means), or training provided by the group. As explained by the ICRC, 'an individual *recruited, trained and equipped* by such a group [...] can be considered to assume a continuous combat function even before he or she first carries out a hostile act'.[135] Other authors have also identified the provision of training, weapons or other

---

129 Interim report on the Situation of Human Rights in the Sudan prepared by Mr. Gáspár Bíró, Special Rapporteur of the Commission on Human Rights (16 October 1995) UN Doc. A/50/569, para. 67.

130 *Ibid*, para. 73.

131 Report of the Secretary-General on Children and Armed Conflict in the Sudan (17 August 2006) S/2006/662, para. 13.

132 K. Schmalenbach, 'International Responsibility for Humanitarian Law Violations by Armed Groups', H. Krieger (ed) *Inducing Compliance with International Humanitarian Law Lessons from the African Great Lakes Region* (Cambridge University Press 2015) 500.

133 Report of the Independent International Commission of Inquiry on the Syrian Arab Republic (8 August 2017) A/HRC/36/55, para. 89(c).

134 Report of the United Nations High Commissioner for Human Rights on the Situation of Human Rights in Libya and on Related Technical Support and Capacity-building Needs' (12 January 2015) A/HRC/28/51, at 16, para. 83(a).

135 N. Melzer, *Interpretative Guidance on the notion of Direct Participation in Hostilities under International Humanitarian Law* (International Committee of the Red Cross 2010) 34.

type of assistance by the group as relevant evidence of a link between the individual and the armed group.[136] With regards to uniforms or insignias, the report of the Commission of Inquiry in Darfur, identified members of the Justice and Equality Movement (JEM) who attacked the town of Kulbus in October 2003 by their 'military desert camouflage uniforms'.[137] The report of the UN Fact-Finding Mission on the Gaza Conflict detailed abuses committed by the Gaza authorities' security services by referring to armed, uniformed, masked men with elements of hierarchical control.[138] According to the report of the Commission of Inquiry in Libya, acts of torture and ill-treatment were committed by opposition armed forces that consisted of 'armed men in green uniforms'.[139] In this regard, Bellal agrees that the specific clothing or uniform could be considered an element which helps us link the violation of an IHL norm with a specific group though notes that this will not be conclusive.[140] Similarly, the final report of the Commission of Inquiry in the Central African Republic identified the attacks carried out by anti-balaka factions as the perpetrators were wearing uniforms and special amulets (*gris-gris*) and committed the attacks with traditional weapons and machetes.[141] In particular, machetes became the main weapons used by the anti-balaka in the killings of Muslim people. In terms of the weapons or the training provided by the armed group, the Commission of Inquiry in Cote d'Ivoire referred to acts of sexual violence committed by armed militiamen who were defined as 'citizens of Côte d'Ivoire recruited and armed to provide military support to an organized group'.[142] In Sri Lanka, the panel of experts in accountability considered that the actions of the LTTE cadre were supported by supply lines, logistical systems and communications equipment.[143]

Thus, these indicators could help in identifying the persons who are acting on behalf of the group and distinguishing them from individuals acting in their private capacities. Moreover, these actions have to be connected with the military efforts of the group as such. Nevertheless, since every armed group is different, those persons will have to be identified on a case-by-case approach.[144]

---

136 G. Gaggioli, 'Targeting Individuals', 914.

137 Report of the International Commission of Inquiry on Darfur to the United Nations Secretary-General (25 January 2005) para. 255.

138 Report of the United Nations Fact-Finding Mission on the Gaza Conflict (25 September 2009) A/HRC/12/48, at 290, para. 1367.

139 Report of the International Commission of Inquiry to Investigate All Alleged Violations of International Human Rights Law in the Libyan Arab Jamahiriya (1 June 2011) A /HRC/17/44, para. 128.

140 A. Bellal, 'Establishing the Direct Responsibility of Non-State Armed Groups for Violations of International Norms: Issues of Attribution' in N. Gal-Or, C. Ryngaert & M. Noortmann. *Responsibilities of the Non-State Actor in Armed Conflict and the Market Place: Theoretical Considerations and Empirical Findings* (Brill Nijhoff 2015) 313.

141 Final Report of the International Commission of Inquiry of the Central African Republic (22 December 2014) S/2014/928, at 77, para. 323, 337, and at 82, para. 361, 363.

142 Report of the International Commission of Inquiry on Côte d'Ivoire (1 July 2011) A /HRC/17/48, paras. 22 and 104.

143 Report of the Secretary-General's Panel of Experts on Accountability in Sri Lanka (31 March 2011) para. 97 and 120.

144 See G. Gaggioli, 'Targeting Individuals', 914.

4.1.2. *Is the notion of membership of armed groups relevant for the purpose of attribution?*

Due to the uncertainty regarding armed groups' structures, another question that has been raised is whether the mere membership is a useful criterion for the purpose of attributing IHL violations to the group. On this matter, in 2002, Zegveld noted that 'the only rule on attribution that can be found in international practice is that members of armed opposition groups can engage the responsibility of such groups'.[145] Similarly, the ICRC in its study on Customary IHL declared that armed groups 'incur responsibility for acts committed by persons forming part of such groups'.[146] However, the notion of membership in an armed group is still unclear and difficult to define because of its context-specific and irregular character. The question of membership has been discussed in relation to the issue of direct participation in hostilities. On this point, the ICRC has offered some guidance on the determination of membership for both state armed forces and organised armed groups.[147] In the case of armed groups, the main difficulty is that membership is not often 'expressed through uniforms, fixed distinctive signs or identification cards'.[148] Therefore, for the determination of membership in armed groups, the ICRC has established that:

> the decisive criterion for individual membership in an organized armed group is whether a person assumes a continuous function for the group involving his or her direct participation in hostilities (hereafter: "continuous combat function").[149]

According to this definition, the continuous combat function involves a lasting integration in the group, acting as the armed forces of such organisation. The ICRC distinguishes two cases. Those individuals who are involved in the preparation, execution or command of operations even before they carry out an armed attack are considered to be exercising a continuous combatant function and, therefore, are members of the group.[150] On the contrary, those individuals who only support the organisation but are not directly involved in the conduct of hostilities are not considered members of that group under IHL. The ICRC clarifies that:

> [t]hus, recruiters, trainers, financiers and propagandists may continuously contribute to the general war effort of a non-State party, but they are not members of an organized armed group belonging to that party unless their function additionally includes activities amounting to direct participation in hostilities.[151]

---

145 L. Zegveld, *Accountability of Armed Opposition Groups*, 153.

146 J. M. Henckaerts & L. Doswald-Beck, *Customary International Humanitarian Law*, 530.

147 N. Melzer, *Interpretative Guidance on the notion of Direct Participation in Hostilities under International Humanitarian Law* (International Committe of the Red Cross 2010).

148 *Ibid*, 33.

149 *Ibid*, 33.

150 *Ibid*, 34.

151 *Ibid*, 34.

However, this definition of membership is made only for the purpose of distinguishing between civilians and combatants (also known as the principle of distinction) and, therefore, determining when to apply the provisions on the protection of civilians and the performance of a legitimate attack, but it does not contemplate the question of attribution of acts to the group. Furthermore, this conception of direct participation in hostilities has been criticised by the doctrine for being too narrow and difficult to apply in practice.[152] For instance, Schmitt notes that participation should be extended to other indirect contributions such as instances of 'capacity building that comprises more than simply enhancing general military capacity in that it can be linked to specific operations, or types of operations, that are relatively imminent'.[153] Watkin also regrets the lack of consideration given by the ICRC in its guidance to the role of logistics in the conduct of military operations. He mentions the example of someone who performs a logistics function on a full-time basis within an organised armed group, which is not clearly addressed by the ICRC guidance as performing a continuous combatant function.[154] Similarly, someone who provides regular supplies to the armed group would not be considered a member according to the guidance as this function would be only supportive but not directly connected with the military operations.[155] Even the ICTY stated in the *Strugar* case that 'conduct amounting to direct or active participation in hostilities is not, however, limited to combat activities as such'.[156]

What is more, the ICRC guidance does not appear to sufficiently take into account the different organisational structures of armed groups. It establishes different criteria for determining the membership of regular armed forces of states and membership of organised armed groups. In the case of states, membership is based on 'domestic law and expressed through formal integration into permanent units distinguishable by uniforms, insignia, and equipment'.[157] On the contrary, for armed groups membership is determined through the performance of a continuous combatant function. However, some armed groups can be organised, armed and dressed like state-based counterparts and they can even engage in conventional operations. For those cases, it seems unreasonable to establish different criteria for the determination of membership, which could result in the application of an unbalanced approach to the rules of IHL.[158]

---

152 M. J. Hopkins, 'Extrapolation of Criminal Law Modes of Liability to Target Analysis under International Humanitarian Law: Developing the Framework for Understanding Direct Participation in Hostilities and Membership in Organized Armed Groups in Non-International Armed Conflict' (2017) 22 *Journal of Conflict and Security Law* 2, 275–310, at 279.

153 M. N. Schmitt, 'Deconstructing Direct Participation in Hostilities: The Constitutive Elements' (2010) 42 *New York University Journal of International Law and Politics*, 697–739, at 727.

154 K. Watkin, 'Opportunity Lost: Organized Armed Groups and the ICRC "Direct Participation in Hostilities Interpretive Guidance' (2009–2010) 42 *New York University Journal of International Law and Politics*, 641–695, at 684–685.

155 *Ibid*, 680.

156 *Prosecutor v. Strugar* (Appeals Chamber Judgment) ICTY Case No. IT-01–42-A, (17 July 2008), para. 176.

157 N. Melzer, *supra note* 147, 25.

158 K. Watlin, *supra note* 154, 674–675.

In sum, the criteria used to determine when a person can be targeted in the conduct of hostilities does not have to be the same as the one used to establish when an act of an individual can be attributed to the armed group. Nevertheless, the limits established by the ICRC in relation to membership for the purpose of direct participation in hostilities are equally relevant for this inquiry. The first limit is that membership cannot be based on abstract criteria such as family ties or clan and tribal associations, which could result in error or arbitrariness.[159] Secondly, membership should be deducted from a permanent role within the group and not only sporadic or spontaneous participation.[160] In consequence, a central consideration should be the permanent participation of a person in the armed activities of the group. In line with this reasoning, some authors claim that membership should be based on objective factors rather than ideological links. From this perspective, in the context of direct participation in hostilities Gaggioli notes that:

> At a minimum, it has to be highlighted that mere ideological bounds with an organized armed group cannot be equated with functional membership. More broadly, functional membership shall not rely on subjective factors, but on objectively verified ones only. The notion of functional membership should also be understood as requiring that an individual has been given a mission *ex ante* and that this individual has assumed it.[161]

Therefore, the definition of 'members of armed groups' suggested by the ICRC in the Interpretative Guidance on the Notion of Direct Participation in Hostilities should be only used for the purpose of determining the legitimate military targets, as it appears too narrow to reflect the full spectrum of members of armed groups that might be relevant to attribution. However, one of the main considerations that should be noted from this Guidance is that those considered 'members' carry out a permanent role within the organisation, which is not based on sporadic participation in their activities. In this regard, the ICRC guidance also keeps a functional approach to the issue of membership which seems to mirror the functional approach of the ILC to the notion of agent.

4.1.3. *Concluding remarks: agency based on a functional approach*

To summarise, both the notion of membership for the purpose of determining direct participation in hostilities and the concepts of organs of states and agents of international organisations for attributional purposes share a common idea: they are not simply based on the mere formal membership and adherence to the group, but on the stable functions that individuals play within an organisation. Therefore, ethnic or ideological bounds or the mere pledging of allegiance are not enough to prove a link between a member and the group.

---

159 N. Melzer, *supra note* 147, 33.
160 *Ibid*, 34.
161 G. Gaggioli, 'Targeting Individuals', 914.

This form of agency has been defined in Article 2(d) of the ARIO where an agent is described as someone 'who is charged by the organization with carrying out, or helping to carry out, one of its functions'.[162] This functional approach was based on the *Reparations* case decided by the ICJ even before international organisations were formally considered subjects of international law. In this case, the action of an agent was understood as 'any person who, whether a paid official or not, and whether permanently employed or not, has been charged by an organ of the organization with carrying out, or helping to carry out, one of its functions – in short, *any person through whom it acts*'.[163] In this context, the actions of agents of international organisations are regarded as those carrying out or *helping to carry out* the functions of the organisation. In other words, they refer to those actions that directly or indirectly contribute to the general aims of the group. Similarly, in the comments submitted to the UN Secretary-General on the Declaration of Minimum Humanitarian Standards, the International Institute of Humanitarian Law suggested that an article be inserted according to which '[a]ny *de jure* or *de facto* authority is responsible for the acts committed by their *agents*, including acts which adversely affect the basic human rights of any person in emergency situations'.[164] This Declaration proposed the establishment of minimum humanitarian standards to be applied in all situations, being an armed conflict or internal disturbances. Although this provision was ultimately not included, it reflects the idea that both recognised legal entities and *de facto* regimes should be responsible for the actions of their agents.

The notion of 'agent' appears to be more flexible than the concept of organ since the concept of agent focuses on the functions rather than the official status of the person or entity. Consequently, in order to attribute acts to armed groups based on this rule, the crucial question is to examine the different roles within the group and the extent to which members act on behalf of the group, rather than only determining the official affiliation to the armed group. In principle, the characterisation of someone as an agent of the armed group should be based on the performance of military actions on behalf of the group. In this regard, the person in question could perform both civil as well as political and military functions but the key element is that he or she is carrying out actions related to the military activities of the group or those obligations derived from international humanitarian law. Therefore, such determinations will have to be done on a case-by-case approach.

Furthermore, these actions could be directly related to the military activities of the group or could constitute auxiliary activities. Actions directly related to the military activities of the group, such as combat actions committed by commanders and fighters, could be attributed to the armed group as such, including *ultra vires* actions. The reason

---

162 Art. 2(d) Draft Articles on the Responsibility of International Organizations, with Commentaries, *Yearbook of the International Law Commission* (2011), Vol. II, Part Two, General commentary.

163 *Reparation for Injuries Suffered in the Service of the United Nations* (Advisory Opinion) [1949] ICJ Rep 174, 11 April 1949, at 177 (emphasis added).

164 Comments on the Declaration of Minimum Humanitarian Standards submitted to the UN Secretary-General, Report of the UN Secretary-General prepared pursuant to Commission Resolution 1995/29 (28 November 1995) UN Doc. E/CN.4/1996/80, 11.

to establish this guarantee is that the units are under the command structure of the group. This rule could be derived from the emerging practice of the UN monitoring bodies in relation to the actions of non-state armed groups. In addition, the actions of other agents of the group could also be potentially attributed to the group if they are performed on a permanent basis. In particular, those persons or entities who carry out additional activities for the group, such as supportive roles (intelligence services, providers of services, training, etc.) or planning activities at the highest level of the organisation should also be considered as acting on behalf of the group.[165] The reason behind this principle is that these actions are not performed on an individual basis but as part of the military efforts of the organisation.

Therefore, in order to attribute violations committed by these persons, there should be a functional link between the conduct of the agent and the functioning of the group. Moreover, the actions that constitute IHL violations have to relate to the military activities of the group, directly or indirectly, even if the person also performs other civilian or political functions on the side. There are some indicators that can help to determine the role of an individual or group as an agent of the armed group. First of all, its inclusion in the internal regulations of the armed group, such as statutes and codes of conduct, could serve as an indication that this person or entity performs military functions for the group. Other indicators that can help determine their role as agents are uniforms or insignias, weapons and other means received from the group, as well as the training provided by the group.

4.2. CONDUCT DIRECTED AND CONTROLLED BY AN ARMED GROUP

The second principle identified above was the attribution of conduct of those persons or entities acting under the direction or control of the armed group by analogy with Article 8 of the ASR. In relation to international organisations, the ARIO did not contain a specific parallel rule, however Article 6 of the ARIO did indicate that '[s]hould persons or groups of persons act under the instructions, or the direction or control, of an international organization, they would have to be regarded as agents according to the definition given in subparagraph (d) of Article 2'.[166] Moreover, Article 7 of the ARIO also refer to external organs or agents under the effective control of the international organisation.[167]

Certain examples in the practice of armed groups appear to validate the application of this rule. For instance, according to the Undertaking of demilitarisation and transformation by the Kosovo Liberation Army (KLA), the KLA was considered to be composed of 'all personnel and organisations within Kosovo, currently *under KLA control*'.[168] The Darfur Peace Agreement also refers to the commitment of both parties,

---

165 On the same opinion see K. Mastorodimos, *supra note* 121, 125.

166 Art. 6 ARIO, Commentary para. 11.

167 Art. 7 ARIO, Commentary paras. 8–12.

168 *Undertaking of demilitarisation and transformation by the KLA (20 June 1999) art. 5(a) available at <https://www.nato.int/kosovo/docu/a990620a.htm> accessed 12 June 2019.*

that is the Government of Sudan and the SPLM/A, to 'ensure that all of the institutions, bodies, commissions, committees and *other entities under their control*, including their members, shall observe the terms of this Agreement'.[169] The Cessation of Hostilities Agreement between the Government of the Republic of Indonesia and the Free Aceh Movement (GAM) goes further and establishes the commitment of both parties to 'control those groups that do not share their objectives but claim to be part of their forces'.[170]

In this context, several authors have also pointed to this possibility. Zegveld has noted that the 'attribution of acts or omissions to smaller armed opposition groups is based on their actual control over individuals, rather than on the existence of a defined state-like structure'.[171] Likewise, Sassòli explains that for smaller armed groups that do not have control of territory, attribution should be based on effective control over persons.[172] The essential question is which standard of control should be applied to consider an act of an individual or entity as being an act of the armed group as such. As concerns states, two theories have been proposed in this regard: the effective control test and the overall control test. Both theories attempt to explain when acts performed by individuals, not having the status of state officials, could be nevertheless legally imputable to the state. The effective control test was first elaborated by the ICJ in the *Nicaragua* case, where it was indicated that the financing, training, equipping of the *contras* and the planning of the operation was not sufficient to attribute the acts to the United States. On the contrary, effective control over the concrete military operation was required for the purpose of attribution.[173] The ICTY proposed a lower threshold, namely, the overall control test, which was not based on specific instructions but on the coordination of the general planning of the military operations of another entity.[174] Later on, the ICJ confirmed and further developed the effective control test in the *Armed Activities* and *Genocide* case.[175] In particular, in the *Genocide* case the Court clarified that:

> [i]t must however be shown that this "effective control" was exercised, or that the State's instructions were given, in respect of each operation in which the alleged violations occurred, not generally in respect of the overall actions taken by the persons or groups of persons having committed the violations.[176]

---

169 Darfur Peace Agreement, Abuja, Nigeria (5 May 2006) art. 32, para. 509.

170 Cessation of Hostilities Framework Agreement between the Government of the Republic of Indonesia and the Free Aceh Movement (9 December 2002) Art. 2(a).

171 L. Zegveld, *Accountability of Armed Opposition Groups*, 155.

172 M. Sàssoli, 'Taking Armed Groups Seriously', 45.

173 *Military and Paramilitary Activities in and against Nicaragua* (Merits) [1984] Judgment ICJ Rep 392, 26 November 1984, para. 115.

174 *Tadić* Appeal Judgment, para. 131.

175 See *Armed Activities on the Territory of the Congo (Democratic Republic of the Congo v Uganda)* (Merits) [2005] Judgment ICJ Rep 168, 19 December 2005, para. 160; *Application of the Convention on the Prevention and Punishment of the Crime of Genocide (Bosnia and Herzegovina v. Yugoslavia)* (Merits) [2007] Judgment, ICJ Rep, 26 February 2007.

176 *Application of the Convention on the Prevention and Punishment of the Crime of Genocide (Bosnia and Herzegovina v. Yugoslavia)* (Merits) [2007] Judgment, ICJ Rep, 26 February 2007, para. 400.

With regards to the possibility of applying a similar rule to armed groups, some authors have argued that it would be inadvisable to use a higher threshold for armed groups than for states, bearing in mind that armed groups are entities with less resources and capabilities.[177] To clarify which standard of direction and control is preferred for the conduct of armed groups it is essential to distinguish between the conduct of individuals and the conduct of a military faction or another entity associated with the armed group. In particular, this distinction serves to acknowledge and incorporate the structural disparity of armed groups. These circumstances will be considered in the following sub-sections.

4.2.1. Conduct of individuals

Following from the discussion in the previous section on the structural disparity of armed groups, it seems necessary to take into account the civilian or military character of the person or entity in question. In this respect, the ICTY has argued for the application of two degrees of control depending on the actions being performed by a 'private individual' or by an 'organised and hierarchical structured group, such as a military unit or, in case of war or civil strife, armed bands of irregulars or rebels'.[178] For the actions of private individuals, the Tribunal indicated that:

> In such a case, it would be necessary to show that the State issued specific instructions concerning the commission of the breach in order to prove – if only by necessary implication – that the individual acted as a *de facto* State agent. Alternatively, it would be necessary to show that the State has publicly given retroactive approval to the action of that individual. A generic authority over the individual would not be sufficient to engage the international responsibility of the State.[179]

In this scenario, private individuals are required to act under the specific instructions of the organisation in question so their conduct could be attributed to such entity. On the contrary, in the case of a military hierarchical group, the Court proposed the aforementioned overall control test by stating:

> Plainly, an organised group differs from an individual in that the former normally has a structure, a chain of command and a set of rules as well as the outward symbols of authority. Normally a member of the group does not act on his own but conforms to the standards prevailing in the group and is subject to the authority of the head of the group. Consequently, for the attribution to a State of acts of these groups it is sufficient to require that the group as a whole be under the overall control of the State.[180]

---

177 K. Mastorodimos (2016), *supra note* 121, 125.
178 *Tadić* Appeal Judgment, paras. 118–120.
179 *Ibid*, para. 118.
180 *Ibid*, para. 120.

Although the ICTY was not dealing with the issue of international responsibility, its reasoning could be useful in identifying the differences between the actions of private individuals and the actions of a military group or faction. In relation to the attribution of acts to armed groups, the effective control test could be better applied to those actions of individuals who do not belong to the structures of the armed group and do not perform their activities, but take part in the conflict in specific moments on behalf of the armed group.[181] According to Verhoeven, the effective control test should be applied to persons who 'do not received financial support, equipment and are not coordinated or assisted in military planning, but at a certain point in time they are directed, controlled or instructed by the insurrectional movement'.[182] On the contrary, as indicated by Mastorodimos, 'an individual/civilian, who wilfully takes part in a battle alongside an ANSA [Armed Non-State Actor], although he does not follow instructions nor is part of the command structure of the ANSA, should not be considered as being under the ANSA's control'.[183] Similarly, the UN Commission of Inquiry in Syria reported killings committed by armed civilians associated with the Free Syrian Army (FSA) and indicated that 'they received information about Syrian civilians reinforcing anti-Government armed groups, which increases problems of effective control even at the level of local FSA groups'.[184] Furthermore, following this reasoning, as individual civilians are expected to comply with specific instructions from the armed group, if they contravene those orders – that is, in case of *ultra vires* acts – conduct is not likely to be attributed to the group.[185]

4.2.2. Conduct of factions and other entities associated with armed groups

More challenging seems to be the determination of the standard of control for the actions of other armed forces affiliated with an armed group, being other insurrectional factions or other entities associated with the armed group. In this context, the standard of direction and control may differ depending on the organisational structure of the armed group. For centralised armed groups, only the actions under the command and control of the armed group could potentially be attributed to the group as such. In this vein, Nohle notes that an armed faction belongs to the armed group 'if its falls under the "command and direction" of that group'. He further explains that 'indicative factors include whether the faction falls under the hierarchical structure, chain of command and disciplinary system of the armed group'.[186] For instance, in the case of the FARC-EP,

---

181 K. Mastorodimos, *supra note* 121, 125.

182 I. Verhoeven, 'International Responsibility of Armed Opposition Groups: Lessons from State Responsibility for Actions of Non-State Armed Groups' in N. Gal-Or, C. Ryngaert, & M. Noortmann (eds) *Responsibilities of the Non-State Actor in Armed Conflict and the Market Place: Theoretical Considerations and Empirical Findings* (Brill Nijhoff 2015) 301–302.

183 K. Mastorodimos, *supra note* 121, 125.

184 Report of the Independent International Commission of Inquiry on the Syrian Arab Republic (22 February 2012) A/HRC/19/69, paras. 108 and 118.

185 S. I. Verhoeven, *supra note* 182, 302; K. Mastorodimos, *supra note* 121, 125.

186 E. Nohle, 'Drawing the Line between Armed Groups under IHL' (2016) *ICRC Law and Conflict* available at <http://blogs.icrc.org/law-and-policy/2016/07/22/drawing-line-armed-groups/> accessed 12 June 2019.

the so-called Bolivarian militias were not included in the FARC-EP's statutes as part of their organisation. These militias had their own statutes and were defined as a military organisation with a hierarchical structure, working in the areas where the FARC-EP had influence.[187] Nevertheless, their statutes indicated that they were under the 'immediate direction' of the FARC-EP's fronts and the EMC, as the governing organ. Consequently, if the rules suggested above are applied, the actions of these militias could be attributed to the FARC-EP. In particular, some of the killings attributed to the FARC-EP in 1998 were carried out by members of their militias.[188] Moreover, two out of the 59 killings of human rights defenders in 2016 were also attributed to FARC-EP militias.[189]

On the contrary, if armed factions are not under the command and control of the group, they are considered splinter and separated factions. This was the case of the SPLM/A with the emergence of the two breakaway SPLA factions – the SPLA-Nasir and SPLA-Torit (or SPLA mainstream). Violations of IHL were attributed separately to each faction during the 1990's by the UN Special Rapporteur on the situation of human rights in Sudan.[190] In addition, in the case of the LTTE in Sri Lanka, the Special Rapporteur on extrajudicial, summary or arbitrary executions also considered the Karuma faction a different entity and violations were attributed to each of them separately.[191]

In the case of decentralised armed groups, it appears that factions or cells are merely considered to be under the overall control of the group, that is, under the general coordination powers of the group. Individual members follow the instructions of local commanders, who retain a high level of autonomy. However, according to Ferraro, legal advisor to the ICRC, 'the notion of overall control does not therefore refer simply to monitoring or checking, but also requires the exercise of some form of authority over the entity in question'.[192] In this regard, the ICTY has clarified the requirement of the overall control test by indicating that:

> [i]n order to attribute the acts of a military or paramilitary group to a State, it must be proved that the State wields overall control over the group, not only by equipping and financing the group, but also by coordinating or helping in the general planning of its military activity. Only then can the State be held internationally accountable for any misconduct of the group.[193]

---

187 The Statutes of the Bolivarian Militias are available in Spanish at <https://www.farc-ep.co/octava-conferencia/estatuto-de-las-milicias-bolivarianas.html> accessed 12 June 2019.

188 Report of the United Nations High Commissioner for Human Rights on the Office in Colombia (16 March 1999) E/CN.4/1999/8, 23, para. 111.

189 Annual Report of the United Nations High Commissioner for Human Rights. Situation of Human Rights in Colombia (23 March 2017) A/HRC/34/3/Add. 3, 9, para. 56.

190 Report of the Special Rapporteur, Mr. Gáspár Bíró, on the Situation of Human Rights in the Sudan' (1 February 1994) paras. 118–119; Report of the Special Rapporteur, Mr. Gáspár Biró, on the Situation of Human Rights in the Sudan' (3 February 1997) E/CN.4/1997/58, para. 26.

191 Report of the Special Rapporteur on Extrajudicial, Summary or Arbitrary Executions, Philip Alston – Mission to Sri Lanka (26 March 2006) E/CN.4/2006/53/Add.5, paras. 15–16, para. 30 and para. 49.

192 T. Ferraro, 'The ICRC's Legal Position on the Notion of Armed Conflict involving Foreign Intervention and on Determining the IHL Applicable to this Type of Conflict' (2015) 97 *International Review of the Red Cross* 1227– 52, 1237.

193 *Tadić* Appeal Judgment, para. 131.

In relation to the threshold that coalitions of armed groups need to reach in order to be considered as one party to an armed conflict, Rodenhäuser has stated that, apart from general coordination powers, the leadership of the group needs to exercise a degree of 'strategic authority'.[194] In his view, this represents a slightly higher threshold because '[w]hile operational coordination requires the ability to coordinate military activities and to distribute logistics, strategic authority signifies leadership's *de facto* authority to determine the overall military objectives and the internal rules that all sub-groups have to follow.[195] Nevertheless, this observation do not necessary require a higher threshold, it could rather be considered as a mere clarification or interpretation of the coordination powers of the leadership. As explained by Ferraro, this concept of authority is more general than the issuance of specific orders and refers to general direction and coordination.[196] Specific instructions will be given by the local commanders in charge of each autonomous cell. Therefore, to attribute actions of different cells or factions to a decentralised armed group, these groups should at least be under the overall control of the armed group. This overall control needs to be understood as the exercise of coordination powers over the military activities of the group as well as the general authority exercised by the leadership over the different sub-groups.

4.2.3. Concluding remarks: agency based on direction and control

To summarise, in addition to the notion of agency based on a functional approach, the second possibility to attribute acts to armed groups is based on the direction and control the group exercises over the person or entity in question. In that respect, this rule could be potentially applied to both centralised and decentralised armed groups. A distinction must nevertheless be drawn between individuals and other military factions. The standard of effective control will be required for the actions of private individuals who do not belong to the internal structures of the group, nor do they perform activities for the group on a regular basis, but who act under the specific instructions of the group. For other armed factions, the rule will depend on the centralised or decentralised nature of the armed group. In the case of centralised armed groups, the actions of other armed entities could be attributed to the group if these factions are under the command and control of the group due to the existence of a strict chain of command. If actions of these armed factions are not under this command and control, they would constitute splinter or separated factions. For decentralised armed groups, the requirement will be, in principle, the overall control over the different factions or cells. This overall control would need to incorporate the general coordination powers of the leadership over the military actions as well as its general authority over the sub-groups or cells.

---

194 T. Rodenhäuser, *Organizing Rebellion*, 84.

195 *Ibid*, 84.

196 T. Ferraro, *supra note* 192, 1237.

4.3. ACKNOWLEDGEMENT OF THE CONDUCT BY THE ARMED GROUP

Finally, the third possible principle of attribution is the acknowledgement of the conduct by the group itself. This principle can be drawn by analogy with Article 11 of the ASR and Article 9 of the ARIO. In the practice of armed groups, we can find several examples of armed groups who have acknowledged their responsibility for specific actions. The work of the UN monitoring bodies has also considered this type of acknowledgement as a way to link certain actions with a particular armed group. In principle, there are no policy or legal reasons against applying this attribution rule for armed groups as well. The acknowledgement of violations by the armed group itself could serve as a complementary or reinforcement tool to attribute violations and could be potentially applied to both centralised and decentralised groups.

4.3.1. Examples from the practice of armed groups

One of the first groups that recognised its responsibility for certain violations was the Sudan People's Liberation Movement/Army (SPLM/A). The representatives of SPLA-Torit and SPLA-Nasir who met the Special Rapporteur of the Commission on Human Rights during his mission in August 1994 admitted the abuses reportedly committed by some of their members.[197] Moreover, according to the mission report of the Secretary-General on children and armed conflict in 2006, 'the SPLA has long acknowledged that it has child soldiers in its ranks'.[198] In addition, in 2011 the SPLA Deputy Chief of Staff for Moral Orientation also acknowledged the presence of children associated with SPLA in the Kordofan State.[199] Palestinian armed factions have also claimed responsibility for a number of attacks, such as rocket and mortar launchings in 2008.[200] More recently, during the Syrian conflict, several armed groups have claimed responsibility for different attacks. In this regard, the Al-Nusrah Front for the People of the Levant acknowledged its responsibility for several suicide bombings against Government forces and senior officials.[201] In addition, anti-government armed groups, like the Free Syrian Army, also claimed responsibility for five bombings in Aleppo and Damascus during 2012 resulting in a number of civilian casualties.[202]

197 Interim Report on the Situation of Human Rights in the Sudan prepared by Mr. Gáspár Bíró Special Rapporteur on the Commission on Human Rights (19 October 1994) A/49/539, para. 87.

198 Report of the Secretary-General on Children and Armed sonflict in the Sudan (17 August 2006) S/2006/662, para. 51.

199 Report of the Secretary-General on Children and Armed Conflict in the Sudan (5 July 2011) S/2011/413, para. 17.

200 Report of the United Nations Fact-Finding Mission on the Gaza Conflict, (25 September 2009) A/HRC/12/48 at 349, para. 1610, and at 353, para. 1629.

201 Report of the Independent International Commission of Inquiry on the Syrian Arab Republic (16 August 2012) A/HRC/21/50, at 8, para. 30.

202 Report of the Independent International Commission of Inquiry on the Syrian Arab Republic (5 February 2012) A/HRC/22/59, Annex XI, 102–103.

Another example that deserves further exploration is the case of the FARC-EP, who has acknowledged its responsibility on several occasions. According to the annual report of the UN High Commissioner for Human Rights in 2000, the FARC-EP acknowledged that they had killed at least 19 people after detaining them in the demilitarized zone during 1999.[203] Additionally, they claimed responsibility for certain attacks by setting off explosives in densely populated urban areas.[204] In 2000, the leadership accepted the charges against the FARC-EP for the lack of respect for IHL in the demilitarized zone.[205] In January 2005, the 29th front of the FARC-EP notified authorities in the indigenous Awá reservation in the municipality of Ricaurte (Nariño) of the death of Efrén Pascal, the reservation Governor, who had been taken hostage in October 2004, and described the murder as a 'regrettable error'.[206] Moreover, the FARC-EP also assumed responsibility for the murder of four members of the public security forces who had been held hostage on the 26th November 2011 in Solano (Caquetá).[207] In 2014, the Office of the High Commissioner encouraged the FARC-EP to issue more statements like the previous ones, stating that:

> During the peace negotiations, FARC-EP indicated that it could acknowledge responsibility for past human rights violations, for example, by declaring that the widespread use of kidnapping might have been a mistake. Further acknowledgements by FARC-EP and other armed groups, as well as actions to stop current violations, are needed.[208]

On the 6th December 2015, the FARC-EP conducted a ceremony in Bojayá (Chocó) to recognise its responsibility and issued a public apology for the civilian deaths and damage caused during a battle with paramilitary forces in 2002 that caused 79 casualties and injured more than a 100 people. This acknowledgement on behalf of the armed group was done in the presence of the High Commissioner for Peace in Colombia, the director of the Victims Unit, the UN Resident Coordinator and Humanitarian Coordinator in Colombia, the representative of the UN High Commissioner for Human Rights, and representatives of the Ombudsman's Office. This symbolic event was considered historic by the High Commissioner.[209] During 2016, the FARC-EP further recognised its responsibility for the practice of kidnapping, the 1994 massacre in La Chinita (Apartadó), the death in captivity in 2009 of 11 legislators in the

203 Report of the United Nations High Commissioner for Human Rights on the Office in Colombia (9 March 2000) E/CN.4/2000/11, at 19, para. 79.

204 *Ibid*, at 21, para. 94.

205 Report of the United Nations High Commissioner for Human Rights on the Human Rights Situation in Colombia (8 February 2001) E/CN.4/2001/15, at 27, para. 129.

206 *Ibid*, Annex III, para. 72.

207 Report of the United Nations High Commissioner for Human Rights on the Situation of Human Rights in Colombia (31 January 2012) A/HRC/19/21/Add.3, Appendix, para. 11 (d).

208 Annual report of the United Nations High Commissioner for Human Rights on the Situation of Human Rights in Colombia (24 January 2014) A /HRC/25/19/Add.3, at 9, para. 41.

209 Annual report of the United Nations High Commissioner for Human Rights on the situation of Human Rights in Colombia (23 June 2016) A/HRC/31/3/Add. 2, at 6, para. 19.

Valle del Cauca, and the assassination of an Afro-Colombian human rights defender in 2015.[210] However, the High Commissioner emphasised that 'challenges remain within the State and FARC-EP concerning the full recognition of their responsibilities for past international human rights and humanitarian law violations, in a manner that satisfies the rights of victims'.[211] He also expressively called on the State and the FARC-EP 'to recognize fully their responsibility for serious violations of human rights and international humanitarian law, in order to generate effective reparations processes based on consensus with victims; and also, to ensure non-repetition of the violations of human rights and international humanitarian law that have characterized the armed conflict'.[212]

As for decentralised armed groups, the FMLN in El Salvador and the anti-balaka groups in CAR have also acknowledged the commission of certain attacks. The FMLN claimed responsibility for a number of extrajudicial executions committed during the internal armed conflict in El Salvador, such as the cases of former guerrilla commander Miguel Castellanos, university lecturer and journalist Peccorini Lettona, and Attorney General of the Republic, García Alvarado.[213] In particular, in the case of García Alvarado, the Truth Commission on El Salvador explained that the 'FMLN took responsibility for Mr. García Alvarado's death, which it attributed to the Fuerzas Armadas de Liberación (FAL), one of its member organizations', clearly establishing the attribution of this violation to the acknowledgement of the conduct.[214] In this case, the FMLN acknowledged the responsibility for the murder committed by another organisation, the FAL, considering it a 'member organization'. In the armed conflict in CAR, the anti-balaka Chief of Staff, with the rank of Lieutenant, directly claimed responsibility for having coordinated the attack carried out in Bangui on the 5th December 2013 and other attacks on the 25th December 2013.[215]

However, other armed groups have systematically denied their responsibility, such as the LTTE in Sri Lanka. According to the Special Rapporteur on extrajudicial, summary or arbitrary executions, the LTTE regularly issued unconvincing denials of responsibility for various killings and failed to denounce any of those which suited their purpose. The Special Rapporteur stressed the difference between denying responsibility and denouncing attacks and called on the LTTE to signal unequivocally its rejection of acts of violence.[216] In this sense, the Special Rapporteur recommended that the LTTE denounce

210 Annual report of the United Nations High Commissioner for Human Rights on the Situation of Human Rights in Colombia (23 March 2017) A/HRC/34/3/Add. 3, at 4, para. 15.

211 *Ibid,* para. 16.

212 Annual report of the United Nations High Commissioner for Human Rights on the Situation of Human Rights in Colombia (23 March 2017) A/HRC/34/3/Add. 3, at 16, para. 106 (a) and (b).

213 UN Security Council, *From Madness to Hope: The 12-year war in El Salvador – Report of the Commission on the Truth for El Salvador* (Annex) S/25500, 1993, 153–155.

214 *Ibid,*155.

215 Office of the Prosecutor, International Criminal Court, 'Situation of the Central African Republic II, Article 53(1) Report' (24 September 2014) 34–35.

216 Report of the Special Rapporteur on Extrajudicial, Summary or Arbitrary Executions, Philip Alston – Mission to Sri Lanka (26 March 2006) E/CN.4/2006/53/Add.5, para. 48.

and condemn any killing attributed to it for which it denied responsibility.[217] On the 15th June 2006, the LTTE issued a statement indicating that 'LTTE condemns this attack on the civilian bus. Directly targeting civilians, as the Kebitigollawe claymore attack has, cannot be justified under any circumstances'.[218] The Special Rapporteur then noted that 'while the statement did not clarify the responsibility of any party, it did demonstrate an important evolution in the acceptance by LTTE of its moral responsibility to denounce attacks on civilians'.[219] However, since then, the LTTE ceased to denounce and condemn killings that have been attributed to it. In particular, the LTTE failed to denounce and condemn other attacks on buses that killed scores of civilians that year.[220]

These examples show that certain armed groups have actually acknowledged and claimed responsibility for a number of attacks committed during NIACs and this could serve as a legitimate basis for attribution of actions. Accordingly, the UN monitoring mechanisms have stressed the necessity for armed groups to acknowledge their actions. Indeed, in some cases, violations have been identified by the endorsement of the group. However, it will be shown below that this acknowledgment has to comply with certain conditions for its validity.

4.3.2. Conditions for the validity of the acknowledgement

By analogy with Article 11 of the ASR and Article 9 of the ARIO, an acknowledgment by an armed group will have to comply with certain conditions. Firstly, as explained in Chapter 3, the acknowledgement has to be more than a mere support or endorsement. Moreover, the armed group has to identify the specific conduct as its own. Consequently, it has to go beyond a general recognition of the facts of the event. Secondly, the act of acknowledgement has to be 'clear and unequivocal'.[221] As regards armed groups, this act could be expressed through a unilateral declaration or a communication sent to an international organisation or an NGO charged with the monitoring of the country situation. If armed groups have offered their commitment to certain primary obligations under IHL – through the issuance of unilateral declarations or the signature of the so-called deeds of commitment – the same reasoning could be applied to those acts that they want to recognise as their own.[222] Acknowledgment could also take place at a later time in judicial proceedings or in truth commissions by the leadership of the armed group.

The UN monitoring mechanisms have encouraged this type of acknowledgment on both sides of the armed conflict. Scholars have also reflected on this possibility.

217 *Ibid.*, para. 84.

218 The Liberation Tigers of Tamil Eelam Peace Secretariat, press release of 15 June 2006.

219 Report of the Special Rapporteur on Extrajudicial, Summary or Arbitrary Executions, Philip Alston – Follow-up To Country Recommendations (14 May 2008) A/HRC/8/3/Add.3, para. 66.

220 *Ibid*, para. 66.

221 Art. 11 ASR, Commentary para. 8.

222 See S. Rondeau, 'Participation of armed groups in the development of the law applicable to armed conflicts' (2011) 93 *International Review of the Red Cross* Vol. 883, 663–667.

In this vein, Verhoeven has pointed out that 'there is no impediment to introduce an identical attribution rule for insurrectional movements: if the movement considers the conduct of sympathisers as its own, there is no reason to deny the responsibility of the movement for such conduct'.[223] As a limitation, Mastorodimos affirms that the '*ex post facto* endorsement' of the wrongful conduct would be considered exceptional.[224] Nevertheless, this principle could be applied as a complementary tool together with the application of the previous rules. Moreover, apart from its function as a rule of attribution for international responsibility, acknowledgment could also serve as a basis for victims to claim reparations.

4.4. KEY IMPLICATIONS FOR THE PROCESS OF ATTRIBUTION OF CONDUCT

The previous part has offered some guidelines into the question of attribution of conduct to armed groups. The development of future principles of attribution would require that the UN monitoring mechanisms involved in the examination of violations committed during NIACs establish a connection between individual members and the group in a more straightforward manner. In particular, they should delimitate under which rule they are attributing such violations, whether this be one based on agency or functional approach, one based on direction or control, acknowledgment of the conduct or other rule. This would help in clarifying the rules of attribution for non-state armed groups in a manner which is consistent with the principle of rule of law, and consequently, would strengthen the legal certainty and the transparency of the monitoring processes. Moreover, a consistent practice in this regard could give rise to the crystallization of customary rules, or at least it could feed into the interpretation of rules applicable to armed groups.

5. CONCLUSIONS

This chapter has argued that, in the process of adjusting the principles of attribution to the conduct of armed groups, a number of factors related to their special characteristics need to be considered. In this connection, it is argued that the concept of armed group for the purposes of NIAC refers exclusively to the military wing of the group. Nevertheless, some members can perform multiple functions within the structures of the armed group, that is, both military and political functions. In addition, as regards the organisational structure of armed groups, two main types of organisation have been identified: centralised and vertical groups armed groups, on the one hand, and decentralised and horizontal armed groups, on the other. Their different structures

223 S. I. Verhoeven, *supra note* 181, 302.
224 K. Mastorodimos, *supra note* 121, 126.

could determine different standards of attribution, in particular with regard to the notion of direction and control. Finally, attribution of conduct will be context-dependent as it is necessary to determine the specific moment when the violation has been committed and the level of organisation of the group.

In relation to the specific rules in question, this study has conceived the attribution of conduct to armed groups based on three principles of attribution: 1) on the conduct of organs and/or agents of the armed group; 2) on the conduct directed and controlled by the armed group; and 3) on the acknowledgement of the conduct by the armed group. These principles can be summarised in the following table.

Table 1. A sketch of principles of attribution of conduct to armed groups as such

<table>
<tr><th>Type of armed group</th><th>Agency based on a functional approach</th><th>Agency based on direction and control</th><th>Acknowledgment of the conduct as its own</th></tr>
<tr><td rowspan="2">Centralised armed group</td><td rowspan="4">– Agents of armed groups based on a permanent role in the organization.
+
– Contribution to military activities (directly or indirectly).

*Indicators:
a) Internal rules
b) Other indicators: uniforms, weapons, training.</td><td>– Individuals under the 'effective control' (specific instructions)</td><td rowspan="4">– Recognition of the specific conduct.
– Clear and unequivocal.
– Expressed through unilateral declarations or communications to international organizations or NGOs.</td></tr>
<tr><td>– Military factions under the command and control.</td></tr>
<tr><td rowspan="2">Decentralised armed group</td><td>– Individuals under the effective control.</td></tr>
<tr><td>– Military factions under the overall control and authority.</td></tr>
</table>

First, in relation to the attribution based on the conduct of organs and agents, this rule seems applicable to armed groups so far as those members of the group are acting as 'agents' of the organisation. This means that members must have a permanent role in the organisation and have to contribute to the armed activities of the group in a direct or indirect manner. Some indicators that aid in identifying the agents of the group based on this functional approach could be the existence of internal rules, or other indicators such as uniforms, weapons or training provided by the group. Moreover, agents should be identified on a case-by-case approach. On the contrary, there are two limits which need to be acknowledged, namely, ethnic or ideological bounds and sporadic participation in the activities of the group are not enough to prove a link between the member and the group.

Second, agency could be also determined based on the standard of direction and control. In the case of civilians who do not belong to the structures of the group and do not perform any permanent function on its behalf, specific instructions are required to attribute their actions to the group as such. In the case of other armed factions or insurrectional movements associated with the armed group, the standard of control would depend on the type of organisational structure. For centralised armed groups, only the actions of those entities under the command and control of the armed group could potentially be attributed to the group as such. For decentralised groups, the standard should be determined on the basis of the overall control and authority of the leadership over the different sub-groups. Finally, according to the third identified principle, the conduct of armed groups could be also attributed if the group expresses acknowledgment of the specific conduct as its own in a clear and unequivocal way.

CHAPTER V
THE OBLIGATION TO PROVIDE REPARATIONS BY ARMED GROUPS

1. INTRODUCTION

As explained in Chapter 2, reparations are the natural consequences of holding a person or entity responsible, both in domestic legal systems and as a general principle of public international law.[1] In the context of armed conflicts, the obligation to provide reparations has a double legal nature. On the one hand, the provision of reparation is one of the main components of ascribing international responsibility to states and international organisations as stated in the ASR and the ARIO respectively.[2] On the other hand, reparations constitute one of the central elements in the field of transitional justice. In particular, they represent a key element to redress the suffering caused to victims of armed conflict.[3] Moreover, reparations can comprise a wide range of measures that go beyond mere financial compensation.

Taking into account the predominantly non-international nature of armed conflicts and the fact that armed groups represent half of the participants involved in these armed conflicts, it would appear logical to address the obligation to provide reparations not only by the state but also by armed groups, as their counterparts. In this sense, some authors have noted that the state-centric system is insufficient in addressing the complex reality of atrocities where different actors are involved.[4] From the point of view of the victim, the suffering caused by IHL violations and the necessity to address their needs remains the same whether the perpetrator is a state or a non-state actor. Furthermore, there could be certain aspects of the reparations that are insufficiently covered by the compensation provided by the state and may require the participation of other non-state entities.[5] According to Dudai, 'overlooking the question of reparations

---

1 I. Brownlie, *Principles of Public International Law* (Oxford University Press 2003) 420–421.

2 See Part Two of the ASR on the content of the international responsbility of a state and Part Three of the ARIO on the content on the international responsibility of an international organisation.

3 See N. Roht-Arriaza, 'Reparations in International Law and Practice' in M. C. Bassiouni (ed) *The Pursuit of International Criminal Justice: A World Study on Conflicts, Victimization, and Post-Conflict Justice* (Intersentia 2010) 655–698.

4 L. Moffett, 'Transitional Justice and Reparations: Remedying the Past?' in C. Lawther, L. Moffett & D. Jacobs (eds) *Research Handbook on Transitional Justice* (Edward Elgar Publishing 2017) 377–400.

5 N. Carrillo-Santarelli, *Direct International Human Rights Obligations of Non-state Actors*, 367.

from armed groups is a major omission, which could leave victims of abuses by armed groups unable to achieve the redress that they seek'.[6]

Nevertheless, the issue of reparations from armed groups presents a series of difficulties. Firstly, some armed groups may not have the material or financial means to provide reparations, nor the political will to do so. In this respect, the International Centre for Transitional Justice has affirmed that 'it is usually not feasible to hold armed groups, whether pro or anti-government, directly accountable for reparations'.[7] Furthermore, armed groups could cease to exist altogether after the armed conflict. In terms of procedure, there is no institutionalised mechanism or forum for victims to claim reparations against armed groups.[8] Notwithstanding these realities, there appears to be a growing practice supporting the obligation of armed groups to provide reparation, as established in some UN reports and peace agreements. Moreover, there have been examples of armed groups committing to provide reparation to victims. In this regard, as Heffes and Frenkel point out, '[r]eparations are an essential element in remedying breaches of international law. Taking NSAGs' practice into account can help to solve both theoretical and practical problems, mostly regarding the lack of formal rules'.[9]

Against this background, this chapter aims to answer the fourth sub-question of this study, namely, 'can the armed group be under an obligation to provide reparations to victims?'. To address this question, this chapter will firstly consider the notion of reparations and then assess the current legal framework regarding reparations for violations committed in armed conflicts, including international humanitarian law, international human rights law, international criminal law and domestic legal systems. The purpose of this exercise is to evaluate whether international treaties, state practice, and the reports from UN monitoring mechanisms have recognised a role for non-state armed groups in the provision of reparations. Secondly, the chapter will look at the practice of armed groups committing to provide certain forms of reparation through peace agreements, unilateral declarations, and codes of conduct. This practice will be also assessed in relation to its normative value and its possible contribution to customary international law. Thirdly, the obligation to provide reparations by armed groups will be explored as a proposal for the progressive development of international law taking into account its possible legal basis. This part will include the exploration of different forms of reparations that could be provided by armed groups as well as possible enforcement mechanisms to incorporate them. In any case, this potential contribution has to be seen in conjunction with the primary efforts carried out by the state. The central objective of this chapter is to evaluate whether the developments in the practice of states and armed

---

6 R. Dudai, 'Closing the Gap: Symbolic Reparations and Armed Groups' (2011) 93 *International Review of the Red Cross* 883, 783–808, at 785 (hereafter R. Dudai. 'Closing the gap').

7 International Centre for Transitional Justice, 'Providing Meaningful Reparations to Victims – Briefing' (December 2009) 2.

8 R. Dudai. 'Closing the gap', 786.

9 E. Heffes & B. E. Frenkel, 'The International Responsibility of Non-State Armed Groups: In Search of the Applicable Rules' (2017) 8 *Goettingen Journal of International Law*, 69.

groups and the additional materials provided by UN monitoring mechanisms could be considered as contributing to customary international law or whether this practice can be used to interpret and clarify an emerging obligation to provide reparations by armed groups.

2. THE NOTION AND FUNCTION OF REPARATIONS IN INTERNATIONAL LAW

The obligation to provide reparation is the classic consequence of the commission of an internationally wrongful act. Already in 1928, the PCIJ in the *Factory at Chorzów* case held that it is 'a principle of international law, and even a general conception of law, that any breach of an engagement involves an obligation to make reparation'.[10] Ferstman has defined reparations in international law as follows:

> Reparation refers to the process and result of remedying the damage or harm caused by an unlawful act. The purpose of reparation is generally understood to reestablish the situation that existed before the harm occurred. It can also serve as a measure to end ongoing breaches and to deter future ones, as a vehicle for reconciliation or to restore relations between the violator and injured parties, as well as a basis to repair or rehabilitate physical and psychological integrity and dignity. In international law, a breach of an international obligation gives rise to a duty to repair the harm caused.[11]

She describes reparation as a comprehensive notion. In this sense, reparation has the main purpose of remedying the damage caused when a violation of an international obligation has occurred. Consequently, responsibility and reparations are intrinsically linked. But reparations can also contribute to reconciliation and rehabilitation. This is particularly relevant in the context of armed conflict and post-conflict situations. As noted by Roht-Arriaza, post-armed conflict or post-dictatorship situations require 'a unique combination of measures of accountability'.[12] In this area, reparations have been considered an important component in the reports of truth and reconciliation commissions and in peace agreements.[13] In particular, in transitional justice contexts as was the case in Germany, Chile and Argentina, a series of administrative reparation programmes were established for massive coverage of victims.[14] Administrative

---

10 *Case concerning the Factory of Chorzóv* (Germany v. Poland) (Merits) PCIJ Report Series A No 17 (13 September 1928) 29.

11 C. Ferstman, 'Reparations' in Oxford Bibliographies (13 June 2017) available at <www.oxfordbibliographies.com/view/document/obo-9780199796953/obo-9780199796953-0003.xml> accessed 10 June 2019.

12 N. Roht-Arriaza, *supra note* 3, 655.

13 See the study of reparations in Truth Commissions conducted by Evans in C. Evans, *The Right of Reparation in International Law for Victims of Armed Conflict* (Cambridge University Press 2012) (hereafter C. Evans, *The Right to Reparation*).

14 N. Roht-Arriaza, *supra note* 3, 663–681.

reparation programmes are processes used by states to provide reparation to a large number of victims of gross violations of international human rights law and/or serious violations of international humanitarian law. As De Greiff affirms 'here "reparations" refers to the attempts to provide benefits directly to the victims of certain types of crimes'.[15]

The notion of reparations is often used synonymously with compensation implying monetary awards. This was the case of the so-called 'war reparations' which referred to the 'payments and other transfers of resources imposed, at the end of an armed conflict [...], in particular under peace treaties or similar arrangements'.[16] However, reparations can take several different forms. According to the ASR and the ARIO, reparations comprise different measures, such as restitution, compensation and satisfaction.[17] Restitution means the reestablishment of the situation to its original state. Compensation refers to those measures that seek to alleviate the harm suffered and usually contain payments and other financial procedures. Satisfaction generally consists of the acknowledgement of the breach, public disclosure of the truth or the expression of formal apologies. As explained by the ILC, the provision of 'full reparation' may require a combination of different forms of reparations depending on the circumstances.[18] Moreover, alongside reparations, the ASR and ARIO contain a further provision relating to cessation and guarantees of non-repetition.[19] Unlike the aforementioned components of reparation, guarantees of non-repetition have a preventive function and serve as future reinforcement of the obligations imposed.

In the context of reparations, one of the most important developments has been the UN Basic Principles and Guidelines on the right to a remedy and reparation for victims of gross violations of International Human Rights Law and serious violations of International Humanitarian Law (UNBPG) adopted by consensus in 2005 by the UN General Assembly.[20] The UNBPG follow a 'victim-based' approach and recognise the victim's right to equal and effective access to justice; adequate, effective and prompt reparation for harm suffered; and access to relevant information concerning violations and reparation mechanisms. In addition to restitution, compensation, satisfaction and guarantees of non-repetition, the UNBPG adds 'rehabilitation' as an additional component of reparation. Rehabilitation refers to those measures that provide 'medical

15 P. De Greiff, 'Justice and Reparations' in P. De Greiff (ed), *The Handbook of Reparations* (Oxford University Press 2008) 453.

16 M. Wood, 'The Rights of Victims to Reparation: The Importance of Clear Thinking' in A. Peters and C. Marxsen (eds) *Reparation for Victims of Armed Conflict: Impulses from the Max Planck Trialogues* (2018) MPIL Research Paper Series, No. 2018–19, 23.

17 Art. 34 ASR; Art. 34 ARIO.

18 Art. 34 ASR, Commentary para. 2.

19 Art. 30 ASR; Art. 30 ARIO.

20 Resolution 60/147 on Basic Principles and Guidelines on the Right to a Remedy and Reparation for Victims of Gross Violations of International Human Rights Law and Serious Violations of International Humanitarian Law adopted and proclaimed by the UN General Assembly on 16 December 2005.

and psychological care as well as legal and social services'.[21] The UNBPG will be further analysed in the following section.

From the above discussion, it is possible to highlight three aspects of reparations that will be relevant for this inquiry. First, the obligation to provide reparations constitutes a general principle of international law when a violation of an international obligation has been committed. Second, reparations have acquired a greater role in the context of armed conflict and post-conflict situations as a measure to alleviate the suffering of victims of human rights and humanitarian law violations. And finally, it is essential to understand that reparations do not only comprise a financial element but also encompasses a series of measures which should address the different needs of victims as well as incorporate a preventive function for the deterrence of future violations.

3. CURRENT LEGAL FRAMEWORK OF REPARATIONS FOR VIOLATIONS COMMITTED IN ARMED CONFLICT

The obligation to provide reparations has its legal basis in domestic tort law and in the law of state responsibility.[22] In international law, reparations were traditionally owed to injured states by other states responsible for breaching an international obligation. By analogy with the ASR, the ARIO also considered international organisations as duty bearers of reparations in the case of the commission of an internationally wrongful act. With the development and growth of international human rights law, individuals have also been entitled to reparations as a result of the actions and omissions of the state. In particular, the jurisprudence of the Inter-American Court of Human Rights has made significant efforts regarding the right to reparations of individuals.[23] In addition, the adoption of the Rome Statute of the International Criminal Court establishes that individuals can also be held responsible to provide reparations to victims of international crimes, when they are prosecuted both in their capacity as state agents and as members of armed groups.[24] In this light, the paradigm of inter-state reparations has been transformed and consequently new duty-bearers and right holders have been incorporated. Particularly, the duty-bearers of the obligation to provide reparation has evolved from considering the state as the only responsible entity to include individuals and international organisations.

Despite this evolution towards a more comprehensive obligation to provide reparations and the development of victim's rights, little attention has been paid to

---

21 UNBPG, Principle 21.

22 N. Roht-Arriaza, *supra note* 3, 657.

23 See C. Evans, *The Right to Reparation*, 66–76. On collective reparations see D. Odier-Contreras Garduno, *Collective reparations: Tensions and Dilemmas Between Collective Reparations with the Individual Right to Receive Reparations* (Intersentia 2018) 121–174.

24 See Art.75(2) Rome Statute and section 5.3.3. of this chapter.

the possibility of incorporating armed groups as duty-holders of this obligation.[25] As Moffett rightly notes, there is still a disconnection between the prevalence of non-international armed conflicts and the abuses committed by those groups, on the one hand, and the lack of interest in regulating their responsibility for reparations, on the other.[26] With that in mind, the following section provides an overview of reparation provisions in the context of armed conflict, looking at the fields of IHL, IHRL, ICL, as well as relevant examples from domestic law. The aim of this mapping exercise is to evaluate whether international treaties, state practice, and the reports from UN monitoring mechanisms have recognised any potential role of non-state armed groups in the provision of reparations.

3.1. INTERNATIONAL HUMANITARIAN LAW

Under IHL, the first provision relating to reparations was introduced by Article 3 of the 1907 Hague Convention (IV) on the Laws and Customs of War on Land which established the obligation of the belligerent party to pay compensation in case of violations of the regulations. This provision was then transposed with a similar wording to Article 91 of Additional Protocol I of the Geneva Conventions regarding international armed conflicts. Moreover, Article 3 of the Protocol to the 1954 Convention for the Protection of Cultural Property in the Event of Armed Conflict referred to restitution, specifically the return of unlawfully taken property. In principle, reparations were meant to be claimed by states against other states in the framework of an international armed conflict.[27] Kalshoven and Greenwood made significant contributions to the interpretation of Article 91 based on the *travaux préparatoires* of the 1907 Hague Convention IV. They clarified that this provision was not only aimed at dealing with inter-state claims but also with the rights of individuals to compensation for the damage caused.[28] In particular, Kalshoven explained that:

---

25 P. Blázquez Rodríguez, 'Does an Armed Group have an Obligation to Provide Reparations to Victims? Construing an Obligation to Provide Reparations for Violations of International Humanitarian Law' in J. Summers & A. Gough (eds) *Non-state actors and International Obligations. Creation, Evolution and Enforcement* (Brill Nijhoff 2018) 407 (hereafter P. Blázquez Rodríguez, 'Does an armed group have an obligation to provide reparations to victims?').

26 L. Moffett 'Beyond Attribution: Responsibility of Armed Non-State Actors for Reparations in Northern Ireland, Colombia and Uganda' in N. Gal-or, C. Ryngaert & M. Noortmann, *Responsibilities of the Non-State Actor in Armed Conflict and the Market Place: Theoretical Considerations and Empirical Findings* (Brill Nijhoff 2015) 323 (heareafter L. Moffett, 'Beyond Attribution').

27 J. P. Pérez-León Acevedo, 'Las Reparaciones en el Derecho Internacional de los Derechos Humanos, Derecho Internacional Humanitario y Derecho Penal Internacional' (2008) 23 *American University International Law Review* 1, 16–17.

28 See C. Greenwood, 'International Humanitarian Law', in F. Kalshoven (ed), *The Centennial of the First International Peace Conference* (Kluwer Law 2000) 250. F. Kalshoven, 'State Responsibility for Warlike Acts of the Armed Forces' (1991) 40 *International and Comparative Law Quarterly* 4, 827–858, at 830–832.

> The records of the conference that adopted the text, i.e. the Second Hague Peace Conference 1907, provide convincing evidence that the delegates sought not so much to lay down a rule relating to the international responsibility of one State vis-a-vis another, as one relating to a State's liability to compensate the losses of individual persons incurred as a consequence of their direct (and harmful) contact with its armed forces.[29]

The 2005 ICRC study on customary IHL has also distinguished between reparations sought by states and reparations sought directly by individuals. In this regard, in the framework of international armed conflicts, reparations for IHL violations have been provided directly to individuals through different procedures: mechanisms set up by inter-state agreements, unilateral state acts such as national legislation, and reparation sought by individuals directly before national courts.[30] In international fora, there have been several examples of compensation awards, such as those awarded by the UN Compensation Commission (1991) to former prisoners of war held by Iraq who were subjected to ill-treatment in violation of the Third Geneva Convention[31]; and the Eritrea-Ethiopia Claims Commission (2000) which was mandated 'to decide through binding arbitration all claims for loss, damage or injury by one Government against the other, and by nationals (including both natural and juridical persons) of one party against the Government of the other party or entities owned or controlled by the other party [...]'.[32]

In relation to NIACs, no similar provision was established in Common Article 3 nor in Additional Protocol II. According to Evans, 'this illustrates a major lacuna in international humanitarian law'.[33] However, the ICRC has specifically affirmed in its 2005 study on customary IHL that state responsibility for reparations has become established as a customary norm both in international and non-international armed conflicts.[34] In this sense, there have been some mechanisms in the framework of NIACs involving claims against states, such as the Agreement on Refugees and Displaced Persons annexed to the Dayton Accords (1995), which established the Commission for Real Property Claims of Displaced Persons and Refugees in Bosnia and Herzegovina[35]; and the Housing and Property Claims Commission in Kosovo (1999).[36] However, with regard to claims against non-state armed groups as counterparties to states in NIACs, the ICRC has noted the uncertainties in relation to these actors, explaining in Rule 150 that:

---

29 F. Kalshoven, *supra note* 28, 830.

30 J. M. Henckaerts & L. Doswald-Beck, *Customary International Humanitarian Law*, 541.

31 United Nations Compensation Commission (UNCC), 'Report and Recommendations made by the Panel of Commissioners concerning Part One of the Second Instalment of Claims for Serious Personal Injury or Death' (15 December 1994) UN Doc. S/AC.26/1999/4.

32 *Eritrea-Ethiopia Claims Commission – Partial Award: Prisoners of War – Ethiopia's Claim 4*; and *Eritrea-Ethiopia Claims Commission – Partial Award: Prisoners of War – Eritrea's Claim 17*, Reports of International Arbitral Awards, Volume XXVI (1 July 2003).

33 C. Evans, *The Right to Reparation*, 31.

34 J. M. Henckaerts & L. Doswald-Beck, *Customary International Humanitarian Law*, 545.

35 Agreement on Refugees and Displaced Persons annexed to the Dayton Accords, Article XI.

36 UNMIK Regulation No. 2000/60, Section 2(2).

> Even if it can be argued that armed opposition groups incur responsibility for acts committed by persons forming part of such groups, the consequences of such responsibility are not clear. In particular, it is unclear to what extent armed opposition groups are under an obligation to make full reparation, even though in many countries victims can bring a civil suit for damages against the offenders.[37]

Notwithstanding these uncertainties, several authors have recognised the obligation to make reparations as a natural consequence of the violation of IHL rules by organised armed groups. Sassòli claims that whenever there is responsibility of the armed group, that group must cease the violation and provide reparations for the injury, in a similar way to a state 'for reasons of pure legal logic'.[38] Likewise, Blázquez Rodríguez argues that the notion of inter-state reparation could be transposed to the relationship between armed opposition groups and individual victims 'who suffered under their unlawful actions'.[39] In fact, the ICRC study has referred to some practice of the United Nations which supported the obligation of armed opposition groups to provide reparation in the late 1990s. Particularly, the ICRC acknowledged three examples:

- The UN Security Council Resolution on Liberia adopted in 1996 called upon 'the leaders of the factions to ensure the immediate return of looted property'.[40]
- The resolution on Afghanistan adopted in 1998 by the UN Commission on Human Rights urged 'all the Afghan parties' to provide effective remedies to the victims of violations of human rights and humanitarian law.[41]
- The 1998 Report of the UN Secretary-General on the causes of conflict and the promotion of durable peace and sustainable development in Africa recommended that 'in order to make warring parties more accountable for their actions [...] international legal machinery be developed to facilitate efforts to find, attach and seize the assets of transgressing parties and their leaders'.[42]

These documents refer to restitution of properties, the provision of effective remedies in general, and financial compensation through the seizure of assets, imposed on the parties to the armed conflict, including states as well as non-state entities. In fact, some recent initiatives appear to go in the same direction by including non-state armed groups in the provision of reparation to victims of IHL and human rights violations. These examples correspond to soft law instruments, such as the UNBPG, the Nairobi declaration on Women's and Girls' Right to a Remedy and Reparation; the Declaration

37 J. M. Henckaerts & L. Doswald-Beck, *Customary International Humanitarian Law*, 550.
38 M. Sassòli, 'Taking Armed Groups Seriously', 43.
39 P. Blázquez Rodríguez, 'Does an armed group have an obligation to provide reparations to victims?' 410.
40 UN Security Council Resolution 1071 (1996) (30 August 1996) para. 8.
41 UN Commission on Human Rights, Resolution 1998/70 on the Situation of Human Rights in Afghanistan, U.N. Doc. E/CN.4/1998/70 (1998), para. 5(d).
42 UN Secretary-General, Report on the Causes of Conflict and the Promotion of Durable Peace and Sustainable Development in Africa (13 April 1998) A/52/871 – S/1998/318, para. 50.

adopted by the International Law Association (ILA) on the issue of Reparations for Victims of Armed Conflict; the reports of UN Commissions of Inquiry and other monitoring mechanisms; and more recently, the 2018 Report on Armed Non-State Actors by the UN Special Rapporteur on extrajudicial, summary or arbitrary killings. These materials and their normative significance are further analysed in the following sections.

3.1.1. *UN Basic Principles and Guidelines on the right to a remedy and reparation for victims of gross violations of International Human Rights Law and serious violations of International Humanitarian Law (UNBPG)*

As explained in its preamble, the UNBPG were not aimed at creating new international obligations but to 'identify mechanisms, modalities, procedures and methods for the implementation of existing legal obligations under international human rights law and international humanitarian law'.[43] The UNBPG refer to both 'gross violations of international human rights law' and 'serious violations of international humanitarian law'. In this context, Bassiouni notes that the principles 'attempted to create a bridge between International Human Rights and Humanitarian Law, because for victims it would be artificial and counterproductive to make separations on the basis of legal definitions'.[44] As for the duty-bearers of the obligation to provide reparation, Principle 15 establishes that:

> '[i]n cases where *a person, a legal person, or other entity* is found liable for reparation to a victim, such party should provide reparation to the victim or compensate the State if the State has already provided reparation to the victim'.[45]

Additionally, Principle 3 affirms the right to equal and effective access to justice 'irrespective of who may ultimately be the bearer of responsibility'.[46] Most authors have interpreted these provisions as the legal basis for the obligation of non-state armed groups to provide reparations to victims.[47] In particular, Van Boven, one of the promotors of the Principles, explained the role of non-state actors in relation to their responsibility towards victims of these violations:

> While the Principles and Guidelines are drawn up on the basis of State responsibility, the issue of responsibility of non-State actors was also raised in the discussions and negotiations, notably insofar as movements or groups exercise effective control over a certain territory and people in that territory, but also with regard to business enterprises exercising economic

43 UNBPG, Preamble, para. 7.

44 M. C. Bassiouni, *International Criminal Law, Volume III: International Enforcement* (3rd ed, Martinus Nijhoff 2008) 673.

45 UNBPG, Principle 15, emphasis added.

46 UNBPG, Principle 3(c).

47 See L. Moffett, 'Beyond Attribution', 331; P. Blázquez Rodríguez, 'Does an armed group have an obligation to provide reparations to victims?', 409.

> power. *It was generally felt that non-State actors are to be held responsible for their policies and practices, allowing victims to seek redress and reparation on the basis of legal liability and human solidarity, and not on the basis of State responsibility.* The Principles and Guidelines provide for equal and effective access to justice, "irrespective of who may ultimately be the bearer of responsibility for the violation" (principle 3 (c)). In this connection reference is also made to the following provision: "In cases where a person, a legal person, or other entity is found liable for reparation to a victim, such party should provide reparation to the victim or compensate the State if the State has already provided reparation to the victim" (principle 15, last sentence). It is a victim-oriented perspective that was kept in mind in extending, albeit in a modest and cautious way, the scope of the Principles and Guidelines *to include the responsibility and liability of non-State actors.*[48]

Here, Van Boven emphasises 'legal liability' of non-state actors and 'human solidarity' as the basis for the duty of non-state actors (including armed groups and corporations) to provide redress to victims. In a similar vein, Carrillo-Santarelli focuses on the victim-oriented approach of the principles and the right of victims to be 'fully' repaired to justify the necessity of non-state participation in the reparation process indicating that 'it would be unfair, discriminatory and unreasonable to argue that victims can only be protected if a State is responsible'.[49] Consequently, although mainly focused on states as the duty bearers of the provision of reparations, the UNBPG acknowledge the potential participation of 'other entities' in the provision of redress to victims. According to Moffett, the UNBPG reflect an emerging customary practice of states and international bodies. He explains that:

> The thinking behind the UNBPG is not void of international practice, but reflects the growing customary practice by States as well as international and regional bodies, such as the reparation provisions within the Rome Statute and the jurisprudence of the regional human rights courts.[50]

In fact, despite being a non-binding instrument, the UNBPG have been applied by truth commissions, referred to in the jurisprudence of different human rights bodies and have also been included in several legal instruments.[51] For instance, the Sierra Leone Truth Commission cited the UNBPG, even in their draft form at that time, and indicated that the principles were 'indicative of the current status of international law of the right to redress of victims of such violations'.[52] The final report of the Timor-Leste Commission for Reception, Truth and Reconciliation also endorsed the UNBPG as an applicable

48 T. Van Boven, 'The United Nations Basic Principles and Guidelines on the Right to a Remedy and Reparation for Victims of Gross Violations of International Human Rights Law and Serious Violations of International Humanitarian Law', *United Nations Audiovisual Library of International Law* (2010) 3, emphasis added.

49 N. Carrillo-Santarelli, *Direct international human rights obligations of non-state actors*, 371–372.

50 L. Moffett, 'Beyond Attribution', 331.

51 See C. Evans, *The Right to Reparation*, 127.

52 Sierra Leone Truth Commission Final Report, Vol. 2, Ch. 4, Reparations, para. 19.

international standard for reparations.[53] Moreover, some commentators have noted that the Principles have served to generate new behavior on remedy and reparations at the domestic and international level, and have also helped treaty monitoring bodies to engage with reparation as part of their mandates.[54] For instance, the UNBPG were considered as inspiration for the incorporation of the right to reparation in Article 26 of the UN Convention for the Protection of All Persons from Enforced Disappearances (2006).[55] They also played an important role in the discussions of the principles on reparation in the *Lubanga* case.[56] In addition, the UNBPG were cited by the UN Committee against Torture which indicated that '[t]he Committee recognizes the elements of full redress under international law and practice as outlined in the Basic Principles and Guidelines [...]'.[57] At the national level, the UNBPG have had an impact on the Colombian domestic legislation on Victims and Land Restitution Law and also on the decisions of the Colombian Constitutional Court.[58] In this respect, Evans has indicated that '[t]he recognition of the Basic Principles on the Right to Reparation for Victims in domestic legislation is significant as it indicates support for this norm and acceptance of a comprehensive concept of reparations'.[59]

Importantly, the UNBPG were adopted by consensus in the UN General Assembly.[60] In principle, in accordance with the findings of the ILC on the issue of customary international law and in particular on the role played by the resolutions adopted by international organisations, one must be cautious about ascribing normative value to a given resolution of the UN General Assembly.[61] Specifically, the ILC has noted that 'the General Assembly is a political organ in which it is often far from clear that their acts carry juridical significance'.[62] However, according to Boyle and Chinkin:

> The degree of support is significant. A resolution adopted by consensus or by unanimous vote will necessarily carry more weight than one supported only by a two-thirds majority

53 'Chega! Final report of the Timor-Leste Commission for Reception, Truth and Reconciliation', Vol. I (November 2013), at 2685.

54 C. Sandoval, 'The Legal Standing and Significance of the Basic Principles and Guidelines on the Right to a Remedy and Reparation' in A. Peters and C. Marxsen (eds) *Reparation for Victims of Armed Conflict: Impulses from the Max Planck Trialogues*, MPIL Research Paper Series, No. 2018-19 (2018), p. 46.

55 *Ibid*, 46.

56 *Prosecutor v. Thomas Lubanga Dyilo* (Trial Chamber I) ICC, No. ICC-01/04-01/06 (7 August 2012) paras. 21, 27, 85, 185.

57 UN Committee against Torture, 'General Comment no. 3: Implementation of Article 14 by States parties' (13 December 2012) CAT/C/GC/3, para. 6.

58 Ley de Victimas y Restitucion de tierras, Ley 1448/2011; Constitutional Court, C- 330/16, Magistrate: Maria Victoria Calle Correa, 23.6.2016, paras. 54.2 and 58.

59 C. Evans, *The Right to Reparation*, 222.

60 Resolution 60/147 on Basic Principles and Guidelines on the Right to a Remedy and Reparation for Victims of Gross Violations of International Human Rights Law and Serious Violations of International Humanitarian Law adopted and proclaimed by the UN General Assembly on 16 December 2005. No State voted against but there were 13 abstentions.

61 Third Report on Identification of Customary International Law by Mr. Michael Wood, Special Rapporteur (27 March 2015) UN A/CN.4/682, paras. 47-48.

62 *Ibid*, para. 47.

of states. Resolutions opposed by even a thirds majority of states. Resolutions opposed by even a small number of states may have little effect if those states are among the ones most immediately affected.[63]

In the case of the UNBPG, the fact that the resolution was adopted with no opposition by states reflects an implied acceptance of the validity of the norm. Moreover, the essential role of the UNBPG was to provide impetus for the further development of state practice and the practice of international organisations. As explained by the ILC, resolutions can be relevant because they may 'exert a strong influence on the development of international customary law'.[64]

3.1.2. The ILA Committee on the issue of Reparations for Victims of Armed Conflict

In May 2003 the ILA established a Committee with the mandate of conducting a general survey of theories and practices relating to compensation for victims of war.[65] After the Rio de Janeiro Conference in 2008, the Committee was renamed to the 'Committee on Reparation for Victims of Armed Conflict'. The ILA Committee decided to draw up two declarations, dividing its task into substantive issues, on the one hand, and procedural issues, on the other. These documents reflect international law as it is progressively developing or as it should be, that is, proposals were made *de lege ferenda*.[66] In 2010, the ILA Committee adopted Resolution No. 2/2010 on the International Law Principles on Reparation for Victims of Armed Conflict addressing the substantive issues. In this resolution, the Committee proposed, in Article 5(2), that '[r]esponsible parties may also include non-State actors other than International Organisations responsible for a violation of rules of international law applicable in armed conflict'.[67] According to the commentary to this article, '[t]he Committee recognizes the possibility that non-State actors are already liable to pay reparation for violations of the law of armed conflict. It strongly encourages the further development of a regime of responsibility for such actors'.[68] It further clarified that '[a] regime of responsibility for non-State actors shall not be interpreted as an acknowledgement of their legitimacy or lawfulness'.[69] The ILA

63 See A. Boyle and C. Chinkin, *The Making of International Law* (Oxford University Press 2007) 226, cited by the ILC, *supra note* 61, at 35.

64 ILC, *supra note* 61, para. 52.

65 See International Law Association, 'Reparation for Victims of Armed Conflict' (2003–2014) available at <www.ila-hq.org/index.php/committees> accessed 15 June 2019.

66 See R. Hofmann, 'The 2010 International Law Association Declaration of International Law Principles on Reparation for Victims of Armed Conflict' in A. Peters and C. Marxsen (eds) *Reparation for Victims of Armed Conflict: Impulses from the Max Planck Trialogues*, MPIL Research Paper Series, No. 2018–19 (2018) 32.

67 International Law Association, Committee on Reparation for Victims of Armed Conflict, Resolution 2/2010 on International Law Principles on Reparation for Victims of Armed Conflict (Substantive Issues) (15–20 August 2010) Art. 5(2).

68 International Law Association, Committee on Reparation for Victims of Armed Conflict, 'The Hague Conference Report: Reparation for Victims of Armed Conflict' (Substantive Issues) (2010), 13.

69 *Ibid*, 13.

acknowledged the emergence of a secondary obligation to make reparation on behalf of non-state actors based on Article 75 of the Rome Statute, the UNBPG and the 2005 Report of the International Commission of Inquiry on Darfur.[70]

In addition, the ILA Committee on Non-state Actors published a report on the obligations and responsibility of non-state actors in 2014. In this report, the ILA took note of the practice of some armed opposition groups (AOG) voluntarily committing themselves to provide reparations to victims and considered reparations as 'desirable consequences of a finding of AOG responsibility'.[71] Although questioning the type of responsibility regime that should be applicable to armed groups, the Committee also suggested that compensation, and in particular, an international indemnity fund composed of blocked assets could be contemplated as a form of reparation for victims.[72] As indicated in Chapter 3, there are additional sources to the traditional sources of international law which can help in clarifying and interpreting international norms. The reports submitted by the ILA can be assimilated to the opinion of highly reputed jurists and therefore, they could constitute supplementary sources of interpretation in relation to the question of reparations by non-state armed groups.

3.1.3. *The Nairobi declaration on Women's and Girls' Right to a Remedy and Reparation*

The Nairobi declaration on Women's and Girls' Right to a Remedy and Reparation was adopted in 2007 by civil society organisations including, among others, the Coalition on Women's Human Rights in Conflict Situations, Urgent Action Fund-Africa, and Rights and Democracy. The innovative element of this declaration is the idea of redefining reparation from a gender perspective. The Declaration briefly considers the responsibility of armed groups and other actors in relation to reparation programmes indicating that:

> The fundamental nature of the struggle against impunity demands that *all reparation programmes must address the responsibility of all actors*, including state actors, foreign governments and inter-governmental bodies, non-governmental actors, such as *armed groups*, multinational companies and individual prospectors and investors.[73]

Although the Declaration considers national governments as bearing the primary responsibility to provide remedy and reparations to victims, it also follows the same philosophy of the UNBPG by including all actors involved as participants of the reparation process. Therefore, the Declaration understands that both states and non-

---

70 The 2005 Report of the International Commission of Inquiry on Darfur and Art. 75 of the Rome Statute will be explored in the following sections.

71 International Law Association Committee on Non-State Actors, 'Third report on the Obligations and Responsibility of Non-State Actors in International Law' (Washington Conference 2014) 10.

72 *Ibid*, 11.

73 Nairobi declaration on Women's and Girls' Right to a Remedy and Reparation, Nairobi, 19–21 March 2007, Preamble, para. 5, emphasis added.

state entities should contribute to reparation efforts. As for its legal value, as a soft-law instrument it is considered a non-binding document. However, it can be seen as an instrument that further develops and improves the content of the UNBPG. As indicated by Couillard '[w]hilst the Nairobi Declaration is in line with the Basic Principles, it further develops certain aspects of the theory of reparation and presents a number of innovative points'.[74] She notes that one of the common elements between the UNBPG and the Declaration is that both instruments include assertions on the need 'to cover crimes committed by any type of actor'.[75] Consequently, the Declaration could serve as a complementary development of the UNBPG by keeping the focus on the necessity to include all relevant actors in the provision of reparation to victims, including armed groups.

3.1.4. UN Commissions of Inquiry and other monitoring mechanisms

The reports of UN Commissions of Inquiry and other monitoring mechanisms have also acknowledged the potential role of armed groups in the provision of redress and reparations to victims of armed conflict. In 1993, the Truth Commission for El Salvador mandated the FMLN to provide compensation to victims in those cases where it was found to have been responsible.[76] On this matter, the Truth Commission directly linked the responsibility of the FMLN for their IHL and human rights violations to the necessity to compensate those victims. Likewise, the UN Commission of Inquiry on Darfur explicitly established the obligation of armed groups to pay compensation to victims in parallel with the obligation of the Sudanese State, explaining that:

> It is in light of this international legal regulation that the obligation of the Sudan to pay compensation for all the crimes perpetrated in Darfur by its agents and officials or de facto organs must be seen. *A similar obligation is incumbent upon rebels* for all crimes they may have committed, whether or not the perpetrators are identified and punished.[77]

According to some authors, this statement clearly foresaw the application of reparation duties to armed groups.[78] In particular, the Commission established the responsibility of the armed groups regardless of whether the individual perpetrators were found and subsequently punished. Moreover, the Commission determined the creation of a Trust Fund based on international voluntary contributions to offer compensation to

---

74 V. Couillard, 'The Nairobi Declaration: Redefining Reparations for Women Victims of Sexual Violence' (2007) 1 *The International Journal of Transitional Justice*, 444–453, at 449.

75 *Ibid*, 449.

76 UN Security Council, 'From Madness to Hope: the 12-year war in El Salvador: Report of the Commission on the Truth for El Salvador' (1993) Annex, S/25500, 177.

77 Report of the International Commission of Inquiry on Darfur to the United Nations Secretary-General, Pursuant to Security Council Resolution 1564 of 18 September 2004 (25 January 2005) para. 600, emphasis added.

78 R. Dudai, 'Closing the gap', 791.

the victims of violations committed by rebels.[79] In the armed conflict in Gaza, the 2009 Report of the UN Fact-Finding Mission noted that the Palestinian Authority had contributed to a compensation package to Palestinian farmers for property damaged during the military operations in Gaza.[80] In addition, the Panel of Experts on Accountability in Sri Lanka also suggested that 'funds acquired by the LTTE from the diaspora and elsewhere, and which still exist, should be secured for the purpose of making reparations to those in the Sri Lanka Tamil community who were victims in the conflict'.[81] More recently, the Commission of Inquiry in Syria recommended that armed groups provide 'effective redress for victims based on international standards'.[82]

While in the case of the FMLN in El Salvador and the rebel groups in Darfur the obligation to provide reparation was based on the legal responsibility of the armed group as a collectivity for the violations of IHL, in the remaining cases the legal basis was not specifically linked to the violations committed by the group. The statements in relation to the non-state armed groups or *de facto* entities in Gaza, Syria and Sri Lanka refer to victims of the conflict rather than victims of concrete violations committed by the armed group. In any case, these examples show the emergent practice of UN Commissions of Inquiry and Fact-Finding Missions in declaring the necessity of contribution of armed groups in the provision of redress and reparations to victims of non-international armed conflicts, together with the primary obligations of the state. More precisely, there appears to be acceptance towards the contribution to 'compensation' as an adequate form of reparation by armed groups when funds are available. As indicated in Chapter 3, the reports from the UN non-judicial monitoring mechanisms are relevant as they have the endorsement of an international organisation, they offer juridical argumentation about the facts examined, and they are reputed sources as they are generally produced by independent experts.[83] As such, they can be used as relevant sources which help clarify and supplement the interpretation of international law.

3.1.5. 2018 Report on Armed Non-State Actors by the UN Special Rapporteur on extrajudicial, summary or arbitrary killings

In 2018, the UN Special Rapporteur on extrajudicial, summary or arbitrary killings published a report on the protection of the right to life focusing on the role of armed

79 Report of the International Commission of Inquiry on Darfur to the United Nations Secretary-General, Pursuant to Security Council Resolution 1564 of 18 September 2004 (25 January 2005) para. 603.

80 Report of the United Nations Fact-Finding Mission on the Gaza Conflict (25 September 2009) A/HRC/12/48, p. 401, para. 1867.

81 Report of the Secretary General's Panel of Experts on Accountability in Sri Lanka (31 March 2011) p. 114, para. 419.

82 Report of the International Commission of Inquiry on the Syrian Arab Republic (5 February 2013) A/HRC/22/59, para. 177 (d).

83 See section 4.2 of Chapter 3.

non-State actors (ANSAs) as perpetrators of violations against this right.[84] In her report, the Special Rapporteur starts by explaining the existence of a protection gap between the UN framework addressing the actions of ANSAs and the accountability deficits for people affected by violations committed by ANSAs.[85] After analysing the existing framework under IHRL, IHL and ICL, she concludes by noting the limitations and deficits and by offering a series of recommendations to address these challenges. In particular, she recommends connecting the collective responsibility of ANSAs and the legal right to reparation of individuals. She further suggests that transitional justice mechanisms such as Truth and Reconciliation Commissions could serve as a tool to implement the collective responsibility of the ANSA. As regards the type of reparations that could be offered by ANSAs, the Special Rapporteur refers to both financial compensation and symbolic reparations. In relation to financial compensation, she proposes 'the possibility to tie forfeiture of ANSAs assets to peace-process, and/or truth and reconciliation' or 'otherwise, there would need to be a means of seizing, for example, ANSAs-held bank accounts'.[86] As for other forms of reparation, she states that:

> [t]here are examples of successful truth and reconciliation commissions involving ANSAs. When they are the perpetrators of right to life violations, ANSAs should provide reparations. Here, the goal is to find out what happened in order to advance community reckoning with the past and public acknowledgment of harm inflicted on victims. NSAs should also provide public apologies, and contribute to national memorials and commemoration ceremonies.[87]

In this matter, the Special Rapporteur advocates for the provision of symbolic reparations and the contribution to the right to truth by non-state armed groups, including the acknowledgment of facts, the offering of public apologies, and other memorials and official ceremonies. In this sense, reparations could serve to the purpose of reconciliation among the communities that have been victim to the atrocities committed during the armed conflict. Consequently, reparations are seen here as a wider instrument rather than a mere tool for financial compensation. Similarly to the reports by the UN Commissions of Inquiry, reports by UN Special Rapporteurs represent relevant sources of interpretation of international provisions. In this case, the focus is on the right to life, and its protection by different branches of international law such as IHL, IHRL and ICL. The innovative element of this report lies in acknowledging the challenges brought about by ANSAs to the protection to the right to life. As indicated in the paragraph above, the Special Rapporteur claims that '[w]hen they are the perpetrators of right to life violations, ANSAs should provide reparations'.[88] In this

---

84 Report of the Special Rapporteur on Extrajudicial, Summary or Arbitrary Executions on Armed non-State Actors: the Protection of the Right to Life (5 June 2018) UN Doc. A/HRC/38/44.

85 *Ibid*, 4, para. 7.

86 *Ibid*, 19, para. 91.

87 *Ibid*, 19, para. 94.

88 *Ibid*, 19, para. 94.

sense, the Special Rapporteur links the violation of the right to life, both during armed conflict and peace situations, to the secondary obligation of armed groups to provide reparation as a consequence of such responsibility.

3.2. INTERNATIONAL HUMAN RIGHTS LAW

In contrast to IHL where the provisions on reparations are sparse, provisions on reparations have been widely developed under IHRL, both at the universal and the regional level. At the international level, Article 8 of the Universal Declaration of Human Rights and Article 2(3a) of the International Covenant on Civil and Political Rights (ICCPR) provide for the right to an effective remedy of individuals whose rights have been violated. Moreover, Article 9(5) and 14(6) of the ICCPR establish a right to compensation in the case of unlawful arrest or detention and reversed or pardoned conviction, respectively. Other human rights treaties also contain provisions regarding different forms of reparations, including Article 14 of the Convention against Torture, Article 39 of the Convention of the Rights of the Child, Article 6 of the Convention on the Elimination of All Forms of Racial Discrimination, and Article 24(4) of the International Convention for the Protection of All Persons from Enforced Disappearance.

At the regional level, Article 13 of the European Convention on Human Rights (ECHR) contemplates the right to an effective remedy and Article 41 ECHR refers to the possibility of affording just satisfaction if the internal law of the State allows only partial reparation. Under the American Convention on Human Rights (ACHR), the provisions on reparations are found in Article 25 regarding the right to an effective remedy and Article 63 on cessation and fair compensation. On the contrary, the African Charter on Human and People's Rights (ACHPR) does not contain an explicit provision regarding the right to an effective remedy granted to individuals. However, Article 27 of the Protocol to the ACHR on the Establishment of an African Court on Human and People's Rights contains references to the provision of remedies, including the payment of fair compensation or reparation.

Human rights jurisprudence has played a major role in the definition and interpretation of different forms of reparation and the right to an effective remedy. In particular, the jurisprudence of the Inter-American Court of Human Rights has been considered the most progressive due to the wide array of modalities of reparations frequently granted and the mechanisms monitoring their enforcement.[89] In light of the lack of enforcement mechanisms under humanitarian law, some scholars have argued

---

[89] J. P. Pérez-León Acevedo, 'The Situation of Reparations in the Inter-American Human Rights System: Analysis and Comparative Considerations' (2016) 20 *ASIL Insights* 15 available at <https://www.asil.org/insights/volume/20/issue/15/situation-reparations-inter-american-human-rights-system-analysis-and> accessed 12 June 2019.

that violations of IHL could be better addressed through human rights mechanisms.[90] In fact, the Inter-American Commission and Court on Human Rights have applied IHL in the context of individual complaints procedures.[91] For instance, in the well-known *Tablada case*, the Commission affirmed its competence to apply IHL based on the overlap between the substantive norms of the American Convention and the 1949 Geneva Conventions.[92] On this matter, the Commission connected humanitarian law issues with the obligation to provide judicial protection indicating that 'the American Convention itself authorizes the Commission to address questions of humanitarian law in cases involving alleged violations of Article 25 [on the right to an effective remedy]'.[93]

Nevertheless, the jurisprudence of human rights bodies has focused mainly on the obligation to provide reparation on behalf of states as parties to human rights treaties and the main holders of human rights obligations. The position of non-state armed groups under these international human rights frameworks regarding reparations remains unclear.[94] This is in part due to the uncertainties regarding the scope of primary human rights obligations of armed groups. States can nevertheless regulate the actions of such groups through the exercise of their domestic civil and criminal law systems, as it will be explained in section 3.4 on domestic remedies.

3.3. INTERNATIONAL CRIMINAL LAW

The question of reparation to victims of armed conflict has traditionally fallen outside the scope of international criminal law. International criminal tribunals have been mainly concerned with the prosecution and punishment of perpetrators, and not so much with how the harm caused by international crimes might be repaired.[95] The Statutes of the Nuremberg and Tokyo Tribunals did not establish any provision on reparations to victims. Likewise, the *ad hoc* tribunals for Rwanda and former Yugoslavia were not authorised to grant remedies to individual victims. The statutes for the International Criminal Tribunal for the former Yugoslavia (ICTY), and the International Criminal Tribunal for Rwanda (ICTR) only contain provisions on restitution of

90 See C. Droege, 'Elective affinities? Human rights and humanitarian law' (2008) 90 *International Review of the Red Cross* 871, 501–548; F. J. Hampson, 'The relationship between international humanitarian law and human rights law from the perspective of a human rights treaty body' (2008) 90 *International Review of the Red Cross* 871, 549–572.

91 On the analysis of cases related to IHL examined by the Inter-American Commission on Human Rights, see L. Zegveld, 'Remedies for victims of violations of international humanitarian law' (2003) 85 *International Review of the Red Cross* 851, 497–526.

92 See L. Zegveld, 'The Inter-American Commission on Human Rights and International Humanitarian Law: A Comment on the Tablada Case' (1998) 324 *International Review of the Red Cross.*

93 *Tablada case,* Inter-American Commission on Human Rights, IACHR Report No. 55/97, Case No. 11.137, Argentina, OEA/Ser/L/V/II.97, Doc. 38 (30 October 1997), para. 163.

94 L. Moffett 'Beyond Attribution', 328.

95 C. McCarthy, *Reparations and victim support in the International Criminal Court* (Cambridge University Press 2012) 47.

property.[96] However, the request for restitution could not be initiated by the victim, but by the Prosecutor or the Chamber. Moreover, the Tribunals were unwilling to use their authority to order restitution. As Mertel describes, '[v]ery little effort has been made to use tribunals as a means of delivering reparations for survivors'.[97]

The adoption of the Rome Statute of the ICC has created a regime for the redress of victims of international crimes. The Rome Statute now recognises the right to reparations for victims of grave breaches of IHL as a result of both international and non-international armed conflict. In this respect, Bassiouni considers the ICC provisions regarding victim's reparation as 'the most promising potential for the development of victims' rights'.[98] According to Article 75(1) of the ICC Statute:

> The Court shall establish principles relating to reparations to, or in respect of, victims, including restitution, compensation and rehabilitation. On this basis, in its decision the Court may, either upon request or on its own motion in exceptional circumstances, determine the scope and extent of any damage, loss and injury to, or in respect of, victims and will state the principles on which it is acting.

Under the ICC Statute, reparation can take the form of restitution, compensation and rehabilitation. According to Article 75(2), reparations can be sought directly against the convicted person or indirectly through the Trust Fund. Consequently, in principle, the duty-bearers of the obligation to provide reparation are the individuals convicted for the commission of international crimes. In this sense, individuals could be both state agents or members of armed groups. The Court may also order that reparations be implemented through the Trust Fund in cases of a) individual awards, where it is impossible or impractical to make awards directly to each victim; b) collective awards; and c) awards made to an intergovernmental, international or national organisation.[99] The Statute also contemplates victim participation in several stages of the proceedings.[100]

The Trust Fund has a two-fold mandate, namely a reparations mandate and an assistance mandate.[101] The reparations mandate refers to the implementation of awards for reparations ordered by the Court against a convicted person. In this first role, reparations are directly linked to the conviction of a particular perpetrator. Under

---

96 Art. 24(3) ICTY Statute and Rule 15 of the Rules of Procedure; Art. 23(3) ICTR Statute and Rule 105 Rules of Procedure.

97 J. Mertel, 'Truth in a Box: The Limits of Justice through Judicial Mechanisms' in I. Amadiume & A. A. An-Naim, *The Politics of Memory. Truth, Healing and Social Justice* (Zed Books 2000) 155.

98 M. C. Bassiouni, 'International Recognition of Victim's Rights' (2006) 6 *Human Rights Law Review* 2, 203–279, at 243.

99 Art. 75(2) of the ICC Statute and Rule 98 of the Rules of Procedure.

100 Art. 68(3) of the Rome Statute states that '[w]here the personal interests of the victims are affected, the Court shall permit their views and concerns to be presented and considered at stages of the proceedings determined to be appropriate by the Court'. See also C. Garbett, 'The International Criminal Court and Restorative Justice: Victims, Participation and the Processes of Justice' (2017) 5 *Restorative Justice* 2, 198–220.

101 REDRESS, 'Making Sense of Reparations at the International Criminal Court' (20 June 2018) Background Paper, 2.

Article 79(2) of the ICC Statute, the Court may order that 'money and other property collected through fines or forfeiture be transferred [...] to the Trust Fund'. However, in most cases convicted persons are likely to be declared impecunious and, therefore, the Trust Fund may use its 'other resources' to complement the award, such as those funds raised through voluntary contributions.[102] Voluntary contributions can be made by governments, international organisations, individuals, corporations and other entities.[103] Secondly, the Trust Fund should also provide victims and their families with 'physical and psychological rehabilitation and/or material support'.[104] Under this assistance mandate, the Trust Fund has been working with local organisations in several countries, including, for example, Northern Uganda and the Democratic Republic of Congo where it has developed rehabilitation assistance projects.[105]

To date, the phase of reparations at the ICC has been only reached in three cases, all related to members of armed groups. These are the *Lubanga*, *Katanga* and *Al Mahdi* cases.

- *Lubanga* case: On the 15th December 2017, Trial Chamber II of the ICC issued a decision setting the amount of Thomas Lubanga Dyilo's liability for collective reparations at USD 10.000.000.[106] The decision completed the Order for Reparations of the 3rd March 2015 in the case of *The Prosecutor v. Thomas Lubanga Dyilo*, which awarded collective reparations to the victims of the war crimes committed by Mr Lubanga.[107]
- *Katanga* case: On the 24th March 2017, Trial Chamber II awarded Mr Katanga's victims individual reparations in the form of symbolic compensation of USD 250 per victim.[108] The Chamber also awarded specific collective reparations in the form of support for housing, support for income-generating activities, education aid and psychological support.
- *Al Mahdi* case: On the 8th March 2018, the Appeals Chamber of the ICC delivered its judgment confirming, for the most, the Reparations Order in *The Prosecutor v. Ahmad Al Faqi Al Mahdi* of the 17th August 2017.[109] Mr Al Mahdi was liable for EUR 2.700.000 in expenses for individual and collective reparations for the community of Timbuktu.

---

102 Rule 56 of the Regulations of the Trust Fund.

103 Rule 21(a) of the Regulations of the Trust Fund.

104 Rule 50(a)(i) of the Regulations of the Trust Fund.

105 On the assistance mandate of the Trust Fund see A. Dutton and F. D. Ni Aolain, 'Between Reparations and Repair: Assessing the Work of the ICC Trust Fund for Victims Under Its Assistance Mandate' (24 September 2018) available at <https://ssrn.com/abstract=3254972> accessed 20 May 2019.

106 *The Prosecutor v. Thomas Lubanga Dyilo* (corrected version of the "Decision Setting the Size of the Reparations Award for which Thomas Lubanga Dyilo is Liable") ICC-01/04-01/06 (21 December 2017).

107 *The Prosecutor v. Thomas Lubanga Dyilo* (Judgment on the appeals against the "Decision establishing the principles and procedures to be applied to reparations" of 7 August 2012 with amended order for reparations (Annex A) and public annexes 1 and 2) ICC-01/04-01/06 A A 2 A 3 (3 March 2015).

108 *The Prosecutor v. Germain Katanga* (Order for Reparations pursuant to Article 75 of the Statute) ICC-01/04-01/07 (24 March 2017).

109 *The Prosecutor v. Ahmad Al Faqi Al Mahdi* (Judgment on the appeal of the victims against the "Reparations Order") ICC-01/12-01/15 A (8 March 2018); *The Prosecutor v. Ahmad Al Faqi Al Mahdi* (Reparation Order) ICC-01/12-01/15 (17 August 2017).

The Court ordered collective reparations in the *Lubanga* case, and a mix of individual and collective reparations in the *Katanga* and *Al-Mahdi* cases. Collective reparations consisted of rehabilitative services and symbolic measures, while individual awards took the form of compensation. Nevertheless, there were several challenges in the implementation of these reparations. For instance, the Court applied 'different approaches in deciding whether it is necessary or appropriate to identify individual beneficiaries and to verify their eligibility in cases where only collective reparations awards are contemplated'.[110] Moreover, 'each of the Chambers have also adopted a different approach with respect to judicial involvement in this process'.[111] Finally, in all three cases the Trust Fund was requested to consider advancing the full amount ordered to reach the implementation phase. According to Evans, '[t]he issue of reparations for victims of armed conflict is difficult to substantiate in terms of individual responsibility'.[112] One of the main difficulties is that individuals are unlikely to have the resources to provide reparations to thousands of victims, and consequently, 'this outcome is asymmetrical to the reality of the commission of such crimes by numerous perpetrators'.[113] Moreover, individual perpetrators lack the capacities held by the state to implement the reparations ordered by the Court.[114] Furthermore, and to reiterate, trials appear to be designed primarily to target perpetrators rather than to respond to victim's needs.[115]

The adoption of reparations provisions in the Rome Statute and the creation of a Trust Fund for victims constitute major developments in international criminal justice and victim's rights. In this context, the only three cases that have reached the reparation phase are directed against members of armed groups. With the acquittal of Gbagbo and the withdrawal of charges in the *Kenyatta* case there is yet to be a conviction under the Rome Statute system that has been pronounced against a state official. So far, the ICL is the only mechanism to address the responsibility of armed groups, although only indirectly through its individual members. In all three cases, the convicted persons have been declared impecunious and the Trust Fund has been called to advance the full amount in order for the implementation phase to be reached.[116] In this regard, with the Trust Fund receiving voluntary contributions from international organisations, corporations and other entities, other possible contributions could be potentially contemplated, such as assets raised from the armed group itself.[117] A similar proposal

110 REDRESS, *supra note* 101, 4.
111 *Ibid*, 4.
112 C. Evans, *The Right to Reparation*, 4.
113 L. Moffett, 'Beyond Attribution', 330–331.
114 O. Amezcua-Noriega, 'Reparation Principles under International Law and their Possible Application by the International Criminal Court: Some Reflections' (2011) Reparations Unit, Transitional Justice Network, Briefing Paper No.1, 8.
115 R. Mani, 'Reparation as a Component of Transitional Justice: Pursuing "Reparative Justice" in the Aftermath of Violent Conflict' in K. De Feyter, S. Parmentier, M. Bossuyt and P. Lemmens (eds) *Out of the Ashes. Reparation for Victims of Gross and Systematic Human Rights Violations* (Intersentia 2005) 62.
116 REDRESS, *supra note* 101, 2.
117 P. Blázquez Rodríguez, 'Does an armed group have an obligation to provide reparations to victims?', 426.

was made by the UN Secretary-General in relation to the necessity to 'facilitate efforts to find, attach and seize the assets of transgressing parties and their leaders' in armed conflicts in Africa.[118] Likewise, the aforementioned report of the UN Special Rapporteur on extrajudicial killings and ANSAs also suggested to seize ANSA-held bank accounts and their assets.[119] Furthermore, the Trust Fund also has the function of assisting in the creation of rehabilitation programmes. Although not explicitly contemplated by the Trust Fund, the contribution of armed groups could be potentially considered in this assistance mandate too.

3.4. REPARATIONS AT THE DOMESTIC LEVEL

Reparations for violations committed during armed conflicts can also be considered at the domestic level. Accordingly, states implement their obligations under international human rights and humanitarian law through their national legal systems.[120] There are two main mechanisms that can be used for obtaining reparations at the domestic level: seeking reparation through judicial litigation or the establishment of national reparation programmes by governments. Judicial litigation refers mainly to civil claims. However, some states provide for the possibility to order reparation in cases linked to criminal prosecution. In this context, 'mechanisms of civil liability have been gaining in popularity over the past decade, both at the national and the international level'.[121]

As for civil remedies, the legal system established in the United States constitutes a representative example. Under the Alien Tort Claims Act (ATCA), US courts can exercise jurisdiction over 'any civil action by an alien for a tort only, committed in violation of the law of nations or a treaty of the United States'.[122] Several claims have been filed under this regime for crimes committed during armed conflict, such as genocide, war crimes, torture or summary executions, amongst others.[123] Most of these cases refer to representatives of foreign states or corporations. However, there have been a number of cases dealing with leaders and members of non-state armed groups. One of the relevant cases is *Kadic v. Karadzic* decided by the Second Circuit Court of Appeal in 1995.[124] In this case, a group of victims from Bosnia and Herzegovina brought actions for damages against Radovan Karadzic, President of the self-proclaimed Bosnian-Serb Republic of Srpska. As the commander of Bosnian-Serb military forces, Karadzic was charged with the commission of systematic human rights and humanitarian law violations, including acts of rape, torture, extrajudicial killing, and genocide. Although the case was initially

---

118 UN Secretary-General, 'Report on the Causes of Conflict and the Promotion of Durable Peace and Sustainable Development in Africa' (13 April 1998) UN Doc A/52/871 – S/1998/318, para. 50.

119 See section 3.1.5 of this chapter.

120 M. C. Bassiouni, *supra note* 98, 266.

121 V. Bílková, 'Direct Responsibility of Armed Opposition Groups', 274.

122 Alien Tort Claims Act (ATCA), 28 USC §1350.

123 M. C. Bassiouni, *supra note* 98, 234–235.

124 *Kadic v. Karadzic* (Opinion of 2nd Circuit re Subject Matter Jurisdiction) United States Court of Appeals for the Second Circuit, 70 F.3d 232, 241 (13 October 1995).

dismissed by the District Court who understood that 'acts committed by non-state actors do not violate the law of nations'[125], the Court of Appeal reversed the decision and held that 'certain forms of conduct violate the law of nations whether undertaken by those acting under the auspices of a state or only as private individuals'.[126] The case was sent back for further proceedings. It was in 2000 when the US District Court ordered Karadzic to pay $4.5 billion in damages to the victims and survivors.[127]

In addition, in *Jane Doe v. Islamic Salvation Front (FIS) and Anwar Haddam*, the Centre for Constitutional Rights and the International Women's Human Rights Law Clinic brought an action against the Islamic Salvation Front (FIS) of Algeria and its leader Anwar Haddam for crimes against humanity and war crimes.[128] Here again, the Court confirmed its jurisdiction under the ATCA over the actions of non-state actors. Nevertheless, the case was finally dismissed for reasons of evidence. In this context, actions under the ATCA could serve as means for victims to claim reparations against individuals and non-state armed groups in the context of violations committed during armed conflict. However, according to Bassiouni, '[w]hile the potential monetary judgments in ATCA cases are substantial, the actual likelihood of attaining full satisfaction from the defendant is minimal'.[129]

Regarding other national jurisdictions, Northern Ireland offers the example of case-law where victims have claimed reparations against members of the IRA, as a non-state armed group. In *Breslin and Others v. Seamus McKenna and Others,* the defendants were seeking reparations for the harm caused by the Omagh bombing in 1998.[130] The Court found four members of the IRA responsible for the bombing and ordered them to pay GBP 1.600.000 to compensate the litigants. In particular, the court referred to the IRA as 'an unincorporated association' and explained the necessity to 'demonstrate that the persons represented should have the same common interest in defending the proceedings in question' so they could be considered as a single defendant.[131]

In Colombia, the Constitutional Court established the joint civil responsibility deriving from a criminal action carried out by an armed group. In the case *Gustavo Gallón y otros* the Constitutional Court indicated that:

> Although criminal liability holds in the individual, civil liability derived from the punishable act admits the element of joint and several liability, not only between those criminally

125 *Doe v. Karadzic*, United States District Court, 866 F. Supp. 734, 735 (S.D.N.Y. 1994) (7 September 1994) at 739.

126 *Kadic v. Karadzic* (Opinion of 2nd Circuit re Subject Matter Jurisdiction) United States Court of Appeals for the Second Circuit, 70 F.3d 232, 241 (13 October 1995) at 239.

127 *Doe v. Karadzic*, United States District Court, 93 Civ. 878 (PKL) (4 October 2000). See comment of this case in M. C. Bassiouni, *International Criminal Law, Volume III: International Enforcement* (3rd ed, Martinus Nijhoff Publishers 2008) 661.

128 *Jane Doe v. Islamic Salvation Front (FIS) and Anwar Haddam*, United States District Court, District of Columbia, 993 F. Supp. 3 (D.D.C.1998) (3 February 1998) dismissed (31 March 2003).

129 M. C. Bassiouni, *supra note* 127, 661.

130 *Breslin and Others v. Seamus McKenna and Others*, NIQB 50 (8 June 2009).

131 *Ibid*, paras. 83–84.

> responsible but also with respect to those who, by judicial decision, have been qualified as members of the specific armed group [...].[132]

In relation to the Fund for the Reparation of Victims created by virtue of Article 54 of the Law 975 of 2005, the court further affirmed that:

> The satisfaction of the principle of reparation requires the observance of an order in the affectation of the resources that make up the fund. Thus, the first ones obliged to repair are the perpetrators of the crimes, and by virtue of the principle of joint and several liability, the specific group to which the perpetrators belong.[133]

Consequently, although individual perpetrators should be the primary duty-bearers of the obligation to provide reparations to victims, the armed group itself should be responsible secondarily. These examples show that, in some national jurisdictions, it is feasible to file civil actions against members of armed groups (and in some cases against the group itself) and hold them responsible to provide reparations. However, the actual likelihood of obtaining full reparation is uncertain.

The second mechanism by which it is possible to seek reparations is through national reparation programmes. As explained earlier, reparation programmes are sometimes created directly by governments to provide a lump sum of money, services and/or a pension for survivors of violations or their family members.[134] These programmes are also contemplated under the UNBPG which state that 'States should endeavour to establish national programmes for reparation and other assistance to victims in the event that the parties liable for the harm suffered are unable or unwilling to meet their obligations'.[135] These programmes allow for securing funds where the responsible person or entity is unable to provide reparations. For these purposes, some states have created special trust funds to provide reparation for victims. In this scenario, funding has also come from the recovery of illegal assets. This was the case of Peru which devoted a portion of assets recovered from corruption; the Philippines with monies recovered from the Marcos estate; or Colombia with assets held by paramilitaries.[136] Similarly to the Trust Fund of the ICC, other possible contributions could be potentially contemplated. For example, illegal assets recovered from the armed group itself, or voluntary contributions from the leadership of the armed group or affiliated associations. As explained by Blázquez-Rodríguez, '[a]lthough this economic contribution to a reparation programme cannot be equated with holding the armed

---

132 *Gustavo Gallón y Otros*, Constitutional Court of Colombia, C-370/2006 (18 May 2006), para. 6.2.4.4.7. Unofficial translation.

133 *Ibid*, para. 6.2.4.4.11. Unofficial translation.

134 N. Roht-Arriaza, *supra note* 3, 663.

135 Principle 16 UNBPG.

136 Office of the UN High Commissioner for Human Rights, 'Rule-of-Law Tools for Post-Conflict States: Reparations Programmes' (United Nations 2008) 33.

group accountable, this and other similar actions could help to establish a link between responsibility and reparations in the eyes of the victims'.[137]

3.5. CONCLUDING REMARKS ON THE FRAMEWORK OF REPARATIONS FOR VIOLATIONS COMMITTED IN ARMED CONFLICT

This section has assessed whether the current international legal framework recognises a role for armed groups in the provision of reparations to victims of IHL violations. Initially, under IHL treaties, provisions regarding compensation were drafted with international armed conflicts and inter-state claims in mind. These provisions are now seen as applicable in both international and non-international armed conflicts as part of customary IHL.[138] Moreover, with the growth and development of human rights treaties, effective remedies and reparations are recognised as rights of individuals to claim against the state. The jurisprudence of the Inter-American Court of Human Rights has been essential in the advancement of this right and in the provision of different forms of reparation. However, human rights frameworks have focused on the state as the main subject responsible for reparations.

As a new feature, with the adoption of the Rome Statute, individual perpetrators of international crimes can also be held responsible for reparations. As a consequence, individuals as well as states are now considered as duty-bearers of the provision of reparations to victims of IHL violations. So far, only three convictions have reached the phase of reparations at the ICC, all of them against members of armed groups. However, the ICC and the Trust Fund are experiencing numerous implementation challenges in this phase. Finally, under domestic law, certain national jurisdictions allow for filing civil actions for damages in relation to criminal convictions of members of non-state armed groups. In some cases, as explained by the Constitutional Court of Colombia, armed groups could be held responsible in a subsidiary manner.

With regards to the role of armed groups in these reparation schemes, their legal position continues to be uncertain. Nonetheless, there are incipient soft law initiatives and monitoring mechanisms that are recognising the obligation of armed groups to provide reparations. In this light, there appears to be a growing acceptance of the necessity that armed groups should contribute to reparations for violations of IHL, in parallel with the primary responsibility of the state. This has been acknowledged by the commentators of the UNBPG, the reports of UN Commissions of Inquiry and Fact-Finding Missions, and other reports by the International Law Association and the UN Special Rapporteur on extrajudicial, summary and arbitrary executions. Although considered soft law instruments, these instruments enjoy significant value.

---

137 P. Blázquez Rodríguez, 'Does an armed group have an obligation to provide reparations to victims?', 425.

138 See J.M. Henckaerts & L. Doswald-Beck, *Customary International Humanitarian Law*, 545–550.

In addition, the UNBPG have played an important role due to their influence in the development of international customary law. The UNBPG have now been cited by international courts, human rights bodies and truth commissions. Moreover, their adoption by consensus in the UN General Assembly represents an implied acceptance by states of the validity of their norms. In relation to the reports from UN bodies, these documents enjoy the endorsement of an international organisation, United Nations, and are produced by independent experts. Therefore, they could constitute supplementary sources of interpretation of international legal provisions. A further possibility can be contemplated under ICL. In particular, once one or several members of an armed group have been convicted, the potential contribution of the armed group itself could be envisaged in the compensation and rehabilitation efforts following conviction. For example, armed groups could contribute to the funding of the Trust Fund for victims or in the rehabilitation programmes established in the field.

In the last twenty years, the legal framework of reparations has been subject to considerable evolution. Although the state continues to be the primary entity responsible for providing reparation to victims under international law, other entities such as international organisations and individuals in the framework of ICL can be now considered as duty-bearers of this secondary obligation. With the rise of non-state armed groups participating in non-international armed conflicts and the continuous atrocities committed by them, the logical next step appears to be incorporating these entities as contributors to the redress of victims of armed conflicts. In fact, the normative basis of such an emerging secondary obligation could be reinforced if the practice of armed groups is also considered indicative of the commitment to provide redress to victims of IHL violations.

4. THE PRACTICE OF ARMED GROUPS REGARDING REPARATIONS

Having examined the legal framework of reparations under international law, this section will review the practice of armed groups who have committed to provide some forms of reparation in peace agreements, unilateral declarations and codes of conduct. Reparations will be considered not only in terms of financial compensation but also in terms of other symbolic forms of reparation, such as apologies and guarantees of non-repetition. The aim of this section is to analyse the potential contribution of armed groups to the provision of reparations as well as to assess the normative value of such practice. In addition, the main challenges and limiting factors are considered in order to best determine how to incorporate these practices into the existing legal framework.

4.1. PEACE AGREEMENTS BETWEEN ARMED GROUPS AND STATES

As examined in Chapter 3, armed groups engage in special agreements and peace agreements with states. Peace agreements are those aimed at ending military violence and sustaining ceasefire among the parties to the conflict. Genuine peace agreements are categorised as 'substantive or framework' agreements and contain several provisions relating to the establishment of 'new constitutional structures addressing governance, elections, and legal and human rights institutions'.[139] There have been several peace processes in the context of non-international armed conflict where armed groups or a cluster of armed groups have committed to abide by provisions on humanitarian law and human rights.[140] Among these provisions, this part will look at those relating to the provision of redress and reparation to victims by both parties to the conflict and, in particular, by armed groups in recent peace agreements.

Philippines

In 2001, the Government of the Republic of the Philippines and the Moro Islamic Liberation Front (MILF) signed the 'Agreement on Peace between the Government of the Republic of the Philippines and the Moro Islamic Liberation Front'.[141] This agreement contains a provision on reparation to victims of the armed conflict in paragraph B-3 which establishes the obligation of both parties to return their properties and compensate in the case of lost or destroyed properties by reason of the armed conflict.[142] Moreover, the MILF also committed to 'determine, lead and manage rehabilitation and development projects in conflict affected areas'.[143] So together with restitution and compensation efforts, the armed group was obliged by the agreement to put in place rehabilitation programmes. These provisions on rehabilitation were later developed in the 'Implementing Guidelines on the Humanitarian, Rehabilitation and Development Aspects of the GRP-MILF Tripoli Agreement on Peace of 2001' and exploratory talks held on the 27th and 28th March 2003.[144]

---

139 C. Bell, 'Peace agreements: their nature and legal status' (2006) 100 *The American Journal of International Law* 373, at 377.

140 S. Sivakumaram, *The Law of Non-International Armed Conflict* (Oxford University Press 2012) 125–133.

141 Agreement on Peace between the Government of the Republic of the Philippines and the Moro Islamic Liberation Front (22 June 2001).

142 Paragraph B-3 of the Agreements establishes that '[t]he Parties shall safely return evacuees to their place of origin; provide all the necessary financial/material and technical assistance to start a new life, as well as allow them to be awarded reparations for their properties lost or destroyed by reason of the conflict'.

143 Paragraph B-2 of the Agreement.

144 See R. G. Buendia, 'The GRP-MILF Peace Talks: Quo Vadis?' in *Southeast Asian Affairs* (2004) Institute of Southeast Asian Studies, 205–221.

Darfur (Sudan)

In 2006, the Government of the Sudan, the Sudan Liberation Movement/Army (SLM/A) and the Justice and Equality Movement (JEM) signed the Darfur Peace Agreement. In this agreement, reparation also focuses on restitution and compensation and recognises the right of victims to 'have their grievances addressed in a comprehensive manner and to receive compensation'.[145] In particular, the parties agreed to create an independent Compensation Commission to deal with claims for compensation together with a Compensation Fund.[146] The agreement requires that the Compensation Commission be composed of 6 members, 2 members to be nominated by each of the parties to the agreement, that is, by the government of Sudan, the SLM/A and the JEM. Awards for compensation included restitution of stolen, lost or destroyed objects; monetary compensation; provision of inputs (crops, livestock, veterinary medicines, agricultural tools, etc); rehabilitation including medical and psychological care; legal assistance and social services; acknowledgment and acceptance of responsibility; guarantees of non-repetition; and traditional forms of compensation. With regard to the potential liability of rebel groups to provide reparations, the International Centre for Transitional Justice affirmed this possibility 'through court actions or as part of a peace agreement in which such groups agree to contribute to a state-administered program of reparations'.[147] Although the compensation commission was ultimately not established, this practice could serve as an example for future reference where armed groups have a role in the distribution of compensation, both as parties to the Commission and as financial contributors.[148]

Uganda

The peace agreement in Uganda was initially signed in Juba, Sudan on the 29th of June 2007 as the 'Agreement on Accountability and Reconciliation between the Government of the Republic of Uganda and the Lord's Resistance Army/Movement' (LRA/M).[149] This agreement contained three provisions regarding reparations that read as follows:

> 9.1. Reparations may include a range of measures such as: rehabilitation; restitution; compensation; guarantees of non-recurrence and other symbolic measures such as apologies, memorials and commemorations. Priority shall be given to members of vulnerable groups.

---

145 Darfur Peace Agreement (5 May 2006) paras. 194, 196 and 199.

146 Darfur Peace Agreement (5 May 2006) paras. 200–213.

147 International Centre for Transitional Justice, 'Reparation and the Darfur Peace Process: Ensuring Victims' Rights' (November 2007), 15.

148 Report of the Special Rapporteur on Extrajudicial, Summary or Arbitrary Executions on Armed non-State Actors: the Protection of the Right to Life (5 June 2018) UN Doc. A/HRC/38/44, para. 91.

149 Agreement on Accountability and Reconciliation between the Government of the Republic of Uganda and the Lord's Resistance Army/Movement, Juba, Sudan (29 June 2007).

9.2. The Parties agree that collective as well as individual reparations should be made to victims through mechanisms to be adopted by the Parties upon further consultation.

9.3. Reparations may be ordered to be made by perpetrators as part of penalties and sanctions in accountability proceedings.[150]

In light of this, both parties committed to contribute to reparation efforts. Moreover, reparations were regarded in a comprehensive manner, including restitution, compensation, rehabilitation and guarantees of non-repetition. Other provisions focused on the necessity to acknowledge and address the suffering of victims.[151] The agreement seemed to acknowledge the position of the UNBPG where both states and non-state entities, in this case armed groups, are responsible to provide reparations based on their responsibilities.[152] Unfortunately, the peace talks broke up in 2008 due to the unwillingness of the LRA to sign the final agreement.

Colombia

After more than fifty years of armed conflict, the Colombian peace agreement was finally signed in 2016 between the Government of Colombia and the FARC-EP.[153] The agreement contains a comprehensive system of reparation for victims of the armed conflict which includes acts of early acknowledgement of collective responsibility and public apology by both the Government and the FARC-EP; reparation programmes established by the Government; collective reparation processes including rural reform plans; a psychosocial rehabilitation plan for coexistence and non-recurrence; collective processes of return of displaced persons and other reparations to victims living abroad; land restitution measures; and strengthening a policy of caring for and comprehensive reparation for victims.[154] In relation to the responsibility of the FARC-EP, it is important to highlight that the group expressively committed to 'to contribute to the material reparation of the victims and in general to their comprehensive reparation, on the basis of the facts identified by the Special Jurisdiction for Peace'.[155] This contribution was to be made through an inventory of all kinds of property and assets. In accordance with the aforementioned provisions, in August 2017, the FARC-EP submitted a list of assets and goods, worth hundreds of millions of dollars, to be used to

150 *Ibid*, paras. 9.1, 9.2, 9.3.

151 *Ibid*, para. 8.1.

152 L. Moffett, 'Beyond Attribution', 344.

153 Final agreement to end the armed conflict and build a stable and lasting peace between the Government of Colombia and the Revolutionary Armed Forces of Colombia – People's Army (FARC-EP) (21 November 2016) available at <http://especiales.presidencia.gov.co/Documents/20170620-dejacion-armas/acuerdos/acuerdo-final-ingles.pdf> accessed 30 May 2019.

154 See H. Olasolo and J. M. F. Ramírez Mendoza, 'The Colombian Integrated System of Truth, Justice, Reparation and Non-Repetition' (2017) 15 *Journal of International Criminal Justice*, 1011–1047.

155 Colombia Peace Agreement (2016) Article 5.1.3.7, at 197.

provide reparation to victims of the conflict.[156] According to the Constitutional Court of Colombia, these assets were to be exclusively used for the reparation of victims and not for the demobilisation or reintegration of members of the armed group.[157] This is the first time that an armed group openly undertook to provide reparation to victims based on their responsibility for the atrocities committed during the armed conflict.

Central African Republic

In February 2019, a peace agreement between the Government of the Central African Republic (CAR) and 14 armed groups was signed.[158] The agreement establishes a series of obligations for armed groups, including the obligation to return buildings and other goods.[159] In addition, the parties agree to contribute to the creation of a trust fund that guarantees the rehabilitation and reparation of victims.[160] Future will tell whether and how this trust fund will develop.

Previously, peace and ceasefire agreements from the 1990s already included restitution measures. For instance, the Somali Agreement on Implementing the Ceasefire and on the Modalities of Disarmament included a provision where the parties to the conflict, the Government and the militias, 'agree in principle that properties unlawfully taken during the fighting shall be returned to the lawful owners'.[161] The Peace Agreement between the Government of the Republic of Sierra Leone and the Revolutionary United Front of Sierra Leone contemplated the release of detainees, which could be regarded as a form of restitution.[162] Moreover, in the framework of the peace process in Guatemala, the Comprehensive Agreement on Human Rights, also referred to the commitment of the parties, the Government of Guatemala and the Unidad Revolucionaria Nacional Guatemalteca to 'recognize that it is a humanitarian duty to compensate and/or assist victims of human rights violations'.[163]

---

156 'Segunda y definitiva entrega de información del listado de bienes y valores de Economía de Guerra de las FARC-EP' (15 August 2017) available at <https://static.iris.net.co/semana/upload/documents/15.08.2017-carta-para-incluir-bienes-fiscalia--esr-1.pdf> accessed 30 May 2019.

157 'Bienes de las FARC sólo se usarán para reparación de víctimas: Corte', *El Tiempo* (4 July 2018) available at <https://www.eltiempo.com/justicia/cortes/corte-constitucional-dice-que-bienes-de-las-farc-solo-se-usaran-en-reparacion-de-victimas-239446> accessed 30 May 2019.

158 Accord politique pour la paix et la reconciliation en Republique Centrafricane (6 February 2019) available at <https://static.rfi.fr/pdf/2019/20190208_accord_paix_reconciliation_rca.pdf?platform=hootsuite&fbclid=IwAR1YNQSuycqWl9ZSrOc8MgIDHHpFe8bBuccrTSBxmkijXoo7GhjcmE_b7JM> accessed 30 May 2019.

159 Article 5(i) of the Agreement.

160 Article 12 of the Agreement.

161 Somali Agreement on Implementing the Ceasefire and on Modalities of Disarmament (15 January 1993) Article III.

162 Peace Agreement between the Government of the Republic of Sierra Leone and the Revolutionary United Front of Sierra Leone, Abidjan (30 November 1996) Article 19. See also K. Mastorodimos, *Armed Non-State Actors in International Humanitarian and Human Rights Law. Foundation and Framework of Obligations, and Rules on Accountability* (Routledge 2015), 127.

163 Comprehensive Agreement on Human Rights, Guatemala (29 March 1994).

These examples demonstrate that armed groups can and have committed to provide different forms of reparation to victims through peace agreements. It is important to emphasize that peace agreements have a hybrid legal nature because, on the one hand, they are signed by states and non-state entities containing a mix of domestic and international legal categories; and on other hand, there is an internationalised implementation.[164] Most of the agreements analysed in this section focus on the restitution of property and compensation when restitution is not possible. The idea of a compensation fund to which armed groups can contribute was envisaged in the Darfur Peace Agreement although it was never established. This idea has now been included in the new CAR Peace Agreement.[165] Other texts also affirm the necessity to establish rehabilitation programmes. The 2016 Colombian Peace Agreement represents the most comprehensive text where both parties to the conflict undertake to provide a whole list of reparation measures to victims, including specific commitments issued by the armed group and a list of assets.[166] It remains to be seen whether these recent instruments are actually implemented and whether they serve the purpose of remedying the damage caused to victims of the armed conflict.

4.2. UNILATERAL DECLARATIONS BY ARMED GROUPS AND SYMBOLIC REPARATIONS

Certain armed groups have also provided measures of satisfaction, also known as symbolic reparations, through public statements in the form of unilateral declarations. In most cases, these examples relate to the offering of public apologies to victims of the armed conflict. As explained above, reparations do not need to exclusively take the form of financial compensation, but they can consist of other intangible mechanisms such as symbolic or moral reparations. Symbolic reparations are contemplated in the ASR and the UNBPG as measures of 'satisfaction'. These measures may include public apologies, such as the acknowledgement of facts and the acceptance of responsibility; full and public disclosure of the truth; the search for the whereabouts of missing persons and for the bodies of those killed; and commemorations and tributes to the victims, among others.[167] As indicated by Dudai, 'the term "symbolic" does not necessarily mean forms of reparations that are less significant – only that they involve a greater intangible element'.[168] Therefore, they focus on the immaterial damage caused to victims.

---

164 C. Bell, *supra note* 139, 408.

165 Accord politique pour la paix et la reconciliation en Republique Centrafricane (6 February 2019), Article 12.

166 Colombia Peace Agreement (2016) Article 5.1.3.7.

167 Principle 22 UNBPG.

168 R. Dudai, 'Closing the gap', 788.

These public statements have been usually pronounced in the context of peace processes or during the hearings of truth commissions. The ICRC study on customary IHL already referred to the apologies issued by the ELN in Colombia as follows:

> In 2001, a provincial arm of the ELN in Colombia publicly apologised for the death of three children and the destruction of civilian houses which resulted from an attack with explosives which members of the ELN had conducted against a police station in the district of San Francisco, Oriente Antioqueño (Industrial Area). The ELN, which itself defined the attack as an "action of war", expressed its deep and sincere condolences to all those who had been affected by the explosion and expressed its willingness to collaborate in the recuperation of the remaining objects.[169]

Also in Colombia, the FARC-EP has offered apologies at different moments during the armed conflict. The last one took place during the peace process in September 2016 where the group recorded a video acknowledging 'with the sentiment of humanity and reconciliation, that during the conflict the FARC-EP also caused great pain with the retention of people for ransom'.[170] As already mentioned, the former SPLA commander and then Vice-President of South Sudan, Riek Machar, confirmed his apology for his 1991 defection from the Sudan People's Liberation Army/Movement, which led to the killing of thousands of people from the Dinka Bor ethnic group.[171] In Sierra Leone, several commanders from the Revolutionary United Front (RUF) offered apologies during the truth commission's public hearings as means of reconciliation.[172] The Guatemalan National Revolutionary Unit also apologised for the abuses it committed during the country's 36-year civil war.[173] In Spain, although not in the context of an armed conflict, ETA recently offered partial apologies to victims in a public statement, but only to 'those citizens without responsibility in the conflict'.[174] In the case of Northern Ireland, the IRA offered other measures of truth-recovery in addition to public apologies.[175] In particular, the IRA assisted in the investigation of the disappearances

169 'Communiqué relative to the events of 9 August 2001' ELN Head Office, Area Industrial cited by J.M. Henckaerts & L. Doswald-Beck (eds), *Customary International Humanitarian Law. Volume II: Practice* (ICRC Cambridge University Press 2005) 3610, para. 365.

170 'Colombia's Farc rebels apologize for "great pain" caused by kidnappings', ***The Guardian*** (12 September 2016) available at <https://www.theguardian.com/world/2016/sep/12/colombias-farc-rebels-apologize-kidnapping-peace-accord> accessed 30 May 2019.

171 'South Sudan VP confirms apology for Bor Massacre', *Sudan Tribune* (3 April 2012) <www.sudantribune.com/South-Sudan-VP-confirms-apology,42124> accessed 30 May 2019.

172 R. Shaw, 'Linking justice with reintegration? Ex-combatants and the Sierra Leone experiment', in R. Shaw and L. Waldorf (eds), *Localizing Transitional Justice: Interventions and Priorities after Mass Violence* (Stanford University Press 2010) 127–129.

173 'Guatemala Rebel Apology', *The New York Times* (14 March 1999) <https://www.nytimes.com/1999/03/14/world/guatemala-rebel-apology.html> accessed 30 May 2019.

174 'ETA lamenta el daño causado y pide "perdón" a parte de las víctimas', ***El País*** <https://elpais.com/politica/2018/04/20/actualidad/1524201219_870285.html> accessed 30 May 2019.

175 'IRA offers "sincere apologies" for 30 years of civilian slaughter', *The Telegraph* (17 July 2002) <https://www.telegraph.co.uk/news/uknews/1401616/IRA-offers-sincere-apologies-for-30-years-of-civilian-slaughter.html> accessed 30 May 2019.

and in finding the whereabouts of those killed and secretly buried.[176] According to Dudai, '[t]he IRA's engagement with the issue of the disappeared demonstrates the capacity of armed groups to provide at least some measures of symbolic reparations'.[177]

The importance of symbolic reparations lies in making the memory of the victims a public matter and helping families to move on.[178] Some authors have recognised the significant role of moral reparations in the efforts to find truth and reconciliation. Moffett notes that '[t]hese more symbolic forms of reparations could be important to victims in finding acknowledgment and truth as to what happened, which could be valued more than money'.[179] Similarly, the Special Rapporteur on extrajudicial, summary or arbitrary executions has encouraged non-state actors to offer public apologies, and contribute to commemoration ceremonies as part of their reparation efforts.[180] However, these measures cannot be regarded as the sole source of reparation to victims but should serve to complement other forms of redress. As indicated by the Report on Reparations Programmes by the Office of the High Commissioner for Human Rights, 'they cannot carry the whole weight of a complicated transition and should always be thought of as one benefit among others'.[181] In addition, apologies should be full and not only limited because partial apologies could jeopardize the attempt to become 'a meaningful, rounded gesture'.[182]

4.3. CODES OF CONDUCT AND INTERNAL RULINGS OF ARMED GROUPS

In addition to peace agreements and unilateral declarations, some measures of reparations have been incorporated as duties in some codes of conduct issued by armed groups. In particular, codes of conduct from insurgent armed groups have been compiled by Bangerter in his work *Internal Control: Codes of Conduct within Insurgent Armed Groups*.[183] In Colombia, the Ejército de Liberación Nacional (ELN) produced a code of conduct which included different provisions on the respect for the civilian population. Among these provisions, one of them stated that '[e]fforts shall be made to avoid damage to civilian property and installations resulting from military

---

176 R. Dudai, 'Closing the gap', 798–801.
177 *Ibid*, 800.
178 Office of the UN High Commissioner for Human Rights, 'Rule-of-Law Tools for Post-Conflict States: Reparations Programmes' (United Nations 2008) 23.
179 L. Moffett, 'Beyond Attribution', 334.
180 Report of the Special Rapporteur on Extrajudicial, Summary or Arbitrary Executions on Armed non-State Actors: the Protection of the Right to Life (5 June 2018) UN Doc. A/HRC/38/44, para. 94.
181 Office of the UN High Commissioner for Human Rights, 'Rule-of-Law Tools for Post-Conflict States: Reparations Programmes' (United Nations 2008) 23.
182 J. Tomlinson (ed), *National Apologies. Mapping the Complexities of Validity: A Practical paper* (The Centre for Peace and Conflict Studies 2012) 11.
183 O. Bangerter, 'Internal Control: Codes of Conduct within Insurgent Armed Groups', Occasional Paper of the Small Arms Survey (Graduate Institute of International and Development Studies 2012).

operations and to make reparations where possible'.[184] Similarly, the New People's Army (NPA) in the Philippines issued their 'Basic Rules' which contained 'Three Rules and Eight Principles'. One of the eight principles was to compensate all damages.[185] In addition, the Revolutionary United Front (RUF) in Sierra Leone developed the 'Eight Codes of Conduct' and included the obligation to 'pay for everything that you demand or damage'.[186] Likewise, the Viet Cong in Vietnam, also known as the National Liberation Front, established its own code of conduct and determined the necessity of their members to return what had been borrowed and make restitution for damaged belongings.[187] Less explicitly, in Uganda, the National Resistance Army Code of Conduct referred to the duty to return anything borrowed from the public.[188]

In all these examples, it seems that the armed group accepts as obligations those related to restitution or compensation for damage caused to civilians. Indeed, these are regarded as the two main forms of reparation generally established for states and international organisations. Moreover, these codes of conduct have been produced by armed groups located in different geographical regions such as Asia, Africa and America which could be considered an important factor in determining the existence of 'general acceptance'. However, these codes of conduct do not clarify whether the damage to which the restitution or compensation applies is the result of mere military operations or whether it is caused by the commission of a violation of international humanitarian law. Indeed, damage could equally be caused by disproportionate or indiscriminate attacks, or the unlawful targeting of civilians.

Alongside the examination of the content of the rules included in these internal rulings, the issuance of codes of conduct could be regarded as guarantees of non-repetition in themselves, as suggested by Mastorodimos.[189] In fact, guarantees of non-repetition are another component of reparation. Assurances of non-repetition are preventive measures taken by the responsible entity to avoid the repetition of the breach. According to Principle 23(b) of the UNBPG, these measures should include, among others, promoting mechanisms for preventing and monitoring social conflicts and their resolution. In the context of transitional justice, guarantees of non-repetition have been translated into 'guarantees of non-recurrence'. As indicated by the former Special Rapporteur De Greiff, guarantees of non-recurrence 'is not a category that designates a measure or a set of measures, but a function that can be played by a variety of initiatives'.[190] The function of this guarantee is essentially the prevention of the recurrence of specific violations.

184 Ejército de Liberación Nacional (ELN), 'Code of War', Colombia 1995. See O. Bangerter, *supra note* 183, 83.

185 New People's Army (NPA), 'Basic Rules', Philippines 1969. See O. Bangerter, *supra note* 183, 72.

186 Revolutionary United Front (RUF), 'Eight Codes of Conduct', Sierra Leone, no date. See O. Bangerter, *supra note* 183, 73–74.

187 Viet Cong, 'Code of Disciplines', Vietnam, no date. See O. Bangerter, *supra note* 183, 75.

188 The National Resistance Army 'Code of Conduct', Uganda, 1982. See O. Bangerter, *supra note* 183, 76–77.

189 K. Mastorodimos, *Armed Non-State Actors in International Humanitarian and Human Rights Law. Foundation and Framework of Obligations, and Rules on Accountability* (Routledge 2015) 128.

190 Report of the Special Rapporteur on the Promotion of Truth, Justice, Reparation and Guarantees of Non-recurrence (23 August 2013) UN Doc. A/68/345, p. 17.

In this regard, guarantees of non-repetition are considered one of the traditional consequences of the responsibility of states and international organisations.[191] In relation to armed groups, these measures have not been systematically studied. However, the inclusion of commitments relating to the prevention of future violations of IHL in the codes of conduct of armed groups could resemble those legislative measures taken by states for the purpose of non-recurrence. In this context, these commitments have been reflected through the signature of the so-called Deeds of Commitment from Geneva Call. For instance, as concerns the prohibition of use of anti-personnel mines, certain armed groups have committed to 'issue the necessary orders and directives to our commanders and fighters for the implementation and enforcement of our commitment'.[192] These directives could be materialised in the issuance of written codes of conduct and could be assimilated to the measures required by states such as 'promoting the observance of codes of conduct and ethical norms, in particular international standards, by public servants [...]'.[193] In a similar vein, in relation to the issue of sexual violence committed during armed conflict, the UN Security Council has called upon parties to the armed conflict to 'make and implement specific and time-bound commitments to combat sexual violence, which should include, inter alia, issuance of clear orders through chains of command prohibiting sexual violence and the prohibition of sexual violence in Codes of Conduct, military field manuals, or equivalent [...]'.[194]

4.4. ASSESSING THE PRACTICE OF ARMED GROUPS

The previous sections have provided some positive examples of armed groups that have voluntarily committed to provide some forms of reparation to victims through peace agreements, unilateral declarations and codes of conduct. These measures have ranged from compensation, restitution, satisfaction (symbolic reparations) to guarantees of non-repetition. The question that arises is whether their practice and views can contribute to the formation of customary law together with the practice of states, or whether it is possible to at least conceive them as interpretative tools.

In answering the first question on their possible contribution to the formation of customary law, Chapter 3 concluded that this practice could have an indirect role in identifying customary international law. Moreover, it was proposed that some weight should be given to this practice when there is convergence with the practice of states.[195] By reviewing the commitments of armed groups in the previous sections, it is possible

---

191 Article 30(b) ASR and ARIO.

192 To date, 50 non-state armed groups have signed this commitment. See Geneva Call, 'Deed of Commitment under Geneva Call for adherence to a total ban on anti-personnel mines and for cooperation in mine action' available at <https://genevacall.org/wp-content/uploads/dlm_uploads/2013/12/DoC-Banning-anti-personnel-mines.pdf> accessed 30 May 2019.

193 Principle 23(f) UNBPG.

194 UN Security Resolution 1960 (16 December 2010) at 3, para. 5.

195 See section 4.1.2 of Chapter 3.

to appreciate an emerging practice and *opinio juris* of armed groups that are willing to provide some measures of reparation to civilians who are victims of non-international armed conflict. However, it is still too early to conclude the consistency and clarity of such practice and *opinio juris*. In particular, a substantive amount of practice and *opinio juris* of armed groups is required to be able to represent 'general acceptance'.[196] In order to be regarded as general acceptance, this practice would need to represent, on the one hand, different organisational structures of armed groups, and on the other hand, different geographical regions.[197] As for the *opinio juris*, clarification is required in relation to whether armed groups undertake to provide reparations based on their responsibility for the commission of IHL violations or based on their mere liability for damages. Future research paths could serve to bring light into these questions.

Another element that needs to be analysed is the process of weighting the practice of armed groups along with that of states. The issue here is that there are no established indicative factors on how to weigh both conducts. It is still premature to affirm that states are willing to accept that armed groups should provide full reparations to victims. However, in relation to peace agreements, there appears to be some convergence between the commitment of states and armed groups. In fact, this could be seen as indicative of some elements of state practice which accept the role of armed groups in the provision of reparations, although they cannot be considered as 'general acceptance' so far. Another question to consider is whether only the views of states that are (or have been) involved in a non-international armed conflict should be examined, or whether all views are relevant. In principle, among the different components of reparations, there seems to be an implied acceptance of the fact that armed groups should restitute those goods and properties illegally taken during the armed conflict. This can be inferred from both peace agreements between states and armed groups, and the own practice of armed groups, as analysed above. As a minimum, the views and conduct of armed groups should be regarded as interpretative tools. As indicated in Chapter 3, their views can be instrumental in adjusting these secondary duties to the capabilities of armed groups. These examples should also be taken as lessons learned for the future development of a general duty to provide reparations by armed groups.

4.5. CHALLENGES AND LIMITING FACTORS RELATING TO REPARATIONS PROVIDED BY ARMED GROUPS

Besides the determination of their normative value, the views and conduct of armed groups could be seen as lessons learned in the development of a potential obligation

---

196 On the concept of general acceptance see J. P. Kelly, 'Customary International Law in Historical Context: The Exercise of Power without General Acceptance' in B. D. Lepard (ed) *Reexamining Customary International Law* (Cambridge University Press 2017), 47–85.

197 In Chapter 3, it was concluded that 'account should be given to a sufficient number of armed groups representing different sizes and geographical regions so the general acceptance of a norm can be properly assessed'.

to provide reparations. In this scenario, there are a number of factors and challenges that require attention. First, in many cases it will be unfeasible to discuss any form of reparation from armed groups. For instance, if the armed group is eliminated as an entity in the aftermath of the conflict or if no military or political structures remain, it makes little sense to demand reparations. As for the moment to demand reparations, although there should be no impediments in claiming compensation during the course of the armed conflict, it seems more feasible to file these actions with the termination of the armed struggle. In this sense, Mastorodimos correctly notes that 'past experiences in armed conflict have shown that only after their effective end will it be possible to establish reparation mechanisms'.[198] Therefore, the provision of reparation as a secondary duty for armed groups will be context-dependent.

Second, another factor to take into account is the organisational structure of the armed group. As explained by Sinno, '[t]he organizational structures of armed groups, whether they develop by accident or by design, affect their strategic choices and performance during the conflict, as well as their ability to enter peace agreements'.[199] He further affirms that, in principle, only centralised organisations with a safe haven will be able to engage in successful peace agreements. As such, centralised armed groups are more likely to undertake reparation duties as part of the peace processes. On the contrary, decentralised armed groups will be less likely to engage in peace agreements 'because of the inability of the leadership to enforce the necessary discipline on the rank and file and because of other structural limitations'.[200]

Third, the previous examples suggested the possibility of creating compensation funds where both parties to the conflict, states and non-state armed groups, could contribute. In practice, however, these funds were either not created or were only supported by the funding of the state. In this regard, the establishment of these types of funds will require further implementation efforts and the regulation of potential contributors through clear rules. The precedent case of the peace agreement in Colombia offers a good example where the assets and goods of the FARC-EP were included in an inventory list. If armed groups are considered contributors of these compensation funds, this will help in creating a sense of trust for victims and will place armed groups alongside the state in terms of the efforts to mitigate the damage caused.

Fourth, although symbolic reparations and other measures of satisfaction can have a positive impact on victims, these measures should be as comprehensive as possible. In this sense, partial apologies by armed groups could be perceived as insufficient and this can lead to demands for further, deeper, and clearer apologies.[201] Moreover, although symbolic reparations could serve to mitigate immaterial or moral damages, they cannot substitute other forms of reparation. As indicated by the ILC commenting on the ASR, 'full reparation may only be achieved in particular cases by the combination of

198 K. Mastorodimos, *supra note* 189, 133.

199 A. H. Sinno, 'Armed groups' Organizational Structure and their Strategic Options' (2011) 93 *International Review of the Red Cross* 882, 311–332, at 312.

200 *Ibid*, 312–313.

201 J. Tomlinson, *supra note* 182, 59.

different forms of reparation'.[202] Consequently, moral reparations should be regarded as a complementary measure to other types of reparation and not in isolation.

Finally, if reparations' duties or other guarantees of non-repetition are established through the voluntary commitments of armed groups, these commitments should be accompanied by a monitoring system. The Geneva Call Deeds of Commitment and the action plans negotiated by the Office of the Special Representative of the Secretary-General for Children and Armed Conflict represent good examples of mechanisms that monitor the conduct of armed groups. These mechanisms have a system in place that could be replicated for further undertakings by non-state armed groups. The monitoring procedure could consist of a reporting system where armed groups indicate the positive steps taken to provide reparations or to prevent violations as a form of non-repetition or also verification missions conducted by the organisation.[203]

4.6. CONCLUDING REMARKS ON THE PRACTICE OF ARMED GROUPS REGARDING REPARATIONS

Some measures of reparations by armed groups have been included in a number of peace agreements resulting from non-international armed conflicts. These peace agreements have been concluded in the Philippines, Darfur (Sudan), Uganda, Colombia, Central African Republic, Somalia and Sierra Leone. These provisions relate mainly to the restitution of property and compensation of damage caused. In some cases, a compensation fund was envisaged but it later suffered problems of implementation. The most comprehensive example was the peace agreement in Colombia, which established a system of reparations, including specific obligations for armed groups. Other provisions of redress consist of symbolic or moral reparations and guarantees of non-repetition. Certain armed groups have offered public apologies to the victims of the conflict through the issuance of unilateral declarations. Moreover, some codes of conduct produced by armed groups have included a duty to restitute and compensate civilians for the damage caused. In fact, the mere issuance of codes of conduct could be considered a measure of non-repetition in certain circumstances, as exemplified by the signature of deeds of commitments in relation to the prohibition of anti-personnel landmines.

Although the normative value of the views and conduct of armed groups remains uncertain, it has been argued that these examples show an emerging practice and acceptance (emerging *opinio juris*) by armed groups to provide reparations to victims. This practice could lead to the formation of a customary norm of international law provided that this acceptance is considered general and, more importantly, provided that the practice of states is also coincident with these views. In particular,

202 Art. 34 ASR, Commentary para. 2.

203 For instance, Geneva Call have self-monitoring systems where armed groups report directly to the organization and they also conduct field missions to verify the compliance in the event of allegations of violations.

a consolidated amount of practice and *opinio juris* of armed groups is required to be able to represent general acceptance together with the practice and *opinio juris* of states. As a minimum, this practice can be used as an interpretative tool and can in fact be considered as lessons learned for the future development of a potential obligation for armed groups. In relation to these lessons learned, a number of limitations and challenges have been identified. These limitations relate to the eventual dissolution of the armed group as a separate entity, the type of organisational structure, possible problems of implementation, the insufficiency of symbolic reparations alone or the lack of monitoring systems. Nevertheless, the examples examined provide significant evidence that proves that armed groups can and have contributed to the redress of victims through different forms of reparation.

5. PROPOSALS FOR THE PROGRESSIVE DEVELOPMENT OF INTERNATIONAL LAW REGARDING ARMED GROUPS AND REPARATIONS

The purpose of this chapter is to answer the research question on whether armed groups can be under an obligation to provide reparations to victims. In this respect, although the current legal framework provided by treaties and customary international law in the fields of IHL, IHRL and ICL does not establish clear duties for armed groups regarding reparations, this appears to be a question of progressive development of international law. For instance, UN Commissions of Inquiry and other monitoring mechanisms have called for the incorporation of armed groups in the provision of reparations to victims of NIACs in parallel with the efforts of the state. Soft law initiatives also seem to promote a broad understanding of the duty holders of this obligation, implying that all actors involved need to contribute in the provision of redress to victims of gross violations of IHL and human rights. Particularly, the ILA Committee on the issue of Reparations in Armed conflict acknowledged the emergence of a secondary obligation to make reparation on behalf of non-state actors based on Article 75 of the Rome Statute, the UNBPG and the 2005 Report of the International Commission of Inquiry on Darfur. Moreover, the 'practice' of armed groups offers examples where certain armed groups have committed to provide some sort of reparation in peace agreements, unilateral declarations and codes of conduct.

However, whether there is existing convergence between the practice of states and armed groups which could lead to the formation of customary international law remains in a premature phase. Additionally, the identification of state practice and *opinio juris* also constitutes a complex endeavour. For instance, 'the evidence of state practice and *opinio juris* may be scattered, difficult to access, incomplete or contradictory'.[204] In any case, it remains to be seen if the duty to provide reparations by armed groups is

[204] A. Boyle and C. Chinkin, ***The Making of International Law*** (Oxford University Press 2007) 163.

crystallised in a substantive manner in the future development of international law. The current study proposes that this issue should be considered in terms of the progressive development of international law. According to the ILC, the progressive development of international law 'encompasses the drafting of legal rules in fields that have not yet been regulated by international law or sufficiently addressed in State practice'.[205] The following sections will examine the obligation to provide reparation by armed groups as a question for the progressive development of international law, taking into account its possible legal basis, its forms and its possible enforcement mechanisms.

5.1. THE OBLIGATION TO PROVIDE REPARATION BY ARMED GROUPS AND ITS LEGAL BASIS

If an emerging obligation to provide reparations by armed groups was to be identified, it would be necessary to establish its legal basis. In this regard, this obligation could derive from the international responsibility of the armed group for the commissions of IHL violations and the principle of full and effective reparation. In relation to the international responsibility of the armed group, the emergent practice analysed above highlights the role of armed groups as a separate and different entity from the state. In this vein, Van Boven affirms that victims could seek reparation from non-state entities under the UNBPG not based on state responsibility but on the 'legal liability' of these non-state actors.[206] In fact, the obligation to provide compensation in international armed conflict is now considered as having customary law status in relation to non-international armed conflicts. Moreover, the establishment of individuals as duty holders of the provision of reparations under ICL opens the door for the inclusion of entities other than the state as carrying this duty. In the context of NIACs, since violations can derive from multiple wrongdoers, reparations should also emanate from the different actors involved in such violations, thereby creating a framework of shared responsibility for reparations.[207] Furthermore, the inclusion of different actors involved in the alleviation of the damage caused could also serve to fight against impunity. This has been indicated by the Nairobi declaration on Women's and Girls' Right to a Remedy and Reparation which stated that 'the fundamental nature of the struggle against impunity demands that all reparation programmes must address the responsibility of all actors'.[208]

Alongside the establishment of the legal responsibility of armed groups, there are important principles and values that call for an inclusive understanding of the provision

205 International Law Commission, 'Codification and Progressive Development of International Law' at <http://legal.un.org/cod/> accessed 15 June 2019.

206 T. Van Boven, *supra note* 48, 3.

207 See P. D'Argent, 'Reparation, Cessation, Assuarances and Guarantees of Non-Repetition' in A. Nollkaemper & I. Plakokefalos (eds), *Principles of Shared Responsibility in International Law: An Appraisal of the State of the Art* (Cambridge University Press 2014) 208–250.

208 Nairobi Declaration on Women's and Girls' Right to a Remedy and Reparation (19–21 March 2007) point 5.

of reparations to victims, namely, the principle of solidarity, the principle of full and effective reparation, the right to truth and the principle of non-discrimination. In this sense, Van Boven has referred to 'human solidarity' as one of the principles constituting the basis of the provision of redress and reparations by non-state actors.[209] Solidarity was defined in the UN General Assembly Resolution 56/151 as follows:

> Solidarity, as a fundamental value, by virtue of which global challenges must be managed in a way that distributes costs and burdens fairly in accordance with basic principles of equity and social justice and ensures that those who suffer or who benefit the least receive help from those who benefit the most.[210]

The notion of solidarity requires a fair distribution of costs and burdens among all participants in the legal system in order to tackle global challenges. This fair distribution of costs and burdens could be applied to the issue of reparations of victims of gross violations of IHL and human rights in relation to those participants in the armed conflict. Additionally, under general international law reparation must be full. The principle of full reparation can be derived from Articles 31 and 34 of the ASR and the ARIO. These provisions require that an entity responsible for a breach is under an obligation to make 'full reparation' for the injury caused. The UNBPG are also based on the principle of full and effective reparation.[211] More precisely, the importance that all participants repair victims relates to the fact that this will contribute to the full protection of victims. As explained by Carrillo-Santarelli:

> It may happen that some of these consequences cannot be eliminated unless the non-state participants repair – e.g. concerning apologies and other forms of satisfaction. Then, their non-liability would be contrary to the necessity of addressing the totality of injuries and of "wholly" protecting victims [...].[212]

There may be victim's needs that are not addressed by the reparation efforts of the state such as the provision of information, acknowledgement of the facts or apologies from the perpetrators. As such, it may be indispensable that non-state armed groups provide complementary remedies. Consequently, in certain instances, unless non-state actors participate in the process of reparation, reparations will not be full and effective. According to Cheng, the principle of integral reparation demands that all proximate consequences of a wrongful act be eliminated in order to make an 'injured party [...] "whole again", because remedies 'should be commensurate with the loss, so that the injured party may be made whole'.[213]

---

209 T. Van Boven, *supra note* 48, 3.

210 UN General Assembly Resolution 56/151 (9 December 2002) para. 3(f).

211 Principle 18 UNBPG.

212 N. Carrillo-Santarelli, *Direct international human rights obligations of non-state actors*, 367.

213 B. Cheng, *General Principles of Law as Applied by International Courts and Tribunals* (Cambridge University Press 2006) 234–240.

With regard to the right to truth, Principle 24 of the UNBPG requires the following measures be provided to the victims:

> Victims and their representatives should be entitled to seek and obtain information on the causes leading to their victimization and on the causes and conditions pertaining to the gross violations of international human rights law and serious violations of international humanitarian law and to learn the truth in regard to these violations.

From this perspective, the right to truth is intrinsically connected with the right to reparation in the form of satisfaction. In particular, the right to truth has been recognised by the Inter-American Court of Human Rights as an essential part of the right to an effective remedy owed to the victims' relatives.[214] The disclosure of the truth could include the identification of the victim's remains and the bodies of those who disappeared. In fact, the origins of the right to truth can be traced to the right of families to know the fate of their relatives, recognised by Articles 32 and 33 of Additional Protocol I to the Geneva Conventions, as well as to the obligations of parties to armed conflicts to search for persons who have been reported missing.[215] In NIACs, the duty to search for the dead can be derived from Article 8 of Additional Protocol II. Moreover, a series of military manuals applicable in NIACs also acknowledge the duty to search for and collect the dead.[216] Rule 117 of the ICRC study on customary IHL affirms the obligation of each party to the conflict to 'take all feasible measures to account for persons reported missing as a result of armed conflict and must provide their family members with any information it has on their fate'.[217] As a procedural right, the right to truth arises after the violation of other substantive rights under IHL and IHRL has taken place.

It is argued that the provision of truth could help in creating 'an historical record, educate people, promote forgiveness and prevent future victimisation'.[218] The right to truth is directly related to reconciliation efforts and has a forward-looking function as it serves to vindicate the memory or status of the victim of the violation; it confronts the past; and it also seeks reform.[219] Attempts to find the truth have been carried out mainly through the establishment of truth commissions and other fact-finding mechanisms. However, in many cases, the voices of non-state actors have not been incorporated into these procedures. For instance, in the case of Peru, although the truth commission recommended the provision of reparation to victims of the violations carried out by the armed groups, the focus was put into the state. The rebel group, Sendero Luminoso,

---

214 T. M. Antkowiak, 'Truth as Right and Remedy in International Human Rights Experience' (2002) 23 *Michigan Journal of International Law* 4, 985–987.

215 Y. Naqvi, 'The right to the truth in international law: fact or fiction?' (2006) 88 *International Review of the Red Cross* 862, 248.

216 J.M. Henckaerts & L. Doswald-Beck, 407.

217 *Ibid*, 421.

218 M. C. Bassiouni, *supra note* 98, 276.

219 M. C. Bassiouni, *supra* note 98, 275.

could not participate in the hearings of the commission.[220] Furthermore, individual perpetrators cannot always be found or identified, or they can be unwilling to tell the truth. In the case of violations committed by armed groups during NIACs, this information could be provided by other members of the group or the group itself. In this sense, it would be essential to make the group responsible and for it to participate in these proceedings.

Therefore, it follows that both psychological and legal elements need to be present to acquire reparation in a comprehensive manner. Nonetheless, there are also a series of obstacles to obtaining reparations. In the case of reparations provided by the state in post-conflict situations, the main problem is determining priorities. Most successor governments that transition from violent conflict and that have witnessed gross violations of IHL and human rights depend heavily on donors to obtain financing as they do not have the adequate resources to provide reparations.[221] The priorities established by donors do not often fit well with the needs and demands of victims. Other issues have emerged in relation to the reparations derived from criminal proceedings at the ICC. International criminal proceedings are long and reparations are directly linked to the conviction of the perpetrator. For instance, the acquittals of Bemba and Gbagbo denied victims expectations of reparations.[222] Moreover, there is a clear unbalanced situation between the focus placed on individual perpetrators and the massive coverage of the victims of armed conflict. This issue has been analysed by Tapia Navarro who claims that 'selected prosecution of the "most responsible ones" in ICL is in open asymmetry with collective reparations as an attempt to address the collective nature of crimes only on the side of the victims'.[223] In this regard, alternative procedures need to be established to involve the armed group as a whole in the provision of redress if the individual perpetrator belonging to that group is unwilling or unable to do so.

Alongside the principle of full and effective reparation, it is also possible to highlight the principle of non-discrimination which is also established in the UNBPG.[224] Traditionally, non-discrimination has referred to issues of sex, gender, ethnicity, race, age, political affiliation, sexual orientation, nationality, religion or disability, among others. However, non-discrimination could also be relevant in relation to the origin or the source of the violation since the Principles acknowledge 'discrimination of any kind or on any ground'. If violations committed by non-state armed groups cannot be

---

220 *Ibid*, 792.

221 M. Schotsmans, 'Victim's Expectations, Needs and Perspectives after Gross and Systematic Human Rights Violations' in K. De Feyter, S. Parmentier, M. Bossuyt and P. Lemmens (eds) *Out of the Ashes: Reparation for Victims of Gross and Systematic Human Rights Violations* (Intersentia 2005) 127–128.

222 *See Press Release from the International Federation for Human Rights, 'The Bemba Case: Heavily criticized, the ICC must maintain victims' legal representation as the establishment of assistance programmes for victims is awaited' (1 October 2018) available at <https://www.fidh.org/en/region/Africa/central-african-republic/the-bemba-case-heavily-criticised-the-icc-must-maintain-victims-legal> accessed 12 June 2019.*

223 N. Tapia Navarro, 'Collective reparations and the limitations of International criminal justice to respond to mass atrocity' (2018) 18 *International Criminal Law Review*, 67–96, at 81.

224 Principle 25 UNBPG.

fully repaired this will lead to discriminatory treatment in comparison to violations committed by states. In conclusion, a victim-oriented approach and the necessity to offer full and effective protection to victims would demand that reparation is also granted by non-state armed groups.

To summarise, the principle of full reparation demands that both material and immaterial needs of victims are addressed by the reparative measures and that these measures cover all types of infringements, whether they be state or non-state violations. There may be victim's needs that are not addressed by the reparation efforts of the state, namely, the provision of information, acknowledgement of facts, and apologies by the perpetrators. As such, in certain cases it may be indispensable that non-state armed groups provide complementary remedies to victims. Besides, the principle of solidarity also requires that global challenges are managed in a way that distributes costs and burdens in a fair manner.

5.2. BROAD INTERPRETATION OF THE NOTION OF REPARATION AND POSSIBLE FORMS OF REPARATION

According to the previous findings, it is argued that the notion of reparation should be interpreted in a broad sense. This broad interpretation has to match a victim-oriented approach and should offer a wide range of measures where armed groups could contribute to covering material as well as immaterial needs. In light of this, reparations should serve to the triple purpose of cessation and non-repetition, restoration, and information. Therefore, reparation can be described as those measures provided by the armed group which cover both the material and immaterial needs of victims and serve one or more of the following purposes: cessation and non-repetition of violations; restoration of the prior situation and alleviation of the damage caused; and the provision of information in relation to the violations committed.

5.2.1. Cessation and non-repetition

First of all, one of the measures that armed groups could take is to cease in the commission of violations and offer guarantees of non-repetition. These components can be traced to Article 30 of the ASR and the ARIO and also from Principles 22(a) and 23 of the UNBPG. In particular, the above sections have provided examples of armed groups that have committed to avoid the commission of future violations of IHL, such as the those who have signed the Geneva Call Deed of Commitment on the prohibition of the use and production of anti-personnel mines and the action plans on the issue of children and armed conflict. In the case of the banning of anti-personnel mines, armed groups committed to cooperate in mine clearance, to allow monitoring and verification processes, and to issue orders to their commanders and fighters. Similarly, in relation to the action plans on children's rights, armed groups committed to release the children identified, issue military command orders and investigate those who recruit and use children. Provisions of non-repetition were also included in the Darfur Peace Agreement and the 2007 peace agreement in Uganda. Further measures of non-repetition similar to these could be taken by armed groups to cease in the commission of IHL violations and ensure the avoidance of future ones.

5.2.2. Restoration: restitution, compensation and rehabilitation

Restoration or the alleviation of the damage caused could take the form of restitution, compensation and rehabilitation. According to Principle 19 of the UNBPG, measures of restitution could consist of the restoration of liberty and other fundamental rights of victims and the return of buildings and other illegally taken properties. These measures have been envisaged in the peace agreements in the Philippines, Darfur, Uganda and the recent agreement in CAR. In 1996, the Security Council called upon the leaders of the factions in Liberia to ensure the return of looted property.[225] There appears to be no opposition in making armed groups responsible for restitution of properties. In fact, armed groups could play a fundamental role in returning property that has been illegally taken or destroyed so that victims can continue living their lives.

Regarding financial compensation, armed groups can also contribute by offering their assets and other belongings as part of the reparations provided, in order to cover both physical and moral damages. The duty of armed groups to provide compensation has been acknowledged by the UN Commission of Inquiry in Darfur and the Panel of Experts for Accountability in Sri Lanka. It has also been contemplated in the peace agreements in the Philippines and Uganda. Moreover, in 1998 the UN Secretary-General recommended to 'find, attach and seize the assets of transgressing parties and their leaders' to make parties to the conflict accountable for their actions.[226] In particular, the 2016 peace agreement in Colombia includes a provision on compensation by the FARC-EP through a list of assets. Finally, rehabilitation measures could also be provided by armed groups, especially in the areas most affected by their actions. This was considered in the peace agreement in the Philippines where the MILF undertook to 'determine, lead and manage rehabilitation and development projects in conflict affected areas'.[227]

5.2.3. Access to information

The necessity to provide information relates both to measures of satisfaction and the right to truth of victims. These measures are established in Article 37 of the ASR and the ARIO and in Principles 22 and 24 of the UNBPG. Measures of satisfaction could consist of the provision of information on the location of dead bodies, persons reported

---

225 UN Security Council, Resolution 1071 (30 August 1996) para. 8.

226 UN Secretary-General, 'Report on the Causes of Conflict and the Promotion of Durable Peace and Sustainable Development in Africa' (13 April 1998) UN Doc A/52/871 – S/1998/318, para. 50.

227 Paragraph B-2 of the Peace Agreement.

missing or the remains of victims; the acknowledgement of facts; the issuance of public apologies; and the celebration of official ceremonies and tributes. In practice, armed groups have offered public apologies to victims on a number of occasions, as was the case in Colombia, Sudan, Guatemala and Sierra Leone. Apart from offering apologies, the IRA in Ireland also assisted in the location of persons reported missing. These measures tackle the immaterial needs of victims and have a specific purpose of reconciliation. As explained above, the UN Special Rapporteur on extrajudicial, summary or arbitrary executions as well as other authors have encouraged armed groups to acknowledge facts and offer apologies as a form of symbolic reparation. Finally, it is important to clarify that all these measures have to be seen as complementary to the performance of the state. Responsibility for reparations has to be regarded as a comprehensive effort which incorporates all the actors involved in the violations committed, whether they be state or non-state entities.

5.3 POSSIBLE IMPLEMENTATION MECHANISMS

At the implementation level, a series of obstacles need to be tackled. As mentioned above, the provision of reparation on behalf of armed groups is only possible if these groups continue to have a separate existence after the conflict, as another type of association or a political entity. The type of organisational structure of the armed group could also be a factor to consider. In this respect, it is easier to reach an agreement with a centralised armed group that has a hierarchical and vertical organisation. Besides, commitments established in written documents or statements need to be complemented with implementation measures that establish the way in which armed groups can contribute to the process of reparations. Those commitments also require a monitoring system in place that contemplates self-reporting by the group and also the possibility of verification missions.

As far as enforcement mechanisms are concerned, armed groups could potentially contribute to reparations through their participation in truth commissions, their financial contribution to the Trust Fund of the ICC or their participation in national reparation programmes and specific compensation funds. As indicated earlier, armed groups have not always been present at the hearings of Truth Commissions so their participation in these proceedings could be essential. Although not being an official judicial mechanism, this could serve as a means to disclose the truth, acknowledge the violations committed and offer apologies and guarantees of non-repetition. In relation to financial compensation, several options are envisaged. Since the Trust Fund of the ICC establishes a system of voluntary contributions, armed groups could potentially offer funds whenever one of its members has been held liable for international crimes committed in the course of the armed conflict. Moreover, armed groups could also contribute to the funds established through national reparations programmes together with the funds of the state. Some national reparations programmes have received funds from assets recovered from corruption or assets held by paramilitaries. Accordingly, contribution from other non-state armed entities could also be envisaged.

In addition, the establishment of a specific compensation fund could be also considered as a possibility. This mechanism was contemplated in the Darfur Peace Agreement which included a Compensation Commission and a Compensation Fund. The Compensation Commission were to include members of the government and members of the two signatory armed groups. Although these measures were ultimately not put in place, this mechanism was considered a good example of a balance in the responsibilities of both parties to the conflict. More recently, the CAR peace agreement between the Government and 14 armed groups has included among its provisions the creation of a Trust Fund for victims. It remains to be determined how this fund will be implemented and if armed groups will also contribute to it.

Finally, domestic legal systems can also offer an alternative to tackle the responsibility of the group to provide compensation. Certain national jurisdictions allow individuals to file actions against 'unincorporated associations' if it is demonstrated 'that the persons represented should have the same common interest in defending the proceedings in question', as was the case in Northern Ireland.[228] In other cases, the group was considered responsible as a secondary actor where the individual belonging to the group was unable to provide compensation due to the principle of joint and several responsibility, as stated by the Constitutional Court in Colombia.[229] Such examples could become tentative proposals for the enforcement of the obligation to provide reparation by non-state armed groups at the domestic level.

6. CONCLUSIONS

This chapter has answered the question of whether armed groups can be under an obligation to provide reparations to victims. The analysis of the current international legal framework provided by treaties and customary international law under IHL, IHRL and ICL has noted the existence of uncertainties regarding the legal duty of armed groups to provide reparations as a secondary obligation. However, the growth of new soft law initiatives adopted by states, the reports of UN Commissions of Inquiry and Fact-Finding Missions, and the practice of certain armed groups place this issue as a question of progressive development of international law. In particular, the UNBPG contemplate the possibility that '*a person, a legal person, or other entity* is found liable for reparation to a victim'.[230] It is important to highlight that the UNBPG were adopted without any opposition by states, and as such, it is possible to consider an implied acceptance of the validity of those principles by states. Furthermore, the fact that Article 75 of the Rome Statute now includes individuals as duty-holders of the

228 *Breslin and Others v. Seamus McKenna and Others*, NIQB 50 (8 June 2009), paras. 83–84.
229 *Gustavo Gallón y Otros*, Constitutional Court of Colombia, C-370/2006 (18 May 2006), para. 6.2.4.4.11.
230 Principle 15, UNBPG.

obligation to provide reparation means that states no longer have the monopoly over reparations.

If we envisage such duty as a question of progressive development of international law, it will be necessary to identify its legal basis, possible forms and possible implementation mechanisms. As for the legal basis of this potential obligation, the international responsibility of the armed group for the commission of IHL violations should be considered the primary source. In addition, the principle of full reparation together with the principle of non-discrimination could reinforce the obligations of armed groups whenever the actions of the state are not sufficient to address the needs of victims, especially those related to moral or immaterial damages. It is foreseen that reparation afforded by armed groups could take the form of restitution, compensation, rehabilitation, satisfaction and guarantees of non-repetition. Nevertheless, these measures will serve to complement the efforts of the state, which will still be the primary guarantor of the duty to provide reparation in accordance with general principles of international law. Finally, as regards implementation mechanisms, these could range from participation of armed groups in the hearings of truth commissions, their financial contribution to the Trust Fund of the ICC, and their participation in national reparation programmes or specific compensation funds. In some cases, victims could also claim reparations from the armed group through civil litigation at the domestic level.

CHAPTER VI
CONCLUSIONS

1. INTRODUCTION

This chapter aims to answer the main research question of this study, namely *how can and should international law develop a responsibility framework for armed groups for violations of international humanitarian law (IHL)?* In order to do so, four sub-questions were formulated:

1. *To what extent is a regime of responsibility for armed groups necessary under international law?*
2. *Which methodology can and should be used to develop a responsibility framework for armed groups under international law?*
3. *In terms of attribution, under which conditions can and should acts of formal or de facto members of an armed group be attributed to the group itself?*
4. *In terms of legal consequences, can the armed group be under an obligation to provide reparation to victims?*

The answers to these sub-questions were provided in Chapters 2 to 5. This concluding chapter summarises the main findings from the four preceding chapters and answers the main research question. The study has advocated for a less state-centric approach to the question of regulation of armed groups taking into consideration certain non-traditional sources of international law. Moreover, this chapter reflects upon the main theoretical issues discussed in the previous chapters and considers the implications that the findings may have on any potential further research into the question of the regulation of armed groups under international law, such as the progressive development of international law.

In conducting the research, this book has tackled the question of the international responsibility of armed groups in a unitary study addressing the following issues: the legal reasons to develop such a responsibility framework; the methods and limitations in doing so; and the main elements to develop a responsibility framework, that is, the imputation or attribution element and the legal consequences. By addressing these elements in a unitary study, the research aims to avoid the problems of fragmentation and eventual conflicting outcomes. Moreover, although the question of international responsibility of armed groups was partially analysed by the scholarship, there was no comprehensive proposal on how to operationalize such responsibility. This study has also deepened the academic discussion regarding the organisational structure of armed groups and their temporal existence, both of which have been considered some of the main challenges in the regulation of armed groups under international law.[1] In addition, the book has considered new materials that could eventually be used for the further study of customary international humanitarian law.

2. TOWARDS A LESS STATE-CENTRIC SYSTEM OF INTERNATIONAL LAW

This study has argued that certain non-traditional sources of international law could be used to interpret and adapt international law to the current conditions of contemporary armed conflict. Moreover, it has been stated that certain notions of international law such as the concept of attribution and the obligation to provide reparations could be applied by analogy to other actors in the international arena such as non-state armed groups. In fact, the emergence of new actors that have a direct or indirect influence in international law has introduced new challenges into the traditional law-making processes as well as the application of international law. In particular, actors other than states are increasing their role in the development and interpretation of international law, for instance, international organisations and international courts and tribunals.[2] In addition, other instruments such as soft law documents are also increasing their influence in international law. As explained by D'Aspremont:

> [...] non-state actors' activities (and the normative outcomes of their actions) cannot entirely be caught by the "net" that international legal scholars have fabricated to catch reality, and definitely do not fall under the existing formal categories of international law.[3]

This makes us wonder whether the traditional state-centric system of international law is still valid to give answer to these challenges. In this regard, this study has tried to combine an intermediate approach to international law which acknowledges the central role of states in the international legal system but also incorporates outputs from international organisations and non-state actors. It has been argued that the adaptation of international law to new realities could be done through the process

---

1 See Fourth report on State responsibility by Mr. Roberto Ago, Special Rapporteur, International Law Commission Yearbook (30 June 1972 and 9 April 1973) UN Doc. A/CN.4/264 and Add.1., para. 154; A. Bellal, 'Establishing the Direct Responsibility of Non-State Armed Groups for Violations of International Norms: Issues of Attribution' in N. Gal-Or, C. Ryngaert & M. Noortmann. *Responsibilities of the Non-State Actor in Armed Conflict and the Market Place: Theoretical Considerations and Empirical Findings* (Brill Nijhoff 2015) 306–307.

2 S. Sivakumaran, 'Beyond States and Non-State Actors: The Role of State-Empowered Entities in the Making and Shaping of International Law' (2017) 55 *Columbia Journal of Transnational Law* 2, 343–394, at 357.

3 J. D'Aspremont (ed), *Participants in the International Legal System – Multiple Perspectives on Non-State Actors in International Law* (Routledge 2011) 1.

of interpretation. In this sense, the role of interpretation could be essential in the development of contemporary international law without challenging the primacy of the traditional sources of international law. This process of interpretation could be done by various interpretative communities in international law depending on the different disciplines of law.[4] Regarding IHL, an important part of this corpus has been developed through the interpretative role of international criminal courts and the work of the ICRC. Moreover, as indicated in this study, other actors are emerging in the task of interpreting IHL, such as independent experts and special rapporteurs.

3. THE NECESSITY OF A RESPONSIBILITY FRAMEWORK FOR ARMED GROUPS UNDER INTERNATIONAL LAW

This study acknowledges the existence of a disconnection between (primary) international obligations of armed groups and secondary norms on international responsibility. This means that while it is clear that armed groups are bound by primary obligations in international law, it is still controversial whether the violation of those obligations (in particular IHL obligations) entails any legal consequences for armed groups as collective entities.[5] In this respect, it is important to highlight that the concept of international responsibility focuses on collective entities, that is, states and international organisations. In addition, the possibility of holding individuals responsible has also been considered under international criminal law. The question remains as to whether other collective entities, such as non-state armed groups, can also be held responsible internationally.

After conducting a systematic review of the current legal framework applicable to armed groups, it was concluded that there were no rules that tackle the responsibility of armed groups as collective entities under international law. The main response given by international law to address the commission of IHL violations by armed groups appears to focus on the criminal responsibility of its individual members, leaving untouched the possible responsibility of the group as a whole. On the other hand, UN monitoring mechanisms have dealt with the actions of armed groups, reporting the strategies and organisational policies of these groups. However, there is no legal framework in place against which the conduct of armed groups qua collective entities could be assessed by these mechanisms. Due to these gaps and inconsistencies, the question arises: 'To what extent is a regime of responsibility for armed groups necessary under international law?'. Or in other words, what are the legal and practical reasons for developing such a regime?

In answering this question, the study has considered a series of principles as evaluative yardsticks: the rule of law, the prevention of impunity and victims' rights to

4 M. Waibel, 'Interpretative Communities in International Law' in A. Bianchi, D. Peat & M. Windsor, (eds) *Interpretation in International Law* (Oxford University Press 2015) 147–165.

5 V. Bílková, 'Direct Responsibility of Armed Opposition Groups', 263.

reparation. First, the lack of clear rules addressing the responsibility of armed groups directly clashes with the idea of an international legal order governed by the rule of law.[6] The rule of law is defined as 'a principle of governance in which all persons, institutions and entities, public and private, including the State itself, are accountable to laws that are publicly promulgated, equally enforced and independently adjudicated, and which are consistent with international human rights norms and standards'.[7] It specifically requires 'measures to ensure adherence to the principles of supremacy of law, equality before the law, accountability to the law, fairness in the application of the law, separation of powers, participation in decision-making, legal certainty, avoidance of arbitrariness and procedural and legal transparency'.[8] Consequently, clarifying the legal framework in this field could contribute to strengthening legal certainty and accountability to the law. It could also help to facilitate the transparency of monitoring compliance and other accountability mechanisms that deal with reporting IHL and IHRL violations during armed conflicts.

Second, since armed conflicts are fought by both states and non-state entities and there are many examples of armed groups committing violations of IHL, it seems necessary to find ways to bring together several aims including the legal consequences of responsibility, the fight against impunity and victims' rights to reparation. In the end, reparations for victims of armed conflict would be better addressed if the respondent is a collective entity, namely a state or an armed group.[9] From the victim's point of view, it is immaterial if the offender is a state agent or a member of an armed group. Moreover, the difficulties in identifying individual perpetrators or leaders should not be an obstacle to providing full reparations to victims. In this regard, impunity is often linked to the denial of effective remedies for victims.

In addition, although ICL has been considered the mainstream answer when dealing with violations of IHL committed by armed groups, there are important reasons to question whether ICL should be considered the ideal mechanism to address violations committed by these groups. In relation to its scope of application, ICL only covers the action of individuals and not groups.[10] With regards to the crimes that are subject to prosecution of international courts and in particular of the ICC, not all violations of IHL are considered international crimes and therefore, punishable.[11] The provisions

---

6 J. K Kleffner, 'The collective accountability of organised armed groups', 259.

7 Report of the UN Secretary-General, 'The Rule of Law and Transitional Justice in Conflict and Post-conflict Societies' (23 August 2004) UN Doc. S/2004/616, para. 6.

8 *Ibid*, para. 6.

9 K. Mastorodimos, *Armed Non-State Actors in International Humanitarian and Human Rights Law. Foundation and Framework of Obligations, and Rules on Accountability* (Routledge 2015) 3.

10 See Art. 25(1) ICC Statute; Art. 6 ICTY Statute; Art. 5 ICTR Statute; Art. 6 Statute of the Special Court for Sierra Leone; Art. 3 Statute Special Tribunal for Lebanon; Art. 29 Extraordinary Chambers in the Courts of Cambodia; Art. 14(1) Special Panels of the Dili District Court East Timor. Interestingly, Art. 46C of the *Protocol on Amendments to the Protocol on the Statute of the African Court of Justice and Human Rights* is entitled 'Corporate Criminal Liability' and establishes that 'the Court shall have jurisdiction over legal persons, with the exception of States.' However, the Protocol is still not in force.

11 V. Bílková, 'Direct Responsibility of Armed Opposition Groups', 273.

of the ICC Statute only cover the most serious violations of the Geneva Conventions and the Additional Protocols, including genocide, war crimes and crimes against humanity. Consequently, some violations do not reach the level of international crimes. Another limitation is that international criminal proceedings seem to focus mainly on retribution and deterrence as their major aims. However, while prosecuting individuals for the commission of international crimes is an important aim in itself, there are other purposes in serving justice, such as truth-seeking, restitution and providing remedies to victims that can be met through additional judicial and non-judicial mechanisms. Finally, criminal proceedings are long and require a strict system of evidence, which often limits victims' access to reparations.

To summarise, ascribing international responsibility to armed groups as collective entities could serve to bridge the so-called 'responsibility gap' by strengthening the rule of law and the right to reparation of victims of non-international armed conflict. If individual criminal responsibility is not sufficient in tackling violations committed by collective entities, and in particular by armed groups, then both levels of responsibility could be complementary. In fact, establishing several layers of responsibility between the individual and the collective entity could be more effective in addressing the whole range of actions carried out by non-state armed groups. Finally, connecting the factual power of armed groups with a coherent response by the international legal order would also serve to fight against impunity.

4. IDENTIFYING A SUITABLE METHODOLOGY TO THE STUDY OF THE INTERNATIONAL RESPONSIBILITY OF ARMED GROUPS

The second research question was exploratory, looking for new fruitful paths in legal research that better incorporate issues of responsibility of armed groups in international law.[12] In particular, the research question posed was '[w]hich methodology can and should be used to develop a responsibility framework for armed groups under international law?'. The aim of the discussion was to inquire into the possible methods that could aid in the development of principles of responsibility for the violations of IHL committed by armed groups. In responding to this question, the study has started by examining the methodology used by the ILC in the drafting process of the principles on international responsibility applicable to states and international organisations. The purpose of this analysis was to extract lessons learned from this procedure and to determine the extent to which possible analogies could be applied to the issue of international responsibility between states and international organisations, on the one hand, and armed groups, on the other.

---

12 M. Van Hoecke (ed) *Methodologies of Legal Research* (Hart Publishing 2011) v.

Analogical legal reasoning has advantages and limitations like any other method of legal reasoning. The main advantage of reasoning by analogy is that it fosters the coherence of the international legal system which also serves the purpose of predictability.[13] Analogous reasoning also has some limitations, however. Particularly, analogous reasoning relies excessively on existing convictions and existing frameworks which may also contain weaknesses.[14] This constitutes an important limitation to be borne in mind. Nevertheless, the application of analogical legal reasoning is preferred in this case as it strikes a fair balance between keeping the unity and coherence of the international legal system and acknowledging the peculiarities and capabilities of organised armed groups.

According to Vöneky, reasoning by analogy has to be conducted in a three-step process: first, comparing the regulated case with the unregulated one; second, exploring the similarities and differences between the proposed cases; and third, assessing whether the similarities are relevant enough.[15] After conducting this three-step process, the present study concluded that as for the similarities between the proposed cases, states, international organisations and armed groups all have to develop a minimum level of organisation in order to operate in a unified manner. In addition, both states and armed groups share parallel obligations under international humanitarian law. In principle, there appears to be no policy reasons against the development of similar rules or guidelines on international responsibility when certain entities have reached a minimum level of organisation and are bound by a limited set of obligations under international law. Nevertheless, one limitation has to be introduced: armed groups differ from states and international organisations in terms of their organisational structure so a plain transposition of the applicable rules was not considered advisable. Accordingly, even if these rules could be taken as a starting point, major adjustments need to be introduced.

Similarly to the work done by the ILC in relation to international organisations, those adjustments would need to take into account the special features of armed groups as well as the relevant practice on the matter. In contrast to the development of rules applicable to international organisations where there was at least certain practice on the matter by both states and international organisations, the practice by these actors in relation to armed groups is more limited. Consequently, one could wonder if the same traditional sources of international law were actually suitable for the introduction of adjustments for armed groups. The traditional sources of international law rarely deal with the conduct of armed groups. However, there are 'other sources' and non-judicial mechanisms that have tackled the conduct of armed groups. In particular, the practice of armed groups has been taken into consideration when discussing the primary

---

13 C. Ahlborn, 'The Use of Analogies in Drafting the Articles on the Responsibility of International Organizations – An Appraisal of the "Copy-Paste Approach" (2012) *SHARES Research Paper* 13, Amsterdam Centre for International Law, 4.

14 C. R. Sunstein, 'On Analogical Reasoning' (1993) 106 *Harvard Law Review* 3, 741–791, 769.

15 S. Vöneky, 'Analogy in International Law', para. 5.

obligations of armed groups.[16] In this line, this material may also contain elements that help clarify secondary rules for armed groups, particularly in relation to the factual organisation of the armed group. Moreover, non-judicial monitoring mechanisms dealing with violations committed by armed groups could also include information that offers assistance in linking the actions of individuals with the group as such.

Indeed, it was demonstrated that the inclusion of other sources of international law for the development of general principles on international responsibility was not actually foreign to the methodology followed by the ILC. Most notably, the ILC considered the decisions of arbitral tribunals and the practice of international organisations as sources of information which did not fit in the classic list contained within Article 38 of the ICJ Statute. Likewise, the practice of armed groups could be considered analogous to the practice and internal rules of international organisations. The reports from UN monitoring mechanisms could be assimilated to the opinion of highly reputed jurists as a supplementary means of interpretation. In addition, these reports enjoy the endorsement of the United Nations.

In conclusion, the study proposes the development of an analogous approach to the issue of international responsibility than the one employed by the ILC in the adaptation of norms to international organisations. This analogous approach is based on common principles of responsibility and attribution shared by states and international organisations but adapted to the specific characteristics of armed groups and the interpretation provided by the practice of armed groups and non-judicial mechanisms that have monitored the conduct of armed groups.

5. THE ATTRIBUTION OF CONDUCT TO ARMED GROUPS AS AN ESSENTIAL ELEMENT OF INTERNATIONAL RESPONSIBILITY

The issue of attribution is a key element for the responsibility of collective entities. The aim of attribution is the determination of the responsible person. Under international law, this connection is not based on a mere exercise of causality but on the development of specific rules that establish the relationship between the individual or the group that performs the act (or the omission) and the entity that carries the burden for the violation committed. According to Zegveld 'the question which acts and omissions can be attributed to armed opposition groups has, however, not been answered in a coherent way by international bodies'.[17] In consequence, an in-depth examination of the potential rules of attribution applicable to armed groups was required. The research question that was answered in this section was: 'Under which conditions can and should acts of formal or *de facto* members of an armed group be attributed to the group itself?'

16 J. M. Henckaerts & L. Doswald-Beck, *Customary International Humanitarian Law*, at xlii.
17 L. Zegveld, *Accountability of armed opposition groups*, 153.

The study also considered whether additional rules of attribution could be applied to the conduct of armed groups.

Following the methodology proposed in Chapter 3, this study analysed the substantive rules of attribution for states and international organisations and extracted the core principles of attribution that could be applied by analogy to other collective entities, including armed groups. These core principles of attribution are:

a) Attribution based on the conduct of organs and agents belonging to the organisation, including *ultra vires* acts.
b) Attribution based on the conduct of other individuals or entities under the direction and control of the organisation.
c) Attribution based on the acknowledgement of conduct as its own by the organisation.[18]

As explained previously, the core principles of attribution could be applied by analogy to armed groups provided that the required adjustments were introduced. Those adjustments relate to the special features of armed groups and the information provided by the so-called practice of armed groups and the reports of non-judicial monitoring mechanisms. Regarding the special features of armed groups, the main factor to be considered was the structural disparity of armed groups.[19] This structural disparity was reflected in a number of elements: the existence of military and political wings; centralised and decentralised types of armed groups; and changes in structure over the course of time. These elements constitute decisive factors to be taken into account when delimiting and adjusting possible rules of attribution. In this respect, the civilian or military character of the individual could determine a different standard of attribution of conduct applicable to the group. The different organisational structure of the armed group will have consequences over the standard of direction and control that is applied to the different members or units, depending on the centralised or decentralised nature of the organisation. Moreover, attribution of conduct is context-dependent, that is, it depends on the specific moment in time when the conduct takes place and the level of organisation of the group at that point. As for the interpretative materials used to adjust those rules, the study considered internal rulings, codes of conduct and unilateral declarations of armed groups. Other indicators and tools of interpretation were found in the reports of UN monitoring bodies that have assessed the conduct of non-state armed groups and the IHL violations committed by them.

In relation to the first rule of attribution based on the conduct of organs and/or agents of the armed group, a functional approach has been proposed. The notion of 'agent' seems to be more flexible than the concept of 'organ' since the former focuses on the functions rather than the official status of the person or entity.[20] Consequently,

18 See section 2.3 of Chapter 4.
19 See section 3.1 of Chapter 4.
20 The concept of 'agent' is established in the ARIO and refers to those persons carrying out activities and acting on behalf of the organisation with independence of their inclusion in the internal structures of the organisation.

for attributing acts to armed groups based on this rule, it is necessary to examine the different roles within the group and to determine the extent to which members are acting on behalf of the group, rather than only establishing their official affiliation to an armed group. In principle, the characterisation of someone as an agent of the armed group should be based on the performance of military actions on behalf of the group.[21]

With regard to the second rule of attribution based on conduct directed and controlled by an armed group, this rule could potentially be applied to both centralised and decentralised armed groups. Besides, a distinction must be drawn between individuals and other military factions. The standard of effective control will be required for the actions of private individuals who do not belong to the internal structures nor perform activities for the group on a regular basis but who act under their specific instructions. For other armed factions, the rule will depend on the centralised or decentralised nature of the armed group. In the case of centralised armed groups, the actions of other armed entities could be considered attributable to the group if these factions are under the command and control of the group due to the existence of a strict chain of command. If the actions of these armed factions are not under this command and control, they would constitute splinter or separated factions. For decentralised armed groups, the requirement will be, in principle, the overall control over the different factions or cells. This overall control would need to incorporate the general coordination powers of the leadership over the military actions as well as its general authority over the sub-groups.[22]

As for the third rule of attribution based on the acknowledgement of the conduct by the armed group, this acknowledgement has to be more than mere support or endorsement. Moreover, the armed group has to identify the specific conduct as its own, going beyond a general recognition of the facts. Secondly, the act of acknowledgement has to be 'clear and unequivocal'.[23] In relation to armed groups, this act could be expressed through a unilateral declaration or a communication sent to an international organisation or an NGO charged with monitoring the country situation. Acknowledgment could also take place in a later moment in judicial proceedings or in truth commissions by the leadership of the armed group.

6. THE LEGAL CONSEQUENCES OF RESPONSIBILITY: THE OBLIGATION TO PROVIDE REPARATIONS BY ARMED GROUPS

The second key element of international responsibility relates to the legal consequences and, in particular, to the obligation to provide reparation. The research question

21 As explained in Chapter 4, only the military wing of the armed group is relevant for the attribution of IHL violations.
22 See T. Rodenhäuser, *Organizing Rebellion*, 84.
23 Art. 11 ASR, Commentary para. 8.

answered in this chapter was: 'can the armed group be under an obligation to provide reparations to victims?'. To answer this query the study conducted an overview of the current legal framework regarding reparations for IHL violations and evaluated whether international treaties, state practice, and the reports from UN monitoring mechanisms have recognised any potential role for non-state armed groups in the provision of reparations. Secondly, the study looked at the practice of armed groups committing to provide certain forms of reparation through peace agreements, unilateral declarations, and codes of conduct. This practice was assessed in relation to its normative value and its possible contribution to customary international law. The following key findings were made.

It was concluded that although the current legal framework provided by treaties and customary international law in the fields of IHL, IHRL and ICL does not establish clear duties on armed groups regarding reparations, this appears to be a question of progressive development of international law. For instance, UN Commissions of Inquiry and other monitoring mechanisms have called for the incorporation of armed groups in the provision of reparations to victims of NIACs in parallel with the efforts of the state.[24] Soft law initiatives also seem to promote a broad understanding of the duty holders of this obligation, implying that all actors involved need to contribute in the provision of redress to victims of gross violations of IHL and human rights. Particularly, the ILA Committee on the issue of Reparations in Armed conflict acknowledged the emergence of a secondary obligation to make reparation on behalf of non-state actors based on Article 75 of the Rome Statute, the UNBPG and the 2005 Report of the International Commission of Inquiry on Darfur.[25]

The 'practice' of armed groups has offered examples where certain armed groups have committed to provide some sort of reparation in peace agreements, unilateral declarations and codes of conduct.[26] By reviewing the commitments of armed groups, it was possible to appreciate an emerging practice and *opinio juris* on behalf of armed groups which were willing to provide some measures of reparation to those civilians who were victims of non-international armed conflicts. However, it is still too early to conclude whether such practice and *opinio juris* can be considered clear and consistent, and whether there is an existing convergence between the practice of states and armed groups that could lead to the formation of customary international law, as it still appears to be in a premature phase. In any case, it remains to be determined if the duty to provide reparations by armed groups is crystallised in a substantive manner in the future development of international law.

A number of lessons learned and limitations were also identified from the study of the practice of armed groups regarding reparations.[27] First, in many cases it will be unfeasible to consider any form of reparation from armed groups. For instance,

[24] See section 3.1.4 of Chapter 5.

[25] International Law Association, Committee on Reparation for Victims of Armed Conflict, The Hague Conference Report 'Reparation for Victims of Armed Conflict (Substantive Issues)' (2010).

[26] See section 4.1 of Chapter 5.

[27] See section 4.5 of Chapter 5.

if the armed group is simply eliminated as an entity in the aftermath of the conflict or if no military or political structures remain, it makes little sense to demand reparations. As for the moment to demand reparations, although there should be no impediments in claiming compensation during the course of the armed conflict, it seems more feasible to file these actions with the termination of the armed struggle. Second, the organisational structure of the armed group will be another circumstance to take into account. Centralised armed groups seem to be more likely to undertake reparation duties as part of the peace processes. On the contrary, decentralised armed groups will be less likely to engage in peace agreements 'because of the inability of the leadership to enforce the necessary discipline on the rank and file and because of other structural limitations'.[28] Third, the establishment of compensation funds to which both parties to the conflict could contribute requires further implementation efforts and the regulation of the potential contributors through clear rules. Fourth, although symbolic reparations and other measures of satisfaction can have a positive impact on victims, they should be regarded as a complementary measure to other components of reparations and not be seen as an isolated effort. Finally, if reparations' duties or other guarantees of non-repetition are established through the voluntary commitments of armed groups, these commitments should be accompanied by a monitoring system.

This study has proposed to consider the provision of reparations by armed groups as a matter of progressive development of international law. In this regard, if an emerging obligation to provide reparations by armed groups is envisaged, it is essential to identify its legal basis. The study argues that this obligation could derive from the international responsibility of the armed group for the commission of violations of IHL and the principle of full reparation to victims. It has also been proposed that the notion of reparation would need to be interpreted broadly. This broad interpretation should follow a victim-oriented approach and offer a wide range of measures allowing for the contribution of armed groups to both material and immaterial needs. In addition, it is foreseen that reparations afforded by armed groups could take the form of restitution, compensation, rehabilitation, satisfaction and guarantees of non-repetition. Nevertheless, these measures will serve to complement the efforts of the state, which will still be the primary guarantor of the provision of reparations in accordance with the general principles of international law. Finally, among the enforcement mechanisms, these could range from their participation in the hearings of truth commissions, their financial contribution to the Trust Fund of the ICC, and their participation in national reparation programmes or specific compensation funds. In some cases, victims could also claim reparations from the armed group through civil litigation at the domestic level.

---

28 A. H. Sinno, 'Armed groups' organizational structure and their strategic options' (2011) 93 *International Review of the Red Cross* 882, 311–332, 312–313.

7. PROGRESSIVE DEVELOPMENT OF INTERNATIONAL LAW AND ARMED GROUPS

Regarding the question of international responsibility of armed groups, this book has focused on two main issues, namely the attribution of and reparations for violations of international humanitarian law. In relation to the issue of attribution of conduct to an armed group, it was concluded that there was no substantive practice on the matter because, on the one hand, ICL only deals with the actions of individuals, and on the other hand, non-judicial monitoring mechanisms do not specifically address the question of attribution of conduct to the armed group as a collectivity. Nonetheless, both ICL and reports from monitoring mechanisms acknowledge the existence of an organisational structure and certain strategies and policies established by the armed group. The existence of such organisational units was the reason to determine that the rules of attribution from states and international organisations could be applied by analogy.

The development of future principles of attribution would require that UN monitoring mechanisms involved in the examination of violations committed during NIAC establish a connection between individual members and the group in a more straightforward manner. More precisely, they should delimitate under which approach or rule – for instance, agency based on a functional approach, agency based on direction or control, acknowledgment of the conduct or any other rules – they are attributing such violations. This would help in clarifying the rules of attribution for non-state armed groups in a manner that is consistent with the principle of the rule of law, and consequently, would strengthen the legal certainty and the transparency of the monitoring processes. Moreover, a consistent practice from UN monitoring mechanisms could give rise to the crystallisation of customary rules or at least it could feed into the interpretation of rules applicable to armed groups. The interaction of states with these reports would be essential. They could submit comments or endorse these reports through subsequent practice. In fact, some authors claim that the lack of response from states could implicitly be treated as acquiescence. This has been noted by Sivakumaran in relation to the output from state-empowered entities such as the ILC and UN human rights bodies. On this matter, he stated that:

> Given that many state-empowered entities have a mandate to make and shape international law, coupled with the general utility of their outputs, members of the community of international lawyers treat the lack of response on the part of States as acquiescence to the output.[29]

The lack of opposition could be considered as an implied acceptance of the content. However, for the creation of substantive state practice, we would need something more than the mere acquiescence.

With regard to the question of reparations, there seems to be an emerging practice on the matter coming from the practice of states and armed groups through peace

[29] S. Sivakuamaran, *supra note* 2, at 385.

agreements, the work of UN monitoring mechanisms and from soft law instruments. However, as was explained, this emerging practice has yet to reach the status of customary international law. More particularly, it is essential to clarify whether the practice of non-state armed groups could contribute to customary international law. So far, the study on customary international law provided by the ILC has only recognised an indirect role to the contribution of non-state actors.[30] As concerns non-state armed groups, the commentary to the draft articles only considered the reactions of states to the conduct of armed groups as being relevant for its possible contribution to customary international law.[31] However, the reply of the Special Rapporteur to the comments of states in the last report was rather ambiguous.[32] Nevertheless, even if we confer any direct or indirect role to the conduct of armed groups in the formation or identification of customary international law, more research efforts will be needed to identify a substantive amount of practice and *opinio juris* of armed groups that will be able to represent 'general acceptance'.[33] In order to be regarded as general acceptance, this practice would need to represent, on the one hand, different organisational structures of armed groups, and on the other hand, different geographical regions.[34] This study has shown that there is an emerging trend from armed groups willing to accept their duty to provide reparations to victims of the armed conflict and that, in fact, certain measures of reparations could be provided by armed groups based on their respective capacities.

In conclusion, it was argued that the provision of reparations by armed groups should be considered a question of progressive development of international law. In this respect, the ILC makes the distinction between codification and progressive development of international law based on the existence or not of sufficient state practice.[35] In relation to the ARIO, the ILC has explicitly claimed that the topic was more an issue of progressive development of international law than a question of codification due to the inexistence of a sufficient amount of practice.[36] Therefore, only subsequent practice by states, international organisations, judicial decisions and other non-judicial mechanisms would determine the crystallisation of this issue as a matter of customary international law.

---

30 International Law Commission Report, 'Sixty-eighth Session' (2016) UN Doc. A/71/10, 89–90, para. 9.

31 *Ibid*, para. 9.

32 Fifth Report on Identification of Customary International Law by Mr. Michael Wood, Special Rapporteur (14 March 2018) A/CN.4/717, 22, para. 49.

33 On the concept of general acceptance see J. P. Kelly, 'Customary International Law in Historical Context: The Exercise of Power without General Acceptance' in B. D. Lepard (ed) *Reexamining Customary International Law* (Cambridge University Press 2017) 47–85.

34 In Chapter 3, it was concluded that 'account should be given to a sufficient number of armed groups representing different sizes and geographical regions so the general acceptance of a norm can be properly assessed'.

35 International Law Commission, 'Codification and Progressive Development of International Law' available at <http://legal.un.org/cod/> accessed 15 June 2019.

36 In the General Commentary of the ARIO, the ILC recognised that '[t]he fact that several of the present draft articles are based on limited practice moves the border between codification and progressive development in the direction of the latter'. See ARIO, General Commentary, 2, para. 5.

8. PROPOSED AVENUES FOR FURTHER RESEARCH

The development of a responsibility framework for armed group as such could also open the door for further research into two interconnected issues, namely the possibility of applying circumstances precluding wrongfulness to armed groups, and the existence of shared responsibility between states and armed groups or between different armed groups. With regard to the first issue, if we accept that rules of attribution could be applied to armed groups, the next question would be the circumstances, if any, that could be used to preclude the wrongfulness of such breaches.[37] In particular, it would be essential to determine if armed groups would be allowed to take countermeasures in response to a breach committed by another entity, probably another state. It has to be noted that circumstances precluding wrongfulness are applicable not only to states but also to international organisations.

The second issue to consider is the possible existence of shared responsibility between states and armed groups or between several armed groups. The reality of contemporary armed conflicts evidences the participation of a myriad of non-state armed groups that contribute to the commission of IHL and human rights violations. In this book, the attribution of violations to armed groups was analysed in an independent way, that is, their contribution to different and separate harmful acts. However, another possibility is that several armed groups contribute to a single harmful outcome. Moreover, certain acts can be committed by armed groups in conjunction or with the assistance of states which also raises the question of shared or joint responsibility.[38] Consequently, there is a need for further research into the different possibilities which can emerge in contemporary armed conflict involving several entities.

9. FINAL REMARKS

This book has aimed to clarify the uncertainties regarding whether armed groups could be held responsible for IHL violations as collectivities and the consequences that this responsibility may have. In order to do so, the book has examined certain common notions of international law, such as attribution and reparations, which could be potentially applied to non-state armed groups if the necessary adjustments are introduced. In particular, it has been argued that the different organisational structures and other special features of armed groups need to be considered if we want to develop a legal framework that is closer to the reality of contemporary armed conflict. In addition, the study has proposed to consider the practice of armed groups (including their unilateral declarations, special agreements, codes of conduct and internal rulings) and the reports of UN monitoring mechanisms as instrumental in the

37 See for instance, E. Heffes, 'The Responsibility of armed opposition groups'.

38 See V. Bílková, 'Armed Opposition Groups and Shared Responsibility' (2015) SHARES Research Paper 62.

process of interpreting and adapting these general concepts to the conduct of armed groups. In doing so, certain notions which were considered obscure or ambiguous such as membership and organs of armed groups, and centralised and decentralised armed groups, have been clarified. Finally, the compilation of practice of armed groups and UN documents included in this study could be considered as relevant material for the further study of customary international humanitarian law.

BIBLIOGRAPHY

ACADEMIC LITERATURE

Ahlborn, C. 'The Use of Analogies in Drafting the Articles on the Responsibility of International Organizations: An Appraisal of the "Copy-Paste Approach"' (2012) *SHARES Research Paper* 13, Amsterdam Centre for International Law, 2012-14.

Ainley, K. 'Excesses of Responsibility: The Limits of Law and The Possibilities of Politics' (2011) 25 *Ethics & International Affairs*, 407-431.

Albin, R. 'Collective responsibility: Organizations as Organic Entities' (2016) 6 *Open Journal of Philosophy*, 392-405.

Alston, P 'The "Not-a-Cat" Syndrome: Can the International Human Rights Regime Accommodate Non-State Actors? in Alston P. (ed), *Non-State Actors and Human Rights* (Oxford University Press 2005).

Alston, P., Morgan-Foster, J. & Abresch, W. 'The Competence of the UN Human Rights Council and its Special Procedures in relation to Armed Conflicts: Extrajudicial executions in the "War on Terror" (2008) 19 *European Journal of International Law* 1, 183-209.

Alvarez, J. 'Book Review of Dan Sarooshi, International Organizations and Their Exercise of Sovereign Powers' (2007) 101 *American Journal of International Law*, 676-677.

Antkowiak, T. M. 'Truth as Right and Remedy in International Human Rights Experience' (2002) 23 *Michigan Journal of International Law* 4.

Anzilotti, D. *Corso di Diritto Internazionale. Vol. 1* (CEDAM, 1955).

Anzilotti, D. *Cours de droit international* (Panthéon-Assas/LGDJ, 1999).

Anzilotti, D. 'La responsabilité internationale des États à raison des dommages soufferts par les étrangers' (1906) *Revue Générale de Droit Internationale Public*, 5-29.

Ambos, K. 'Superior Responsibility' in Cassese A., Gaeta P., Jones J. R. W. D. (eds) *The Rome Statute of the International Criminal Court: A Commentary, Vol. 3* (Oxford University Press 2002).

Ambos, K. 'The ICC and Common Purpose: What Contribution is Required Under Article 25(3)(d)?' in Stahn, C. (ed), *The Law and Practice of the ICC: A Critical Account of Challenges and Achievements* (Oxford University Press 2015).

Amoroso, D. 'Armed Opposition Groups' (and Foreign Fighters) Abidance by International Human Rights Law: The Issue of Compliance in Syria and Iraq' in de Guttry, A, Capone F and Paulussen, C. (eds) *Foreign fighters under international law and beyond* (TMC Asser Press 2016).

Azzarello C. & Niederhauser M. 'The Independent Humanitarian Fact-Finding Commission: Has the "Sleeping Beauty" Awoken?' in *ICRC Humanitarian Law & Policy* (January 2018).

Badar, M.L. "Just Convict Everyone!" – Joint Perpetration: From Tadic to Stakic and Back Again' (2006) 6 *International Criminal Law Review*, 293-302.

Bangerter, O. 'Internal Control. Codes of Conduct within Insurgent Armed Groups', Occasional Paper of the Small Arms Survey (Graduate Institute of International and Development Studies 2012).

Bartels, R. 'From *Jus In Bello* to *Jus Post Bellum*: When do Non-International Armed Conflicts End?' in Stahn, C., Easterday, J. S. and Iverson J. (ed) *Jus Post Bellum: Mapping the Normative Foundations* (Oxford University Press 2014).

Bassiouni, M.C. (ed), *International Criminal Law. Volume 1: Crimes* (Transnational 1999).

Bassiouni, M.C. *International Criminal Law, Volume III: International Enforcement* ((3rd ed, Martinus Nijhoff 2008)

Bassiouni, M. C., 'International Recognition of Victim's Rights' (2006) 6 *Human Rights Law Review* 2, 203–279.

Bassiouni, M.C. (ed) *The Pursuit of International Criminal Justice: A World Study on Conflicts, Victimization, and Post-Conflict Justice* (Intersentia 2010).

Bell, C. *Peace Agreements and Human Rights* (Oxford University Press 2000).

Bell, C. 'Peace agreements: their nature and legal status' (2006) 100 *The American Journal of International Law* 373.

Bellal, A. 'Establishing the Direct Responsibility of Non-State Armed Groups for Violations of International Norms: Issues of Attribution' in Gal-or, N. Ryngaert, C. & Noortmann, M. *Responsibilities of the Non-State Actor in Armed Conflict and the Market Place: Theoretical Considerations and Empirical Findings* (Brill Nijhoff 2015).

Bellal, 'Non-State Armed Groups in Transitional Justice Processes Adapting to New Realities of Conflict', in Duthie R. and Seils P. (eds), *Justice Mosaics: How Context Shapes Transitional Justice in Fractured Societies* (ICTJ 2017).

Bellal A. and Heffes, E. 'Yes, I do": Binding Armed Non-State Actors to IHL and Human Rights norms through their consent' (2018) 12 *Human Rights & International Legal Discourse* 1, 120–136.

Bigi, G. 'Joint Criminal Enterprise in the Jurisprudence of the International Criminal Tribunal for the Former Yugoslavia and the Prosecution of Senior Political and Military Leaders: The *Krajišnik* Case' in von Bogdandy A. and Wolfrum R. (eds.), *Max Planck Yearbook of United Nations Law*, Volume 14 (Koninklijke Brill 2010) 51–83.

Bílková, V. 'Establishing Direct Responsibility of Armed Opposition Groups for Violations of International Humanitarian Law? in Gal-Or, N., Ryngaert, C. & Noortmann, M. *Responsibilities of the Non-State Actor in Armed Conflict and the Market Place: Theoretical Considerations and Empirical Findings* (Brill Nijhoff 2015).

Blázquez Rodríguez, P. 'Does and armed group have an obligation to provide reparations to victims? Construing an obligation to provide reparations for violations of International Humanitarian Law' in Summers J. & Gough A. (ed) *Non-state actors and International Obligations. Creation, Evolution and Enforcement* (Brill Nijhoff 2018).

Boyle A. and Chinkin, C. *The Making of International Law* (Oxford University Press 2007).

Brownlie, I. *Principles of Public International Law* (Clarendon Press 1998)

Brownlie, I. *Principles of Public International Law* (Oxford University Press 2008).

Buchan, R. 'The Mavi Marmara Incident and the Application of International Humanitarian Law by Quasi-Judicial Bodies', in Jinks D. *et al* (eds), *Applying International Humanitarian Law in Judicial and Quasi- Judicial Bodies: International and Domestic Aspects* (Springer 2014).

Burnett, K. R. *Case Studies in Insurgency and Revolutionary Warfare - Colombia (1964 - 2009)* (United States Army Special Operations Command, John Hopkins University. National Security Analysis Department, 2014).

Butler, C.K., Gluch T. & Mitchell, NJ. 'Security Forces and Sexual Violence: A Cross-National Analysis of a Principal-Agent Argument' (2007) 44 *Journal of Peace Research* 6, 669–687.

Cahin, G. 'Attribution of conduct to the State: insurrectional movements' in Crawford J., Pellet A & Olleson S. (eds), *The law of international responsibility* (Oxford University Press 2010).

Carrillo-Santarelli, N. *Direct International Human Rights Obligations of Non-State Actors: A Legal and Ethical Necessity* (Wolf Legal Publishers 2017).

Cassese, A. 'The Nicaragua and Tadić Tests Revisited in Light of the ICJ Judgment on Genocide in Bosnia' (2007) 18 *European Journal of International Law* 4, 649–668.

Cassese, A. 'The status of rebels under the 1977 Geneva Protocol on Non-International Armed Conflicts' (1981) 30 *International and Comparative Law Quarterly* 2, 416–439.

Cheng, B. *General Principles of Law as Applied by International Courts and Tribunals* (Cambridge University Press 2006).

Clapham, A. 'Extending International Criminal Law beyond the Individual to Corporations and Armed Opposition Groups' (2008) 6 *Journal of International Criminal Justice*, 899–926.

Clapham, A. 'Focusing on Armed Non-State Actors' in Clapham A. & Gaeta, P. *The Oxford Handbook of International Law in Armed Conflict* (Oxford University Press 2014) 766–810.

Clapham, A. *Human Rights Obligations of Non-State Actors* (Oxford University Press 2006).

Clapham, A. 'Human rights obligations of non-state actors in conflict situations' (2006) 88 *International Review of the Red Cross* 863, 491–523.

Clapham, A. 'The Rights and Responsibilities of Armed Non-State Actors: The Legal Landscape & Issues Surrounding Engagement', *Geneva Academy of International Humanitarian Law and Human Rights* (February 2010).

Condorelli, L. & Kress, C. 'The rules of attribution: General Considerations' in Crawford J., Pellet A. & Olleson S. (eds), *The law of international responsibility, Oxford commentaries on international law* (Oxford University Press 2010).

Constantinides, A. 'Human Rights Obligations and Accountability of Armed Opposition Groups: The Practice of the UN Security Council' (2010) 4 *Human Rights and International Legal Discourse*, 89–110.

Cooper, D.E. 'Collective Responsibility (A defense)' in L. May & S. Hoffman, *Collective responsibility. Five decades of debate in theoretical and Applied Ethics* (Rowman & Littlefield 1991).

Couillard, V. 'The Nairobi Declaration: Redefining Reparations for Women Victims of Sexual Violence' (2007) 1 *The International Journal of Transitional Justice*, 444–453.

Crawford, J. *State responsibility. The General Part* (Cambridge University Press 2013).

Darcy, S. *Collective responsibility and Accountability under International Law* (Transnational 2007).

Darcy, S. 'Imputed Criminal Liability and the Goals of International Justice' (2007) 20 *Leiden Journal of International Law* 2, 377–404.

Darcy, S. 'Laying the Foundations: Commissions of Inquiry and the Development of International Law', in Henderson C. (ed), *Commissions of Inquiry: Problems and Prospects* (Hart Publishing 2017).

D'Argent, P. 'Reparation, Cessation, Assuarances and Guarantees of Non-Repetition' in Nollkaemper A. & Plakokefalos, I. *Principles of Shared Responsibility in International Law. An Appraisal of the State of the Art* (Cambridge University Press 2014).

D'Aspremont, J. *Formalism and the Sources of International Law: A Theory of the Ascertainment of Legal Rules* (Oxford University Press 2011).

D'Aspremont, J. 'Non-State Actors and the Social Practice of International Law', in M. Noortmann, A. Reinisch and C. Ryngaert (eds), *Non-state Actors in International Law* (Hart Publishing 2015).

D'Aspremont, J. (ed), *Participants in the International Legal System – Multiple Perspectives on Non-State Actors in International Law* (Routledge 2011).

Daugirdas, K. 'Reputation and the International Responsibility of International Organizations' (2015) 25 *European Journal of International Law 4*, 991–1018.

De Frouville, O. 'Attribution of Conduct to the State: Private Individuals' in Crawford J., Pellet A. & Olleson, S. (eds) *The law of international responsibility* (Oxford University Press 2010).

De Greiff, P. 'Justice and Reparations' in P. De Greiff, *The Handbook of Reparations* (Oxford University Press 2008).

Dinstein, Y. *Non- International Armed Conflicts in International Law* (Cambridge University Press 2014).

Droege, C. 'Elective affinities? Human rights and humanitarian law' (2008) 90 *International Review of the Red Cross* 871, 501–548.

Droege, C. 'The Interplay between International Humanitarian Law and International Human Rights Law in Situations of Armed Conflict' (2007) 40 *Israel Law Review* 2, 310–355.

Drumbl, M.A. *Atrocity, Punishment and International Law* (Cambridge University Press 2007).

Drumbl, M.A. 'Collective responsibility and post-conflict justice' in Isaacs T. & Vernon R. (eds) *Accountability for Collective Wrongdoing* (Cambridge University Press 2011).

Dudai, R. 'Closing the gap: symbolic reparations and armed groups' (2011) 93 *International Review of the Red Cross* 883, 783–808.

Dumberry, P. 'New State Responsibility for Internationally Wrongful Acts by an Insurrectional Movement' (2006) 17 *The European Journal of International Law* 3, 605–621.

Eagleton, C. *The Responsibility of States in International Law* (The New York University Press 1928).

Evans, C. *The Right of Reparation in International Law for Victims of Armed Conflict* (Cambridge University Press 2012).

Fair, C. C. *Urban Battle Fields of South Asia. Lessons Learned from Sri Lanka, India and Pakistan* (Rand Corporation 2004).

Feinberg, J. 'Collective Responsibility (Another Defense)' in May L. & Hoffman S., *Collective responsibility. Five decades of debate in theoretical and Applied Ethics* (Rowman & Littlefield 1991).

Ferraro, T. 'The ICRC's Legal Position on the Notion of Armed Conflict involving Foreign Intervention and on Determining the IHL Applicable to this Type of Conflict' (2015) 97 *International Review of the Red Cross* 1227– 52.

Ferro Medina J. G. & Uribe Ramón, G. *El orden de la Guerra: las FARC-EP entre la organización y la política* (Centro Editorial Javariano 2002).

Fortin, K. *Accountability of Armed Groups under Human Rights Law* (Oxford University Press 2017).

Fortin, K. 'How to Cope with Diversity While Preserving Unity in Customary International Law? Some Insights from International Humanitarian Law' (2018) 23 *Journal of Conflict & Security Law* 3, 337–358.

Fortin, K. 'The Application of Human Rights Law to Everyday Civilian Life Under Rebel Control' (2016) 63 *Netherlands International Law Review* 2, 161–181.

Gaggioli, G. 'Targeting Individuals belonging to an armed group' (2018) 51 *Vanderbilt Journal of Transnational Law* 3, 901–917.

Gates, S. 'Recruitment and Allegiance: The Microfoundations of Rebellion' (2002) 46 *Journal of Conflict Resolution* 1, 111–130.

Goelland-Debbas, V. 'Responsibility and the United Nations Charter' in Crawford J., Pellet A. & Olleson, S. (eds) *The law of international responsibility* (Oxford University Press 2010).

Greenwood, C. 'International Humanitarian Law', in Kalshoven F. (ed.), *The Centennial of the First International Peace Conference* (Kluwer Law 2000).

Grotius, H. *De Iure Belli ac Pacis* (1625) (Oceana Publications Wildy & Son 1964)

Gutiérrez Sanín F. & Giustozzi, A. 'Networks and Armies: Structuring Rebellion in Colombia and Afghanistan' (2010) 33 *Studies in Conflict & Terrorism* 9, 836–853.

Haer, R. *Armed Group Structure and Violence in Civil Wars: The Organizational Dynamics of Civilian Killing* (Routledge 2015).

Hampson, F. J. 'The relationship between international humanitarian law and human rights law from the perspective of a human rights treaty body' (2008) 90 *International Review of the Red Cross* 871, 549–572.

Hardwood, C. 'Contributions of International Commissions of Inquiry to Transitional Justice' (2016) *Grotius Centre working paper* 2016/054-ICL.

Hart, H.L.A. *Punishment and Responsibility. Essays in the Philosophy of Law* (Oxford University Press 2008).

Hayner, P. B. 'Fifteen Truth Commissions – 1974 to 1994: A Comparative Study (1994) 16 *Human Rights Quarterly* 4, 597–655.

Heffes, E. 'The Responsibility of armed opposition groups for violations of International Humanitarian Law: Challenging the State-Centric System of International Law' (2013) 4 *Journal of International Humanitarian Legal Studies*, 81–107.

Heffes E. & Frenkel, B. E. 'The International Responsibility of Non-state Armed Groups: In Search of the Applicable Rules' (2017) 8 *Goettingen Journal of International Law* 1, 39–72.

Heffter, A. W. *Le Droit International Public de l'Europe, tr. par Jules Bergson* (E.H. Schrœder 1857).

Henckaerts J. M. & Doswald-Beck, L. *Customary International Humanitarian Law* (Cambridge University Press 2005).

Hiemstra H. and Nohle E. 'The Role of Non-State Armed Groups in the Development and Interpretation of International Humanitarian Law' (2017) 20 *Yearbook of International Humanitarian Law*, 3–35.

Higgins, R. *Problems and Process. International Law and How We Use it* (Clarendon Press 1994).

Hofmann, R. 'The 2010 International Law Association Declaration of International Law Principles on Reparation for Victims of Armed Conflict' in Peters, A. & Marxsen C. (eds) *Reparation for Victims of Armed Conflict: Impulses from the Max Planck Trialogues,* MPIL Research Paper Series | No. 2018-19 (2018).

Hollis, D. B. 'Interpretation' in J. D'Aspremont & S. Singh (eds) *Concepts for International Law. Contributions to Disciplinary Thought* (Edward Elgar Publishing 2019).

Hopkins, M.J. 'Extrapolation of Criminal Law Modes of Liability to Target Analysis under International Humanitarian Law: Developing the Framework for Understanding Direct Participation in Hostilities and Membership in Organized Armed Groups in Non-International Armed Conflict' (2017) 22 *Journal of Conflict and Security Law* 2, 275–310.

Jaspers, K. *The Question of German Guilt. Perspective in Continental Philosophy* (2nd edition, Fordham University Press 2001).

Johnson, D. H. 'The Sudan People's Liberation Army and the Problem of Factionalism', in Clapham C. S., *African Guerrillas. Eritrea, Tigrai, Sudan, Somalia, Uganda, Rwanda, Congo-Zaire, Liberia, Sierra Leone* (Indiana University Press 1998).

Jonas D. S. and Saunders, T. N. 'The Object and Purpose of a Treaty: Three Interpretive Methods' (2010) 43 *Vanderbilt Journal of Transnational Law* 3, 565–609.

Kalshoven, F. 'State Responsibility for Warlike Acts of the Armed Forces' (1991) 40 *International and Comparative Law Quarterly* 4, 827–858.

Kelly, J. P. 'Customary International Law in Historical Context. The Exercise of Power without General Acceptance' in Lepard B.D. (ed) *Reexamining Customary International Law* (Cambridge University Press 2017) 47–85.

Klabbers, J. *An Introduction to International Institutional Law* (2nd edn Cambridge University Press 2009).

Klabbers, J. '(I Can't Get No) Recognition: Subjects Doctrine and the Emergence of Non-State Actors', in Petman J. & Klabbers J. (eds) *Nordic Cosmopolitanism: Essays in International Law for Martii Koskenniemi* (Martinus Nijhoff 2003) 351–69.

Kleffner, J.K. 'The Applicability of International Humanitarian Law to Organized Armed Groups' (2011) 93 *International Review of the Red Cross* 882, 443–461.

Kleffner, J.K. 'The collective accountability of organized armed groups for system crimes', in Nollkaemper A. & Van der Wilt H., *System Criminality in International Law* (Cambridge University Press 2015).

Klein, P. 'The attribution of acts to international organizations' in Crawford J., Pellet A. & Olleson, S. (eds) *The law of international responsibility* (Oxford University Press 2010).

Kolb, R. *Interprétation et création du droit international. Esquisse d'une herméneutique juridique moderne pour le droit international public* (Bruylant 2006).

Kooijmans, P. 'The Security Council and Non-State Entities as Parties to Conflicts', in Kwellens K (ed), *International Law: Theory and Practice, Essays in Honour of Eric Suy* (Martinus Nijhoff 1998).

Koutroulis, V. 'The Prohibition of the Use of Force in Arbitrations and Fact-Finding Reports' in Weller M. (ed), *The Oxford Handbook of the Use of Force in International Law* (Oxford University Press 2015).

La Rosa A. & Wuerzner, C. 'Armed groups, sanctions and the implementation of international humanitarian law' (2008) 90 *International Review of the Red Cross* 870, 327–341.

Lauterpacht, H. 'Recognition of Insurgents as a *De Facto* Government' (1939) 3 *Modern Law Review*, 1–20.

Mack, M. *Increasing respect for International Humanitarian Law in Non-International Armed Conflict* (ICRC, Geneva 2008).

Mampilly, Z. C. *Rebel Rulers. Insurgent Governance and Civilian Life during War* (Cornell University Press 2011).

Mani, R. 'Reparation as a component of transitional justice: Pursuing "Reparative Justice" in the Aftermath of Violent Conflict' in De Feyter K., Parmentier S., Bossuyt M. and Lemmens

P. (eds) *Out of the Ashes. Reparation for Victims of Gross and Systematic Human Rights Violations* (Intersentia 2005).

Márquez Carrasco, C., Íñigo Álvarez, L. Loozen, N. & Salmón E., *Survey study on human rights violations in conflict settings*, EU FP7 Research Project, Deliverable No. 10.1 (30 September 2014).

Mastorodimos, K. *Armed Non-State Actors in International Humanitarian and Human Rights Law. Foundation and Framework of Obligations, and Rules on Accountability* (Routledge 2015).

May L. & Hoffman, S. *Collective responsibility. Five decades of debate in theoretical and Applied Ethics* (Rowman & Littlefield 1991).

McCarthy, C. *Reparations and victim support in the International Criminal Court* (Cambridge University Press 2012).

McQuinn, B. 'DDR and the Internal Organization of Non-State Armed Groups' (2016) *Stability: International Journal of Security and Development* X(X): X, 1–24.

Mégret, F. 'The Subjects of International Criminal Law' in Kastner P. (ed), *International Criminal Law in Context* (Taylor and Francis 2017).

Mellena, G. F. *Collective responsibility* (Brill Rodopi 1997).

Melzer, N. *Interpretative Guidance on the notion of Direct Participation in Hostilities under International Humanitarian Law* (ICRC, Geneva 2010).

Mertel, J. 'Truth in a Box: The Limits of Justice through Judicial Mechanisms' in Amadiume I. & An-Naim A. A., *The Politics of Memory. Truth, Healing and Social Justice* (Zed Books 2000).

Miller, G. 'The Political Evolution of Principal-Agent Models' (2005) 8 *Annual Review of Political Science 1*, 203–225.

Moffett, L. 'Beyond Attribution: Responsibility of Armed Non-State Actors for Reparations in Northern Ireland, Colombia and Uganda in Gal-or, N. Ryngaert, C. & Noortmann, M. *Responsibilities of the Non-State Actor in Armed Conflict and the Market Place: Theoretical Considerations and Empirical Findings* (Brill Nijhoff 2015).

Moffett, L. 'Transitional justice and reparations: Remedying the past?' in Lawther C., Moffett L. & Jacobs, D. *Research Handbook on Transitional Justice* (Edward Elgar Publishing 2017) 377–400.

Moir, L. *The Law of Internal Armed Conflict* (Oxford University Press 2002).

Möldner, M. 'Responsibility of International Organizations. Introducing the ILC's DARIO' (2012) 16 *Max Planck Yearbook of United Nations Law*, 281–328.

Murray, D. *Human Rights Obligations of Non-State Armed Groups* (Hart Publishing 2016).

Naqvi, Y. 'The right to the truth in international law: fact or fiction?' (2006) 88 *International Review of the Red Cross* 862.

Nollkaemper, A. 'Concurrence between Individual Responsibility and State Responsibility in International Law' (2003) 52 *International and Comparative Law Quarterly*, 615–640.

Nollkaemper, A. 'Power and responsibility' (2014) Amsterdam Law School Legal Studies Research Paper No. 2014–35.

Nollkaemper, A. 'Responsibility' (2017) Amsterdam Law School Legal Studies Research Paper No. 2017–04.

Noortmann, N., Reinisch, A. & Ryngaert, C. *Non-State Actors in International Law* (Hart Publishing 2015).

Nyamutata, C. 'Engaging or Shaming? An Analysis of UN's Naming and Shaming of Child Abusers in Armed Conflict' (2013) 4 *Journal of International Humanitarian Legal Studies* 1, 151–173.
Odier-Contreras Garduno, D. *Collective reparations. Tensions and Dilemmas Between Collective Reparations with the Individual Right to Receive Reparations* (Intersentia 2018).
Ohlin, J.D. 'Three Conceptual Problems with the Doctrine of Joint Criminal Enterprise' (2007) 5 *Journal of International Criminal Justice*, 69–90.
Olleson, S. 'The Impact of the ILC's Articles on Responsibility of States for Internationally Wrongful Acts – Preliminary Draft' (British Institute of International and Comparative Law 2007).
Olasolo H. and Ramírez Mendoza, J.M.F. 'The Colombian Integrated System of Truth, Justice, Reparation and Non-Repetition' (2017) 15 *Journal of International Criminal Justice*, 1011–1047.
Oppenheim, L. *International Law: A Treatise, Vol. I* (Longmans, Green & Co. 1912).
Oppenheim, L. *International Law: A Treatise, Vol. I* (7th edn, Longmans, Green & Co. 1948).
Ortega, M. M. *Acciones y reacciones estratégicas adaptaciones de las FARC a las innovaciones operacionales de las Fuerzas Armadas de Colombia durante la política de defensa y seguridad democrática* (Universidad de los Andes 2011).
Paasivirta E. & Kuijper, P. 'Does one size fit all?: The European Community and the responsibility of international organizations' (2005) 36 *Netherlands Yearbook of International Law* 1, 169–226.
Parkinson S.E. and Zaks, S. 'Militant and Rebel Organization(s)' (2018) 50 *Comparative Politics* 2, 271–293.
Pellet, A. 'The definition of Responsibility in International Law' in Crawford J., Pellet A & Olleson, S. (eds) *The law of international responsibility* (Oxford University Press 2010).
Pérez-León Acevedo, J.P. 'Las Reparaciones en el Derecho Internacional de los Derechos Humanos, Derecho Internacional Humanitario y Derecho Penal Internacional' (2008) 23 *American University International Law Review* 1.
Pérez-León Acevedo, J. P., 'The Situation of Reparations in the Inter-American Human Rights System: Analysis and Comparative Considerations' (2016) 20 *ASIL Insights* 15.
Petit, P. 'Responsibility incorporated' (2007) 38 *Netherlands Journal of Legal Philosophy* 2, 90–117.
Pierik, R. 'Shared responsibility in international law. A normative-philosophical analysis' in Nollkaemper A., *A Distribution of responsibility in international law* (Cambridge University Press 2015).
Podder S. 'Understanding the Legitimacy of Armed Groups: A Relational Perspective' (2017) 28 *Small Wars & Insurgencies* 4–5, 686–708.
Pronto, A.N. 'Some thoughts on the Making of International Law' (2008) 19 *The European Journal of International Law* 3, 601–616.
Provost, R. 'Interpretation in International Law as a Transcultural Project' in Bianchi A., Peat, D. and Windsor, M. *Interpretation in International Law* (Oxford University Press 2015).
Richards, J. 'An Institutional History of the Liberation Tigers of Tamil Eelam (LTTE)', *The Centre on Conflict, Development and Peacebuilding*, CCDP Working Paper (2014).
Roberts A. & Sivakumaran, S. 'Lawmaking by Nonstate Actors: Engaging Armed Groups in the Creation of International Humanitarian Law' (2012) 37 *Yale Journal of International Law* 1, 107–152.

Rodenhäuser, T. *Organizing Rebellion: Non-State Armed Groups under International Humanitarian Law, Human Rights Law, and International Criminal Law* (Oxford University Press 2018).

Rondeau, S. 'Participation of armed groups in the development of the law applicable to armed conflicts' (2011) 93 *International Review of the Red Cross* 883, 649–672.

Roht-Arriaza N., 'Reparations in International Law and Practice' in Bassiouni, M.C. *The Pursuit of International Criminal Justice: A World Study on Conflicts, Victimization, and Post-Conflict Justice* (Intersentia 2010).

Ryngaert, C. 'Non-state actors in International Humanitarian Law' in D'Aspremont, J. *Participants in the International Legal System. Multiple perspectives on Non-State Actors in International Law* (Routledge 2011) 284–294.

Ryngaert, C. & Van De Meulebroucke, A. 'Enhancing and Enforcing Compliance with International Humanitarian Law by Non-State Armed Groups: an Inquiry into some Mechanisms' (2012) 16 *Journal of Conflict & Security Law* 3, 443–472.

Sabahi, B. *Compensation and Restitution in Investor-State Arbitration: Principles and Practice* (Oxford University Press 2011).

Sandoval, C. 'The Legal Standing and Significance of the Basic Principles and Guidelines on the Right to a Remedy and Reparation' in Peters, A. & Marxsen C. (eds) *Reparation for Victims of Armed Conflict: Impulses from the Max Planck Trialogues,* MPIL Research Paper Series | No. 2018–19 (2018).

Sassòli, M. 'State responsibility for violations of international humanitarian law' (2002) 84 *International Review of the Red Cross* 846, 401–434.

Sassòli, M. 'Taking Armed Groups Seriously: Ways to Improve Their Compliance with International Humanitarian Law' (2010) 1 *Journal of International Humanitarian Legal Studies,* 5–51.

Sassòli, M., Bouvier A. A. & Quintin, A. *How does law protect in war? Cases, Documents and Teaching Materials on Contemporary Practice in International Humanitarian Law,* Vol. II Cases and documents (ICRC, Geneva 2011).

Schmalenbach, K. 'International responsibility for humanitarian law violations by armed groups' in Krieger, H. *Inducing Compliance with International Humanitarian Law. Lessons from the African Great Lake Region* (Cambridge University Press 2015).

Schotsmans, M. 'Victim's Expectations, Needs and Perspectives after Gross and Systematic Human Rights Violations' in De Feyter K., Parmentier S., Bossuyt M. and Lemmens, P. (eds) *Out of the Ashes. Reparation for Victims of Gross and Systematic Human Rights Violations* (Intersentia 2005).

Schmitt, M. N. 'Deconstructing Direct Participation in Hostilities: The Constitutive Elements' (2010) 42 *New York University Journal of International Law and Politics,* 697–739.

Schwarzenberger, G. 'The Inductive Approach to International Law' (1947) 60 *Harvard Law Review* 4, 539–570.

Shaw, R. 'Linking justice with reintegration? Ex-combatants and the Sierra Leone experiment', in Shaw R. and Waldorf L. (eds), *Localizing Transitional Justice: Interventions and Priorities after Mass Violence* (Stanford University Press 2010).

Shelton, D. (ed) *Commitment and Compliance: The Role of Non-Binding Norms in the International Legal System* (Oxford University Press 2000).

Sinclair, K. 'Legal Reasoning: In Search of an Adequate Theory of Argument' (1971) 59 *California Law Review* 3, 821–858.

Sinno, A.H. 'Armed groups' organizational structure and their strategic options' (2011) 93 *International Review of the Red Cross* 882, 311-332.

Sivakumaran, S. 'Beyond States and Non-State Actors: The Role of State-Empowered Entities in the Making and Shaping of International Law' (2017) 55 *Columbia Journal of Transnational Law* 2, 343–394.

Sivakumaran, S. 'Binding Armed Opposition Groups' (2006) 55 *International & Comparative Law Quarterly* 2, 369–394.

S. Sivakumaran, 'Re-envisaging the International Law of Internal Armed Conflict' (2011) 22 *European Journal of International Law* 1, 219–264.

Sivakumaran, S. 'Techniques in International Law-Making: Extrapolation, Analogy, Form and the Emergence of an International Law of Disaster Relief' (2017) 28 *European Journal of International Law* 4, 1097–1132.

Sivakumaran, S. *The Law of Non-International Armed Conflict* (Oxford University Press 2012).

Smeulers, A. 'Punishing the Enemies of All Mankind' (2008) 21 *Leiden Journal of International Law* 4, 971–993.

Subedi, S.P., Wheatley, S. Mukherjee, A. & Ngane, S. 'The role of the special rapporteurs of the United Nations Human Rights Council in the development and promotion of international human rights norms' (2011) 15 *The International Journal of Human Rights* 2, 155–161.

Sunstein, C. R. 'On Analogical Reasoning' (1993) 106 *Harvard Law Review* 3, 741–791.

Tapia Navarro, N. 'Collective reparations and the limitations of International criminal justice to respond to mass atrocity' (2018) 18 *International Criminal Law Review*, 67–96.

Terpstra N. and Frerks, G. 'Rebel Governance and Legitimacy: Understanding the Impact of Rebel Legitimation on Civilian Compliance with the LTTE Rule' (2017) 19 *Civil Wars* 3, 279–307.

Thompson, D.F. 'Responsibility for Failures of Government: The Problem of Many Hands' (2014) 44 *American Review of Public Administration* 3, 259–273.

Tomlinson J. (ed), *National Apologies. Mapping the Complexities of Validity: a Practical paper* (The Centre for Peace and Conflict Studies 2012).

Triepel, H. *Droit International et Droit Interne* (Pédone 1920).

Triepel, H. *Völkerrecht und Landesrecht* (C.L. Hirschfeld 1899).

Van Essen, J. '*De Facto* Regimes in International Law' (2012) 28 *Utrecht Journal of International and European Law* 74, 31–49.

Vattel, E. *Le Droit des Gens ou Principes de la loi naturelle, appliqués à la conduite et aux affaires des Nations et des Souverains*, Vol. 1 (London 1758).

Venkze, I. 'Semantic Authority' (2016) *Amsterdam Center for International Law No. 2016-03, Amsterdam Law School Research Paper No. 2016-06.*

Verhoeven, S.I. 'International responsibility of armed opposition groups. Lessons from State responsibility for actions of Non-State Armed Groups' in N. Gal-Or, C. Ryngaert, & M. Noortmann, M. *Responsibilities of the Non-State Actor in Armed Conflict and the Market Place: Theoretical Considerations and Empirical Findings* (Brill Nijhoff 2015).

Vadi, V. *Analogies in International Investment Law and Arbitration* (Cambridge University Press 2015).

Vierruci, L. 'Applicability of the Conventions by Means of Ad Hoc Agreements', in Clapham, A., Gaeta P. & Sassòli M.(eds) *The 1949 Geneva Conventions: A Commentary* (Oxford University Press 2015).

Vinci, A. *Armed Groups and the Balance of Power: The International Relations of Terrorists, Warlords and Insurgents* (1st edn, Routledge 2008).
Waibel, M. 'Interpretative Communities in International Law' in Bianchi A., Peat, D. &. Windsor, M. *Interpretation in International Law* (Oxford University Press 2015).
Watkin, K. 'Opportunity Lost: Organized Armed Groups and the ICRC "Direct Participation in Hostilities Interpretive Guidance' (2009–2010) 42 *New York University Journal of International Law and Politics*, 641–695.
Weinstein, J. M. *Inside Rebellion. The Politics of Insurgent Violence* (Cambridge University Press 2007).
Wiebelhaus-Brahm, E. 'Truth Commissons and other Investigative Bodies' in Bassiouni M. C. (ed) *The Pursuit of International Criminal Justice: A World Study on Conflicts, Victimization, and Post-Conflict Justice* (Intersentia 2010) 477–574.
Wood, M. 'The Rights of Victims to Reparation: The Importance of Clear Thinking' in Peters, A. & Marxsen C. (eds) *Reparation for Victims of Armed Conflict: Impulses from the Max Planck Trialogues* (2018) MPIL Research Paper Series | No. 2018–19.
Worster, W.T. 'The inductive and deductive methods in Customary International Law analysis: traditional and modern approaches' (2014) 45 *Georgetown Journal of International Law*, 445–521.
Zacklin, R. 'Responsabilité des organisations internationales' in Société Française pour le Droit International, *La responsabilité dans le système international* (Pedone 1991).
Zegveld, L. *Accountability of Armed Opposition Groups in International Law* (Cambridge University Press 2002).
Zegveld, L. 'Remedies for victims of violations of international humanitarian law' (2003) 85 *International Review of the Red Cross* 851, 497–526.
Zegveld, L. 'The Inter-American Commission on Human Rights and international humanitarian law: A Comment on the Tablada Case' (1998) 324 *International Review of the Red Cross.*

EUROPEAN UNION

Council Decision 2005/930/EC of 21 December 2005 implementing Art. 2(3) of Regulation (EC) No. 2580/2001 on specific restrictive measures directed against certain persons and entities with a view to combating terrorism and repealing Decision 2005/848/EC.
European Parliament Resolution of 6 September 2001, on measures to promote a commitment by non-State actors to a total ban on anti-personnel landmines, B5–0542, 0561, 0568, 0575, 0590 and 0599/2001.

INTERNATIONAL LAW ASSOCIATION

International Law Association, 'Final Report on Accountability of International Organizations' (Berlin Conference 2004).
International Law Association Committee on Non-State Actors, 'Final report on Non-state actors' (Johannesburg Conference 2016).

International Law Association Committee on Non-State Actors, 'Third report on the Obligations and Responsibility of Non-State Actors in International Law' (Washington Conference 2014).

International Law Association, Committee on Reparation for Victims of Armed Conflict, Resolution 2/2010 on International Law Principles on Reparation for Victims of Armed Conflict (Substantive Issues) (15–20 August 2010).

International Law Association, Committee on Reparation for Victims of Armed Conflict 'The Hague Conference Report: Reparation for Victims of Armed Conflict' (Substantive Issues) (2010).

INTERNATIONAL LAW COMMISSION

Draft Articles on Responsibility of States for Internationally Wrongful Acts, with commentaries 2001, *Yearbook of the International Law Commission* (2001), UN Doc. No. A/56/83.

Draft Articles on the Responsibility of International Organizations, with Commentaries, *Yearbook of the International Law Commission* (2011), UN Doc. No. A/66/10.

Fifth Report on Identification of Customary International Law by Mr. Michael Wood, Special Rapporteur (14 March 2018) UN Doc. A/CN.4/717 18–19.

Fifth Report on State Responsibility by Mr. Roberto Ago, Special Rapporteur: The Internationally Wrongful Act of the State – Source of International Responsibility (continued) (22 March, 14 April and 4 May 1976) UN Doc. A/CN.4/291 and Add. 1 & 2 and Corr. 1

First report on State responsibility by James Crawford, Special Rapporteur (24 April, 1, 5, 11 and 26 May, 22 and 24 July, 12 August 1998) UN. Doc. A/CN.4/490 and Add. 1–7

First report on State Responsibility by Roberto Ago, Special Rapporteur – Review of Previous Work on Codification of the Topic of the International Responsibility of States (7 May 1969 and 20 January 1970) UN. Doc. A/CN.4/217 and Corr. 1 and Add. 1.

First Report on Responsibility of International Organizations by Giorgio Gaja, Special Rapporteur (26 March 2013) UN Doc. A/CN.4/532.

Fourth report on State responsibility by Mr. Roberto Ago, Special Rapporteur, International Law Commission Yearbook (30 June 1972 and 9 April 1973) UN Doc. A/CN.4/264 and Add.1.

International Law Commission Report, Fifty-fourth Session (2002), UN Doc. A/57/10.

International Law Commission Report, Sixty-eighth Session (2016), UN Doc. A/71/10.

International Law Commission Yearbook (1963), Vol. II, UN Doc. A/CN.4/SER.A/1963/ADD.1.

International Law Commission Yearbook (1996), Vol. II (2), UN. Doc. A/CN.4/SER.A/1996/ Add.l (Part 2).

Report of the Commission to the General Assembly on the Work of its Fifty-Fourth Session, Vol. II, Part II, Yearbook of the International Law Commission (2002).

Report on International Responsibility by Mr. F. V. Garcia-Amador, Special Rapporteur (20 January 1956), UN Doc. A/CN.4/96.

Second Report on Identification of Customary International Law by Mr. Michael Wood, Special Rapporteur (22 May 2014) UN Doc. A/CN.4/672.

Second Report on Responsibility of International Organizations by Mr. Giorgio Gaja, Special Rapporteur (2 April 2004) UN Doc. A/CN.4/541.

Second Report on State Responsibility by Mr. Roberto Ago, Special Rapporteur: The Origin of International Responsibility (20 April 1970) UN Doc. A/CN.4/233.

Third Report on Identification of Customary International Law by Mr. Michael Wood, Special Rapporteur (27 March 2015) UN Doc. A/CN.4/682.

Third Report on State responsibility by Mr. Roberto Ago, Special Rapporteur: The Internationally Wrongful Act of the State – Source of International Responsibility (5 March, 7 April, 28 April and 18 May 1971) UN Doc. A/CN.4/246 and Add. 1–3.

UNITED NATIONS DOCUMENTS

GENERAL ASSEMBLY

UN General Assembly, Resolution 67/1 Declaration of the High-level Meeting of the General Assembly on the Rule of Law at the National and International Levels (30 November 2012).

HUMAN RIGHTS COUNCIL AND FORMER COMMISSION ON HUMAN RIGHTS

Interim report on the Situation of Human Rights in the Sudan prepared by Mr. Gáspár Bíró, Special Rapporteur of the Commission on Human Rights (16 October 1995) UN Doc. A/50/569.

Report of the Commission of Inquiry on Burundi (11 August 2017) A/HRC/36/54.

Report of the International Commission of Inquiry on Côte d'Ivoire (1 July 2011) A /HRC/17/48.

Report of the International Commission of Inquiry on Libya (2 March 2012) A/HRC/19/68.

Report of the Independent International Commission of Inquiry on the Syrian Arab Republic (22 February 2012) A/HRC/19/69.

Report of the Independent International Commission of Inquiry on the Syrian Arab Republic (16 August 2012) A/HRC/21/50.

Report of the International Commission of Inquiry on the Syrian Arab Republic (5 February 2013) A/HRC/22/59.

Report of the Independent International Commission of Inquiry on the Syrian Arab Republic (8 August 2017) A/HRC/36/55.

Report of the International Commission of Inquiry to Investigate All Alleged Violations of International Human Rights Law in the Libyan Arab Jamahiriya (1 June 2011) A / HRC/17/44.

Report of the Special Rapporteur, Mr. Gáspár Bíró, on the Situation of Human Rights in the Sudan (1 February 1994).

Report of the Special Rapporteur, Mr. Gáspár Biró, on the Situation of Human Rights in the Sudan (3 February 1997) E/CN.4/1997/58.

Report of the Special Rapporteur on Extrajudicial, Summary or Arbitrary Executions, Philip Alston – Mission to Sri Lanka (26 March 2006) E/CN.4/2006/53/Add.5.

Report of the Special Rapporteur on Extrajudicial, Summary or Arbitrary Executions, Philip Alston – Follow-up To Country Recommendations (14 May 2008) A/HRC/8/3/Add.3.

Report of the Special Rapporteur on Extrajudicial, Summary or Arbitrary Executions on Armed Non-State Actors: the Protection of the Right to Life (5 June 2018) UN Doc. A/HRC/38/44.

Report of the Special Rapporteur on the Promotion of Truth, Justice, Reparation and Guarantees of Non-recurrence (23 August 2013) UN Doc. A/68/345.
Report of the United Nations Fact-Finding Mission on the Gaza Conflict (25 September 2009) A/HRC/12/48.
UN Human Rights Council Resolution 9/9 'Protection of human rights of civilians in armed conflict' (18 September 2008) A/HRC/RES/9/9.

OFFICE OF THE HIGH COMMISSIONER OF HUMAN RIGHTS

Annual report of the United Nations High Commissioner for Human Rights on the Situation of Human Rights in Colombia (24 January 2014) A /HRC/25/19/Add.3.
Annual report of the United Nations High Commissioner for Human Rights on the situation of Human Rights in Colombia (23 June 2016) A/HRC/31/3/Add. 2.
Annual Report of the United Nations High Commissioner for Human Rights. Situation of Human Rights in Colombia (23 March 2017) A/HRC/34/3/Add. 3.
Report of the Office of the United Nations High Commissioner for Human Rights on the human rights situation in Iraq in light of the abuses committed by the so-called Islamic State in Iraq and the Levant and associated groups (13 March 2015) A/HRC/28/18.
Report of the United Nations High Commissioner for Human Rights (12 September 2013), A/HRC/24/59, para. 25.
Report of the United Nations High Commissioner for Human Rights on the Office in Colombia (16 March 1999) E/CN.4/1999/8, 23.
Report of the United Nations High Commissioner for Human Rights on the Office in Colombia (9 March 2000) E/CN.4/2000/11.
Report of the United Nations High Commissioner for Human Rights on the Human Rights Situation in Colombia (8 February 2001) E/CN.4/2001/15.
Report of the United Nations High Commissioner for Human Rights on the Situation of Human Rights in Colombia (16 May 2006) E/CN.4/2006/9.
Report of the United Nations High Commissioner for Human Rights on the Situation of Human Rights in Colombia (31 January 2012) A/HRC/19/21/Add.3.
Report of the United Nations High Commissioner for Human Rights on the Situation of Human Rights in Colombia (23 January 2015) A/HRC/28/3/Add. 3, at 11, para. 46.
Report of the United Nations High Commissioner for Human Rights on the Situation of Human Rights in Libya and on Related Technical Support and Capacity-building Needs' (12 January 2015) A/HRC/28/51.
Office of the UN High Commissioner for Human Rights, 'Rule-of-Law Tools for Post-Conflict States: Reparations Programmes' (United Nations 2008).

REPORTS OF COMMISSIONS OF INQUIRY OF THE SECRETARY-GENERAL

Final report of the International Commission of Inquiry on the Central African Republic (22 December 2014) S/2014/928.

Report of the International Commission of Inquiry on Darfur to the United Nations Secretary-General, Pursuant to Security Council Resolution 1564 of 18 September 2004, Geneva (25 January 2005).

UN SECRETARY-GENERAL

Report of the Secretary-General on Children in Armed Conflict (26 April 2012) A /66/782–S /2012/26.
Report of the Secretary-General on Children in Armed Conflict (16 May 2018) A/72/865–S/2018/465.
Report of the Secretary-General on Children and Armed Conflict in the Sudan (17 August 2006) S/2006/662.
Report of the Secretary-General on Children and Armed Conflict in the Sudan (5 July 2011) S/2011/413.
Report of the Secretary-General on Conflict-related Sexual Violence (13 January 2012) A /66/657–S /2012/33.
Report of the Secretary-General on Conflict-related Sexual Violence (15 April 2017) S/2017/249.
Report of the Secretary-General on Conflict-related Sexual Violence (23 March 2018) S/2018/250.
UN Secretary-General, Report on the Causes of Conflict and the Promotion of Durable Peace and Sustainable Development in Africa (13 April 1998) A/52/871 – S/1998/318.
Report of the Secretary-General on the Protection of Civilians in Armed Conflict (28 May 2004) S/2004/431.
Report of the Secretary-General on the Protection of Civilians in Armed Conflict (29 May 2009) UN Doc. S/2009/277.
Report of the Secretary-General on the Protection of Civilians in Armed Conflict (10 November 2010) S/2010/579.
Report of the Secretary-General on the Protection of Civilians in Armed Conflict (22 May 2012) S/2012/376.
Report of the Secretary-General on the Protection of Civilians in Armed Conflict (18 June 2015) S/2015/453
Report of the Secretary-General on the Protection of Civilians in Armed Conflict (10 May 2017) S/2017/414
Report of the Secretary-General's Panel of Experts on Accountability in Sri Lanka (31 March 2011).
Report of the UN Secretary-General prepared pursuant to Commission Resolution 1995/29 (28 November 1995) UN Doc. E/CN.4/1996/80.
Report of the UN Secretary-General, The rule of law and transitional justice in conflict and post-conflict societies (23 August 2004) UN Doc. S/2004/616.

UN SECURITY COUNCIL

UN Security Council, 'From Madness to Hope: The 12-year war in El Salvador: Report of the Commission on the Truth for El Salvador' (1 April 1993) Annex, UN Doc. S/25500.

UN Security Council Resolution 942 (1994), UN Doc. S/RES/942 (1994).
UN Security Council Resolution 1071 (1996), UN Doc S/RES/1071 (1996).
UN Security Council Resolution 1132 (1997), UN Doc. S/RES/1132 (1997).
UN Security Council Resolution 1171 (1998), UN Doc. S/RES/1171 (1998).
UN Security Council Resolution 1214 (1998), UN Doc. S/RES/1214 (1998).
UN Security Council Resolution 1216 (1998), UN Doc. S/RES/1216 (1998).
UN Security Council Resolution 1267 (1999), UN Doc. S/RES/1267 (1999).
UN Security Council Resolution 1493 (2003), UN Doc. S/RES/1493 (2003).
UN Security Council Resolution 1564 (2004), UN Doc. S/RES/1564 (2004)
UN Security Council Resolution 1807 (2008), UN Doc. S/RES/1807 (2008).
UN Security Council Resolution 2127 (2013), UN Doc. S/RES/2127 (2013).

NEWSPAPERS AND PRESS RELEASES

'Bienes de las FARC sólo se usarán para reparación de víctimas: Corte', *El Tiempo* (4 July 2018) at <https://www.eltiempo.com/justicia/cortes/corte-constitucional-dice-que-bienes-de-las-farc-solo-se-usaran-en-reparacion-de-victimas-239446>

'Colombia's Farc rebels apologize for "great pain" caused by kidnappings', *The Guardian* (12 September 2016) at <https://www.theguardian.com/world/2016/sep/12/colombias-farc-rebels-apologize-kidnapping-peace-accord>

'ETA lamenta el daño causado y pide "perdón" a parte de las víctimas', *El País* <https://elpais.com/politica/2018/04/20/actualidad/1524201219_870285.html≥

'Guatemala Rebel Apology', *The New York Times* (14 March 1999) <https://www.nytimes.com/1999/03/14/world/guatemala-rebel-apology.html≥

'IRA offers "sincere apologies" for 30 years of civilian slaughter', *The Telegraph* (17 July 2002) <https://www.telegraph.co.uk/news/uknews/1401616/IRA-offers-sincere-apologies-for-30-years-of-civilian-slaughter.html≥

'Libya admits Lockerbie blame', *BBC News* (16 August 2003) at <http://news.bbc.co.uk/2/hi/uk_news/scotland/3155523.stm≥

Press Release from the International Federation for Human Rights, 'The Bemba Case: Heavily criticized, the ICC must maintain victims' legal representation as the establishment of assistance programmes for victims is awaited' (1 October 2018) at <https://www.fidh.org/en/region/Africa/central-african-republic/the-bemba-case-heavily-criticised-the-icc-must-maintain-victims-legal>

'South Sudan VP confirms apology for Bor Massacre', *Sudan Tribune* (3 April 2012) <www.sudantribune.com/South-Sudan-VP-confirms-apology,42124>

'Who are the FARC?' *BBC News* (24 November 2016) at <www.bbc.com/news/world-latin-america-36605769>

OTHER REPORTS AND DOCUMENTS

Buchanan (ed) C., *Viewpoints: Volume 2 – Negotiating Disarmament* (Centre for Humanitarian Dialogue, November 2008).

Clark, K. 'The Layha: Calling the Taleban to Account – Appendix 1: The Taleban Codes of Conduct in English'. AAN Thematic Report 6/2011, Afghanistan Analysts Network (June 2011).
Colombo Embassy Cable 1987, 'Inside the LTTE: A Look at the Tiger's Command Structure'.
Constitution of the National Democratic Front of the Philippines (July 1994).
Chega! 'Final report of the Timor-Leste Commission for Reception, Truth and Reconciliation' (November 2013).
Ejército de Liberación Nacional (ELN), 'Code of War', Colombia 1995.
Fifteen-Point Programme of the SPLM, Vision and Programme of the Sudan People's Liberation Movement (SPLM), SPLM Political Secretariat, Yei and New Cush, New Sudan, March 1998
Final Report of Sierra Leone's the Truth and Reconciliation Commission (2004).
Geneva Academy of International Humanitarian Law and Human Rights, *Reactions to Norms. Armed Groups and the Protection of Civilians* (Geneva 2014).
Geneva Academy of International Humanitarian Law and Human Rights, 'Non-international armed conflicts in Libya' in *RULAC: Rule of Law in Armed Conflicts* (2018).
Geneva Call, 'Deed of Commitment under Geneva Call for adherence to a total ban on anti-personnel mines and for cooperation in mine action'.
Guatemala Memoria del Silencio, Resumen ejecutivo, conclusiones y recomendaciones (27 April 1999) UN Doc. A/53/928.
Inter-American Commission on Human Rights, Third Report on the Situation of Human Rights in Colombia (1999), OEA/Ser.L/V/II.102, Doc. 9 rev. 1
International Centre for Transitional Justice, 'Providing Meaningful Reparations to Victims – Briefing' (December 2009).
International Committee of the Red Cross, *The Roots of Restraint in War* (Geneva, 2018)
Mouvement de Libération du Congo, 'Statuts du Mouvement de Libération du Congo' (1999).
New People's Army (NPA), 'Basic Rules', Philippines 1969.
Office of the Prosecutor, International Criminal Court, 'Situation of the Central African Republic II, Article 53(1) Report' (24 September 2014).
REDRESS, 'Making Sense of Reparations at the International Criminal Court' (20 June 2018) Background Paper.
Report of the Truth and Reconciliation Commission in Peru (2003).
Revolutionary United Front (RUF), 'Eight Codes of Conduct', Sierra Leone, no date.
Statutes of the Bolivarian Militias of the Revolutionary Armed Forces of Colombia, People's Army (FARC-EP).
Statutes of the Revolutionary Armed Forces of Colombia, People's Army (FARC-EP).
The National Resistance Army 'Code of Conduct', Uganda, 1982.
Truth and Reconciliation Commission of Liberia, 'Final Report: Volume II: Consolidated Final Report' (2009).
Undertaking of demilitarisation and transformation by the KLA (20 June 1999)
Viet Cong, 'Code of Disciplines', Vietnam, no date.

TABLE OF INSTRUMENTS

African Charter on Human and People's Rights (1982) OAU Doc. CAB/LEG/67/3 rev. 5, 21 ILM 58

American Convention on Human Rights (1969) OAS Treaty Series No. 36, 1144 UNTS 123

Basic Principles and Guidelines on the Right to a Remedy and Reparation for Victims of Gross Violations of International Human Rights Law and Serious Violations of International Humanitarian Law (2005) C.H.R. res. 2005/35, U.N. Doc. E/CN.4/2005/ L.10/Add.11

European Convention for the Protection of Human Rights and Fundamental Freedoms (1950) ETS 5, UNTS vol. 213, 222

Geneva Conventions (1949) 75 UNTS 31, 75, 85, 287

Hague Convention for the Protection of Cultural Property in the Event of Armed Conflict (1954) 249 UNTS 215

Hague Convention IV Respecting the Laws and Customs of War on Land (1907) U.S.T.S. 539, 2 A.J.I.L. Supp. 90

International Covenant on Civil and Political Rights (1966) UNTS vol. 999, 171 and vol. 1057, 407

Protocol Additional to the Geneva Conventions of 12 August 1949, and relating to the Protection of Victims of International Armed Conflicts (Protocol I) (1977) 1125 UNTS 3

Protocol Additional to the Geneva Conventions of 12 August 1949, and relating to the Protection of Victims of Non-International Armed Conflicts (Protocol II) (1977) 1125 UNTS 609

Rome Statute of the International Criminal Court (1998) UNTS vol. 2187, 3

Statute of the International Court of Justice (1945) 33 UNTS 993

Statute of the International Criminal Tribunal for the Former Yugoslavia (1993) U.N. Doc. S/25704 at 36, annex (1993) and S/25704/Add.1 (1993), adopted by Security Council on 25 May 1993, U.N. Doc. S/RES/827.

Statute of the International Criminal Tribunal for Rwanda (1994) U.N. Doc. S/RES/955 (1994), 33 I.L.M. 1598, 1600.

Vienna Convention on the Law of Treaties (1969) 1155 UNTS 331

UN General Assembly, Universal Declaration of Human Rights (1948) UN. Doc. No. GA/ RES/217A(III)

TABLE OF CASES

INTERNATIONAL COURT OF JUSTICE

Application of the Convention on the Prevention and Punishment of the Crime of Genocide (Bosnia and Herzegovina v. Yugoslavia) (Merits) [2007] Judgment, ICJ Rep, 26 February 2007.

Legal Consequences of the Construction of a Wall in the Occupied Palestinian Territory (Advisory Opinion) [2004] ICJ Rep 136, 9 July 2004.

Military and Paramilitary Activities in and against Nicaragua (Merits) [1984] Judgment ICJ Rep 392, 26 November 1984.

Nuclear Tests (Australia v. France) [1974] ICJ Rep 253, 20 December 1974.

Reparation for Injuries Suffered in the Service of the United Nations (Advisory Opinion) [1949] ICJ Rep 174, 11 April 1949.

PERMANENT COURT OF INTERNATIONAL JUSTICE

Case Concerning the Factory at Chorzów (Germany v Poland) (Merits) PCIJ Rep Series A No 17, 13 September 1928.

Questions relating to Settlers of German Origin in Poland (Advisory Opinion) PCIJ Series B no 6, 10 September 1923.

EUROPEAN COURT OF HUMAN RIGHTS

Behrami and Behrami v. France and *Saramati v. France, Germany and Norway* (Decision on Admissibility) European Court of Human Rights, Application No 71412/01 and 78166/01 (2 May 2007).

INTER-AMERICAN COMMISSION ON AND COURT OF HUMAN RIGHTS

Tablada case, Inter-American Commission on Human Rights, IACHR Report No. 55/97, Case No. 11.137, Argentina, OEA/Ser/L/V/II.97, Doc. 38 (30 October 1997).

INTERNATIONAL CRIMINAL COURT

The Prosecutor v. Ahmad Al Faqi Al Mahdi (Reparation Order) ICC-01/12-01/15 (17 August 2017).

Prosecutor v. Ahmad Al Faqi Al Mahdi (Judgment on the appeal of the victims against the 'Reparations Order'), ICC-01/12-01/15 A (8 March 2018).

Prosecutor v. Germain Katanga (Order for Reparations pursuant to Article 75 of the Statute) ICC-01/04-01/07 (24 March 2017).

Prosecutor v. Mbarushimana (Decision on the confirmation of charges) ICC-01/04-01/10-465-Red (16 December 2011).

Prosecutor v. Thomas Lubanga Dyilo (Decision on the Applications for Participation in the Proceedings Submitted by VPRS 1 to VPRS 6) Pre-Trial Chamber I, ICC-01/04-01/06 (29 June 2006).

Prosecutor v. Thomas Lubanga Dyilo (Decision on Sentence pursuant to Article 76 of the Statute) ICC-01/04-01/06-2901 (10 July 2012).

Prosecutor v. Thomas Lubanga Dyilo (Judgment on the appeals against the 'Decision establishing the principles and procedures to be applied to reparations' of 7 August 2012 with AMENDED order for reparations (Annex A) and public annexes 1 and 2), ICC-01/04-01/06 A A 2 A 3 (3 March 2015).

Prosecutor v. Thomas Lubanga Dyilo (Corrected version of the 'Decision Setting the Size of the Reparations Award for which Thomas Lubanga Dyilo is Liable') ICC-01/04-01/06 (21 December 2017).

INTERNATIONAL CRIMINAL COURT FOR THE FORMER YUGOSLAVIA

Prosecutor v. Blaškić (Judgment) ICTY Case No. IT-95-14-A (29 July 2004).

Prosecutor v. Boškoski & Tarčulovski (Trial Judgment) Case No. ICTY-04-82-T (10 July 2008).

Prosecutor v. Strugar (Appeals Chamber Judgment) ICTY Case No. IT-01-42-A (17 July 2008).

Prosecutor v. Tadić, (Trial Judgment) ICTY Case No. IT-94-I-T (7 May 1997).

Prosecutor v. Tadić (Appeal Chamber Jurisdiction Decision) ICTY Case No. IT-94-I-T (15 July 1999).

Prosecutor v. Tadić (Decision on the Defence Motion for Interlocutory Appeal on Jurisdiction) ICTY Case No. IT-94-I-T (2 October 1995).

Prosecutor v. Orić, (Judgment) ICTY Case No. IT- 03-68- T (30 June 2006).

SPECIAL COURT FOR SIERRA LEONE

Prosecutor v. Sam Hinga Norman (Decision on Preliminary Motion Based on Lack of Jurisdiction) (Child Recruitment) Case No. SCSL-2004-14-AR72(E) (31 May 2004).

INTERNATIONAL CLAIMS COMMISSIONS

Claim of Finnish shipowners against Great Britain in respect of the use of certain Finnish vessels during the war (Finland, Great Britain), Reports of International Arbitral Awards, Volume III (9 May 1934).

Claim of the Salvador Commercial Company ("El Triunfo Company"), Reports of International Arbitral Awards, Volume XV (8 May 1902).

Eritrea-Ethiopia Claims Commission – Partial Award: Prisoners of War – Ethiopia's Claim 4; and *Eritrea-Ethiopia Claims Commission – Partial Award: Prisoners of War – Eritrea's Claim 17*, Reports of International Arbitral Awards, Volume XXVI (1 July 2003).

N. Henriquez case, Mixed Claims Commission (Netherlands-Venezuela), Reports of International Arbitral Awards, Volume X (28 February 1903).

Sambiaggio case, Mixed Claims Commission (Italy-Venezuela), Reports of International Arbitral Awards, Volume X (13 February and 7 May 1903).

Sentence arbitrale sur la réclamation numéro 2, présentée par Don Luis Chiessa, Reports of International Arbitral Awards, Volume XV (30 September 1901).

NATIONAL COURTS

COLOMBIA

Gustavo Gallón y Otros, Constitutional Court of Colombia, C-370/2006 (18 May 2006).

NORTHERN IRELAND

Breslin and Others v. Seamus McKenna and Others, NIQB 50 (8 June 2009).

THE NETHERLANDS

Mothers of Srebrenica et al. v. State of The Netherlands and the United Nations, Supreme Court of The Netherlands, Judgment, Case no. 10/04437 (13 April 2012).

The State of the Netherlands v. Hasan Nuhanovic, Supreme Court of The Netherlands, Judgment, Case no. 12/03324 (6 September 2013).

UNITED KINGDOM

Her Majesty's Advocate v Al Megrahi, Scottish High Court of Justiciary at Camp Zeist (The Netherlands) 40 ILM 582 (31 January 2001).

R. (on the application of Al-Jedda) v. Secretary of State for Defence [2007] UKHL 58.

UNITED STATES

Doe v. Karadzic, United States District Court, 866 F. Supp. 734, 735 (S.D.N.Y. 1994) (7 September 1994).

Doe v. Karadzic, United States District Court, 93 Civ. 878 (PKL) (4 October 2000).

Jane Doe v. Islamic Salvation Front (FIS) and Anwar Haddam, United States District Court, District of Columbia, 993 F. Supp. 3 (D.D.C.1998) (3 February 1998) dismissed (31 March 2003).

Kadic v. Karadzic (Opinion of 2nd Circuit re Subject Matter Jurisdiction) United States Court of Appeals for the Second Circuit, 70 F.3d 232, 241 (13 October 1995).

ANNEX I: PEACE AND CEASEFIRE AGREEMENTS

Accord politique pour la paix et la reconciliation en Republique Centrafricane (6 February 2019).

Agreement on Accountability and Reconciliation between the Government of the Republic of Uganda and the Lord's Resistance Army/Movement, Juba, Sudan (29 June 2007).

Agreement on Peace between the Government of the Republic of the Philippines and the Moro Islamic Liberation Front (22 June 2001).

Cessation of Hostilities Framework Agreement between the Government of the Republic of Indonesia and the Free Aceh Movement (9 December 2002).

Comprehensive Agreement on Human Rights, Guatemala (29 March 1994).

Darfur Peace Agreement (5 May 2006, Abuja, Nigeria).

Final agreement to end the armed conflict and build a stable and lasting peace between the Government of Colombia and the Revolutionary Armed Forces of Colombia – People's Army (FARC-EP) (21 November 2016).

Peace Agreement between the Government of the Republic of Sierra Leone and the Revolutionary United Front of Sierra Leone, Abidjan (30 November 1996).

Somali Agreement on Implementing the Ceasefire and on Modalities of Disarmament (15 January 1993).

CURRICULUM VITAE

Laura Íñigo Álvarez is a researcher in Public International Law at the University of Seville. Her research focuses on the responsibility of non-state armed groups for violations of international humanitarian law and the legal consequences of such responsibility. She conducted her research as part of a Joint Doctorate Agreement between Utrecht University and the University of Seville from 2016 to 2019. Currently, she is a contributor to Oxford Reports on International Law in Domestic Courts. She is also a member of the European Society of International Law (ESIL) and the Spanish Bar Association.

Laura obtained her Law Degree (*Licenciatura en Derecho*) and her LL.M *cum laude* at the University of Seville. She further studied at KU Leuven during an academic year focusing on European and human rights law and participated in courses at the Hague Academy of International Law. In 2013, Laura was awarded for having one of the best university grades in her city by the Seville City Council. Before joining Utrecht University, Laura was a junior researcher of the EU Project FRAME 'Fostering Human Rights among European (internal and external) Policies' where she contributed to Work Package 10 dealing with EU external policies in response to conflicts and crisis situations and exploring ways to prevent and overcome violence through the integration of human rights, humanitarian law and democracy/rule of law principles.

She has also conducted research in the field of business and human rights as a member of the working group of the Research Network 'The European Union and Non-State Actors' and the Research Project 'The Implementation of the UN Guiding Principles on Business and Human Rights by the EU and its Member States' funded by the Spanish Ministry of Economy and Competitiveness. She was a teaching assistant to the European Master's Programme in Human Rights and Democratization (EMA) at the University of Seville for three years. Prior to this, she was a legal intern at various NGOs and law firms in Spain, including Asociación Internacional de Juristas *Inter Iuris* and Montero Aramburu Abogados.

Human Rights Research Series

The Human Rights Research Series' central research theme is the nature and meaning of international standards in the fi eld of human rights, their application and promotion in the national legal order, their interplay with national standards, and the international supervision of such application. Anyone directly involved in the defi nition, study, implementation, monitoring, or enforcement of human rights will fi nd this series an indispensable reference tool.
The Series is published together with the world famous Netherlands Network for Human Rights Research (formerly School of Human Rights Research), a joint eff ort by human rights researchers in the Netherlands.

Published titles within the Series:

79. Malu Beijer, *The Limits of Fundamental Rights Protection by the EU*
ISBN 978-1-78068-455-0
80. Marie Elske Gispen, *Human Rights and Drug Control*
ISBN 978-1-78068-454-3
81. Bart van der Sloot, *Privacy as Virtue: Moving Beyond the Individual in the Age of Big Data*
ISBN 978-1-78068-505-2
82. Mohammad Hadi Zakerhossein, *Situation Selection Regime at the International Criminal Court*
ISBN 978-1-78068-618-9
83. Yi Zhang, *Advancing the Right to Health Care in China. Towards Accountability*
ISBN 978-1-78068-677-6
84. Diana Itza Odier-Contreras Garduño, *Collective Reparations.Tensions and Dilemmas Between Collective Reparations and the Individual Right to Receive Reparations*
ISBN 978-1-78068-705-6
85. Daphina Misiedjan, *Towards a Sustainable Human Right to Water. Supporting vulnerable people and protecting water resources*
ISBN 978-1-78068-612-7
86. Benedicta Deogratias, *Trapped in a Religious Marriage*
ISBN 978-1-78068-842-8
87. Kasim Balarabe, *Realising the Right to Water and Sanitation in Nigeria*
ISBN 978-1-78068-901-2
88. Leonie Huijbers, *Process-based Fundamental Rights Review*
ISBN 978-1-78068-887-9
89. Vincent Willem Vleugel, *Culture in the State Reporting Procedure of the UN Human Rights Treaty Bodies. How the HRC, the CESCR and the CEDAWCee use human rights as a sword to protect and promote culture, and as a shield to protect against harmful culture*
ISBN 978-1-83970-006-4

www.ingramcontent.com/pod-product-compliance
Ingram Content Group UK Ltd.
Pitfield, Milton Keynes, MK11 3LW, UK
UKHW051922100926
8556IPUK00021B/1315